XSLT

Doug Tidwell

O'REILLY®

Beijing · Cambridge · Farnham · Köln · Paris · Sebastopol · Taipei · Tokyo

XSLT

by Doug Tidwell

Published by O'Reilly & Associates, Inc., 1005 Gravenstein Highway North, Sebastopol, CA 95472.

Editor: Simon St.Laurent

Production Editor: Ann Schirmer

Cover Designer: Edie Freedman

Printing History:

August 2001: First Edition.

ISBN: 0-596-00053-7

[C] [8/03]

XSLT

To my family— my wonderful wife, Sheri Castle, and
our amazing daughter, Lily—for their support and understanding.
Nothing I do would be possible without their help.

Table of Contents

Preface

Organization of This Book

The heart of this book is designed to take you through the basics of XSLT and help you solve problems with this exciting new technology. It contains the following chapters:

Chapter 1, Getting Started
: Covers the basics of XML and discusses how to install the Xalan stylesheet engine.

Chapter 2, The Obligatory Hello World Example
: Takes a look at an XML-tagged "Hello World" document, then examines stylesheets that transform it into other things.

Chapter 3, XPath: A Syntax for Describing Needles and Haystacks
: Covers the basics of XPath, the language used to describe parts of an XML document.

Chapter 4, Branching and Control Elements
: Discusses the logic elements of XSLT (`<xsl:if>` and `<xsl:choose>`) and how they work.

Chapter 5, Creating Links and Cross-References
: Covers the different ways to build links between elements in XML documents. Using XPath to describe relationships between related elements is also covered.

Chapter 6, Sorting and Grouping Elements
: Goes over the `<xsl:sort>` element and discusses various ways to sort elements in an XML document. It also talks about how to do grouping with various XSLT elements and functions.

Chapter 7, Combining XML Documents
: Discusses the `document()` function, which allows you to combine several XML documents, then write a stylesheet that works against the collection of documents.

Chapter 8, Extending XSLT
: Explains how you can write extension elements and extension functions. Although XSLT and XPath are extremely powerful and flexible, there are still times when you need to do something that isn't provided by the language itself.

Chapter 9, Case Study: The Toot-O-Matic
: Goes through a complicated case study that puts XSLT through its paces. The chapter reviews the Toot-O-Matic, an XSLT tool that generates a wide range of output documents from a single file.

The last section of the book contains reference information:

Appendix A, XSLT Reference
: An alphabetical listing of all the elements defined by XSLT, with a discussion of all attributes of those elements and how they were designed to be used.

Appendix B, XPath Reference
: A listing of various aspects of XPath, including datatypes, axes, node types, and operators.

Appendix C, XSLT and XPath Function Reference
: An alphabetical listing of all the functions defined by XPath and XSLT.

Appendix D, XSLT Guide
: A series of "How do I . . . ?" questions, with brief examples and/or references to sections of the book that explain how to do common tasks.

Glossary
: A glossary of terms used in XSLT, XPath, and XML in general.

Where I'm Coming From

Before we begin, it's only fair that I tell you my biases.

I Believe in Open, Platform-Neutral, Standards-Based Computing

If any part of your business life ties you down to anything closed, proprietary, or platform-specific, I encourage you to make some changes. This book shows you how to take charge of your data and move it from one place to another on your terms, not your software vendor's. XML is shifting the balance of power from software vendors to software users. If your tools force you to work in unnatural ways or refuse to let you have your data when and where you want it, you don't have to take it anymore.

I Assume You're Busy

This book is written for developers who want to learn how to use XSLT to solve problems. Throughout the book, we'll transform XML-tagged data into a variety of useful things. If a particular bit of arcana from the specifications doesn't relate to any practical problem I can think of, it's probably mentioned in the reference section only.

I Don't Care Which Standards-Compliant Tools You Use

Most examples in this book are done with Apache's Xalan XSLT engine, which is free, open source, cross-platform, and standards compliant. I use Xalan for two reasons: I've been using it longer than the others out there, and it has more developers working on it than any other XSLT engine I'm aware of. Unless otherwise stated, all examples in this book also work with Michael Kay's Saxon, Microsoft's XSLT tools, James Clark's XT, and Oracle's XML parser.

My job as an author and a teacher is to show you how to use free, standards-compliant tools to simplify your life. I'm not here to sell you a parser, an XSLT processor, a toaster, or anything else, so please use whatever tools you like. I encourage you to take a look at all of the tools out there and find your own preferences.

The XSLT processors mentioned in this book are:

Xalan
: Xalan is the Apache XML Project's XSLT engine. It was originally built on the LotusXSL code base. It's available at *http://xml.apache.org/xalan/*. Every example in this book was developed and tested using Xalan. Except where noted, examples should work on all other standards-compliant XSLT processors as well, although I haven't tested other tools as thoroughly.

Saxon
: Saxon was written by Michael Kay, an XSLT author and a frequent contributor to the XSLT mailing list. You can find it at *http://saxon.sourceforge.net.*

Microsoft's XSLT tools
: As of this writing, Microsoft's XSLT processor is part of the MSXML parser, available at *http://www.microsoft.com/xml.* (This site seems to be redesigned frequently, so be prepared to spend some time looking. Also, there are rumors that the packaging and names of the tools may change.) The most exciting

thing about this processor is that it can be integrated with the Internet Explorer browser, allowing you to transform XML documents on a client machine. By merely pointing your browser at an XML document, you can have the document transformed and rendered as HTML automatically. (For this to work, you must associate a stylesheet with the XML document. See the section "Associating stylesheets with XML documents" in Chapter 1 for more information.)

XT
XT was written by James Clark, the editor of the XSLT specification and the co-editor of the XPath specification. You can find it at *http://www.jclark.com/xml/xt.html.* Much of the code in XT was written to test the XSLT and XPath specs as they were developed. (Even though it is still a very popular XSLT processor, XT is no longer actively developed.)

Oracle
Oracle's XML parser is different from most because it includes the XSLT processor and the XML parser in a single package. It's free at Oracle's TechNet site (*http://technet.oracle.com/tech/xml*), although you do have to register before you can download it.

XSLT Is a Tool, Not a Religion

An old adage says that to a person with a hammer, everything looks like a nail. I don't claim that XSLT is the solution to every business problem you'll encounter. The next chapter discusses reasons why XML and XSLT were created, the design decisions behind XSLT, and tries to identify the kinds of problems XSLT is designed to solve. All chapters in this book illustrate common scenarios in which XSLT is extremely powerful and useful.

That being said, if a particular tool does something better than XSLT does, by all means, use that other tool. XSLT is a powerful addition to your tool box, but that doesn't mean you should throw out all your other tools.

Conventions Used in This Book

Items appearing in this book are sometimes given a special appearance to set them apart from the regular text. Here's how they look:

Italic
Used for citations of books and articles, commands, email addresses, and URLs

`Constant width`
Used for literals, constant values, code listings, and XML markup

`Constant-width bold`
: Used to indicate user input

`Constant-width italic`
: Used for replaceable parameter and variable names

This icon represents a tip, suggestion, or general note.

This icon represents a warning or caution.

How to Contact Us

We have tested and verified the information in this book to the best of our ability, but you may find that features have changed (or even that we have made mistakes!). Please let us know about any errors you find, as well as your suggestions for future editions, by writing to:

O'Reilly & Associates, Inc.
101 Morris Street
Sebastopol, CA 95472
(800) 998-9938 (in the United States or Canada)
(707) 829-0515 (international/local)
(707) 829-0104 (fax)

To ask technical questions or comment on the book, send email to:

bookquestions@oreilly.com

The web site for this book lists examples, errata, and plans for future editions. You can access this page at:

http://www.oreilly.com/catalog/xslt

For more information about our books, conferences, software, resource centers, and the O'Reilly Network, see our web site:

http://www.oreilly.com

Acknowledgments

First and foremost, I'd like to thank the reviewers of this book. David Marston of Lotus was the lead reviewer; David, thank you so much for your comments, wisdom, and knowledge. Along the way, I also got a lot of good feedback and encouragement from Tony Colle, Slavko Malesvic, Dr. Joe Molitoris, Shane O'Donnell, Andy Piper, Sreenivas Ramarao, Mike Riley, and Willie Wheeler. This book is significantly better because of your comments and other efforts.

I'd also like to thank my teammates at developerWorks for encouraging me to undertake this project. Taking on an additional full-time job hasn't been easy, but their advice, flexibility, and understanding as I've tried to balance my responsibilities has been invaluable. Even more valuable is the fact that I'm surrounded by some of the most interesting, creative, and remarkable people I've ever known. You guys rule.

For the times I've been at home (in Raleigh, North Carolina), I've depended on my nutritional advisors at Schiano's Pizza: "Hey, you want your usual?" (Slight pause.) "Yeah, that'd be great, thanks." Nothing's as comforting as a couple of slices. If you're within a day's drive of Raleigh, I strongly encourage you to visit.

Finally, I'd like to thank the staff at O'Reilly, especially Laurie Petrycki and Simon St.Laurent. Laurie, thank you for convincing me to take on this project and for sticking with me when my ability to find the time to write was in doubt. Simon, I've enjoyed reading your books for years; it's been an honor to work with you. Your guidance, technical insight, patience, and suggestions were invaluable.

Thanks so much to all of you!

1

Getting Started

In this chapter, we review the design rationale behind XSLT and XPath and discuss the basics of XML. We also talk about other web standards and how they relate to XSLT and XPath. We conclude the chapter with a brief discussion of how to set up an XSLT processor on your machine so you can work with the examples throughout the book.

The Design of XSLT

XML has gone from working group to entrenched buzzword in record time. Its flexibility as a language for presenting structured data has made it the lingua franca for data interchange. Early adopters used programming interfaces such as the Document Object Model (DOM) and the Simple API for XML (SAX) to parse and process XML documents. As XML becomes mainstream, however, it's clear that the average web citizen can't be expected to hack Java, Visual Basic, Perl, or Python code to work with documents. What's needed is a flexible, powerful, yet relatively simple, language capable of processing XML.

What's needed is XSLT.

XSLT, the Extensible Stylesheet Language for Transformations, is an official recommendation of the World Wide Web Consortium (W3C). It provides a flexible, powerful language for transforming XML documents into something else. That something else can be an HTML document, another XML document, a Portable Document Format (PDF) file, a Scalable Vector Graphics (SVG) file, a Virtual Reality Modeling Language (VRML) file, Java code, a flat text file, a JPEG file, or most anything you want. You write an XSLT stylesheet to define the rules for transforming an XML document, and the XSLT processor does the work.

The W3C has defined two families of standards for stylesheets. The oldest and simplest is Cascading Style Sheets (CSS), a mechanism used to define various properties of markup elements. Although CSS can be used with XML, it is most often used to style HTML documents. I can use CSS properties to define that certain elements be rendered in blue, or in 58-point type, or in boldface. That's all well and good, but there are many things that CSS can't do:

- CSS can't change the order in which elements appear in a document. If you want to sort certain elements or filter elements based on a certain property, CSS won't do the job.
- CSS can't do computations. If you want to calculate and output a value (maybe you want to add up the numeric value of all `<price>` elements in a document), CSS won't do the job.
- CSS can't combine multiple documents. If you want to combine 53 purchase order documents and print a summary of all items ordered in those purchase orders, CSS won't do the job.

Don't take this section as a criticism of CSS; XSLT and CSS were designed for different purposes. One fairly common use of XSLT is to generate an HTML document that contains CSS elements. See the section "The XPath View of an XML Document" in Chapter 3 for an example that uses XSLT to generate CSS properties.

XSLT was created to be a more powerful, flexible language for transforming documents. In this book, we go through all the features of XSLT and discuss each of them in terms of practical examples. Some of XSLT's design goals specify that:

- An XSLT stylesheet should be an XML document. This means that you can write a stylesheet that transforms a second stylesheet into another stylesheet (we actually do this in Chapter 4). This kind of recursive thinking is common in XSLT.
- The XSLT language should be based on pattern matching. Most of our stylesheets consist of rules (called templates in XSLT) used to transform a document. Each rule says, "When you see part of a document that looks like this, here's how you convert it into something else." This is probably different from any programming you've previously done.

- XSLT should be designed to be free of side effects. In other words, XSLT is designed to be optimized so that many different stylesheet rules could be applied simultaneously. The biggest impact of this is that variables can't be modified. Once a variable is initialized, you can't change its value; if variables could be changed, then processing one stylesheet rule might have side effects that impact other stylesheet rules. This is almost certainly different from any programming you've previously done.

  XSLT is heavily influenced by the design of *functional programming languages*, such as Lisp, Scheme, and Haskell. These languages also feature immutable variables. Instead of defining the templates of XSLT, functional programming languages define programs as a series of functions, each of which generates a well-defined output (free from side effects, of course) in response to a well-defined input. The goal is to execute the instructions of a given XSLT template without affecting the execution of any other XSLT template.

- Instead of looping, XSLT uses iteration and recursion. Given that variables can't be changed, how do you do something like a `for` or `do-while` loop? XSLT uses two equivalent techniques: iteration and recursion. *Iteration* means that you can write an XSLT template that says, "get all the things that look like this, and here's what I want you to do with each of them." Although that's different from a `do-while` loop, usually what you do in a procedural language is something like, "do this while there are any items left to process." In that case, iteration does exactly what you want.

  Recursion takes some getting used to. If you must implement something like a `for` statement (`for i=1 to 10 do`, for example), recursion is the way to go. There are a number of examples of recursion throughout the book; you can flip ahead to the section "A Stylesheet That Emulates a for Loop" in Chapter 4 for more information.

Given these design goals, what are XSLT's strengths? Here are some scenarios:

- Your web site needs to deliver information to a variety of devices. You need to support ordinary desktop browsers, as well as pagers, mobile phones, and other low-resolution, low-function devices. It would be great if you could create your information in structured documents, then transform those documents into all the formats you need.
- You need to exchange data with your partners, but all of you use different database systems. It would be great if you could define a common XML data format, then transform documents written in that format into the import files you need (SQL statements, comma-separated values, etc.).

- To stay on the cutting edge, your web site gets a complete visual redesign every few months. Even though things such as server-side includes and CSS can help, they can't do everything. It would be great if your data were in a flexible format that could be transformed into any look and feel, simplifying the redesign process.
- You have documents in several different formats. All the documents are machine-readable, but it's a hassle to write programs to parse and process all of them. It would be great if you could combine all of the documents into a single format, then generate summary documents and reports based on that collection of documents. It would be even better if the report could contain calculated values, automatically generated graphics, and formatting for high-quality printing.

Throughout the book, we'll demonstrate XSLT solutions for problems just like these. Most chapters focus on particular techniques, such as sorting, grouping, and generating links between pieces of data. We wrap up with a case study that discusses a real-world content-management scenario and illustrates how XSLT was used to solve a number of problems.

XML Basics

Almost everything we do in this book deals with XML documents. XSLT stylesheets are XML documents themselves, and they're designed to transform an XML document into something else. If you don't have much experience with XML, we'll review the basics here. For more information on XML, check out Erik T. Ray's *Learning XML* (O'Reilly, 2001) and Elliotte Rusty Harold and W. Scott Means's *XML in a Nutshell* (O'Reilly, 2001).

XML's Heritage

XML's heritage is in the Standard Generalized Markup Language (SGML). Created by Dr. Charles Goldfarb in the 1970s, SGML is widely used in high-end publishing systems. Unfortunately, SGML's perceived complexity prevented its widespread adoption across the industry (SGML also stands for "sounds great, maybe later"). SGML got a boost when Tim Berners-Lee based HTML on SGML. Overnight, the whole computing industry was using a markup language to build documents and applications.

The problem with HTML is that its tags were designed for the interaction between humans and machines. When the Web was invented in the late 1980s, that was just fine. As the Web moved into all aspects of our lives, HTML was asked to do lots of strange things. We've all built HTML pages with awkward table structures, 1-pixel GIFs, and other nonsense just to get the page to look right in the browser. XML is designed to get us out of this rut and back into the world of structured documents.

Whatever its limitations, HTML is the most popular markup language ever created. Given its popularity, why do we need XML? Consider this extremely informative HTML element:

```
<td>12304</td>
```

What does this fascinating piece of content represent?

- Is it the postal code for Schenectady, New York?
- Is it the number of light bulbs replaced each month in Las Vegas?
- Is it the number of Volkswagens sold in Hong Kong last year?
- Is it the number of tons of steel in the Sydney Harbour Bridge?

The answer: maybe, maybe not. The point of this silly example is that there's no structure to this data. Even if we included the entire table, it takes intelligence (real, live intelligence, the kind between your ears) to make sense of this data. If you saw this cell in a table next to another cell that contained the text "Schenectady," and the heading above the table read "Postal Codes for the State of New York," as a human being, you could interpret the contents of this cell correctly. On the other hand, if you wanted to write a piece of code that took any HTML table and attempted to determine whether any of the cells in the table contained postal codes, you'd find that difficult, to say the least.

Most HTML pages have one goal in mind: the appearance of the document. Veterans of the markup industry know that this is definitely not the way to create content. The *separation of content and presentation* is a long-established tenet of the publishing industry; unfortunately, most HTML pages aren't even close to approaching this ideal. An XML document should contain information, marked up with tags that describe what all the pieces of information are, as well as the relationship between those items. Presenting the document (also known as *rendering*) involves rules and decisions separate from the document itself. As we work through dozens of sample documents and applications, you'll see how delaying the rendering decisions as long as possible has significant advantages.

Let's look at another marked-up document. Consider this:

```
<?xml version="1.0"?>
<postalcodes>
  <title>Most-used postal codes in November 2000</title>
  <item>
    <city>Schenectady</city>
    <postalcode>12304</postalcode>
```

```
    <usage-count>2039</usage-count>
  </item>
  <item>
    <city>Kuala Lumpur</city>
    <postalcode>57000</postalcode>
    <usage-count>1983</usage-count>
  </item>
  <item>
    <city>London</city>
    <postalcode>SW1P 4RG</postalcode>
    <usage-count>1722</usage-count>
  </item>
  ...
</postalcodes>
```

Although we're still in the realm of contrived examples, it would be fairly easy to write a piece of code to find the postal codes in any document that used this set of tags (as opposed to HTML's `<table>`, `<tr>`, `<td>`, etc.). Our code would look for the contents of any `<postalcode>` elements in the document. (Not to get ahead of ourselves here, but writing an XSLT stylesheet to do this might take all of 30 minutes, including a 25-minute nap.) A well-designed XML document identifies each piece of data in the document and models the relationships between those pieces of data. This means we can be confident that we're processing an XML document correctly.

Again, the key idea here is that we're separating content from presentation. Our XML document clearly delineates the pieces of data and puts them into a format we can parse easily. In this book, we illustrate a number of techniques for transforming this XML document into a variety of formats. Among other things, we can transform the item `<postalcode>12304</postalcode>` into `<td>12304</td>`.

XML Document Rules

Continuing our trip through the basics of XML, there are several rules you need to keep in mind when creating XML documents. All stylesheets we develop in this book are themselves XML documents, so all the rules of XML documents apply to everything we do. The rules are pretty simple, even though the vast majority of HTML documents don't follow them.

One important point: The XML 1.0 specification makes it clear that when an XML parser finds an XML document that breaks the rules, the parser is supposed to throw an exception and stop. The parser is not allowed to guess what the document structure should actually be. This specification avoids recreating the HTML world, where lots of ugly documents are still rendered by the average browser.

An XML document must be contained in a single element

The first element in your XML document must contain the entire document. That first element is called the *document element* or the *root element.* If more than one document element is in the document, the XML parser throws an exception. This XML document is perfectly legal:

```
<?xml version="1.0"?>
<greeting>
  Hello, World!
</greeting>
```

(To be precise, this document is *well-formed.* XML documents are described as *well-formed* and *valid*; we'll define those terms in a minute.) This XML document isn't legal at all:

```
<?xml version="1.0"?>
<greeting>
  Hello, World!
</greeting>
<greeting>
  Hey, Y'all!
</greeting>
```

There are two root elements in this document, so an XML parser refuses to process it. Also, be aware that the XML declaration (the `<?xml version="1.0"?>` part, more on this in a minute) isn't an element at all.

All elements must be nested

If you start one element inside another, you have to end it there, too. An HTML browser is happy to render this document:

```
<b>I really, <i>really</b> like XML.</i>
```

But an XML parser will throw an exception when it sees this document. If you want the same effect, you would need to code this:

```
<b>I really, <i>really</i></b><i> like XML.</i>
```

All attributes must be quoted

You can quote the attributes with either single quotes or double quotes. These two XML tags are equivalent:

```
<a href="http://www.oreilly.com">
<a href='http://www.oreilly.com'>
```

If you need to define an attribute with the value `"Doug's car"`, you can use single quotes inside double quotes, as we just did. If you need both single and double quotes in an attribute, use the predefined entities `"` for double quotes and `'` for single quotes.

One more note: XML doesn't allow attributes without values. In other words, HTML elements like `<ol compact>` aren't valid in XML. To code this element in XML, you'd have to give the attribute a value, as in `<ol compact="yes">`.

XML tags are case-sensitive

In HTML, `<h1>` and `<H1>` are the same. In XML, they're not. If you try to end an `<h1>` element with `</H1>`, the parser will throw an exception.

All end tags are required

This is another area where most HTML documents break. Your browser doesn't care whether you don't have a `</p>` or `</br>` tag, but your XML parser does.

Empty tags can contain the end marker

In other words, these two XML fragments are identical:

```
<lily age="6"></lily>

<lily age="6"/>
```

Notice that there is nothing, not even whitespace, between the start tag and the end tag in the first example; that's what makes this an empty tag.

XML declarations

Some XML documents begin with an *XML declaration.* An XML declaration is a line similar to this:

```
<?xml version="1.0" encoding="ISO-8859-1"?>
```

If no `encoding` is specified, the XML parser assumes you're using UTF-8, a Unicode standard that uses different numbers of bytes to represent virtually every character and ideograph from the world's languages. Be aware that each parser supports a different set of encodings, so you need to check your parser's documentation to find out what your options are.

Document Type Definitions (DTDs) and XML Schemas

All of the rules we've discussed so far apply to all XML documents. In addition, you can use DTDs and Schemas to define other constraints for your XML documents. DTDs and Schemas are metalanguages that let you define the characteristics of an XML vocabulary. For example, you might want to specify that any XML document describing a purchase order must begin with a `<po>` element, and the `<po>` element in turn contains a `<customer-id>` element, one or more `<item-ordered>` elements, and an `<order-date>` element. In addition, each `<item-ordered>` element must contain a `part-number` attribute and a `quantity` attribute.

Here's a sample DTD that defines the constraints we just mentioned:

```
<?xml version="1.0" encoding="UTF-8"?>

<!ELEMENT po (customer-id , item-ordered+ , order-date)>

<!ELEMENT customer-id (#PCDATA)>

<!ELEMENT item-ordered EMPTY>

<!ATTLIST item-ordered  part-number CDATA  #REQUIRED
                        quantity    CDATA  #REQUIRED >
<!ELEMENT order-date EMPTY>

<!ATTLIST order-date  day   CDATA  #REQUIRED
                      month CDATA  #REQUIRED
                      year  CDATA  #REQUIRED >
```

And here's an XML Schema that defines the same document type:

```
<?xml version="1.0" encoding="UTF-8"?>
<xsd:schema xmlns:xsd="http://www.w3.org/2000/10/XMLSchema">

  <xsd:element name="po">
    <xsd:complexType>
      <xsd:sequence>
        <xsd:element ref="customer-id"/>
        <xsd:element ref="item-ordered" maxOccurs="unbounded"/>
        <xsd:element ref="order-date"/>
      </xsd:sequence>
    </xsd:complexType>
  </xsd:element>

  <xsd:element name="customer-id" type="xsd:string"/>

  <xsd:element name="item-ordered">
    <xsd:complexType>
      <xsd:attribute name="part-number" use="required">
        <xsd:simpleType>
          <xsd:restriction base="xsd:string">
            <xsd:pattern value="[0-9]{5}-[0-9]{4}-[0-9]{5}"/>
          </xsd:restriction>
        </xsd:simpleType>
      </xsd:attribute>
      <xsd:attribute name="quantity" use="required" type="xsd:integer"/>
    </xsd:complexType>
  </xsd:element>
```

```
    <xsd:element name="order-date">
      <xsd:complexType>
        <xsd:attribute name="day" use="required">
          <xsd:simpleType>
            <xsd:restriction base="xsd:integer">
              <xsd:maxInclusive value="31"/>
            </xsd:restriction>
          </xsd:simpleType>
        </xsd:attribute>
        <xsd:attribute name="month" use="required">
          <xsd:simpleType>
            <xsd:restriction base="xsd:integer">
              <xsd:maxInclusive value="12"/>
            </xsd:restriction>
          </xsd:simpleType>
        </xsd:attribute>
        <xsd:attribute name="year" use="required">
          <xsd:simpleType>
            <xsd:restriction base="xsd:integer">
              <xsd:maxInclusive value="2100"/>
            </xsd:restriction>
          </xsd:simpleType>
        </xsd:attribute>
      </xsd:complexType>
    </xsd:element>
  </xsd:schema>
```

Schemas have two significant advantages over DTDs:

- *They can define datatypes and other complex structures that are difficult or impossible to do in a DTD.* In the previous example, we defined various constraints for the data in our XML documents. We defined that the `day` attribute must be an integer between 1 and 31, and the `month` attribute must be an integer between 1 and 12. We also used a regular expression to define a `part-number` attribute as a five-digit number, a dash, a four-digit number, a dash, and another five-digit number. None of those things are possible in a DTD.
- *Schemas are themselves XML documents.* Since they are XML documents, we can write XSLT stylesheets to manipulate them. There are products in the marketplace today that take a schema and generate documentation from it. Figure 1-1 shows some sample output generated from our schema.

  Generating this output is relatively straightforward because the tool transforms an XML document. The schema defines a variety of elements and attributes and constraints on valid data, all of which can be easily converted into other formats, such as the HTML shown in Figure 1-1.

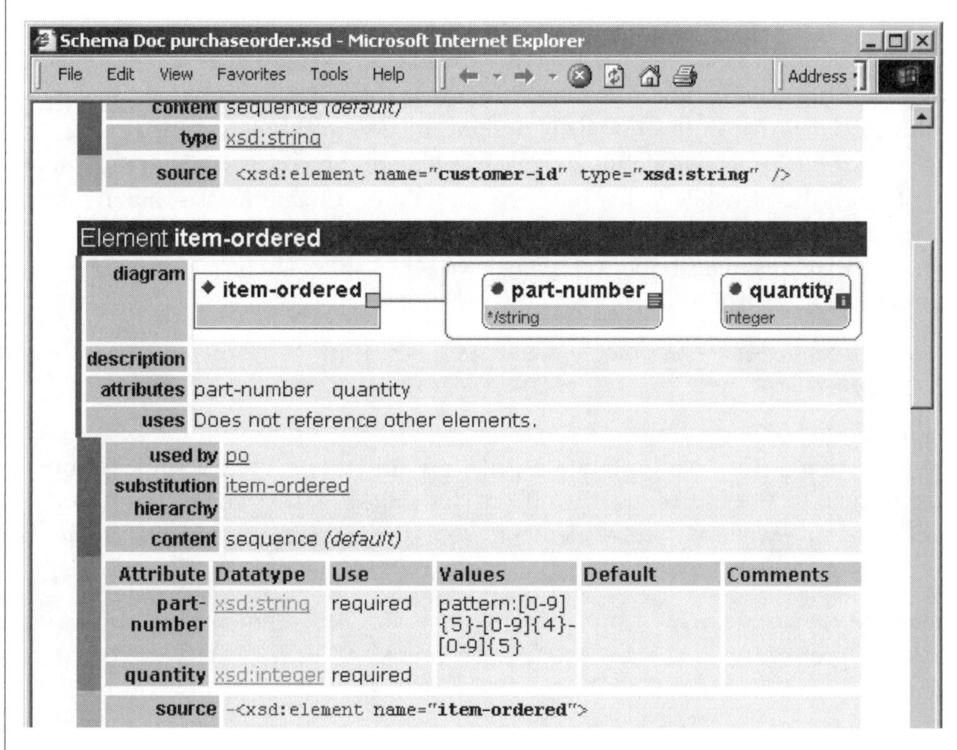

Figure 1-1. Automatically generated XML Schema documentation

Well-formed versus valid documents

Any XML document that follows the rules described here is said to be *well-formed.* In addition, if an XML document references a set of rules that define how the document is structured (either a DTD or an XML Schema), and it follows all those rules, it is said to be a *valid* document.

All valid documents are well-formed; on the other hand, not all well-formed documents are valid.

Tags versus elements

Although many people use the two terms interchangably, a tag is different from an element. A tag is the text between the angle brackets (< and >). There are start tags, end tags, and empty tags. A tag consists of a tag name and, if it is a start tag or an empty tag, some optional attributes. (Unlike other markup languages, end tags in XML cannot contain attributes.) An element consists of the start tag for the element, the end tag for the element, and everything in between. This might include text, other elements, and comments, as well as other things such as entity references and processing instructions.

Namespaces

A final XML topic we'll mention here is *namespaces*. Namespaces are designed to distinguish between two tags that have the same name. For example, if I design an XML vocabulary for books and you design an XML vocabulary for paintings, it's likely that both of us will define a `<title>` element. My `<title>` element refers to the title of a book, while yours refers to the title of a painting. If someone needs to create an XML document that refers to both books and paintings, they can use a namespace to distinguish between the two `<title>` elements. Namespaces are defined and used as follows:

```
<xyz xmlns:books="http://www.myco.com/books.dtd"
     xmlns:paintings="http://www.yourco.com/paintings.xsd">
```

In this example, the `xmlns:books` attribute associates a string with the `books` DTD, and the `xmlns:paintings` attribute associates a string with the `paintings` schema. This means that a `title` element from the `books` DTD would be coded as `<books:title>`, while a `title` element from the `paintings` schema would be referred to as `<paintings:title>`.

I mention namespaces here primarily because all XSLT elements we use in this book are prefixed with the `xsl` namespace prefix. All stylesheets we write begin like this:

```
<?xml version="1.0"?>
<xsl:stylesheet xmlns:xsl="http://www.w3.org/1999/XSL/Transform" version="1.0">
```

This opening associates the `xsl` namespace prefix with the string `http://www.w3.org/1999/XSL/Transform`. The value of the namespace prefix doesn't matter; we could start our stylesheets like this:

```
<?xml version="1.0"?>
<pdq:stylesheet xmlns:pdq="http://www.w3.org/1999/XSL/Transform" version="1.0">
```

What matters is the string to which the namespace prefix is mapped. Also keep in mind that all XSLT stylesheets use namespace prefixes to process the XML elements they contain. By default, anything that doesn't use the `xsl` namespace prefix is not processed—it's written to the result tree. We'll discuss these topics in more detail as we go through the book.

DOM and SAX

The two most popular APIs used to parse XML documents are the Document Object Model (DOM) and the Simple API for XML (SAX). DOM is an official recommendation of the W3C (available at *http://www.w3.org/TR/REC-DOM-Level-1*), while SAX is a de facto standard created by David Megginson and others on the

XML-DEV mailing list (*http://lists.xml.org/archives*). We'll discuss these two APIs briefly here. We won't use them much in this book, but discussing them will give you some insight into how most XSLT processors work.

See *http://www.megginson.com/SAX/* for the SAX standard. (Make sure the letters `SAX` are in uppercase.) If you'd like to learn more about the XML-DEV mailing list, send email with "subscribe xml-dev" in the body of the message to *majordomo@xml.org*. You can also check out *http://www.lists.ic.ac.uk/hypermail/xml-dev* to see the XML-DEV mailing list archives.

DOM

DOM is designed to build a tree view of your document. Remember that all XML documents must be contained in a single element; that single element becomes the root of the tree. The DOM specification defines several language-neutral interfaces, described here:

`Node`
: This interface is the base datatype of the DOM. `Element`, `document`, `text`, `comment`, and `attr` all extend the `Node` interface.

`Document`
: This object contains the DOM representation of the XML document. Given a `Document` object, you can get the root of the tree (the `Document` element); from the root, you can move through the tree to find all elements, attributes, text, comments, processing instructions, etc., in the XML document.

`Element`
: This interface represents an element in an XML document.

`Attr`
: This interface represents an attribute of an element in an XML document.

`Text`
: This interface represents a piece of text from the XML document. Any text in your XML document becomes a `Text` node. This means that the text of a DOM object is a child of the object, not a property of it. The text of an `Element` is represented as a `Text` child of an `Element` object; the text of an `Attr` is also represented that way.

`Comment`
: This interface represents a comment in the XML document. A comment begins with `<!--` and ends with `-->`. The only restriction on its contents is that two consecutive hyphens (`--`) can appear only at the start or end of the comment.

Other than that, a comment can include angle brackets (< >), ampersands (&), single or double quotation marks (' "), and anything else.

`ProcessingInstruction`
: This interface represents a processing instruction in the XML document. Processing instructions look like this:

```
<?xml-stylesheet href="case-study.xsl" type="text/xsl"?>
<?cocoon-process type="xslt"?>
```

Processing instructions contain processor-specific information. The first of the two PIs (PI is XML jargon—feel free to drop this into casual conversations to impress your friends) is the standard way to associate an XSLT stylesheet with an XML document (more on this in a minute). The second PI is used by Cocoon, an XML publishing framework from the Apache Software Foundation. (If you're not familiar with Cocoon, look at the Cocoon home page at *http://xml.apache.org/cocoon*.)

When you parse an XML document with a DOM parser, it:

- Creates objects (`Elements`, `Attr`, `Text`, `Comments`) representing the contents of the document. These objects implement the interfaces defined in the DOM specification.
- Arranges these objects in a tree. Each `Element` in the XML document has some properties (such as the element's name), and may also have some children.
- Parses the entire document before control returns to your code. This means that for large documents, there is a significant delay while the document is parsed.

The most significant thing about the DOM is that it is based on a tree view of your document. An XSLT processor uses a very similar tree view (with some slight differences, such as the fact that not everything we deal with in XPath and XSLT has the same root element). Understanding how a DOM parser works makes it easier to understand how an XSLT processor views your document.

A sample DOM tree. DOM, XSLT, and XPath all use tree structures to represent data from an XML document. For this reason, it's important to have at least a casual knowledge of how DOM builds a tree structure. Our earlier `<postalcodes>` document is shown as a DOM tree in Figure 1-2.

The image in Figure 1-2 was produced by the DOMit servlet, an XML validation service available at *http://www-106.ibm.com/developerworks/features/xmlvalidatorform.html*.

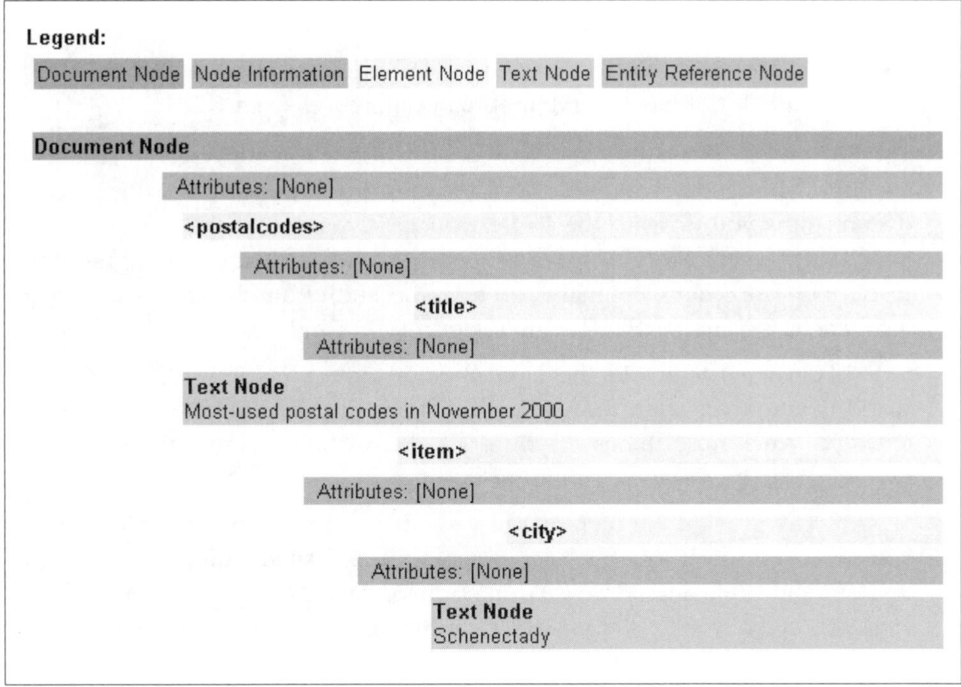

Figure 1-2. DOM tree representation of an XML document

If we want to find different parts of our XML document, sort the subtrees based on the first character of the text of the `<postalcode>` element, or select only the subtrees in which the text of the `<usage-count>` element has a numeric value greater than 500, we have to start at the top of the DOM tree and work our way down through the root element's descendants. When we write XSLT stylesheets, we also start at the root of the tree and work our way down.

To be honest, the DOM tree built for our document is more complicated than our beautiful picture indicates. The whitespace characters in our document (carriage return/line feed, tabs, spaces, etc.) become `Text` nodes. Normally it's a good idea to remove this whitespace so the DOM tree won't be littered with these useless `Text` nodes, but I included them here to give you a sense of the XML document's structure.

SAX

The Simple API for XML was developed by David Megginson and others on the XML-DEV mailing list. It has several important differences from DOM:

- The SAX API is interactive. As a SAX parser processes your document, it sends events to your code. You don't have to wait for the parser to finish the entire document as you do with the DOM; you get events from the parser immediately. These events let you know when the parser finds the start of the document, the start of an element, some text, the end of an element, a processing instruction, the end of the document, etc.
- SAX is designed to avoid the large memory footprint of DOM. In the SAX world, you're told when the parser finds things in the XML document; it's up to you to save those things. If you don't do anything to store the data found by the parser, it goes into the bit bucket.
- SAX doesn't provide the hierarchical view of the document that DOM does. If you need to know a lot about the structure of an XML document and the context of a given element, SAX isn't much help. Each SAX event is stateless; that is, a SAX event won't tell you, "Here's some text for the `<postalcode>` element I mentioned earlier." A SAX parser only tells you, "Here's some text." If you need to know about an XML document's structure, you have to keep track of that information yourself.

The best thing about SAX is that it is interactive. Most of the transformations currently done with XSLT take place on the server. As of this writing, most XSLT processors are based on DOM parsers. In the near future, however, we'll see XSLT processors based on SAX parsers. This means that the processor can start generating results almost as soon as the parse of the source document begins, resulting in better throughput and creating the perception of faster service. Because DOM, XPath, and XSLT all use trees to represent XML documents, DOM is more relevant to our discussions here. Nevertheless, it's useful to know how SAX parsers work, especially as SAX-based XSLT processors begin to rear their speedy little heads.

XML Standards

When we talk about writing stylesheets, we'll work with two standards: XSLT and XPath. XSLT defines a set of primitives used to describe a document transformation, while XPath defines a syntax for describing locations in XML documents. When we write stylesheets, we'll use XSLT to tell the processor what to do, and we'll use XPath to tell the processor what to do it to. Both standards are available at the W3C's web site; see *http://www.w3.org/TR/xslt* and *http://www.w3.org/TR/xpath* for more information.

There are other XML-related standards, of course. We'll discuss them here briefly, with a short mention of how (or whether) they relate to our work with XSLT and XPath.

XML 1.0

XML 1.0 is the foundation upon which everything else is built. See *http://www.w3.org/TR/REC-xml.*

The Extensible Stylesheet Language (XSL)

Also called the *Formatting Objects specification* or *XSL-FO*, this standard deals with rendering XML elements. Although most people think of rendering as formatting for a browser or a printed page, researchers use the specification to render XML elements as Braille or as audio files. (That being said, the main market for this technology is in producing high-quality printed output.) As of this writing, the XSL-FO specification is a Candidate Recommendation at the W3C. A couple of our examples in this book use formatting objects and the Apache XML Project's Formatting Object to PDF translator (FOP) tool; see *http://xml.apache.org/fop* for more information on FOP. For more information on XSL, see *http://www.w3.org/TR/xsl.*

XML Schemas

In our earlier examples, we had a brief example of an XML Schema. Part 1 of the specification deals with XML document structures; it contains XML elements that define what can appear in an XML document. You use these elements to specify which elements can be nested inside others, how many times each element can appear, the attributes of those elements, and other features. Part 2 of the specification defines basic datatypes used in XML Schemas and rules for deriving new datatypes from existing ones.

The two specifications are available at *http://www.w3.org/TR/xmlschema-1* and *http://www.w3.org/TR/xmlschema-2.* For a good introduction to XML Schemas, see the XML Schema Primer, available at *http://www.w3.org/TR/xmlschema-0.*

The Simple API for XML (SAX)

The SAX API defines the events and interfaces used to interact with a SAX parser. SAX and DOM are the most common APIs used to work with XML documents. See *http://www.megginson.com/SAX/* for the complete specification. (Note that the letters "SAX" must be in uppercase.)

Document Object Model (DOM) Level 1

The DOM, as we discussed earlier, is a programming API for documents. It defines a set of interfaces and methods used to view an XML document as a tree structure. XSLT and XPath use a similar tree view of XML documents. See *http://www.w3.org/TR/REC-DOM-Level-1* for more information.

Document Object Model (DOM) Level 2

The DOM Level 2 standard builds on DOM Level 1. It adds several new features:

- HTML support, providing a DOM view of HTML documents
- CSS and stylesheet interfaces
- Document events
- Tree traversal methods
- Range selection methods
- Views of DOM trees, in which the view is separate from the DOM itself

The new features of DOM Level 2 don't affect our work directly. If you read the specification, you'll see that certain features, such as views, stylesheet interfaces, and tree traversal, provide features useful to an XSLT processor. Although future XSLT processors will be built on XML parsers that provide these functions, that won't change any of the techniques we cover in this book. See *http://www.w3.org/TR/DOM-Level-2* for the complete specification.

Namespaces in XML

As we mentioned earlier, namespaces provide a way to avoid name collisions when two XML elements have the same name. See *http://www.w3.org/TR/REC-xml-names* for more information.

Associating stylesheets with XML documents

It's possible to reference an XSLT stylesheet within an XML document. This specification uses processing instructions to define one or more stylesheets that should be used to transform an XML document. You can define different stylesheets to be used for different browsers. See *http://www.w3.org/TR/xml-stylesheet* for complete information. Here's the start of an XML document, with two associated stylesheets:

```
<?xml version="1.0"?>
<?xml-stylesheet href="docbook/html/docbook.xsl" type="text/xsl"?>
<?xml-stylesheet href="docbook/wap/docbook.xsl"  type="text/xsl" media="wap"?>
```

In this example, the first stylesheet is the default because it doesn't have a `media` attribute. The second stylesheet will be used when the `User-Agent` field from the HTTP header contains the string `wap`, identifying the requester of a document as a

WAP browser. The advantage of this technique is that you can define several different stylesheets within a particular document and have each stylesheet generate useful results for different browser or client types. The disadvantage of this technique is that we're effectively putting rendering instructions into our XML document, something we prefer to avoid.

If you use Microsoft Internet Explorer Version 5.0 or higher, you can install the Microsoft's XSLT processor so that opening an XML document in your browser will cause it to be transformed and rendered automatically. For more details on how to install and configure the XML tools to work with the brower, see *http://www.microsoft.com/xml*. In the previous example, if we opened an XML document that began this way, the browser would transform the XML document according to the rules defined in *docbook/html/docbook.xsl* and render the results as if it were any HTML page.

Scalable Vector Graphics (SVG)

The SVG specification defines an XML vocabulary for vector graphics. Described by some as "PostScript with angle brackets," it allows you to define images that can be scaled to any size or resolution. See *http://www.w3.org/TR/SVG/* for details.

Canonical XML Version 1.0

Sometimes comparing two XML documents is necessary (when digitally signing an XML document, for example). The Canonical XML specification defines a canonical form of XML that makes comparing two documents easy. See *http://www.w3.org/TR/xml-c14n* for the complete specification.

XML digital signatures

A joint effort of the W3C and the Internet Engineering Task Force (IETF), XML digital signatures provide a mechanism for storing digital signatures in an XML document. The XML document then provides an envelope used to store, send, and retrieve digital signatures for any kind of digital resource. The latest draft of the specification can be found at *http://www.w3.org/TR/xmldsig-core*.

XML Pointer Language (XPointer) Version 1.0

XPointer provides a way to identify a fragment of a web resource. It uses XPath to identify fragments. For details, see *http://www.w3.org/TR/xptr*.

XML Linking Language (XLink) Version 1.0

XLink defines an XML vocabulary for linking to other web resources within an XML document. It supports the unidirectional links we're all familiar with in HTML, as well as more sophisticated links. See *http://www.w3.org/TR/xlink/*.

Installing Xalan

In this section, I'll show you how to install the Xalan XSLT processor. In the next chapter, we'll create our first stylesheet and use it to transform an XML document.

The installation process is pretty simple, assuming you already have a Java Runtime Environment (JRE) installed on your machine. Although very little of the code we look at in this book uses Java, the Xalan XSLT processor itself is written in Java. Once you've installed the JRE, go to *http://xml.apache.org/xalan* and download the latest stable build of the code. (If you're feeling brave, feel free to download last night's build instead.)

Once the Xalan *.zip* or *.gzip* file is downloaded, unpack it and add three files to your CLASSPATH. The three files include the *.jar* file for the Xerces parser, the *.jar* file for the Xalan stylesheet engine itself, and the *.jar* file for the Bean Scripting Framework. As of this writing, the *.jar* files are named *xerces.jar*, *xalan.jar*, and *bsf.jar*.

To make sure Xalan is installed correctly, go to a command prompt and type the following command:

```
java org.apache.xalan.xslt.Process
```

This is a Java class, so everything is case sensitive. You should see an error message like this:

```
java org.apache.xalan.xslt.Process
=xslproc options:
    -IN inputXMLURL
   [-XSL XSLTransformationURL]
   [-OUT outputURL]
   [-LXCIN compiledStylesheetFileNameIn]
   [-LXCOUT compiledStylesheetFileNameOutOut]
```

If you got this error message, you're all set! You're ready for the next chapter, in which we'll build our very first XSLT stylesheet.

Summary

In this chapter, we've gone over the basics of XML and talked about DOM and SAX, two standards that are commonly used by XSLT processors. We also talked about other technology standards and how to install the Xalan stylesheet processor. At this point, you've got everything you need to build and use your first stylesheets, something we'll do in the next chapter.

2

The Obligatory Hello World Example

In future chapters, we'll spend much time talking about XSLT, XPath, and various advanced functions used to transform XML documents. First, though, we'll go through a short example to illustrate how stylesheets work.

Goals of This Chapter

By the end of this chapter, you should know:

- How to create a basic stylesheet
- How to use a stylesheet to transform an XML document
- How a stylesheet processor uses a stylesheet to transform an XML document
- The structure of an XSLT stylesheet

Transforming Hello World

Continuing the tradition of Hello World examples begun by Brian Kernighan and Dennis Ritchie in *The C Programming Language* (Prentice Hall, 1988), we'll transform a Hello World XML document.

Our Sample Document

First, we'll look at our sample document. This simple XML document, courtesy of the XML 1.0 specification, contains the famous friendly greeting to the world:

```
<?xml version="1.0"?>
<greeting>
  Hello, World!
</greeting>
```

What we'd like to do is transform this fascinating document into something we can view in an ordinary household browser.

A Sample Stylesheet

Here's an XSLT stylesheet that defines how to transform the XML document:

```
<xsl:stylesheet
     xmlns:xsl="http://www.w3.org/1999/XSL/Transform"
     version="1.0">
  <xsl:output method="html"/>

  <xsl:template match="/">
    <xsl:apply-templates select="greeting"/>
  </xsl:template>

  <xsl:template match="greeting">
    <html>
      <body>
        <h1>
          <xsl:value-of select="."/>
        </h1>
      </body>
    </html>
  </xsl:template>
</xsl:stylesheet>
```

We'll talk about these elements and what they do in just a minute. Keep in mind that the stylesheet is itself an XML document, so we have to follow all of the document rules we discussed in the previous chapter.

Transforming the XML Document

To transform the XML document using the XSLT stylesheet, run this command:

```
java org.apache.xalan.xslt.Process -in greeting.xml -xsl greeting.xsl
  -out greeting.html
```

This command transforms the document *greeting.xml*, using the templates found in the stylesheet *greeting.xsl*. The results of the transformation are written to the file *greeting.html*. Check the output file in your favorite browser to make sure the transform worked correctly.

Stylesheet Results

The XSLT processor generates these results:

```
<html>
<body>
<h1>
  Hello, World!
```

```
</h1>
</body>
</html>
```

When rendered in a browser, our output document looks like Figure 2-1.

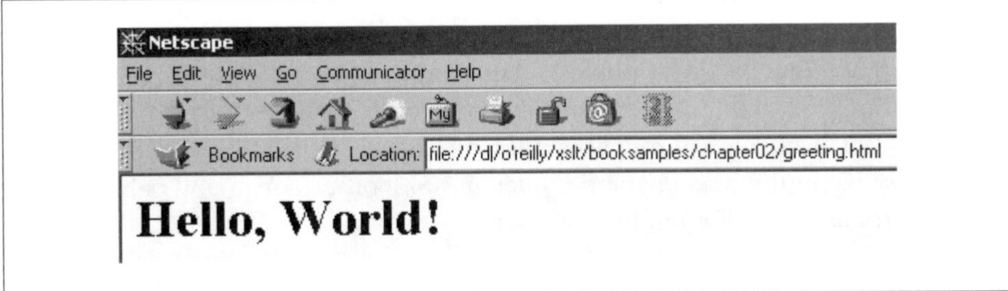

Figure 2-1. HTML version of our Hello World file

Congratulations! You've now used XSLT to transform an XML document.

How a Stylesheet Is Processed

Now that we're giddy with the excitement of having transformed an XML document, let's discuss the stylesheet and how it works. A big part of the XSLT learning curve is figuring out how stylesheets are processed. To make this clear, we'll go through the steps taken by the stylesheet processor to create the HTML document we want.

Parsing the Stylesheet

Before the XSLT processor can process your stylesheet, it has to read it. Conceptually, it doesn't matter how the XSLT processor stores the information from your stylesheet. For our purposes, we'll just assume that the XSLT processor can magically find anything it needs in our stylesheet. (If you really must know, Xalan uses an optimized table structure to represent the stylesheet; other processors may use that approach or something else.)

Our stylesheet contains three items: an `<xsl:output>` element that specifies HTML as the output format and two `<xsl:template>` elements that specify how parts of our XML document should be transformed.

Parsing the Transformee

Now that the XSLT processor has processed the stylesheet, it needs to read the document it's supposed to transform. The XSLT processor builds a tree view from the XML source. This tree view is what we'll keep in mind when we build our stylesheets.

Lather, Rinse, Repeat

Finally, we're ready to begin the actual work of transforming the XML document. The XSLT processor may set some properties based on your stylesheet (in the previous example, it would set its output method to HTML), then it begins processing as follows:

- Do I have any nodes to process? The nodes to process are represented by something called the *context*. Initially the context is the root of the XML document, but it changes throughout the stylesheet. We'll talk about the context extensively in the next chapter. (Note: all XSLT processors enjoy being anthropomorphized, so I'll often refer to them this way.)

While any nodes are in the context, do the following:

- Get the next node from the context. Do I have any `<xsl:template>`s that match it? (In our example, the next node is the root node, represented in XPath syntax by `/`.) There is a template that matches this node—it's the one that begins `<xsl:template match="/">`.
- If one or more `<xsl:template>`s match, pick the right one and process it. (The right one is the most specific template. For example, `<xsl:template match="/html/body/h1/p">` is more specific than `<xsl:template match="p">`. See the discussion of the `<xsl:template>` element for more information.) If no `<xsl:template>`s match, the XSLT processor uses some built-in rules. See the section "Built-in Template Rules" later in this chapter for more information.

Notice that this is a recursive processing model. We process the current node by finding the right `xsl:template` for it. That `xsl:template` may in turn invoke other `xsl:templates`, which invoke `xsl:templates` as well. This model takes some getting used to, but it is actually quite elegant once you're accustomed to it.

If it helps, you can think of the root template (`<xsl:template match="/">`) as the `main` method in a C, C++, or Java program. No matter how much code you've written, everything starts in `main`. Similarly, no matter how many `<xsl:template>`s you've defined in your stylesheet, everything starts in `<xsl:template match="/">`.

Walking Through Our Example

Let's revisit our example and see how the XSLT processor transforms our document:

1. The XSLT stylesheet is parsed and converted into a tree structure.
2. The XML document is also parsed and converted into a tree structure. (Don't worry too much about what that tree looks like or how it works; for now, just assume that the XSLT processor knows everything that's in the XML document and the XSLT stylesheet. After the first two steps are done, when we describe various things using XSLT and XPath, the processor knows what we're talking about.)
3. The XSLT processor is now at the root of the XML document. This is the original context.
4. There is an `xsl:template` that matches the document root:

   ```
   <xsl:template match="/">
     <xsl:apply-templates select="greeting"/>
   </xsl:template>
   ```

   A single forward slash (/) is an *XPath expression* that means "the root of the document."
5. Now the process begins again inside the `xsl:template`. Our only instruction here is to apply whatever `xsl:templates` might apply to any `greeting` elements in the current context. The current context inside this template is defined by the `match` attribute of the `xsl:template` element. This means the XSLT processor is looking for any `greeting` elements at the document root.

   Because one `greeting` element is at the document root, the XSLT processor must deal with it. (If more than one element matches in the current context, the XSLT processor deals with each one in the order in which they appear in the document; this is known as *document order*.) Looking at the `greeting` element, the `xsl:template` that applies to it is the second `xsl:template` in our stylesheet:

   ```
   <xsl:template match="greeting">
     <html>
       <body>
         <h1>
           <xsl:value-of select="."/>
         </h1>
       </body>
     </html>
   </xsl:template>
   ```

6. Now we're in the `xsl:template` for the `greeting` element. The first three elements in this `xsl:template` (`<html>`, `<body>`, and `<h1>`) are HTML elements. Because they're not defined with a namespace declaration, the XSLT processor passes those HTML elements through to the output stream unaltered.

   The middle of our `xsl:template` is an `xsl:value-of` element. This element writes the value of something to the output stream. In this case, we're using the XPath expression `.` (a single period) to indicate the current node. The XSLT processor looks at the current node (the `greeting` element we're currently processing) and outputs its text.

   Because our stylesheet is an XML document (we're really harping on that, aren't we?), we have to end the `<h1>`, `<body>`, and `<html>` elements here. At this point, we're done with this template, so control returns to the template that invoked us.

7. Now we're back in the template for the root element. We've processed all the `<greeting>` elements, so we're finished with this template.

8. No more elements are in the current context (there is only one root element), so the XSLT processor is done.

Stylesheet Structure

As the final part of our introduction to XSLT, we'll look at the contents of the stylesheet itself. We'll explain all the things in our stylesheet and discuss other approaches we could have taken.

The <xsl:stylesheet> Element

The `<xsl:stylesheet>` element is typically the root element of an XSLT stylesheet.

```
<xsl:stylesheet
    xmlns:xsl="http://www.w3.org/1999/XSL/Transform"
    version="1.0">
```

First of all, the `<xsl:stylesheet>` element defines the version of XSLT we're using, along with a definition of the `xsl` namespace. To be compliant with the XSLT specification, your stylesheet should always begin with this element, coded exactly as shown here. Some stylesheet processors, notably Xalan, issue a warning message if your `<xsl:stylesheet>` element doesn't have these two attributes with these two values. For all examples in this book, we'll start the stylesheet with this exact element, defining other namespaces as needed.

The <xsl:output> Element

Next, we specify the output method. The XSLT specification defines three output methods: `xml`, `html`, and `text`. We're creating an HTML document, so HTML is the output method we want to use. In addition to these three methods, an XSLT processor is free to define its own output methods, so check your XSLT processor's documentation to see if you have any other options.

```
<xsl:output method="html"/>
```

A variety of attributes are used with the different output methods. For example, if you're using `method="xml"`, you can use `doctype-public` and `doctype-system` to define the public and system identifiers to be used in the the document type declaration. If you're using `method="xml"` or `method="html"`, you can use the `indent` attribute to control whether or not the output document is indented. The discussion of the `<xsl:output>` element in Appendix A has all the details.

Our First <xsl:template>

Our first template matches `"/"`, the XPath expression for the document's root element.

```
<xsl:template match="/">
  <xsl:apply-templates select="greeting"/>
</xsl:template>
```

The <xsl:template> for <greeting> Elements

The second `<xsl:template>` element processes any `<greeting>` elements in our XML source document.

```
<xsl:template match="greeting">
  <html>
    <body>
      <h1>
        <xsl:value-of select="."/>
      </h1>
    </body>
  </html>
</xsl:template>
```

Built-in Template Rules

Although most stylesheets we'll develop in this book explicitly define how various XML elements should be transformed, XSLT does define several built-in template rules that apply in the absence of any specific rules. These rules have a lower priority than any other templates, so they're always overridden when you define your own templates. The built-in templates are listed here.

Built-in template rule for element and root nodes

This template processes the root node and any of its children. This processing ensures that recursive processing will continue, even if no template is declared for a given element.

```
<xsl:template match="*|/">
  <xsl:apply-templates/>
</xsl:template>
```

This means that if the structure of a document looks like this:

```
<?xml version="1.0"?>
<x>
  <y>
    <z/>
  </y>
</z>
```

The built-in template rule for element and root nodes means that we could write a template with `match="z"` and the `<z>` element will still be processed, even if there are no template rules for the `<x>` and `<y>` elements.

Built-in template rule for modes

This template ensures that element and root nodes are processed, regardless of any mode that might be in effect. (See the section "Templates à la Mode" in Chapter 4 for more information on the `mode` attribute.)

```
<xsl:template match="*|/" mode="x">
  <xsl:apply-templates mode="x"/>
</xsl:template>
```

Built-in template rule for text and attribute nodes

This template copies the text of all text and attribute nodes to the output tree. Be aware that you have to actually select the text and attribute nodes for this rule to be invoked.

```
<xsl:template match="text()|@*">
  <xsl:value-of select="."/>
</xsl:template>
```

Built-in template rule for comment and processing instruction nodes

This template does nothing.

```
<xsl:template match="comment()|processing-instruction()"/>
```

Built-in template rule for namespace nodes

This template also does nothing.

```
<xsl:template match="namespace()"/>
```

Top-Level Elements

To this point, we haven't actually talked about our source document or how we're going to transform it. We're simply setting up some properties for the transform. There are other elements we can put at the start of our stylesheet. Any element whose parent is the `<xsl:stylesheet>` element is called a *top-level element*. Here is a brief discussion of the other top-level elements:

`<xsl:include>` *and* `<xsl:import>`
: These elements refer to another stylesheet. The other stylesheet and all of its contents are included in the current stylesheet. The main difference between `<xsl:import>` and `<xsl:include>` is that a template, variable, or anything else imported with `<xsl:import>` has a lower priority than the things in the current stylesheet. This gives you a mechanism to subclass stylesheets, if you want to think about this from an object-oriented point of view. You can import another stylesheet that contains common templates, but any templates in the *importing* stylesheet will be used instead of any templates in the imported stylesheet. Another difference is that `<xsl:import>` can only appear at the beginning of a stylesheet, while `<xsl:include>` can appear anywhere.

`<xsl:strip-space>` *and* `<xsl:preserve-space>`
: These elements contain a space-separated list of elements from which whitespace should be removed or preserved in the output. To define these elements globally, use `<xsl:strip-space elements="*"/>` or `<xsl:preserve-space elements="*"/>`. If we want to specify that whitespace be removed for all elements except for `<greeting>` elements and `<salutation>` elements, we would add this markup to our stylesheet:

```
<xsl:strip-space elements="*"/>
<xsl:preserve-space elements="greeting salutation"/>
```

`<xsl:key>`
: This element defines a key, which is similar to defining an index on a database. We'll talk more about the `<xsl:key>` element and the `key()` function in the section "Generating Links with the key() Function" in Chapter 5.

`<xsl:variable>`
: This element defines a variable. Any `<xsl:variable>` that appears as a top-level element is global to the entire stylesheet. Variables are discussed extensively in the section "Variables" in Chapter 4.

`<xsl:param>`
: This element defines a parameter. As with `<xsl:variable>`, any `<xsl:param>` that is a top-level element is global to the entire stylesheet. Parameters are discussed extensively in the section "Parameters" in Chapter 4.

Other stuff
: More obscure elements that can appear as top-level elements are `<xsl:decimal-format>`, `<xsl:namespace-alias>`, and `<xsl:attribute-set>`. All are discussed in Appendix A.

Other Approaches

One mantra of the Perl community is, "There's more than one way to do it." That's true with XSLT stylesheets, as well. We could have written our stylesheet like this:

```
<xsl:stylesheet
    xmlns:xsl="http://www.w3.org/1999/XSL/Transform"
    version="1.0">
  <xsl:output method="html"/>

  <xsl:template match="/">
    <html>
      <body>
        <xsl:apply-templates select="greeting"/>
      </body>
    </html>
  </xsl:template>

  <xsl:template match="greeting">
    <h1>
      <xsl:value-of select="."/>
    </h1>
  </xsl:template>
</xsl:stylesheet>
```

In this version, we put the wrapper elements for the HTML document in the template for the root element. One of the things you should think about as you build your stylesheets is where to put elements like `<html>` and `<body>`. Let's say our XML document looked like this instead:

```
<?xml version="1.0"?>
<greetings>
  <greeting>Hello, World!</greeting>
  <greeting>Hey, Y'all!</greeting>
</greetings>
```

In this case, we would have to put the <html> and <body> elements in the <xsl:template> for the root element. If they were in the <xsl:template> for the <greeting> element, the output document would have multiple <html> elements, something that isn't valid in an HTML document. Our updated stylesheet would look like this:

```
<xsl:stylesheet
    xmlns:xsl="http://www.w3.org/1999/XSL/Transform"
    version="1.0">
  <xsl:output method="html"/>

  <xsl:template match="/">
    <html>
      <body>
        <xsl:apply-templates select="greetings/greeting"/>
      </body>
    </html>
  </xsl:template>

  <xsl:template match="greeting">
    <h1>
      <xsl:value-of select="."/>
    </h1>
  </xsl:template>
</xsl:stylesheet>
```

Notice that we had to modify our XPath expression; what was originally `greeting` is now `greetings/greeting`. As we develop stylesheets, we'll have to make sure our XPath expressions match the document structure. When you get unexpected results, or no results, an incorrect XPath expression is usually the cause.

As a final example, we could also write our stylesheet with only one `xsl:template`:

```
<xsl:stylesheet xmlns:xsl="http://www.w3.org/1999/XSL/Transform" version="1.0">
  <xsl:output method="html"/>

  <xsl:template match="/">
    <html>
      <body>
        <h1>
          <xsl:value-of select="greeting"/>
        </h1>
      </body>
    </html>
  </xsl:template>
</xsl:stylesheet>
```

Although this is the shortest of our sample stylesheets, our examples will tend to feature a number of short templates, each of which defines a simple transform for a few elements. This approach makes your stylesheets much easier to understand, maintain, and reuse. The more transformations you cram into each `xsl:template`, the more difficult it is to debug your stylesheets, and the more difficult it is to reuse the templates elsewhere.

Sample Gallery

Before we get into more advanced topics, we'll transform our Hello World document in other ways. We'll look through simple stylesheets that convert our small XML document into the following things:

- A Scalable Vector Graphics (SVG) File
- A PDF file
- A Java program
- A Virtual Reality Modeling Language (VRML) file

The Hello World SVG File

Our first example will convert our Hello World document into an SVG file:

```
<?xml version="1.0"?>
<xsl:stylesheet version="1.0"
  xmlns:xsl="http://www.w3.org/1999/XSL/Transform">

  <xsl:output method="xml"
    doctype-public="-//W3C//DTD SVG 20001102//EN"
    doctype-system=
      "http://www.w3.org/TR/2000/CR-SVG-20001102/DTD/svg-20001102.dtd"/>

  <xsl:template match="/">
    <svg width="8cm" height="4cm">
      <g>
        <defs>
          <radialGradient id="MyGradient"
            cx="4cm" cy="2cm" r="3cm" fx="4cm" fy="2cm">
            <stop offset="0%" style="stop-color:red"/>
            <stop offset="50%" style="stop-color:blue"/>
            <stop offset="100%" style="stop-color:red"/>
          </radialGradient>
        </defs>
        <rect style="fill:url(#MyGradient); stroke:black"
          x="1cm" y="1cm" width="6cm" height="2cm"/>
        <text x="4cm" y="2.2cm" text-anchor="middle"
          style="font-family:Verdana; font-size:24;
          font-weight:bold; fill:black">
          <xsl:apply-templates select="greeting"/>
        </text>
      </g>
    </svg>
  </xsl:template>
```

```
    <xsl:template match="greeting">
      <xsl:value-of select="."/>
    </xsl:template>

  </xsl:stylesheet>
```

As you can see from this stylesheet, most of the code here simply sets up the structure of the SVG document. This is typical of many stylesheets; once you learn what the output format should be, you merely extract content from the XML source document and insert it into the output document at the correct spot. When we transform the Hello World document with this stylesheet, here are the results:

```
<?xml version="1.0" encoding="UTF-8"?>
<!DOCTYPE svg PUBLIC "-//W3C//DTD SVG 20001102//EN"
        "http://www.w3.org/TR/2000/CR-SVG-20001102/DTD/svg-20001102.dtd">
<svg height="4cm" width="8cm">
  <g>
    <defs>
      <radialGradient fy="2cm" fx="4cm" r="3cm" cy="2cm"
        cx="4cm" id="MyGradient">
        <stop style="stop-color:red" offset="0%"/>
        <stop style="stop-color:blue" offset="50%"/>
        <stop style="stop-color:red" offset="100%"/>
      </radialGradient>
    </defs>
    <rect height="2cm" width="6cm" y="1cm" x="1cm"
        style="fill:url(#MyGradient); stroke:black"/>
    <text style="font-family:Verdana; font-size:24;
        font-weight:bold; fill:black"
        text-anchor="middle" y="2.2cm" x="4cm">
  Hello, World!
    </text>
  </g>
</svg>
```

When rendered in an SVG viewer, our Hello World document looks like Figure 2-2.

Figure 2-2. SVG version of our Hello World file

This screen capture was made using the Adobe SVG plug-in inside the Internet Explorer browser. You can find the plug-in at *http://www.adobe.com/svg/*.

We used Xalan to generate the SVG file:

```
java org.apache.xalan.xslt.Process -in greeting.xml -xsl svg-greeting.xsl
  -out greeting.svg
```

(This command should all be on a single line.)

The Hello World PDF File

To convert the Hello World file into a PDF file, we'll first convert our XML file into formatting objects. The Extensible Stylesheet Language for Formatting Objects (XSL-FO) is an XML vocabulary that describes how content should be rendered. Here is our stylesheet:

```
<?xml version="1.0"?>
<xsl:stylesheet version="1.0"
  xmlns:xsl="http://www.w3.org/1999/XSL/Transform"
  xmlns:fo="http://www.w3.org/1999/XSL/Format">

  <xsl:output method="xml"/>

  <xsl:template match="/">
    <fo:root xmlns:fo="http://www.w3.org/1999/XSL/Format">
      <fo:layout-master-set>
        <fo:simple-page-master margin-right="75pt" margin-left="75pt"
          page-height="11in" page-width="8.5in"
          margin-bottom="25pt" margin-top="25pt" master-name="main">
          <fo:region-before extent="25pt"/>
          <fo:region-body margin-top="50pt" margin-bottom="50pt"/>
          <fo:region-after extent="25pt"/>
        </fo:simple-page-master>
        <fo:page-sequence-master master-name="standard">
          <fo:repeatable-page-master-alternatives>
            <fo:conditional-page-master-reference
              master-name="main" odd-or-even="any"/>
          </fo:repeatable-page-master-alternatives>
        </fo:page-sequence-master>
      </fo:layout-master-set>

      <fo:page-sequence master-name="standard">
        <fo:flow flow-name="xsl-region-body">
          <xsl:apply-templates select="greeting"/>
        </fo:flow>
      </fo:page-sequence>
    </fo:root>
  </xsl:template>
```

```
  <xsl:template match="greeting">
    <fo:block line-height="40pt" font-size="36pt" text-align="center">
      <xsl:value-of select="."/>
    </fo:block>
  </xsl:template>

</xsl:stylesheet>
```

This stylesheet converts our Hello World document into the following XML file:

```
<?xml version="1.0" encoding="UTF-8"?>
<fo:root xmlns:fo="http://www.w3.org/1999/XSL/Format">
  <fo:layout-master-set>
    <fo:simple-page-master master-name="main" margin-top="25pt"
        margin-bottom="25pt" page-width="8.5in" page-height="11in"
        margin-left="75pt" margin-right="75pt">
      <fo:region-before extent="25pt"/>
      <fo:region-body margin-bottom="50pt" margin-top="50pt"/>
      <fo:region-after extent="25pt"/>
    </fo:simple-page-master>
    <fo:page-sequence-master master-name="standard">
      <fo:repeatable-page-master-alternatives>
        <fo:conditional-page-master-reference odd-or-even="any"
        master-name="main"/>
      </fo:repeatable-page-master-alternatives>
    </fo:page-sequence-master>
  </fo:layout-master-set>
  <fo:page-sequence master-name="standard">
    <fo:flow flow-name="xsl-region-body">
      <fo:block text-align="center" font-size="36pt" line-height="40pt">
  Hello, World!
      </fo:block>
    </fo:flow>
  </fo:page-sequence>
</fo:root>
```

We generated this file of formatting objects with this command:

```
java org.apache.xalan.xslt.Process -in greeting.xml -xsl fo-greeting.xsl
  -out greeting.fo
```

This lengthy set of tags uses formatting objects to describe the size of the page, the margins, font sizes, line heights, etc., along with the text extracted from our XML source document. Now that we have the formatting objects, we can use the Apache XML Project's FOP tool. After converting the formatting objects to PDF, the PDF file looks like Figure 2-3.

Here's the command used to convert our file of formatting objects into a PDF file:

```
java org.apache.fop.apps.CommandLine greeting.fo greeting.pdf
```

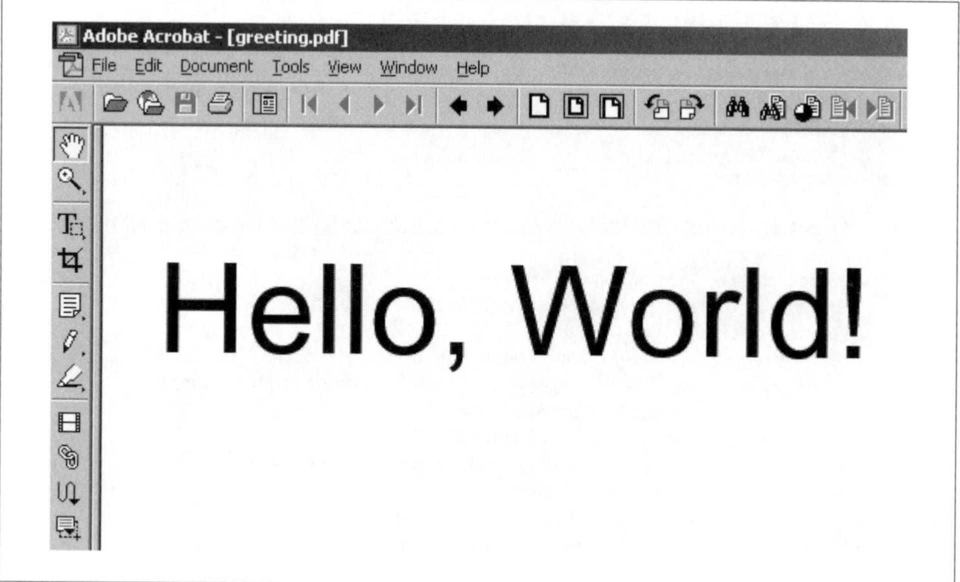

Figure 2-3. PDF version of our Hello World file

The Hello World Java Program

Our last two transformations don't involve XML vocabularies at all; they use XSLT to convert the Hello World document into other formats. Next, we'll transform our XML source document into the source code for a Java program. When the program is compiled and executed, it prints the message from the XML document to the console. Here's our stylesheet:

```
<?xml version="1.0"?>
<xsl:stylesheet version="1.0"
  xmlns:xsl="http://www.w3.org/1999/XSL/Transform">

  <xsl:output method="text"/>

  <xsl:template match="/">
    <xsl:text>
public class Greeting
{
  public static void main(String[] argv)
  {
    </xsl:text>
    <xsl:apply-templates select="greeting"/>
    <xsl:text>
  }
}
    </xsl:text>
  </xsl:template>
```

```
  <xsl:template match="greeting">
    <xsl:text>System.out.println("</xsl:text>
    <xsl:value-of select="normalize-space()"/>
    <xsl:text>");</xsl:text>
  </xsl:template>

</xsl:stylesheet>
```

(Notice that we used `<xsl:output method="text">` to generate text, not markup.) Our stylesheet produces these results:

```
public class Greeting
{
  public static void main(String[] argv)
  {
    System.out.println("Hello, World!");
  }
}
```

We generated this Java code with the following command:

```
java org.apache.xalan.xslt.Process -in greeting.xml -xsl java-greeting.xsl
  -out Greeting.java
```

(Notice that the name of the generated file must start with an uppercase letter; Java requires that the name of the file must match the name of the class it contains. Also, this command should be entered on a single line.) When executed, our generated Java program looks like this:

```
C:\> java Greeting
Hello, World!
```

Although generating Java code from an XML document may seem strange, it is actually a common technique. The FOP tool from the Apache XML Project does this; it defines a number of properties in XML, then generates the Java source code to create class definitions and `get` and `set` methods for each of those properties.

The Hello World VRML File

For our final transformation, we'll create a VRML file from our XML source document. Here's the stylesheet that does the trick:

```
<?xml version="1.0"?>
<xsl:stylesheet version="1.0"
  xmlns:xsl="http://www.w3.org/1999/XSL/Transform">

  <xsl:output method="text"/>

  <xsl:template match="/">
    <xsl:text>#VRML V2.0 utf8
```

```
Shape
{
  geometry ElevationGrid
  {
    xDimension 9
    zDimension 9
    xSpacing 1
    zSpacing 1
    height
    [
      0 0 0 0 0 0 0 0 0
      0 0 0 0 0 0 0 0 0
      0 0 0 0 0 0 0 0 0
      0 0 0 0 0 0 0 0 0
      0 0 0 0 0 0 0 0 0
      0 0 0 0 0 0 0 0 0
      0 0 0 0 0 0 0 0 0
      0 0 0 0 0 0 0 0 0
      0 0 0 0 0 0 0 0 0
    ]
    colorPerVertex FALSE
    color Color
    {
      color
      [
        0 0 0, 1 1 1, 0 0 0, 1 1 1, 0 0 0, 1 1 1, 0 0 0, 1 1 1,
        1 1 1, 0 0 0, 1 1 1, 0 0 0, 1 1 1, 0 0 0, 1 1 1, 0 0 0,
        0 0 0, 1 1 1, 0 0 0, 1 1 1, 0 0 0, 1 1 1, 0 0 0, 1 1 1,
        1 1 1, 0 0 0, 1 1 1, 0 0 0, 1 1 1, 0 0 0, 1 1 1, 0 0 0,
        0 0 0, 1 1 1, 0 0 0, 1 1 1, 0 0 0, 1 1 1, 0 0 0, 1 1 1,
        1 1 1, 0 0 0, 1 1 1, 0 0 0, 1 1 1, 0 0 0, 1 1 1, 0 0 0,
        0 0 0, 1 1 1, 0 0 0, 1 1 1, 0 0 0, 1 1 1, 0 0 0, 1 1 1,
        1 1 1, 0 0 0, 1 1 1, 0 0 0, 1 1 1, 0 0 0, 1 1 1, 0 0 0,
      ]
    }
  }
}

Transform
{
  translation 4.5 1 4
  children
  [
    Shape
    {
      geometry Text
      {
    </xsl:text>
    <xsl:apply-templates select="greeting"/>
    <xsl:text>
        fontStyle FontStyle
```

```
          {
            justify "MIDDLE"
            style "BOLD"
          }
        }
      }
    ]
  }

  NavigationInfo
  {
    type ["EXAMINE","ANY"]
  }

  Viewpoint
  {
    position 4 1 10
  }
      </xsl:text>
    </xsl:template>

    <xsl:template match="greeting">
      <xsl:text>string"</xsl:text>
      <xsl:value-of select="normalize-space()"/>
      <xsl:text>"</xsl:text>
    </xsl:template>

  </xsl:stylesheet>
```

We generate our VRML document with the following command:

```
java org.apache.xalan.xslt.Process -in greeting.xml -xsl vrml-greeting.xsl
  -out greeting.wrl
```

As with our earlier stylesheet, our VRML-generating template is mostly boilerplate, with content from the XML source document added at the appropriate point. The `<xsl:apply-templates>` element is replaced with the value of the `<greeting>` element. The VRML code here draws a checkerboard, then draws the text from the XML document above it, floating in midair in the center of the document. A couple of views of the VRML version of our XML document are shown in Figure 2-4.

Although we haven't discussed any of the specific vocabularies or file formats we've used here, hopefully you understand that you can transform your XML documents into any useful format you can think of. Through the rest of the book, we'll cover several common tasks you can solve with XSLT, all of which build on the basics we've discussed here.

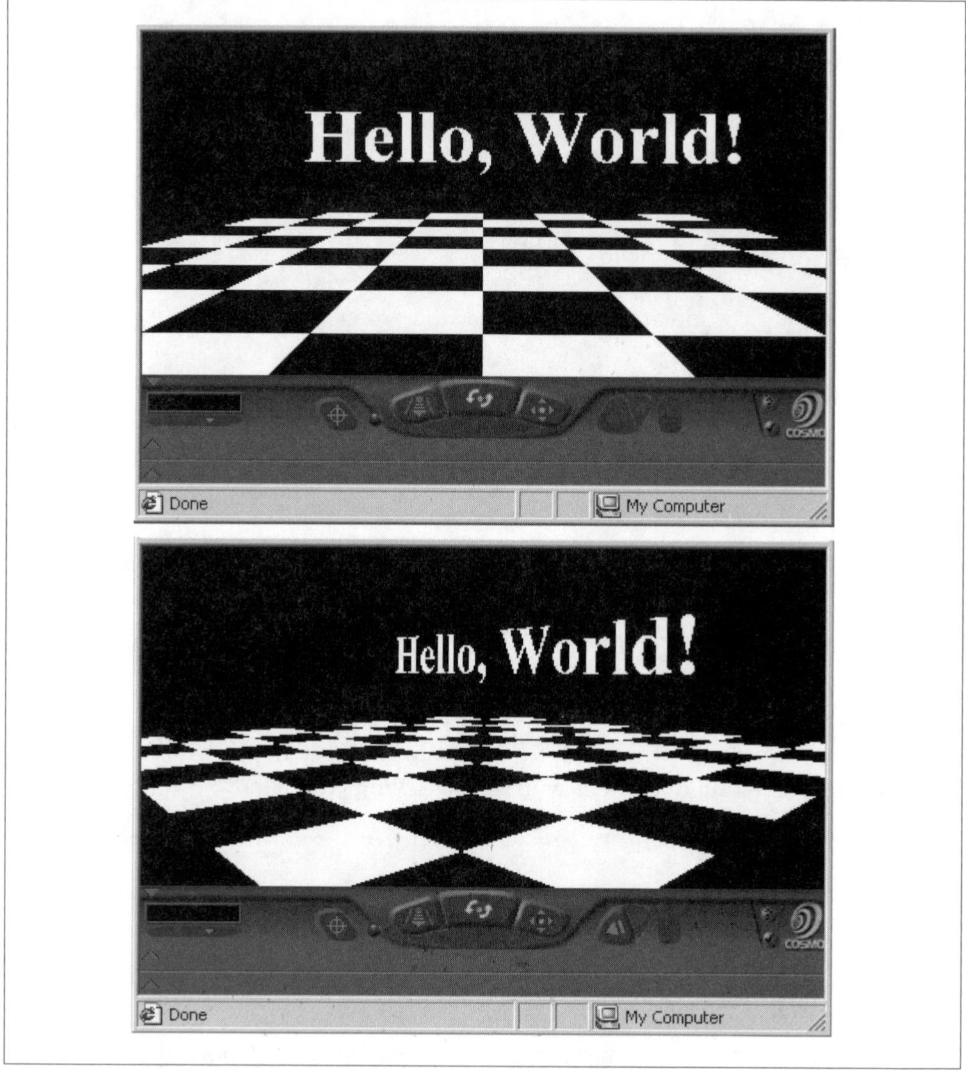

Figure 2-4. Two views of the VRML version of our Hello World document

Summary

Although our stylesheets here are trivial, they are much simpler than the corresponding procedural code (written in Visual Basic, C++, Java, etc.) to transform any `<greeting>` elements similarly. We've gone over the basics of what stylesheets are and how they work.

As we go through this book, we'll demonstrate the incredible range of things you can do in XSLT stylesheets, including:

- Using logic, branching, and control statements
- Sorting and grouping elements
- Linking and cross-referencing elements
- Creating master documents that embed other XML documents, then sort, filter, group, and format the combined documents.
- Adding new functions to the XSLT stylesheet processor with XSLT's extension mechanism

XSLT has an extremely active user community. To see just how active, visit the XSL-List site at *http://www.mulberrytech.com/xsl/xsl-list/index.html.*

Before we dive in to those topics, we need to talk about XPath, the syntax that describes what parts of an XML document we want to transform into all of these different things.

3

XPath: A Syntax for Describing Needles and Haystacks

XPath is a syntax used to describe parts of an XML document. With XPath, you can refer to the first `<para>` element, the `quantity` attribute of the `<part-number>` element, all `<first-name>` elements that contain the text `"Joe"`, and many other variations. An XSLT stylesheet uses XPath expressions in the `match` and `select` attributes of various elements to indicate how a document should be transformed. In this chapter, we'll discuss XPath in all its glory.

XPath is designed to be used inside an attribute in an XML document. The syntax is a mix of basic programming language expressions (such as `$x*6`) and Unix-like path expressions (such as `/sonnet/author/last-name`). In addition to the basic syntax, XPath provides a set of useful functions that allow you to find out various things about the document.

One important point, though: XPath works with the parsed version of your XML document. That means that some details of the original document aren't accessible to you from XPath. For example, entity references are resolved beforehand by the XSLT processor before instructions in our stylesheet are evaluated. CDATA sections are converted to text, as well. That means we have no way of knowing if a text node in an XPath tree was in the original XML document as text, as an entity reference, or as part of a CDATA section. As you get used to thinking about your XML documents in terms of XPath expressions, this situation won't be a problem, but it may confuse you at first.

The XPath Data Model

XPath views an XML document as a tree of nodes. This tree is very similar to a Document Object Model (DOM) tree, so if you're familiar with the DOM, you should have some understanding of how to build basic XPath expressions. (To be precise, this is a conceptual tree; an XSLT processor or anything else that implements the XPath standard doesn't have to build an actual tree.) There are seven kinds of nodes in XPath:

- The root node (one per document)
- Element nodes
- Attribute nodes
- Text nodes
- Comment nodes
- Processing instruction nodes
- Namespace nodes

We'll talk about all the different node types in terms of the following document:

```
<?xml version="1.0"?>
<?xml-stylesheet href="sonnet.xsl" type="text/xsl"?>
<?cocoon-process type="xslt"?>

<!DOCTYPE sonnet [
  <!ELEMENT sonnet (auth:author, title, lines)>
  <!ATTLIST sonnet public-domain CDATA "yes"
            type (Shakespearean | Petrarchan) "Shakespearean">
<!ELEMENT auth:author  (last-name,first-name,nationality,
                        year-of-birth?,year-of-death?)>
<!ELEMENT last-name (#PCDATA)>
<!ELEMENT first-name (#PCDATA)>
<!ELEMENT nationality (#PCDATA)>
<!ELEMENT year-of-birth (#PCDATA)>
<!ELEMENT year-of-death (#PCDATA)>
<!ELEMENT title (#PCDATA)>
<!ELEMENT lines (line,line,line,line,
                 line,line,line,line,
                 line,line,line,line,
                 line,line)>
<!ELEMENT line (#PCDATA)>
]>

<!-- Default sonnet type is Shakespearean, the other allowable -->
<!-- type is "Petrarchan."                                     -->
<sonnet type="Shakespearean">
  <auth:author xmlns:auth="http://www.authors.com/">
    <last-name>Shakespeare</last-name>
    <first-name>William</first-name>
```

```
      <nationality>British</nationality>
      <year-of-birth>1564</year-of-birth>
      <year-of-death>1616</year-of-death>
    </auth:author>
    <!-- Is there an official title for this sonnet?  They're
         sometimes named after the first line.                 -->
    <title>Sonnet 130</title>
    <lines>
      <line>My mistress' eyes are nothing like the sun,</line>
      <line>Coral is far more red than her lips red.</line>
      <line>If snow be white, why then her breasts are dun,</line>
      <line>If hairs be wires, black wires grow on her head.</line>
      <line>I have seen roses damasked, red and white,</line>
      <line>But no such roses see I in her cheeks.</line>
      <line>And in some perfumes is there more delight</line>
      <line>Than in the breath that from my mistress reeks.</line>
      <line>I love to hear her speak, yet well I know</line>
      <line>That music hath a far more pleasing sound.</line>
      <line>I grant I never saw a goddess go,</line>
      <line>My mistress when she walks, treads on the ground.</line>
      <line>And yet, by Heaven, I think my love as rare</line>
      <line>As any she belied with false compare.</line>
    </lines>
  </sonnet>
  <!-- The title of Sting's 1987 album "Nothing like the sun" is  -->
  <!-- from line 1 of this sonnet.                                 -->
```

The Root Node

The root node is the XPath node that contains the entire document. In our example, the root node contains the <sonnet> element; it's not the <sonnet> element itself. In an XPath expression, the root node is specified with a single slash (/).

Unlike other nodes, the root node has no parent. It always has at least one child, the document element. The root node also contains comments or processing instructions that are outside the document element. In our sample document, the two processing instructions named `xml-stylesheet` and `cocoon-process` are both children of the root node, as are the comment that appears before the <sonnet> tag and the comment that appears after the </sonnet> tag. The string value of the root node (returned by `<xsl:value-of select="/" />`, for example), is the concatenation of all text nodes of the root node's descendants.

Element Nodes

Every element in the original XML document is represented by an XPath element node. In the previous document, an element node exists for the <sonnet> element, the <auth:author> element, the <last-name> element, etc. An element node's children include text nodes, element nodes, comment nodes, and processing instruction nodes that occur within that element in the original document.

An element node's string value (returned by <xsl:value-of select="sonnet">, for example) is the concatenation of the text of this node and all of its children, in document order (the order in which they appear in the original document). All entity references (such as <) and character references (such as 4) in the text are resolved automatically; you can't access the entity or character references from XPath.

The name of an element node (returned by the XPath name() function) is the element name and any namespace in effect. In the previous example, the name() of the <sonnet> element is sonnet. The name() of the <auth:author> element is auth:author, and the name() of the <last-name> element is auth:last-name (any element contained in the <author> element is from the auth namespace unless specifically declared otherwise). Other XPath functions, such as local-name() and namespace-uri(), return other information about the name of the element node.

Attribute Nodes

At a minimum, an element node is the parent of one attribute node for each attribute in the XML source document. In our sample document, the element node corresponding to the <sonnet> element is the parent of an attribute node with a name of type and a value of Shakespearean. A couple of complications for attribute nodes exist, however:

- Although an element node is the parent of its attribute nodes, those attribute nodes are not children of their parent. The children of an element are the text, element, comment, and processing instruction nodes contained in the original element. If you want a document's attributes, you must ask for them specifically. That relationship seems odd at first, but you'll find that treating an element's attributes separately is usually what you want to do.
- If a DTD or schema defines default values for certain attributes, those attributes don't have to appear in the XML document. For example, we could have declared that a Shakespearean sonnet is the default type, so that the tag <sonnet type="Shakespearean"> is functionally equivalent to <sonnet>. Under normal circumstances, XPath creates an attribute node for all attributes with default values, whether they actually appear in the document or not. If the type is defined as #IMPLIED, both of the <sonnet> elements we just mentioned will have an attribute node with a name of type and a value of Shakespearean. Of course, if the document codes a value other than the default (<sonnet type="Petrarchan">, for example), the attribute node's value will be whatever was coded in the document.

To make this situation even worse, an XML parser isn't required to read an external DTD. If it doesn't, then any attribute nodes that represent default values not coded in the document won't exist. Fortunately, XSLT has some branching elements (`<xsl:if>` and `<xsl:choose>`) that can help you deal with these ambiguities; we'll discuss those in Chapter 4.

- The XML 1.0 specification defines two attributes (`xml:lang` and `xml:space`) that work like default namespaces. In other words, if the `<auth:author>` element in our sample document contains the attribute `xml:lang="en_us"`, that attribute applies to all elements contained inside `<auth:author>`. Even though that attribute might apply to the `<last-name>` element, `<last-name>` won't have an attribute node named `xml:lang`. Similarly, the `xml:space` defines whether whitespace in an element should be preserved; valid values for this attribute are `preserve` and `default`. Whether these attributes are in effect for a given element or not, the only attribute nodes an element node contains are those tagged in the document and those defined with a default value in the DTD.

  For more information on language codes and whitespace handling, see the discussions of the XPath `lang()` function and the XSLT `<xsl:preserve-space>` and `<xsl:strip-space>` elements.

Text Nodes

Text nodes are refreshingly simple; they contain text from an element. If the original text in the XML document contained entity or character references, they are resolved before the XPath text node is created. The text node is text, pure and simple. A text node is required to contain as much text as possible; the next or previous node can't be a text node.

You might have noticed that there are no CDATA nodes in this list. If your XML document contains text in a CDATA section, you can access the contents of the CDATA section as a text node. You have no way of knowing if a given text node was originally a CDATA section. Similarly, all entity references are resolved before anything in your stylesheet is evaluated, so you have no way of knowing if a given piece of text originally contained entity references.

Comment Nodes

A comment node is also very simple—it contains some text. Every comment in the source document (except for comments in the DTD) becomes a comment node. The text of the comment node (returned by the `text()` node test) contains everything inside the comment, except the opening `<!--` and the closing `-->`.

Processing Instruction Nodes

A processing instruction node has two parts, a name (returned by the `name()` function) and a string value. The string value is everything after the name, including whitespace, but not including the `?>` that closes the processing instruction.

Namespace Nodes

Namespace nodes are almost never used in XSLT stylesheets; they exist primarily for the XSLT processor's benefit. Remember that the declaration of a namespace (such as `xmlns:auth="http://www.authors.net"`), even though it is technically an attribute in the XML source, becomes a namespace node, not an attribute node.

Location Paths

One of the most common uses of XPath is to create *location paths*. A location path describes the location of something in an XML document. In our examples in the previous chapter, we used location paths on the `match` and `select` attributes of various XSLT elements. Those location paths described the parts of the XML document we wanted to work with. Most of the XPath expressions you'll use are location paths, and most of them are pretty simple. Before we dive in to the wonders of XPath, we need to discuss the *context*.

The Context

One of the most important concepts in XPath is the context. Everything we do in XPath is interpreted with respect to the context. You can think of an XML document as a hierarchy of directories in a filesystem. In our sonnet example, we could imagine that `sonnet` is a directory at the root level of the filesystem. The `sonnet` directory would, in turn, contain directories named `auth:author`, `title`, and `lines`. In this example, the context would be the current directory. If I go to a command line and execute a particular command (such as `dir *.js`), the results I get vary depending on the current directory. Similarly, the results of evaluating an XPath expression will probably vary based on the context.

Most of the time, we can think of the context as the node in the tree from which any expression is evaluated. To be completely accurate, the context consists of five things:

- The context node (the "current directory"). The XPath expression is evaluated from this node.
- Two integers, the *context position* and the *context size*. These integers are important when we're processing a group of nodes. For example, we could write an XPath expression that selects all of the `<li>` elements in a given

document. The context size refers to the number of `<li>` items selected by that expression, and the context position refers to the position of the `<li>` we're currently processing.

- A set of variables. This set includes names and values of all variables that are currently in scope.
- A set of all the functions available to XPath expressions. Some of these functions are defined by the XPath and XSLT standards themselves; others might be extension functions defined by whomever created the stylesheet. (You'll read more about extension functions in Chapter 8.)
- A set of all the namespace declarations currently in scope.

Having said all that, most of the time you can ignore everything but the context node. To use our command line analogy one more time, if you're at a command line, you have a current directory; you also have (depending on your operating system) a number of environment variables defined. For most commands, you can focus on the current directory and ignore the environment variables.

Simple Location Paths

Now that we've talked about what a context is and why it matters, we'll look at some location paths. We'll start with a variety of simple location paths; as we go along, we'll look at more complex location paths that use all the various features of XPath. We already looked at one of the simplest XPath expressions:

```
<xsl:template match="/">
```

This template selects the root node of the document. We saw another simple XPath expression in the `<xsl:value-of>` element:

```
<xsl:value-of select="."/>
```

This template selects the context node, represented by a period. To complete our tour of very simple location paths, we can use the double period (`..`) to select the *parent* of the context node:

```
<xsl:value-of select=".."/>
```

All these XPath expressions have one thing in common: they don't use element names. As you might have noticed in our Hello World example, you can use element names to select elements that have a particular name:

```
<xsl:apply-templates select="greeting"/>
```

In this example, we select all of the <greeting> elements in the current context and apply the appropriate template to each of them. Turning to our XML sonnet, we can create location paths that specify more than one level in the document hierarchy:

```
<xsl:apply-templates select="lines/line/">
```

This example selects all <line> elements that are contained in any <lines> elements in the current context. If the current context doesn't have any <lines> elements, then this expression returns an empty node-set. If the current context has plenty of <lines> elements, but none of them contain any <line> elements, this expression also returns an empty node-set.

Relative and Absolute Expressions

The XPath specification talks about two kinds of XPath expressions, *relative* and *absolute*. Our previous example is a relative XPath expression because the nodes it specifies depend on the current context. An absolute XPath expression begins with a slash (/), which tells the XSLT processor to start at the root of the document, regardless of the current context. In other words, you can evaluate an absolute XPath expression from any context node you want, and the results will be the same. Here's an absolute XPath expression:

```
<xsl:apply-templates select="/sonnet/lines/line"/>
```

The good thing about an absolute expression is that you don't have to worry about the context node. Another benefit is that it makes it easy for the XSLT processor to find all nodes that match this expression: what we've said in this expression is that there must be a <sonnet> element at the root of the document, that element must contain at least one <lines> element, and that at least one of those <lines> elements must contain at least one <line> element. If any of those conditions fail, the XSLT processor can stop looking through the tree and return an empty node-set.

A possible disadvantage of using absolute XPath expressions is that it could make your templates more difficult to reuse. Both of these templates process <line> elements, but the second one is more difficult to reuse:

```
<xsl:template match="line">
  ...
</xsl:template>

<xsl:template match="/sonnet/lines/line">
  ...
</xsl:template>
```

If the second template has wonderful code for processing `<line>` elements, but your document contains `<line>` elements that don't match the absolute XPath expression, you can't reuse that template. You should keep that in mind as you design your templates.

Selecting Things Besides Elements with Location Paths

Up until now, we've discussed XPath expressions that used either element names (`/sonnet/lines/line`) or special characters (`/` or `..`) to select elements from an XML document. Obviously, XML documents contain things other than elements; we'll talk about how to select those other things here.

Selecting attributes

To select an attribute, use the at-sign (`@`) along with the attribute name. In our sample sonnet, you can select the `type` attribute of the `<sonnet>` element with the XPath expression `/sonnet/@type`. If the context node is the `<sonnet>` element itself, then the relative XPath expression `@type` does the same thing.

Selecting the text of an element

To select the text of an element, use the XPath node test `text()`. The XPath expression `/sonnet/auth:author/last-name/text()` selects the text of the `last-name` element in our example document. Be aware that the text of an element is the concatenation of all of its text nodes. Thus, the XPath expression `/sonnet/auth:author/text()` returns the following text:

```
ShakespeareWilliamBritish15641616
```

That's probably not the output you want; if you want to provide spacing, line breaks, or other formatting, you need to use the `text()` node test against all the child nodes individually.

Selecting comments, processing instructions, and namespace nodes

By this point, we've covered most of the things you're ever likely to do with an XPath expression. You can use a couple of other XPath node tests to describe parts of an XML document. The `comment()` and `processing-instruction()` node tests allow you to select comments and processing instructions from the XML document. Going back to our sample sonnet, the XPath expression `/processing-instruction()` returns the two processing instructions (named `xml-stylesheet` and `cocoon-process`). The expression `/sonnet/comment()` returns the comment node that begins, "Is there an official title for this sonnet?"

Processing comment nodes in this way can actually be useful. If you've entered comments into an XML document, you can use the `comment()` node test to display your comments only when you want. Here's an XSLT template you could use:

```
<xsl:template match="comment()">
  <span class="comment">
    <p><xsl:value-of select="."/></p>
  </span>
</xsl:template>
```

Elsewhere in your stylesheet, you could define CSS attributes to print comments in a large, bold, purple font. To remove all comments from your output document, simply go to your stylesheet and comment out any `<xsl:apply-templates select="comment()"/>` statements.

XPath has one other kind of node, the rarely used *namespace node*. To retrieve namespace nodes, you have to use something called the namespace axis; we'll discuss axes soon. One note about namespace nodes, if you ever have to use them: When matching namespace nodes, the namespace prefix isn't important. As an example, our sample sonnet used the `auth` namespace prefix, which maps to the value `http://www.authors.com/`. If a stylesheet uses the namespace prefix `writers` to refer to the same URL, then the XPath expression `/sonnet/writers::*` would return the `<auth:author>` element. Even though the namespace prefixes are different, the URLs they refer to are the same.

Having said all that, the chances that you'll ever need to use namespace nodes are pretty slim.

Using Wildcards

XPath features three wildcards:

- The asterisk (*), which selects all element nodes in the current context. Be aware that the asterisk wildcard selects element nodes only; attributes, text nodes, comments, or processing instructions aren't included. You can also use a namespace prefix with an asterisk: in our sample sonnet, the XPath expression `auth:*` returns all element nodes in the current context that are associated with the namespace URL `http://www.authors.com`.
- The at-sign and asterisk (`@*`), which selects all attribute nodes in the current context. You can use a namespace prefix with the attribute wildcard. In our sample sonnet, `@auth:*` returns all attribute nodes in the current context that are associated with the namespace URL `http://www.authors.com`.
- The `node()` node test, which selects all nodes in the current context, regardless of type. This includes elements, text, comments, processing instructions, attributes, and namespace nodes.

In addition to these wildcards, XPath includes the double slash (`//`), which indicates that zero or more elements may occur between the slashes. For example, the XPath expression `//line` selects all `<line>` elements, regardless of where they appear in the document. This is an absolute XPath expression because it begins with a slash. You can also use the double slash at any point in an XPath expression; the expression `/sonnet//line` selects all `<line>` elements that are descendants of the `<sonnet>` element at the root of the XML document. The expressions `/sonnet//line` and `/sonnet/descendant-or-self::line` are equivalent.

The double slash (`//`) is a very powerful operator, but be aware that it can make your stylesheets incredibly inefficient. If we use the XPath expression `//line`, the XSLT processor has to check every node in the document to see if there are any `<line>` elements. The more specific you can be in your XPath expressions, the less work the XSLT processor has to do, and the faster your stylesheets will execute. Thinking back to our filesystem metaphor, if I go to a Windows command prompt and type **`dir/s c:\*.xml`**, the operating system has to look in every subdirectory for any **.xml* files that might be there. However, if I type **`dir /s c:\doug\projects\xml-docs\*.xml`**, the operating system has far fewer places to look, and the command will execute much faster.

Axes

To this point, we've been able to select child elements, attributes, text, comments, and processing instructions with some fairly simple XPath expressions. Obviously, we might want to select many other things, such as:

- All ancestors of the context node
- All descendants of the context node
- All previous siblings or following siblings of the context node (siblings are nodes that have the same parent)

To select these things, XPath provides a number of *axes* that let you specify various collections of nodes. There are thirteen axes in all; we'll discuss all of them here, even though most of them won't be particularly useful to you. To use an axis in an XPath expression, type the name of the axis, a double colon (`::`), and the name of the element you want to select, if any.

Before we define all of the axes, though, we need to talk about XPath's unabbreviated syntax.

Unabbreviated syntax

To this point, all the XPath expressions we've looked at used the XPath *abbreviated syntax*. Most of the time, that's what you'll use; however, most of the lesser-used axes can only be specified with the unabbreviated syntax. For example, when we wrote an XPath expression to select all of the `<line>` elements in the current context, we used the abbreviated syntax:

```
<xsl:apply-templates select="line"/>
```

If you really enjoy typing, you can use the unabbreviated syntax to specify that you want all of the `<line>` children of the current context:

```
<xsl:apply-templates select="child::line"/>
```

We'll go through all of the axes now, pointing out which ones have an abbreviated syntax.

Axis roll call

The following list contains all of the axes defined by the XPath standard, with a brief description of each one.

`child` *axis*
: Contains the children of the context node. As we've already mentioned, the XPath expression `child::lines/child::line` is equivalent to `lines/line`. If an XPath expression (such as `/sonnet`) doesn't have an axis specifier, the `child` axis is used by default. The children of the context node include all comment, element, processing instruction, and text nodes. Attribute and namespace nodes are not considered children of the context node.

`parent` *axis*
: Contains the parent of the context node, if there is one. (If the context node is the root node, the `parent` axis returns an empty node-set.) This axis can be abbreviated with a double period (`..`). The expressions `parent::sonnet` and `../sonnet` are equivalent. If the context node does not have a `<sonnet>` element as its parent, these XPath expressions return an empty node-set.

`self` *axis*
: Contains the context node itself. The `self` axis can be abbreviated with a single period (`.`). The expressions `self::*` and `.` are equivalent.

`attribute` *axis*
: Contains the attributes of the context node. If the context node is not an element node, this axis is empty. The `attribute` axis can be abbreviated with the at-sign (`@`). The expressions `attribute::type` and `@type` are equivalent.

`ancestor` *axis*
: Contains the parent of the context node, the parent's parent, etc. The `ancestor` axis always contains the root node unless the context node is the root node.

`ancestor-or-self` *axis*
: Contains the context node, its parent, its parent's parent, and so on. This axis always includes the root node.

`descendant` *axis*
: Contains all children of the context node, all children of all the children of the context node, and so on. The children are all of the comment, element, processing instruction, and text nodes beneath the context node. In other words, the `descendant` axis does not include attribute or namespace nodes. (As we discussed earlier, although an attribute node has an element node as a parent, an attribute node is not considered a child of that element.)

`descendant-or-self` *axis*
: Contains the context node and all the children of the context node, all the children of all the children of the context node, all the children of the children of all the children of the context node, and so on. As always, the children of the context node include all comment, element, processing instruction, and text nodes; attribute and namespace nodes are not included.

`preceding-sibling` *axis*
: Contains all preceding siblings of the context node; in other words, all nodes that have the same parent as the context node and appear before the context node in the XML document. If the context node is an attribute node or a namespace node, the `preceding-sibling` axis is empty.

`following-sibling` *axis*
: Contains all the following siblings of the context node; in other words, all nodes that have the same parent as the context node and appear after the context node in the XML document. If the context node is an attribute node or a namespace node, the `following-sibling` axis is empty.

`preceding` *axis*
: Contains all nodes that appear before the context node in the document, except ancestors, attribute nodes, and namespace nodes.

`following` *axis*
: Contains all nodes that appear after the context node in the document, except descendants, attribute nodes, and namespace nodes.

`namespace` *axis*
: Contains the namespace nodes of the context node. If the context node is not an element node, this axis is empty.

Predicates

There's one more aspect of XPath expressions that we haven't discussed: *predicates*. Predicates are filters that restrict the nodes selected by an XPath expression. Each predicate is evaluated and converted to a Boolean value (either `true` or `false`). If the predicate is `true` for a given node, that node will be selected; otherwise, the node is not selected. Predicates always appear inside square brackets (`[]`). Here's an example:

```
<xsl:apply-templates select="line[3]"/>
```

This expression selects the third `<line>` element in the current context. If there are two or fewer `<line>` elements in the current context, this XPath expression returns an empty node-set. Several things can be part of a predicate; we'll go through them here.

Numbers in predicates

A number inside square brackets selects nodes that have a particular position. For example, the XPath expression `line[7]` selects the seventh `<line>` element in the context node. XPath also provides the boolean `and` and `or` operators as well as the union operator (`|`) to combine predicates. The expression `line[position()=3 and @style]` matches all `<line>` elements that occur third and have a `style` attribute, while `line[position()=3 or @style]` matches all `<line>` elements that either occur third or have a `style` attribute. With the union operator, the expression `line[3|7]` matches all third and seventh `<line>` elements in the current context, as does the more verbose `line[3] | line[7]`.

Functions in predicates

In addition to numbers, we can use XPath and XSLT functions inside predicates. Here are some examples:

`line[last()]`
: Selects the last `<line>` element in the current context.

`line[position() mod 2 = 0]`
: Selects all even-numbered `<line>` elements. (The `mod` operator returns the remainder after a division; the `position` of any even-numbered element divided by 2 has a remainder of 0.)

`sonnet[@type="Shakespearean"]`
: Selects all `<sonnet>` elements that have a `type` attribute with the value `Shakespearean`.

`ancestor::table[@border="1"]`
: Selects all `<table>` ancestors of the current context that have a `border` attribute with the value `1`.

`count(/body/table[@border="1"])`
: Returns the number of `<table>` elements with a `border` attribute equal to `1` that are children of `<body>` elements that are children of the root node. Notice that in this case we're using an XPath predicate expression as an argument to a function.

Attribute Value Templates

Although they're technically defined in the XSLT specification (in section 7.6.2, to be exact), we'll discuss attribute value templates here. An attribute value template is an XPath expression that is evaluated, and the result of that evaluation replaces the attribute value template. For example, we could create an HTML `<table>` element like this:

```
<table border="{@size}"/>
```

In this example, the XPath expression `@size` is evaluated, and its value, whatever that happens to be, is inserted into the output tree as the value of the `border` attribute. Attribute value templates can be used in any literal result elements in your stylesheet (for HTML elements and other things that aren't part of the XSLT namespace, for example). You can also use attribute value templates in the following XSLT attributes:

- The `name` and `namespace` attributes of the `<xsl:attribute>` element
- The `name` and `namespace` attributes of the `<xsl:element>` element
- The `format`, `lang`, `letter-value`, `grouping-separator`, and `grouping-size` attributes of the `<xsl:number>` element
- The `name` attribute of the `<xsl:processing-instruction>` element
- The `lang`, `data-type`, `order`, and `case-order` attributes of the `<xsl:sort>` element

XPath Datatypes

An XPath expression returns one of four datatypes:

`node-set`
: Represents a set of nodes. The set can be empty, or it can contain any number of nodes.

`boolean`
: Represents the value `true` or `false`. Be aware that the `true` or `false` strings have no special meaning or value in XPath; see the section "Boolean examples" in Chapter 4 for a more detailed discussion of boolean values.

`number`
: Represents a floating-point number. All numbers in XPath and XSLT are implemented as floating-point numbers; the `integer` (or `int`) datatype does not exist in XPath and XSLT. Specifically, all numbers are implemented as IEEE 754 floating-point numbers, the same standard used by the Java `float` and `double` primitive types. In addition to ordinary numbers, there are five special values for numbers: positive and negative infinity, positive and negative zero, and `NaN`, the special symbol for anything that is not a number.

`string`
: Represents zero or more characters, as defined in the XML specification.

These datatypes are usually simple, and with the exception of node-sets, converting between types is usually straightforward. We won't discuss these datatypes in any more detail here; instead, we'll discuss datatypes and conversions as we need them to do specific tasks.

The XPath View of an XML Document

Before we leave the subject of XPath, we'll look at a stylesheet that generates a pictorial view of a document. The stylesheet has to distinguish between all of the different XPath node types, including any rarely used `namespace` nodes.

Output View

Figure 3-1 shows the output of our stylesheet. In this graphical view of the document, the nested HTML tables illustrate which nodes are contained inside of others, as well as the sequence in which these nodes occur in the original document. In the section of the document visible in Figure 3-1, the root of the document contains, in order, two processing instructions and two comments, followed by the `<sonnet>` element. The `<sonnet>` element, in turn, contains two attributes and an `<auth:author>` element. The `<auth:author>` element contains a namespace node and an element. Be aware that this stylesheet has its limitations; if you throw a very large XML document at it, it will generate an HTML file with many levels of nested tables—probably more levels than your browser can handle.

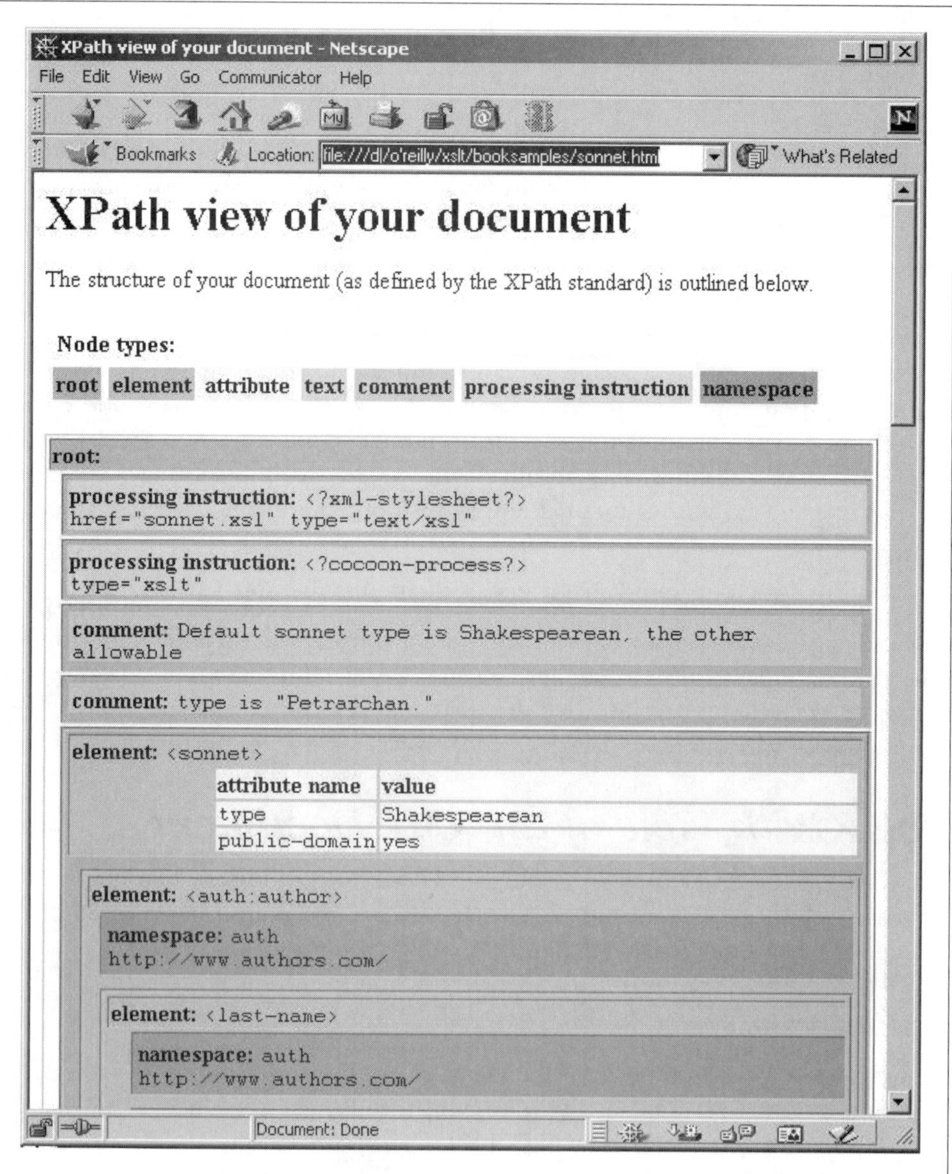

Figure 3-1. XPath tree view of an XML document

The Stylesheet

Now we'll take a look at the stylesheet and how it works. The stylesheet creates a number of nested tables to illustrate the XPath view of the document. We begin by writing the basic HTML elements to the output stream and creating a legend for our nested tree view:

```
<xsl:template match="/">
  <html>
    <head>
      <title>XPath view of your document</title>
      <style type="text/css">
        <xsl:comment>
          span.literal         { font-family: Courier, monospace; }
        </xsl:comment>
      </style>
    </head>
    <body>
      <h1>XPath view of your document</h1>
      <p>The structure of your document (as defined by
         the XPath standard) is outlined below.</p>
      <table cellspacing="5" cellpadding="2" border="0">
        <tr>
          <td colspan="7">
            <b>Node types:</b>
          </td>
        </tr>
        <tr>
          <td bgcolor="#99CCCC"><b>root</b></td>
          <td bgcolor="#CCCC99"><b>element</b></td>
          <td bgcolor="#FFFF99"><b>attribute</b></td>
          <td bgcolor="#FFCC99"><b>text</b></td>
          <td bgcolor="#CCCCFF"><b>comment</b></td>
          <td bgcolor="#99FF99"><b>processing instruction</b></td>
          <td bgcolor="#CC99CC"><b>namespace</b></td>
        </tr>
      </table>
      <br />
```

Having created the legend for our document, we select all the different types of nodes and represent them:

```
<xsl:for-each select="namespace::*">
  ...
</xsl:for-each>
<xsl:for-each select="*|comment()|processing-instruction()|text()">
          ...
        </xsl:for-each>
```

The only difficult thing here was remembering to get all of the namespace nodes. These nodes are rarely used (with the exception of this example, I've never needed them), and they can only be selected with the `namespace::` axis. Also, we process the attribute nodes when we process their element node parents; that's why the `select` attribute just shown doesn't have `@*` in it.

Here's the complete stylesheet:

```
<?xml version="1.0"?>
<xsl:stylesheet version="1.0" xmlns:xsl="http://www.w3.org/1999/XSL/Transform">

  <xsl:output method="html"/>

  <xsl:template match="/">
    <html>
      <head>
        <title>XPath view of your document</title>
        <style type="text/css">
          <xsl:comment>
            span.literal         { font-family: Courier, monospace; }
          </xsl:comment>
        </style>
      </head>
      <body>
        <h1>XPath view of your document</h1>
        <p>The structure of your document (as defined by
          the XPath standard) is outlined below.</p>
        <table cellspacing="5" cellpadding="2" border="0">
          <tr>
            <td colspan="7">
              <b>Node types:</b>
            </td>
          </tr>
          <tr>
            <td bgcolor="#99CCCC"><b>root</b></td>
            <td bgcolor="#CCCC99"><b>element</b></td>
            <td bgcolor="#FFFF99"><b>attribute</b></td>
            <td bgcolor="#FFCC99"><b>text</b></td>
            <td bgcolor="#CCCCFF"><b>comment</b></td>
            <td bgcolor="#99FF99"><b>processing instruction</b></td>
            <td bgcolor="#CC99CC"><b>namespace</b></td>
          </tr>
        </table>
        <br />
        <table width="100%" border="1" bgcolor="#99CCCC" cellspacing="2">
          <tr bgcolor="#99CCCC">
            <td colspan="2">
              <b>root:</b>
            </td>
          </tr>
          <xsl:for-each select="namespace::*">
            <tr bgcolor="#CC99CC">
              <td width="15">   </td>
```

```
          <td>
            <xsl:call-template name="namespace-node"/>
          </td>
        </tr>
      </xsl:for-each>
      <xsl:for-each select="*|comment()|processing-instruction()|text()">
        <tr bgcolor="#99CCCC">
          <td width="15">   </td>
          <td>
            <xsl:apply-templates select="."/>
          </td>
        </tr>
      </xsl:for-each>
    </table>
  </body>
</html>
</xsl:template>

<xsl:template match="comment()">
  <table width="100%" cellspacing="2">
    <tr>
      <td bgcolor="#CCCCFF">
        <b>comment: </b>
        <span class="literal">
          <xsl:value-of select="."/>
        </span>
      </td>
    </tr>
  </table>
</xsl:template>

<xsl:template match="processing-instruction()">
  <table border="0" width="100%" cellspacing="2">
    <tr>
      <td bgcolor="#99FF99">
        <b>processing instruction: </b>
        <span class="literal">
          <xsl:text>&lt;?</xsl:text>
          <xsl:value-of select="name()"/>
          <xsl:text>?&gt;</xsl:text>
          <br />
          <xsl:value-of select="."/>
        </span>
      </td>
    </tr>
  </table>
</xsl:template>

<xsl:template match="text()">
  <xsl:if test="string-length(normalize-space(.))">
    <tr>
      <td bgcolor="#CCCC99" width="15">    </td>
      <td bgcolor="#FFCC99" width="100%">
        <b>text: </b>
```

```
          <span class="literal">
            <xsl:value-of select="."/>
          </span>
        </td>
      </tr>
    </xsl:if>
  </xsl:template>

  <xsl:template name="namespace-node">
    <table border="0" width="100%" cellspacing="2">
      <tr>
        <td bgcolor="#CC99CC">
          <b>namespace: </b>
          <span class="literal">
            <xsl:value-of select="name()"/>
          </span>
          <br />
          <span class="literal">
            <xsl:value-of select="."/>
          </span>
        </td>
      </tr>
    </table>
  </xsl:template>

  <xsl:template match="*">
    <table border="1" width="100%" cellspacing="2">
      <xsl:choose>
        <xsl:when test="count(@*) &gt; 0">
          <tr>
            <td bgcolor="#CCCC99" colspan="2">
              <b>element: </b>
              <span class="literal">
                <xsl:text>&lt;</xsl:text>
                <xsl:value-of select="name()"/>
                <xsl:text>&gt;</xsl:text>
              </span>
              <table border="0" width="100%" cellspacing="2">
                <tr>
                  <td bgcolor="#CCCC99" width="15">   </td>
                  <td bgcolor="#FFFF99" width="20%">
                    <b>attribute name</b>
                  </td>
                  <td bgcolor="#FFFF99">
                    <b>value</b>
                  </td>
                </tr>
                <xsl:for-each select="@*">
                  <tr>
                    <td bgcolor="#CCCC99" width="15">   </td>
                    <td bgcolor="#FFFF99" width="20%">
                      <span class="literal">
                        <xsl:value-of select="name()"/>
                      </span>
```

```
                    </td>
                    <td bgcolor="#FFFF99">
                      <span class="literal">
                        <xsl:value-of select="."/>
                      </span>
                    </td>
                  </tr>
                </xsl:for-each>
              </table>
            </td>
          </tr>
        </xsl:when>
        <xsl:otherwise>
          <tr>
            <td bgcolor="#CCCC99" colspan="2">
              <b>element: </b>
              <span class="literal">
                <xsl:text>&lt;</xsl:text>
                <xsl:value-of select="name()"/>
                <xsl:text>&gt;</xsl:text>
              </span>
            </td>
          </tr>
        </xsl:otherwise>
      </xsl:choose>
      <xsl:for-each select="namespace::*">
        <tr>
          <td bgcolor="#CCCC99" width="15">    </td>
          <td bgcolor="#CC99CC">
            <xsl:call-template name="namespace-node"/>
          </td>
        </tr>
      </xsl:for-each>
      <xsl:for-each select="*|comment()|processing-instruction()|text()">
        <tr bgcolor="#CCCC99">
          <td width="15">   </td>
          <td>
            <xsl:apply-templates select="."/>
          </td>
        </tr>
      </xsl:for-each>
    </table>
  </xsl:template>

</xsl:stylesheet>
```

Before we leave this example, there are a couple of other techniques worth mentioning here. First, notice that we used CSS to format some of the output. XSLT and CSS aren't mutually exclusive; you can use XSLT to generate CSS as part of an HTML page, as we demonstrated here. Second, we used wildcard expressions like `*` and `@*` to process all the elements and attributes in our document. Use of these expressions allows us to apply this stylesheet to any XML document, regardless of the tags it uses. Because we use these wildcard expressions, we have to use the name() function to get the name of the element or attribute we're currently working with. Third, notice that we used conditional logic and the expression count(@*) > 0 to determine whether a given element has attributes. We'll talk more about conditional logic in the next chapter.

Summary

We've covered the basics of XPath. Hopefully, at this point you're comfortable with the idea of writing XPath expressions to describe parts of an XML document. As we go through the following chapters, you'll see XPath expressions used in a variety of ways, all of which build on the basics we've discussed here. You'll probably spend most of your debugging time working on the XPath expressions in your stylesheets. Very few of the things we'll do in the rest of the book are possible without precise XPath expressions.

4

Branching and Control Elements

So far, we've done some straightforward transformations and we've been able to do some reasonably sophisticated things. To do truly useful work, though, we'll need to use logic in our stylesheets. In this chapter, we'll discuss the XSLT elements that allow you to do just that. Although you'll see several XML elements that look like constructs from other programming languages, they're not exactly the same. As we go along, we'll discuss what makes XSLT different and how to do common tasks with your stylesheets.

Goals of This Chapter

By the end of this chapter, you should:

- Know the XSLT elements used for branching and control
- Understand the differences between XSLT's branching elements and similar constructs in other programming languages
- Know how to invoke XSLT templates by name and how to pass parameters to them, if you want
- Know how to use XSLT variables
- Understand how to use recursion to get around the "limitations" of XSLT's branching and control elements

Branching Elements of XSLT

Three XSLT elements are used for branching: <xsl:if>, <xsl:choose>, and <xsl:for-each>. The first two are much like the if and case statements you may be familiar with from other languages, while the for-each element is significantly different from the for or do-while structures in other languages. We'll discuss all of them here.

The <xsl:if> Element

The <xsl:if> element looks like this:

```
<xsl:if test="count(zone) &gt; 2">
  <xsl:text>Applicable zones: </xsl:text>
  <xsl:apply-templates select="zone"/>
</xsl:if>
```

The <xsl:if> element, surprisingly enough, implements an if statement. The element has only one attribute, test. If the value of test evaluates to the boolean value true, then all elements inside the <xsl:if> are processed. If test evaluates to false, then the contents of the <xsl:if> element are ignored. (If you want to implement an if-then-else statement, check out the <xsl:choose> element described in the next section.)

Notice that we used > instead of > in the attribute value. You're always safe using > here, although some XSLT processors process the greater-than sign correctly if you use > instead. If you need to use the less-than operator (<), you'll have to use the < entity. The same holds true for the less-than-or-equal operator (<=) and the greater-than-or-equal (>=) operators. See the section "Boolean Operators" for more information on this topic.

Converting to boolean values

The <xsl:if> element is pretty simple, but it's the first time we've had to deal with *boolean values*. These values will come up later, so we might as well discuss them here. Attributes like the test attribute of the <xsl:if> element convert whatever their values happen to be into a boolean value. If that boolean value is true, the <xsl:if> element is processed. (The <xsl:when> element, which we'll discuss in just a minute, has a test attribute as well.)

Here's the rundown of how various datatypes are converted to boolean values:

number
: If a number is positive or negative zero, it is false. If a numeric value is NaN (not a number; if I try to use the string "blue" as a number, the result is NaN), it is false. If a number has any other value, it is true.

node-set
: An empty node-set is false, a non-empty node-set is true.

string
: A zero-length string is false; a string whose length is not zero is true.

These rules are defined in Section 4.3 of the XPath specification.

Boolean examples

Here are some examples that illustrate how boolean values evaluate the test attribute:

<xsl:if test="count(zone) >= 2">
: This is a boolean expression because it uses the greater-than-or-equal boolean operator. If the count() function returns a value greater than or equal to 2, the test attribute is true. Otherwise, the test attribute is false.

<xsl:if test="$x">
: The variable x is evaluated. If it is a string, then the test attribute is true only if the string has a length greater than zero. If it is a node-set, then the test attribute is true only if the node-set has at least one member. If it is a number, then the test attribute is true only if the number is anything other than positive zero, negative zero, or NaN. (Of course, if x is a boolean value, true is true and false is false.)

<xsl:if test="true()">
: The boolean function true() always returns the boolean value true. Therefore, this test attribute is always true.

<xsl:if test="true">
: This example is a trick. This test attribute is true only if there is at least one <true> element in the current context. The XSLT processor interprets the value true as an XPath expression that specifies all <true> elements in the current context. The strings true and false don't have any special significance in XSLT.

`<xsl:if test="'true'">`
: This `test` attribute is always `true`. Notice that in this case we used single quotes inside double quotes to specify that this is a literal string, not an element name. This `test` attribute is always `true` because the string has a length greater than zero, *not* because its value happens to be the word "true."

`<xsl:if test="'false'">`
: Another trick example; this `test` attribute is always `true`. As before, we used single quotes inside double quotes to specify that this is a literal string. Because the string has a length greater than zero, the `test` attribute is always `true`. The value of the nonempty string, confusing as it is, doesn't matter.

`<xsl:if test="not(3)">`
: This `test` attribute is always `false`. The literal `3` evaluates to `true`, so its negation is `false`. On the other hand, the expressions `not(0)` and `not(-0)` are always `true`.

`<xsl:if test="false()">`
: This `test` attribute is always `false`. The boolean function `false()` always returns the boolean value `false`.

`<xsl:if test="section/section">`
: The XPath expression `section/section` returns a node-set. If the current context contains one or more `<section>` elements that contain a `<section>` element in turn, the `test` attribute is `true`. If no such elements exist in the current context, the `test` attribute is `false`.

The <xsl:choose> Element

The `<xsl:choose>` element is the equivalent of a `case` or `switch` statement in other programming languages. You can also use it to implement an if-then-else statement. An `<xsl:choose>` contains at least one `<xsl:when>` element (logically equivalent to an `<xsl:if>` element), with an optional `<xsl:otherwise>` element. The `test` attribute of each `<xsl:when>` element is evaluated until the XSLT processor finds one that evaluates to `true`. When that happens, the contents of that `<xsl:when>` element are evaluated. If none of the `<xsl:when>` elements have a test that is `true`, the contents of the `<xsl:otherwise>` element (if there is one) are processed.

Here's how these XSLT elements compare to the `switch` or `select/case` statements you might know from other languages:

- The C, C++, and Java `switch` statement is roughly equivalent to the `<xsl:choose>` element. The one exception is that procedural languages tend to use fallthrough processing. In other words, if a branch of the `switch` statement evaluates to `true`, the runtime executes everything until it encounters a `break` statement, even if some of that code is part of other branches. The `<xsl:choose>` element doesn't work that way. If a given `<xsl:when>` evaluates to `true`, only the statements inside that `<xsl:when>` are evaluated.

- The Java `case` statement is equivalent to the `<xsl:when>` element. In Java, if a given `case` statement does not end with a `break` statement, the following case is executed as well. Again, this is not the case with XSLT; only the contents of the first `<xsl:when>` element that is `true` are processed.
- The Java and C++ `default` statement is equivalent to the `<xsl:otherwise>` element.

<xsl:choose> example

Here's a sample `<xsl:choose>` element that sets the background color of the table's rows. If the `bgcolor` attribute is coded on the `<table-row>` element, the value of that attribute is used as the color; otherwise, the sample uses the `position()` function and the `mod` operator to cycle the colors between `papayawhip`, `mintcream`, `lavender`, and `whitesmoke`.

```
<xsl:template match="table-row">
  <tr>
    <xsl:attribute name="bgcolor">
     <xsl:choose>
        <xsl:when test="@bgcolor">
          <xsl:value-of select="@bgcolor"/>
        </xsl:when>
        <xsl:when test="position() mod 4 = 0">
          <xsl:text>papayawhip</xsl:text>
        </xsl:when>
        <xsl:when test="position() mod 4 = 1">
          <xsl:text>mintcream</xsl:text>
        </xsl:when>
        <xsl:when test="position() mod 4 = 2">
          <xsl:text>lavender</xsl:text>
        </xsl:when>
        <xsl:otherwise>
          <xsl:text>whitesmoke</xsl:text>
        </xsl:otherwise>
      </xsl:choose>
    </xsl:attribute>
    <xsl:apply-templates select="*"/>
  </tr>
</xsl:template>
```

In this sample, we use `<xsl:choose>` to generate the value of the `bgcolor` attribute of the `<tr>` element. Our first test is to see if the `bgcolor` attribute of the `<table-row>` element exists; if it does, we use that value for the background color and the

`<xsl:otherwise>` and other `<xsl:when>` elements are ignored. (If the `bgcolor` attribute is coded, the XPath expression `@bgcolor` returns a node-set containing a single attribute node.)

The next three `<xsl:when>` elements check the position of the current `<table-row>` element. The use of the `mod` operator here is the most efficient way to cycle between the various options. Finally, we use an `<xsl:otherwise>` element to specify `whitesmoke` as the default case. If `position() mod 4 = 3`, the background color will be `whitesmoke`.

A couple of minor details: in this example, we could replace the `<xsl:otherwise>` element with `<xsl:when test="position() mod 4 = 3">`; that is logically equivalent to the example as coded previously. For obfuscation bonus points, we could code the second `<xsl:when>` element as `<xsl:when test="not(position() mod 4)">`. (Remember that the boolean negation of zero is `true`.)

The <xsl:for-each> Element

If you want to process all the nodes that match a certain criteria, you can use the `<xsl:for-each>` element. Be aware that this isn't a traditional `for` loop; you can't ask the XSLT processor to do something like this:

```
for i = 1 to 10 do
```

The `<xsl:for-each>` element lets you select a set of nodes, then do something with each of them. Let me mention again that this is not the same as a traditional `for` loop. Another important point is that the current node changes with each iteration through the `<xsl:for-each>` element. We'll go through some examples to illustrate this.

<xsl:for-each> example

Here's a sample that selects all `<section>` elements inside a `<tutorial>` element and then uses a second `<xsl:for-each>` element to select all the `<panel>` elements inside each `<section>` element:

```
<xsl:template match="tutorial">
  <xsl:for-each select="section">
    <h1>
      <xsl:text>Section </xsl:text>
      <xsl:value-of select="position()"/>
      <xsl:text>. </xsl:text>
      <xsl:value-of select="title"/>
    </h1>
    <ul>
      <xsl:for-each select="panel">
        <li>
          <xsl:value-of select="position()"/>
```

```
          <xsl:text>. </xsl:text>
          <xsl:value-of select="title"/>
        </li>
      </xsl:for-each>
    </ul>
  </xsl:for-each>
</xsl:template>
```

Given this XML document:

```
<tutorial>
  <section>
    <title>Gene Splicing for Young People</title>
    <panel>
      <title>Introduction</title>
      <!-- ... -->
    </panel>
    <panel>
      <title>Discovering the secrets of life and creation</title>
      <!-- ... -->
    </panel>
    <panel>
      <title>"I created him for good, but he's turned out evil!"</title>
      <!-- ... -->
    </panel>
    <panel>
      <title>When angry mobs storm your castle</title>
      <!-- ... -->
    </panel>
  </section>
</tutorial>
```

The previous template produces these results:

```
<h1>Section 1. Gene Splicing for Young People</h1>
<ul>
  <li>1. Introduction</li>
  <li>2. Discovering the secrets of life and creation</li>
  <li>3. "I created him for good, but he's turned out evil!"</li>
  <li>4. When angry mobs storm your castle</li>
</ul>
```

Each time a `select` attribute is processed, it is evaluated in terms of the current node. As the XSLT processor cycles through all the `<xsl:section>` and `<xsl:panel>` elements, each of them in turn becomes the current node. By using iteration, we've generated a table of contents with a very simple template.

Invoking Templates by Name

Up to this point, we've always used XSLT's <xsl:apply-templates> element to invoke other templates. You can think of this as a limited form of *polymorphism;* a single instruction is invoked a number of times, and the XSLT processor uses each node in the node-set to determine which <xsl:template> to invoke. Most of the time, this is what we want. However, sometimes we want to invoke a particular template. XSLT allows us to do this with the <xsl:call-template> element.

How It Works

To invoke a template by name, two things have to happen:

- The template you want to invoke has to have a name.
- You use the <xsl:call-template> element to invoke the named template.

Here's how to do this. Say we have a template named *createMasthead* that creates the masthead of a web page. Whenever we create an HTML page for our web site, we want to invoke the *createMasthead* template to create the masthead. Here's what our stylesheet would look like:

```
<xsl:template name="createMasthead">
  <!-- interesting stuff that generates the masthead goes here -->
</xsl:template>
...
<xsl:template match="/">
  <html>
    <head>
      <title><xsl:value-of select="title"/></title>
    </head>
    <body>
      <xsl:call-template name="createMasthead"/>
...
```

Named templates are extremely useful for defining commonly used markup. For example, say you're using an XSLT stylesheet to create web pages with a particular look and feel. You can write named templates that create the header, footer, navigation areas, or other items that define how your web page will look. Every time you need to create a web page, simply use <xsl:call-template> to invoke those templates and create the look and feel you want.

Even better, if you put those named templates in a separate stylesheet and import the stylesheet (with either <xsl:import> or <xsl:include>), you can create a set of stylesheets that generate the look and feel of the web site you want. If you decide to redesign your web site, redesign the stylesheets that define the common graphical and layout elements. Change those stylesheets, regenerate your web site, and voila! You will see an instantly updated web site. (See Chapter 9 for an example.)

Templates à la Mode

The XSLT `<xsl:template>` element has a `mode` attribute that lets you process the same set of nodes several times. For example, we might want to process `<h1>` elements one way when we generate a table of contents, and another way when we process the document as a whole. We could use the `mode` attribute to define different templates for different purposes:

```
<xsl:template match="h1" mode="build-toc">
  <!-- Template to process the <h1> element for table of contents -->
</xsl:template>

<xsl:template match="h1" mode="process-text">
  <!-- Template to process the <h1> element along with the rest   -->
  <!-- of the document                                                 -->
</xsl:template>
```

We can then start applying templates with the `mode` attribute:

```
<xsl:template match="/">
  <html>
    <body>
      <h1>Table of Contents</h1>
      <ul>
        <xsl:apply-templates select="h1" mode="build-toc"/>
      </ul>
      <xsl:apply-templates select="*" mode="process-text"/>
    </body>
  </html>
</xsl:template>
```

This style of coding makes maintenance much easier; if the table of contents isn't generated correctly, the templates with `mode="build-toc"` are the obvious place to start debugging. See Chapter 9 for a more detailed discussion of the `mode` attribute.

Parameters

The XSLT `<xsl:param>` and `<xsl:with-param>` elements allow you to pass parameters to a template. You can pass templates with either the `<call-template>` element or the `<apply-templates>` element; we'll discuss the details in this section.

Defining a Parameter in a Template

To define a parameter in a template, use the `<xsl:param>` element. Here's an example of a template that defines two parameters:

```
<xsl:template name="calcuateArea">
  <xsl:param name="width"/>
  <xsl:param name="height"/>
```

```
  <xsl:value-of select="$width * $height"/>
</xsl:template>
```

Conceptually, this is a lot like writing code in a traditional programming language, isn't it? Our template here defines two parameters, `width` and `height`, and outputs their product.

If you want, you can define a default value for a parameter. There are two ways to define a default value; the simplest is to use a `select` attribute on the `<xsl:param>` element:

```
<template name="addTableCell">
  <xsl:param name="bgColor" select="'blue'"/>
  <xsl:param name="width" select="150"/>
  <xsl:param name="content"/>
  <td width="{$width}" bgcolor="{$bgColor}">
    <xsl:apply-templates select="$content"/>
  </td>
</template>
```

In this example, the default values of the parameters `bgColor` and `width` are `'blue'` and `150`, respectively. If we invoke this template without specifying values for these parameters, the default values are used. Also notice that we generated the values of the `width` and `bgcolor` attributes of the HTML `<td>` tag with attribute value templates, the values in curly braces. For more information, see the section "Attribute Value Templates" in Chapter 3.

Notice that in the previous sample, we put single quotes around the value `blue`, but we didn't do it around the value `150`. Without the single quotes around `blue`, the XSLT processor assumes we want to select all the `<blue>` elements in the current context, which is probably not what we want. The XSLT processor is clever enough to realize that the value `150` can't be an XML element name (the XML 1.0 Specification says element names can't begin with numbers), so we don't need the single quotes around a numeric value.

Try to keep this in mind when you're using parameters. You'll probably forget it at some point, and you'll probably go nuts trying to figure out the strange behavior you're getting from the XSLT processor.

The second way to define a default value for a parameter is to include content inside the `<xsl:param>` element:

```
<template name="addTableCell">
  <xsl:param name="bgColor">
    <xsl:text>blue</xsl:text>
  </xsl:param>
  <xsl:param name="width">
```

```
    <xsl:value-of select="7+8"/><xsl:text>0</xsl:text>
  </xsl:param>
  <xsl:param name="content"/>
  <td width="{$width}" bgcolor="{$bgColor}">
    <xsl:apply-templates select="$content"/>
  </td>
</template>
```

In this example, we used `<xsl:text>` and `<xsl:value-of>` elements to define the default values of the parameters. Out of sheer perverseness, we defined the value of `width` as the concatenation of the numeric expression `7+8`, followed by the string "0". This example produces the same results as the previous one.

Passing Parameters

If we invoke a template by name, which is similar to calling a subroutine, we'll need to pass parameters to those templates. We do this with the `<xsl:with-param>` element. For example, let's say we want to call a template named *draw-box*, and pass the parameters `startX`, `startY`, `endX`, and `endY` to it. Here's what we'd do:

```
<xsl:call-template name="draw-box">
  <xsl:with-param name="startX" select="50"/>
  <xsl:with-param name="startY" select="50"/>
  <xsl:with-param name="endX" select="97"/>
  <xsl:with-param name="endY" select="144"/>
</xsl:call-template>
```

In this sample, we've called the template named draw-box with the four parameters we mentioned earlier. Notice that up until now, `<xsl:call-template>` has always been an empty tag; here, though, the parameters are the content of the `<xsl:call-template>` element. (If you want, you can do the same thing with `<xsl:apply-templates>`.) We used the `<xsl:with-param>` element with the `<xsl:call-template>` element here, but you can also use it with `<xsl:apply-templates>`.

If we're going to pass parameters to a template, we have to set up the template so that it expects the parameters we're passing. To do this, we'll use the `<xsl:param>` element inside the template. Here are some examples:

```
<xsl:template name="draw-box">
<xsl:param name="startX"/>
<xsl:param name="startY" select="'0'"/>
<xsl:param name="endX">
10
</xsl:param>
<xsl:param name="endY">
10
</xsl:param>
...
</xsl:template>
```

A couple of notes about the <xsl:param> element:

- If you define any <xsl:param> elements in a template, they must be the first thing in the template.
- The <xsl:param> element allows you to define a default value for the parameter. If the calling template doesn't supply a value, the default is used instead. The last three <xsl:param> elements in our previous example define default values.
- The <xsl:param> element has the same content model as <xsl:variable>. With no content and no select attribute, the default value of the parameter is an empty string (""). With a select attribute, the default value of the parameter is the value of the select attribute. If the <xsl:param> element contains content, the default value of the parameter is the content of the <xsl:param> element.

Global Parameters

XSLT allows you to define parameters whose scope is the entire stylesheet. You can define default values for these parameters and you can pass values to those parameters externally to the stylesheet. Before we talk about how to pass in values for global parameters, we'll show you how to create them. Any parameters that are top-level elements (any <xsl:param> elements whose parent is <xsl:stylesheet>) are global parameters. Here's an example:

```
<?xml version="1.0"?>
<xsl:stylesheet version="1.0" xmlns:xsl="http://www.w3.org/1999/XSL/Transform">

  <xsl:output method="text"/>

  <xsl:param name="startX"/>
  <xsl:param name="baseColor"/>

  <xsl:variable name="newline">
<xsl:text>
</xsl:text>
  </xsl:variable>

  <xsl:template match="/">
    <xsl:value-of select="$newline"/>
    <xsl:text>Global parameters example</xsl:text>

    <xsl:value-of select="$newline"/>
    <xsl:value-of select="$newline"/>
    <xsl:text>The value of startX is: </xsl:text>
    <xsl:value-of select="$startX"/>
    <xsl:value-of select="$newline"/>
    <xsl:text>The value of baseColor is: </xsl:text>
```

```
    <xsl:value-of select="$baseColor"/>
    <xsl:value-of select="$newline"/>
  </xsl:template>

</xsl:stylesheet>
```

How you pass values for global parameters depends on the XSLT processor you're using. We'll go through some examples here for all the usual suspects. Let's say we want to pass the numeric value `50` as the value for `startX`, and the string value `magenta` as the default value for `baseColor`. Here are the commands you'd use to do that.

Xalan

To pass global parameters to Xalan, you can define them on the Xalan command line:

```
java org.apache.xalan.xslt.Process -in xyz.xml -xsl params.xsl
  -param startX 50 -param baseColor magenta
```

(This command should be on a single line.)

XT

If you're using James Clark's XSLT processor, you can pass parameters like this:

```
java com.jclark.xsl.sax.Driver xyz.xml params.xsl startX=50 baseColor=magenta
```

Microsoft's XSLT tools

Microsoft's XSLT tools support external parameters like this:

```
msxsl xyz.xml params.xsl startX=50 baseColor=magenta
```

Saxon

Saxon supports external parameters like this:

```
java com.icl.saxon.StyleSheet xyz.xml params.xsl startX=50 baseColor=magenta
```

Oracle

If you're using Oracle's parser, stylesheet parameters are passed like this:

```
java oracle.xml.parser.v2.oraxsl -p startX=50 -p baseColor='magenta' xyz.xml
params.xsl
```

(This command should be on a single line.) Notice that for the Oracle parser, we had to put single quotes around the text value `magenta`.

Using this stylesheet with any XML document and any of the XSLT processors listed here produces these results:

```
Global parameters example

The value of startX is: 50
The value of baseColor is: magenta
```

Setting global parameters in a Java program

If your XSLT engine supports the Transformation API for XML (TrAX), you can embed the XSLT processor and set global parameters in your code. Here's an example that uses TrAX support:

```
import java.io.File;
import javax.xml.transform.Transformer;
import javax.xml.transform.TransformerConfigurationException;
import javax.xml.transform.TransformerException;
import javax.xml.transform.TransformerFactory;
import javax.xml.transform.stream.StreamResult;
import javax.xml.transform.stream.StreamSource;

public class GlobalParameters
{
  public static void parseAndProcess(String sourceID,
                                     String xslID,
                                     String outputID)
  {
    try
    {
      TransformerFactory tfactory = TransformerFactory.newInstance();

      Transformer transformer
        = tfactory.newTransformer(new StreamSource(xslID));

      // Use the setParameter method to set global parameters
      transformer.setParameter("startX", new Integer(50));
      transformer.setParameter("baseColor", "magenta");

      transformer.transform(new StreamSource(new File(sourceID)),
                            new StreamResult(new File(outputID)));
    }
    catch (TransformerConfigurationException tce)
    {
      System.err.println("Exception: " + tce);
    }
    catch (TransformerException te)
    {
      System.err.println("Exception: " + te);
    }
  }
```

```
    public static void main(String argv[])
      throws java.io.IOException,
             org.xml.sax.SAXException
    {
      GlobalParameters gp = new GlobalParameters();
      gp.parseAndProcess("xyz.xml", "params.xsl", "output.text");
    }
  }
```

Notice that we used the `setParameter` method to set global parameters for the `Transformer` object before we invoke the `transform` method. This transformation generates the following results in *output.text*:

```
Global parameters example

The value of startX is: 50
The value of baseColor is: magenta
```

Variables

If we use logic to control the flow of our stylesheets, we'll probably want to store temporary results along the way. In other words, we'll need to use variables. XSLT provides the `<xsl:variable>` element, which allows you to store a value and associate it with a name.

The `<xsl:variable>` element can be used in three ways. The simplest form of the element creates a new variable whose value is an empty string (`""`). Here's how it looks:

```
<xsl:variable name="x"/>
```

This element creates a new variable named `x`, whose value is an empty string. (Please hold your applause until the end of the section.)

You can also create a variable by adding a `select` attribute to the `<xsl:variable>` element:

```
<xsl:variable name="favouriteColour" select="'blue'"/>
```

In this case, we've set the value of the variable to be the string "blue". Notice that we put single quotes around the value. These quotes ensure that the literal value `blue` is used as the value of the variable. If we had left out the single quotes, this would mean the value of the variable is that of all the `<blue>` elements in the current context, which definitely isn't what we want here.

Some XSLT processors don't require you to put single quotes around a literal value if the literal value begins with a number. This is because the XML specification states that XML element names can't begin with a number. If I say the value should be 35, Xalan, XT, and Saxon all assume that I mean 35 as a literal value, not as an element name. Although this works with many XSLT processors, you're safer to put the single quotes around the numeric values anyway. A further aside: the value here is the string "35", although it can be converted to a number easily.

The third way to use the <xsl:variable> element is to put content inside it. Here's a brief example:

```
<xsl:variable name="y">
  <xsl:choose>
    <xsl:when test="$x &gt; 7">
      <xsl:text>13</xsl:text>
    </xsl:when>
    <xsl:otherwise>
      <xsl:text>15</xsl:text>
    </xsl:otherwise>
  </xsl:choose>
</xsl:variable>
```

In this more complicated example, the content of the variable y depends on the test attribute of the <xsl:when> element. This is the equivalent of this procedural programming construct:

```
int y;
if (x > 7)
  y = 13;
else
  y = 15;
```

Are These Things Really Variables?

Although these XSLT variables are called variables, they're not variables in the traditional sense of procedural programming languages like C++ or Java. Remember that earlier we said one goal behind the design of the stylesheet language is to avoid side effects in execution? Well, one of the most common side effects used in most procedural languages is changing the value of a variable. If we write our stylesheet so that the results depend on the varying values of different variables, the stylesheet engine would be forced to evaluate the templates in a certain order.

XSLT variables are more like variables in the traditional mathematical sense. In mathematics, we can define a function called `square(x)` that returns the value of a number (represented by `x`) multiplied by itself. In other words, `square(2.5)` returns `6.25`. In this context, we understand that `x` can be any number; we also understand that the `square` function can't change the value of `x`.

It takes a while to get used to this concept, but you'll get there. Trust me on this.

Variable Scope

An `<xsl:variable>` element is scoped to the element that contains it. If an `<xsl:variable>` element is a top-level element (its parent is `<xsl:stylesheet>`), it is global, and its value is visible everywhere in the stylesheet. You can also use an `<xsl:variable>` element to override the value of a global variable locally.

Using Recursion to Do Most Anything

Writing an XSLT stylesheet is different from programming in other languages. If you didn't believe that before, you probably do now. We'll finish this chapter with a couple of examples that demonstrate how to use recursion to solve the kinds of problems that you're probably used to solving with procedural programming languages.

Implementing a String Replace Function

To demonstrate how to use recursion to solve problems, we'll write a string replace function. This is sometimes useful when you need to escape certain characters or substrings in your output. The stylesheet we'll develop here transforms an XML document into a set of SQL statements that will be executed at a Windows command prompt. We have to do several things:

Put a caret (`^`) *in front of all ampersands* (`&`)

On the Windows NT and Windows 2000 command prompt, the ampersand means that the current command has ended and another is beginning. For example, this command creates a new directory called *xslt* and changes the current directory to the newly created one:

```
mkdir xslt & chdir xslt
```

If we create a SQL statement that contains an ampersand, we'll need to escape the ampersand so it's processed as a literal character, not as an operator. If we insert the value `Jones & Son` as the value of the company field in a row of the database, we need to change it to `Jones ^& Son` before we try to run the SQL command.

Put a caret (`^`)*) in front of all vertical bars* (`|`)
: The vertical bar is the pipe operator on Windows systems, so we need to escape it if we want it interpreted as literal text instead of an operator.

Replace any single quote (`'`) *with two single quotes* (`''`)
: This is a requirement of our database system.

Procedural design

Three functions we could use in our template are `concat()`, `substring-before()`, and `substring-after()`. To replace an ampersand with a caret and an ampersand, this would do the trick:

```
<xsl:value-of select="concat(substring-before(., '&amp;'), '^&amp;',
                              substring-after(., '&amp;'))"/>
```

The obvious problem with this step is that it only replaces the first occurrence of the ampersand. If there are two ampersands, or three, or three hundred, we need to call this method once for each ampersand in the original string. Because of the way variables work, we can't do what we'd do in a procedural language:

```
private static String strChange(String string, String from, String to)
{
  String before = "", after = "";
  int    index;

  index = string.indexOf(from);
  while (index >= 0)
  {
    before = string.substring(0, index);
    after = string.substring(index + from.length());
    string = before + to + after;

    index = string.indexOf(from, index + to.length());
  }

  return string;
}
```

Recursive design

To implement a string replace function with recursion, we take a modified version of the approach we used here. We build the replaced string in three pieces:

- Everything up to the first occurrence of the substring we're replacing. If the substring doesn't exist in the main string, then this is the entire string.
- The replacement substring. If the substring we're replacing doesn't exist in the main string, then this is blank.

- Everything after the first occurrence of the substring. If the substring doesn't exist in the main string, then this is blank.

The third portion is where we use recursion. If the substring we're replacing occurs in that part of the main string, we call the substring replace function on the last of the string. The key here, as with all recursive functions, is that we have an exit case, a condition in which we don't recurse. If the substring doesn't occur in the last portion of the string, we're done.

Here's the design in pseudocode:

```
replaceSubstring(originalString, substring, replacementString)
{
  if (contains(originalString, substring))
    firstOfString = substring-before(originalString, substring)
  else
    firstOfString = originalString

  if (contains(originalString, substring))
    middleOfString = replacementString
  else
    middleOfString = ""

  if (contains(originalString, substring))
  {
    if (contains(substring-after(originalString, substring), substring))
     lastOfString = replaceString(substring-after(originalString, substring),
                                  substring, replacementString)
    else
      lastOfString = substring-after(originalString, substring)
  }
  concat(firstOfString, middleOfString, lastOfString)
}
```

In the recursive approach, the function calls itself whenever there's at least one more occurrence of the substring. Each time the function calls itself, the `originalString` parameter is a little smaller, until eventually we've processed the complete string. Here's the complete template:

```
<xsl:template name="replace-substring">
  <xsl:param name="original"/>
  <xsl:param name="substring"/>
  <xsl:param name="replacement" select="''"/>
  <xsl:variable name="first">
    <xsl:choose>
      <xsl:when test="contains($original, $substring)">
        <xsl:value-of select="substring-before($original, $substring)"/>
      </xsl:when>
      <xsl:otherwise>
        <xsl:value-of select="$original"/>
      </xsl:otherwise>
    </xsl:choose>
```

```
    </xsl:variable>
    <xsl:variable name="middle">
      <xsl:choose>
        <xsl:when test="contains($original, $substring)">
          <xsl:value-of select="$replacement"/>
        </xsl:when>
        <xsl:otherwise>
          <xsl:text></xsl:text>
        </xsl:otherwise>
      </xsl:choose>
    </xsl:variable>
    <xsl:variable name="last">
      <xsl:choose>
        <xsl:when test="contains($original, $substring)">
          <xsl:choose>
            <xsl:when test="contains(substring-after($original, $substring),
                                     $substring)">
              <xsl:call-template name="replace-substring">
                <xsl:with-param name="original">
                  <xsl:value-of select="substring-after($original, $substring)"/>
                </xsl:with-param>
                <xsl:with-param name="substring">
                  <xsl:value-of select="$substring"/>
                </xsl:with-param>
                <xsl:with-param name="replacement">
                  <xsl:value-of select="$replacement"/>
                </xsl:with-param>
              </xsl:call-template>
            </xsl:when>
            <xsl:otherwise>
              <xsl:value-of select="substring-after($original, $substring)"/>
            </xsl:otherwise>
          </xsl:choose>
        </xsl:when>
        <xsl:otherwise>
          <xsl:text></xsl:text>
        </xsl:otherwise>
      </xsl:choose>
    </xsl:variable>
    <xsl:value-of select="concat($first, $middle, $last)"/>
  </xsl:template>
```

This style of programming takes some getting used to, but whatever you want to do can usually be done. Our example here is a good illustration of the techniques we've discussed in this chapter, including branching statements, variables, invoking templates by name, and passing parameters.

A Stylesheet That Emulates a for Loop

We stressed earlier that the `xsl:for-each` element is not a `for` loop; it's merely an iterator across a group of nodes. However, if you simply must implement a `for` loop, there's a way to do it. (Get ready to use recursion, though.)

Template Design

Our design here is to create a named template that will take some arguments, then act as a `for` loop processor. If you think about a traditional `for` loop, it has several properties:

- One or more initialization statements. These statements are processed before the `for` loop begins. Typically the initialization statements refer to an *index variable* that is used to determine whether the loop should continue.
- An increment statement. This statement specifies how the index variable should be updated after each pass through the loop.
- A boolean expression. If the expression is `true`, the loop continues; if it is ever `false`, the loop exits.

Let's take a sample from the world of Java and C++:

```
for (int i=0; i<length; i++)
```

In this scintillating example, the initialization statement is `i=0`, the index variable (the variable whose value determines whether we're done or not) is `i`, the boolean expression we use to test whether the loop should continue is `i<length`, and the increment statement is `i++`.

For our purposes here, we're going to make several simplifying assumptions. (Feel free, dear reader, to make the example as complicated as you wish.) Here are the shortcuts we'll take:

- Rather than use an initialization statement, we'll require the caller to set the value of the local variable `i` when it invokes our `for` loop processor.
- Rather than specify an increment statement such as `i++`, we'll require the caller to set the value of the local variable `increment`. The default value for this variable is `1`; it can be any negative or positive integer, however. The value of this variable will be added to the current value of `i` after each iteration through our loop.

- Rather than allow any conceivable boolean expression, we'll require the caller to pass in two parameters; operator and testValue. The allowable values for the operator variable are =, < (coded as <), > (coded as >), <> (coded as <>), <= (coded as <=), and >= (coded as >=). We're doing things this way because there isn't a way to ask the XSLT processor to evaluate a literal (such as i<length) as if it were part of the stylesheet.

Implementation

Let's look at the parameters for our for loop template:

```
<xsl:param name="i"         select="1"/>
<xsl:param name="increment" select="1"/>
<xsl:param name="operator"  select="="/>
<xsl:param name="testValue" select="1"/>
```

Our for template uses four parameters: the index variable, the increment, the comparison operator, and the test value. To emulate this C++ statement:

```
for (int i=1; i<=10; i++)
```

You'd use this markup:

```
<xsl:call-template name="for-loop">
  <xsl:with-param name="i"         select="1"/>
  <xsl:with-param name="increment" select="1"/>
  <xsl:with-param name="operator"  select="&lt;="/>
  <xsl:with-param name="testValue" select="10"/>
</xsl:call-template>
```

To demonstrate our stylesheet, our first version simply prints out the value of our index variable each time through the loop:

```
Transforming...
Iteration 1: i=1
Iteration 2: i=2
Iteration 3: i=3
Iteration 4: i=4
Iteration 5: i=5
Iteration 6: i=6
Iteration 7: i=7
Iteration 8: i=8
Iteration 9: i=9
Iteration 10: i=10
transform took 260 milliseconds
XSLProcessor: done
```

Here's the markup you'd use to emulate the Java statement `for (int i=10; i>0; i-=2)`:

```
<xsl:call-template name="for-loop">
  <xsl:with-param name="i"         select="10"/>
  <xsl:with-param name="increment" select="-2"/>
  <xsl:with-param name="operator"  select="&gt;"/>
  <xsl:with-param name="testValue" select="0"/>
</xsl:call-template>
```

In this case, the values of `i` decrease from `10` to `0`:

```
Transforming...
Iteration 1: i=10
Iteration 2: i=8
Iteration 3: i=6
Iteration 4: i=4
Iteration 5: i=2
transform took 110 milliseconds
XSLProcessor: done
```

The Complete Example

Here's our complete stylesheet:

```
<?xml version="1.0"?>
<xsl:stylesheet xmlns:xsl="http://www.w3.org/1999/XSL/Transform" version="1.0">

  <xsl:output method="text"/>

  <xsl:variable name="newline">
<xsl:text>
</xsl:text>
  </xsl:variable>

  <xsl:template name="for-loop">
    <xsl:param name="i"         select="1"/>
    <xsl:param name="increment" select="1"/>
    <xsl:param name="operator"  select="="/>
    <xsl:param name="testValue" select="1"/>
    <xsl:param name="iteration" select="1"/>

    <xsl:variable name="testPassed">
      <xsl:choose>
        <xsl:when test="starts-with($operator, '!=')">
          <xsl:if test="$i != $testValue">
            <xsl:text>true</xsl:text>
          </xsl:if>
        </xsl:when>
        <xsl:when test="starts-with($operator, '<=')">
          <xsl:if test="$i <= $testValue">
            <xsl:text>true</xsl:text>
          </xsl:if>
```

```
    </xsl:when>
    <xsl:when test="starts-with($operator, '>=')">
      <xsl:if test="$i >= $testValue">
        <xsl:text>true</xsl:text>
      </xsl:if>
    </xsl:when>
    <xsl:when test="starts-with($operator, '=')">
      <xsl:if test="$i = $testValue">
        <xsl:text>true</xsl:text>
      </xsl:if>
    </xsl:when>
    <xsl:when test="starts-with($operator, '<')">
      <xsl:if test="$i < $testValue">
        <xsl:text>true</xsl:text>
      </xsl:if>
    </xsl:when>
    <xsl:when test="starts-with($operator, '>')">
      <xsl:if test="$i > $testValue">
        <xsl:text>true</xsl:text>
      </xsl:if>
    </xsl:when>
    <xsl:otherwise>
      <xsl:message terminate="yes">
        <xsl:text>Sorry, the for-loop emulator only </xsl:text>
        <xsl:text>handles six operators </xsl:text>
        <xsl:value-of select="$newline"/>
        <xsl:text>(< | > | = | <= | >= | !=). </xsl:text>
        <xsl:text>The value </xsl:text>
        <xsl:value-of select="$operator"/>
        <xsl:text> is not allowed.</xsl:text>
        <xsl:value-of select="$newline"/>
      </xsl:message>
    </xsl:otherwise>
  </xsl:choose>
</xsl:variable>

<xsl:if test="$testPassed='true'">
  <!-- Put your logic here, whatever it might be. For the purpose      -->
  <!-- of our example, we'll just write some text to the output stream. -->

  <xsl:text>Iteration </xsl:text><xsl:value-of select="$iteration"/>
  <xsl:text>: i=</xsl:text>
  <xsl:value-of select="$i"/><xsl:value-of select="$newline"/>

  <!-- Your logic should end here; don't change the rest of this        -->
  <!-- template!                                                        -->

  <!-- Now for the important part: we increment the index variable and  -->
  <!-- loop. Notice that we're passing the incremented value, not       -->
  <!-- changing the variable itself.                                    -->

  <xsl:call-template name="for-loop">
    <xsl:with-param name="i"         select="$i + $increment"/>
    <xsl:with-param name="increment" select="$increment"/>
```

```
        <xsl:with-param name="operator"  select="$operator"/>
        <xsl:with-param name="testValue" select="$testValue"/>
        <xsl:with-param name="iteration" select="$iteration + 1"/>
      </xsl:call-template>
    </xsl:if>
  </xsl:template>

  <xsl:template match="/">
    <xsl:call-template name="for-loop">
      <xsl:with-param name="i"         select="'10'"/>
      <xsl:with-param name="increment" select="'-2'"/>
      <xsl:with-param name="operator"  select="'>'"/>
      <xsl:with-param name="testValue" select="'0'"/>
    </xsl:call-template>
  </xsl:template>

</xsl:stylesheet>
```

If you want to modify the `for` loop to do something useful, put your code between these comments:

```
<!-- Put your logic here, whatever it might be. For the purpose      -->
<!-- of our example, we'll just write some text to the output stream. -->

<xsl:text>Iteration </xsl:text><xsl:value-of select="$iteration"/>
<xsl:text>: i=</xsl:text>
<xsl:value-of select="$i"/><xsl:value-of select="$newline"/>

<!-- Your logic should end here; don't change the rest of this        -->
<!-- template!                                                        -->
```

A Stylesheet That Generates a Stylesheet That Emulates a for Loop

We've emulated a `for` loop now, but what about a stylesheet that generates another stylesheet that emulates the `for` loop? As we beat this dead horse one more time, we'll create a stylesheet that generates the iteration for us, along with an XML syntax that automates the process.

XML Input

Here's the XML template we'll use to generate the stylesheet:

```
<?xml version="1.0"?>
<html xmlns:xsl="http://www.w3.org/1999/XSL/Transform">
  <head>
    <title>Text generated by our for loop processor</title>
  </head>
  <body>
    <h1>Text generated by our for loop processor</h1>
    <table border="1">
```

```
        <tr>
          <th>Iteration #</th>
          <th>Value of <i>i</i></th>
        </tr>
        <for-loop index-variable="0" increment="1"
         operator="<=" test-value="10">
          <tr>
            <td align="center">
              <xsl:value-of select="$iteration"/>
            </td>
            <td align="center">
              <xsl:value-of select="$i"/>
            </td>
          </tr>
        </for-loop>
      </table>
    </body>
  </html>
```

Template Design

The design of our stylesheet-generating stylesheet is as follows:

1. Output the <xsl:stylesheet> element.
2. Generate the for-loop template. This will be a named template that we'll invoke while processing the rest of the document.
3. Generate the root element template. To do this, everything except the <for-loop> element is copied to the output document. The <for-loop> element will be converted into a call to the for-loop template we generated in the previous step.
4. Close out the <xsl:stylesheet> element.

Complications

There are a couple of complications in producing our stylesheet-generating stylesheet. First, we need to have some way to distinguish among the XSLT elements in the stylesheet being processed and the XSLT elements we're generating. Here's one way to do it:

```
<xsl:element name="xsl:template"
  namespace="http://www.w3.org/1999/XSL/Transform">
  <xsl:attribute name="name">for-loop</xsl:attribute>
  <xsl:element name="xsl:param"
  namespace="http://www.w3.org/1999/XSL/Transform">
    <xsl:attribute name="name">i</xsl:attribute>
    <xsl:attribute name="select">
      <xsl:value-of select="@index-variable"/>
    </xsl:attribute>
  </xsl:element>
```

```
<xsl:element name="xsl:param" namespace="http://www.w3.org/1999/XSL/Transform">
  <xsl:attribute name="name">increment</xsl:attribute>
  <xsl:attribute name="select">
    <xsl:value-of select="@increment"/>
  </xsl:attribute>
</xsl:element>
<xsl:element name="xsl:param" namespace="http://www.w3.org/1999/XSL/Transform">
  <xsl:attribute name="name">operator</xsl:attribute>
  <xsl:attribute name="select">
    <xsl:text>'</xsl:text>
    <xsl:value-of select="@operator"/>
    <xsl:text>'</xsl:text>
  </xsl:attribute>
</xsl:element>
<xsl:element name="xsl:param" namespace="http://www.w3.org/1999/XSL/Transform">
  <xsl:attribute name="name">testValue</xsl:attribute>
  <xsl:attribute name="select">
    <xsl:value-of select="@test-value"/>
  </xsl:attribute>
</xsl:element>
<xsl:element name="xsl:param" namespace="http://www.w3.org/1999/XSL/Transform">
  <xsl:attribute name="name">iteration</xsl:attribute>
  <xsl:attribute name="select">1</xsl:attribute>
</xsl:element>
...
```

This lengthy listing generates this simple XML fragment:

```
<ns1:template name="for-loop">
  <ns1:param name="i" select="0"/>
  <ns1:param name="increment" select="1"/>
  <ns1:param name="operator" select="'<='"/>
  <ns1:param name="testValue" select="10"/>
  <ns1:param name="iteration" select="1"/>
  ...
```

This approach works, but we're doing an awful lot of work to create some fairly simple elements. For all the XSLT elements we're generating with <xsl:element> elements, we have to declare the namespace for each one. The obvious way of handling this would be to generate a namespace declaration on the <xsl:stylesheet> element:

```
<xsl:attribute name="xmlns:xsl">
  http://www.w3.org/1999/XSL/Transform
</xsl:attribute>
```

Unfortunately, the XSLT specification states (in section 7.1.3) that this isn't legal. What we did in our previous example was add the namespace attribute to all XSLT elements we need to generate. (The XSLT processor is not required to use the namespace prefix we specified in the <xsl:element>, by the way.) To help us get around this awkward problem, the XSLT specification provides the <xsl:namespace-alias> element. This provision allows us to define an alias for the XSLT namespace (or any other namespace we want to use); we'll use the normal XSLT namespace for the stylesheet elements we use, and we'll use the alias for the stylesheet elements we generating. Here's how our new stylesheet looks:

```
<?xml version="1.0"?>
<xsl:stylesheet version="1.0"
  xmlns:xsl="http://www.w3.org/1999/XSL/Transform"
  xmlns:xslout="can be anything, doesn't matter">

  <xsl:output method="xml" indent="yes"/>

  <xsl:namespace-alias stylesheet-prefix="xslout" result-prefix="xsl"/>

  <xsl:template match="*|@*|text()|comment()|processing-instruction()">
    <xsl:copy>
      <xsl:apply-templates
        select="*|@*|text()|comment()|processing-instruction()"/>
    </xsl:copy>
  </xsl:template>

  <xsl:template match="for-loop">
    <xslout:call-template name="for-loop">
      <xslout:with-param name="i" select="{@index-variable}"/>
      <xslout:with-param name="increment" select="{@increment}"/>
      <xslout:with-param name="operator">
        <xsl:attribute name="select">
          <xsl:text>'</xsl:text>
          <xsl:value-of select="@operator"/>
          <xsl:text>'</xsl:text>
        </xsl:attribute>
      </xslout:with-param>
      <xslout:with-param name="testValue" select="{@test-value}"/>
    </xslout:call-template>
  </xsl:template>

  <xsl:template match="for-loop" mode="generate-template">
    <xslout:variable name="newline">
<xslout:text>
</xslout:text>
    </xslout:variable>

    <xslout:template name="for-loop">
      <xslout:param name="i" select="@index-variable"/>
      <xslout:param name="increment" select="@increment"/>
      <xslout:param name="operator" select="@operator"/>
      <xslout:param name="testValue" select="@test-value"/>
      <xslout:param name="iteration" select="1"/>

      <xslout:variable name="testPassed">
        <xslout:choose>
          <xslout:when test="starts-with($operator, '!=')">
            <xslout:if test="$i != $testValue">
              <xslout:text>true</xslout:text>
```

```
      </xslout:if>
    </xslout:when>
    <xslout:when test="starts-with($operator, '<=')">
      <xslout:if test="$i <= $testValue">
        <xslout:text>true</xslout:text>
      </xslout:if>
    </xslout:when>
    <xslout:when test="starts-with($operator, '>=')">
      <xslout:if test="$i >= $testValue">
        <xslout:text>true</xslout:text>
      </xslout:if>
    </xslout:when>
    <xslout:when test="starts-with($operator, '=')">
      <xslout:if test="$i = $testValue">
        <xslout:text>true</xslout:text>
      </xslout:if>
    </xslout:when>
    <xslout:when test="starts-with($operator, '<')">
      <xslout:if test="$i < $testValue">
        <xslout:text>true</xslout:text>
      </xslout:if>
    </xslout:when>
    <xslout:when test="starts-with($operator, '>')">
      <xslout:if test="$i > $testValue">
        <xslout:text>true</xslout:text>
      </xslout:if>
    </xslout:when>
    <xslout:otherwise>
      <xslout:message terminate="yes">
        <xslout:text>Sorry, the for-loop emulator only </xslout:text>
        <xslout:text>handles six operators </xslout:text>
        <xslout:value-of select="$newline"/>
        <xslout:text>(< | > | = | <= | >= | !=).  </xslout:text>
        <xslout:text>The value </xslout:text>
        <xslout:value-of select="$operator"/>
        <xslout:text> is not allowed.</xslout:text>
        <xslout:value-of select="$newline"/>
      </xslout:message>
    </xslout:otherwise>
  </xslout:choose>
</xslout:variable>

<xslout:if test="$testPassed='true'">
  <xslout:comment>From your stylesheet:</xslout:comment>

  <xsl:apply-templates select="*"/>

  <xslout:comment>End of text from your stylesheet</xslout:comment>

  <xslout:call-template name="for-loop">
    <xslout:with-param name="i" select="$i + $increment"/>
    <xslout:with-param name="increment" select="$increment"/>
    <xslout:with-param name="operator" select="$operator"/>
    <xslout:with-param name="testValue" select="$testValue"/>
```

```
          <xslout:with-param name="iteration" select="$iteration + 1"/>
        </xslout:call-template>
      </xslout:if>
    </xslout:template>
  </xsl:template>

  <xsl:template match="/">
    <xslout:stylesheet version="1.0">
      <xsl:apply-templates select="//for-loop" mode="generate-template"/>
      <xslout:template match="/">
        <xsl:apply-templates select="*"/>
      </xslout:template>
    </xslout:stylesheet>
  </xsl:template>

</xsl:stylesheet>
```

Throughout our stylesheet, we used the usual `xsl` namespace for the stylesheet elements we use, and the `xslout` namespace for the stylesheet elements we generate. Notice that though we define the `xslout` namespace on the `<xsl:namespace-alias>` element, we still have to declare it on the `<xsl:stylesheet>` element. Also note that the value we define for the `xslout` namespace doesn't matter; the value referred to by the `<xsl:namespace-alias>` is used instead.

Here is the stylesheet generated by our stylesheet-generating stylesheet:

```
<?xml version="1.0" encoding="UTF-8"?>
<xslout:stylesheet xmlns:xslout="http://www.w3.org/1999/XSL/Transform"
  version="1.0">
<xslout:variable name="newline">
<xslout:text/>
</xslout:variable>
<xslout:template name="for-loop">
<xslout:param select="@index-variable" name="i"/>
<xslout:param select="@increment" name="increment"/>
<xslout:param select="@operator" name="operator"/>
<xslout:param select="@test-value" name="testValue"/>
<xslout:param select="1" name="iteration"/>
<xslout:variable name="testPassed">
<xslout:choose>
<xslout:when test="starts-with($operator, '!=')">
<xslout:if test="$i != $testValue">
<xslout:text>true</xslout:text>
</xslout:if>
</xslout:when>
<xslout:when test="starts-with($operator, '<=')">
<xslout:if test="$i <= $testValue">
<xslout:text>true</xslout:text>
</xslout:if>
</xslout:when>
<xslout:when test="starts-with($operator, '>=')">
<xslout:if test="$i >= $testValue">
<xslout:text>true</xslout:text>
```

```
</xslout:if>
</xslout:when>
<xslout:when test="starts-with($operator, '=')">
<xslout:if test="$i = $testValue">
<xslout:text>true</xslout:text>
</xslout:if>
</xslout:when>
<xslout:when test="starts-with($operator, '<')">
<xslout:if test="$i < $testValue">
<xslout:text>true</xslout:text>
</xslout:if>
</xslout:when>
<xslout:when test="starts-with($operator, '>')">
<xslout:if test="$i > $testValue">
<xslout:text>true</xslout:text>
</xslout:if>
</xslout:when>
<xslout:otherwise>
<xslout:message terminate="yes">
<xslout:text>Sorry, the for-loop emulator only </xslout:text>
<xslout:text>handles six operators </xslout:text>
<xslout:value-of select="$newline"/>
<xslout:text>(< | > | = | <= | >= | !=).  </xslout:text>
<xslout:text>The value </xslout:text>
<xslout:value-of select="$operator"/>
<xslout:text> is not allowed.</xslout:text>
<xslout:value-of select="$newline"/>
</xslout:message>
</xslout:otherwise>
</xslout:choose>
</xslout:variable>
<xslout:if test="$testPassed='true'">
<xslout:comment>From your stylesheet:</xslout:comment>
<tr xmlns:xsl="http://www.w3.org/1999/XSL/Transform">
          <td align="center">
            <xsl:value-of select="$iteration"/>
          </td>
          <td align="center">
            <xsl:value-of select="$i"/>
          </td>
        </tr>
<xslout:comment>End of text from your stylesheet</xslout:comment>
<xslout:call-template name="for-loop">
<xslout:with-param select="$i + $increment" name="i"/>
<xslout:with-param select="$increment" name="increment"/>
<xslout:with-param select="$operator" name="operator"/>
<xslout:with-param select="$testValue" name="testValue"/>
<xslout:with-param select="$iteration + 1" name="iteration"/>
</xslout:call-template>
</xslout:if>
</xslout:template>
<xslout:template match="/">
<html xmlns:xsl="http://www.w3.org/1999/XSL/Transform">
  <head>
```

```
      <title>Text generated by our for loop processor</title>
    </head>
    <body>
      <h1>Text generated by our for loop processor</h1>
      <table border="1">
        <tr>
          <th>Iteration #</th>
          <th>Value of <i>i</i>
</th>
        </tr>
        <xslout:call-template name="for-loop">
<xslout:with-param select="0" name="i"/>
<xslout:with-param select="1" name="increment"/>
<xslout:with-param name="operator" select="'<='"/>
<xslout:with-param select="10" name="testValue"/>
</xslout:call-template>
      </table>
    </body>
</html>
</xslout:template>
</xslout:stylesheet>
```

When we execute the generated stylesheet, it produces the following HTML document. (When rendered in a browser, the document generated by the stylesheet generated by our other stylesheet looks like Figure 4-1.)

```
<html>
<head>
<META http-equiv="Content-Type" content="text/html; charset=UTF-8">
<title>Text generated by our for loop processor</title>
</head>
<body>
<h1>Text generated by our for loop processor</h1>
<table border="1">
<tr>
<th>Iteration #</th><th>Value of <i>i</i></th>
</tr>
<tr>
<td align="center">1</td><td align="center">0</td>
</tr>
<tr>
<td align="center">2</td><td align="center">1</td>
</tr>
<tr>
<td align="center">3</td><td align="center">2</td>
</tr>
<tr>
<td align="center">4</td><td align="center">3</td>
</tr>
<tr>
<td align="center">5</td><td align="center">4</td>
</tr>
<tr>
<td align="center">6</td><td align="center">5</td>
```

```
</tr>
<tr>
<td align="center">7</td><td align="center">6</td>
</tr>
<tr>
<td align="center">8</td><td align="center">7</td>
</tr>
<tr>
<td align="center">9</td><td align="center">8</td>
</tr>
<tr>
<td align="center">10</td><td align="center">9</td>
</tr>
<tr>
<td align="center">11</td><td align="center">10</td>
</tr>
</table>
</body>
</html>
```

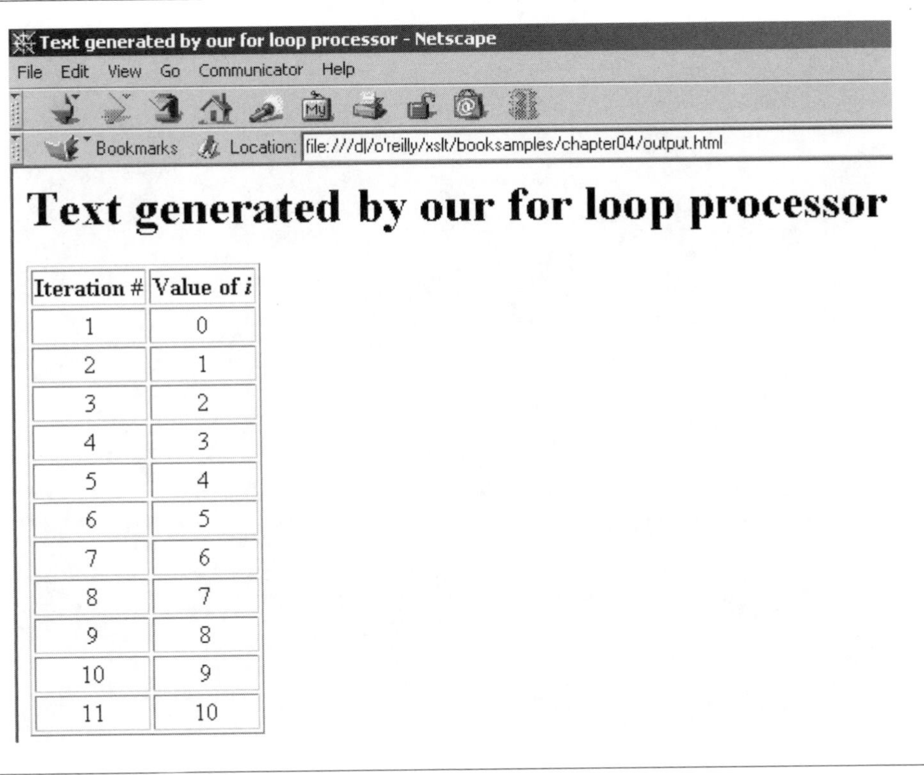

Figure 4-1. HTML document generated by our generated stylesheet

Notice in the generated document that the HTML `<title>` and `<h1>` values come directly from the XML template, as do the table headings and the definition of the HTML table itself.

Summary

We've covered a lot of ground in this chapter, haven't we? We've gone over all of the basic elements you need to add logic and branching to your stylesheets. We discussed some of the similarities between XSLT and other programming languages you might know; more importantly, we discussed how XSLT is different from most of the code you've probably written. In particular, the use of recursion and the principles of variables that don't change take some getting used to. Despite the learning curve, most of the common tasks you'll need to do will be similar to the exercises we've gone through in this chapter. Now that we've covered these basic elements, we'll talk about links and references, discovering ways to build links between different parts of an XML document.

5

Creating Links and Cross-References

If you're creating a web site, publishing a book, or creating an XML transaction, chances are many pieces of information will refer to other things. This chapter discusses a several ways to link XML elements. It reviews three techniques:

- Using the `id()` function
- Doing more advanced linking with the `key()` function
- Generating links in unstructured documents

Generating Links with the id() Function

Our first attempt at linking will be with the XPath `id()` function.

The ID, IDREF, and IDREFs Datatypes

Three of the basic datatypes supported by XML Document Type Definitions (DTDs) are `ID`, `IDREF`, and `IDREFS`. Here's a simple DTD that illustrates these datatypes:

```
<!--glossary.dtd-->
<!--The containing tag for the entire glossary-->
<!ELEMENT glossary  (glentry+) >

<!--A glossary entry-->
<!ELEMENT glentry  (term,defn+) >

<!--The word being defined-->
<!ELEMENT term  (#PCDATA) >
```

```
<!--The id is used for cross-referencing, and the
    xreftext is the text used by cross-references.-->
<!ATTLIST term
              id  ID    #REQUIRED
              xreftext  CDATA    #IMPLIED  >

<!--The definition of the term-->
<!ELEMENT defn  (#PCDATA | xref | seealso)* >

<!--A cross-reference to another term-->
<!ELEMENT xref   EMPTY  >

<!--refid is the ID of the referenced term-->
<!ATTLIST xref
              refid  IDREF    #REQUIRED >

<!--seealso refers to one or more other definitions-->
<!ELEMENT seealso EMPTY>
<!ATTLIST seealso
                refids   IDREFS  #REQUIRED >
```

In this DTD, each `<term>` element is required to have an `id` attribute, and each `<xref>` element must have an `refid` attribute. The `ID` and `IDREF` datatypes work according to two rules:

- Each value of the `id` attribute must be unique.
- Each value of the `refid` attribute must match a value of an `id` attribute elsewhere in the document.

To round out our example, the `<seealso>` element contains an attribute of type `IDREFS`. This datatype contains one or more values, each of which must match a value of an `ID` elsewhere in the document. Multiple values, if present, are separated by whitespace.

There are some complications of `ID` and related datatypes, but we'll discuss them later. For now, we'll focus on how the `id()` function works.

An XML Document in Need of Links

To illustrate the value of linking, we'll use a small glossary written in XML. The glossary contains some `<glentry>` elements, each of which contains a single `<term>` and one or more `<defn>` elements. In addition, a definition is allowed to contain a cross-reference (`<xref>`) to another `<term>`. Here's a short sample document:

```
<?xml version="1.0" ?>
<!DOCTYPE glossary SYSTEM "glossary.dtd">
<glossary>
  <glentry>
    <term id="applet">applet</term>
```

```
  <defn>
    An application program,
    written in the Java programming language, that can be
    retrieved from a web server and executed by a web browser.
    A reference to an applet appears in the markup for a web
    page, in the same way that a reference to a graphics
    file appears; a browser retrieves an applet in the same
    way that it retrieves a graphics file.
    For security reasons, an applet's access rights are limited
    in two ways: the applet cannot access the file system of the
    client upon which it is executing, and the applet's
    communication across the network is limited to the server
    from which it was downloaded.
    Contrast with <xref refid="servlet"/>.
    <seealso refids="wildcard-char DMZlong pattern-matching"/>
  </defn>
</glentry>

<glentry>
  <term id="DMZlong" xreftext="demilitarized zone">demilitarized
    zone (DMZ)</term>
  <defn>
    In network security, a network that is isolated from, and
    serves as a neutral zone between, a trusted network (for example,
    a private intranet) and an untrusted network (for example, the
    Internet). One or more secure gateways usually control access
    to the DMZ from the trusted or the untrusted network.
  </defn>
</glentry>

<glentry>
  <term id="DMZ">DMZ</term>
  <defn>
    See <xref refid="DMZlong"/>.
  </defn>
</glentry>

<glentry>
  <term id="pattern-matching">pattern-matching character</term>
  <defn>
    A special character such as an asterisk (*) or a question mark
    (?) that can be used to represent zero or more characters.
    Any character or set of characters can replace a pattern-matching
    character.
  </defn>
</glentry>

<glentry>
  <term id="servlet">servlet</term>
  <defn>
    An application program, written in the Java programming language,
    that is executed on a web server. A reference to a servlet
    appears in the markup for a web page, in the same way that a
    reference to a graphics file appears. The web server executes
```

```
      the servlet and sends the results of the execution (if there are
      any) to the web browser. Contrast with <xref refid="applet" />.
    </defn>
  </glentry>

  <glentry>
    <term id="wildcard-char">wildcard character</term>
    <defn>
      See <xref refid="pattern-matching"/>.
    </defn>
  </glentry>
</glossary>
```

In this XML listing, each <term> element has an id attribute that identifies it uniquely. Many <xref> elements also refer to other terms in the listing. Notice that each time we refer to another term, we don't use the actual text of the referenced term. When we write our stylesheet, we'll use the XPath id function to retrieve the text of the referenced term; if the name of a term changes (as buzzwords go in and out of fashion, some marketing genius might want to rename the "pattern-matching character," for example), we can rerun our stylesheet and be confident that all references to the new term contain the correct text.

Finally, some <term> elements have an xreftext element because some of the actual terms are longer than we'd like to use in a cross-reference. When we have an <xref> to the term ASCII (American Standard Code for Information Interchange), it would get pretty tedious if the entire text of the term appeared throughout our document. For this term, we'll use the xreftext attribute's value, ensuring that the cross-reference contains the less-intimidating text ASCII.

A Stylesheet That Uses the id() Function

Let's look at our desired output. What we want is an HTML document, such as that shown in Figure 5-1, that displays the various definitions in an easy-to-read format, with the cross-references formatted as hyperlinks.

In the HTML document, we'll need to address several things in our stylesheet:

- The <title> and the <h1> contain the first and last terms in the glossary. We can use XPath expressions to generate that information.
- The <xref> elements have been replaced with the xreftext attribute of the referenced <term> element, if there is one. If that attribute doesn't exist, <xref> is replaced by the text of the <term> element. We'll use the id() function to find the referenced <term>, and we'll use XSLT's control elements to check if the xreftext attribute exists.

- The hyperlinks generated from the `<xref>` elements refer to a named anchor point elsewhere in the HTML document. If `<xref>` elements refer to a given `<term>`, we have to create a named anchor (`<a name=". . .">`) at the location of the referenced `<term>`. To simplify things, we'll generate a named anchor for each term automatically, using the `id` attribute (required to be unique by our DTD) as the name of the anchor.
- We need to process any `<seealso>` elements, as well. These elements are handled similarly to the `<xref>` elements, the main difference being that the `refids` attribute of the `<seealso>` element can refer to more than one glossary entry.

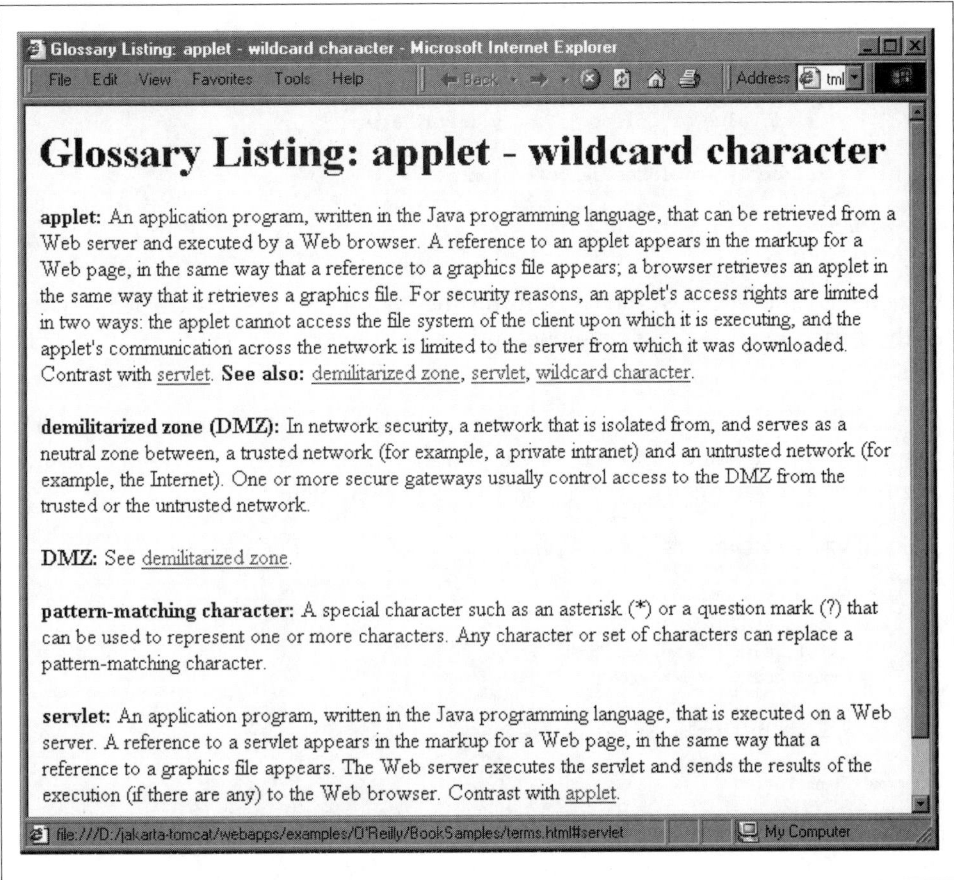

Figure 5-1. HTML document with generated cross-references

Here's the template that takes care of our first task, generating the HTML <title> and the <h1>:

```
<xsl:template match="glossary">
  <html>
    <head>
      <title>
        <xsl:text>Glossary Listing: </xsl:text>
        <xsl:value-of select="glentry[1]/term"/>
        <xsl:text> - </xsl:text>
        <xsl:value-of select="glentry[last()]/term"/>
      </title>
    </head>
    <body>
      <h1>
        <xsl:text>Glossary Listing: </xsl:text>
        <xsl:value-of select="glentry[1]/term"/>
        <xsl:text> - </xsl:text>
        <xsl:value-of select="glentry[last()]/term"/>
      </h1>
      <xsl:apply-templates select="glentry"/>
    </body>
  </html>
</xsl:template>
```

We generate the <title> and <h1> using the XPath expressions `glentry[1]/term` for the first <term> in the document, and using `glentry[last()]/term` for the last term.

Our next step is to process all the <glentry> elements. We'll generate an HTML paragraph for each one, and then we'll generate a named anchor point, using the `id` attribute as the name of the anchor. Here's the template:

```
<xsl:template match="glentry">
  <p>
    <b>
      <a name="{@id}"/>
      <xsl:value-of select="term"/>
      <xsl:text>: </xsl:text>
    </b>
    <xsl:apply-templates select="defn"/>
  </p>
</xsl:template>
```

In this template, we're using an *attribute value template* to generate the `name` attribute of the HTML <a> element. The XPath expression `@id` retrieves the `id` attribute of the <glentry> element we're currently processing. We use this attribute to generate a named anchor. We then write the term itself in bold and apply the template for the <defn> element. In our output document, each glossary entry contains a paragraph with the highlighted term and its definition.

The name attribute of this HTML <a> element is generated with an attribute value template. See the section "Attribute Value Templates" for more information.

Our next step is to process the cross-reference. Here's the template for the <xref> element:

```
<xsl:template match="xref">
  <a href="#{@refid}">
    <xsl:choose>
      <xsl:when test="id(@refid)/@xreftext">
        <xsl:value-of select="id(@refid)/@xreftext"/>
      </xsl:when>
      <xsl:otherwise>
        <xsl:value-of select="id(@refid)"/>
      </xsl:otherwise>
    </xsl:choose>
  </a>
</xsl:template>
```

We create the <a> element in two steps:

- Create the href attribute. It must refer to the correctly named anchor in the HTML document.
- Create the text of the link. This text is the word or phrase that appears in the browser; clicking on the link should take the user to the referenced term.

For the first step, we know that the href attribute must contain a hash mark (#) followed by the name of the anchor point. Because we generated all the named anchors from the id attributes of the various <glentry> elements, we know the name of the anchor point is the same as the id.

Now all that's left is for us to retrieve the text. This retrieval is the most complicated part of the process (relatively speaking, anyway). Remember that we want to use the xreftext attribute of the <term> element, if there is one, and use the text of the <term> element, otherwise. To implement an if-then-else statement, we use the <xsl:choose> element. In the previous sample, we used a test expression of id(@refid)/@xreftext to see if the xreftext attribute exists. (Remember, an empty node-set is considered false. If the attribute doesn't exist, the node-set will be empty and the <xsl:otherwise> element will be evaluated.) If the test is true, we use id(@refid)/@xreftext to retrieve the cross-reference text. The first part of the XPath expression (id(@refid)) returns the node that has an ID that matches the value @refid; the second part (@xreftext) retrieves the xreftext attribute of that node. We insert the text of the xreftext attribute inside the <a> element.

Finally, we handle any <seealso> elements. The difference here is that the `refids` attribute can reference any number of glossary terms, so we'll use the `id()` function differently. Here's the template for <seealso>:

```
<xsl:template match="seealso">
  <b>
    <xsl:text>See also: </xsl:text>
  </b>
  <xsl:for-each select="id(@refids)">
    <a href="#{@id}">
      <xsl:choose>
        <xsl:when test="@xreftext">
          <xsl:value-of select="@xreftext"/>
        </xsl:when>
        <xsl:otherwise>
          <xsl:value-of select="."/>
        </xsl:otherwise>
      </xsl:choose>
    </a>
    <xsl:if test="not(position()=last())">
      <xsl:text>, </xsl:text>
    </xsl:if>
  </xsl:for-each>
  <xsl:text>. </xsl:text>
</xsl:template>
```

There are a couple of important differences here. First, we call the `id()` function in an `<xsl:for-each>` element. Calling the `id()` function with an attribute of type `IDREFS` returns a node-set; each node in the node-set is the match for one of the `ID`s in the attribute.

The second difference is that referencing the correctly named anchor is more difficult. When we processed the `<xref>` element, we knew that the correct anchor name was the value of the `refid` attribute. When processing <seealso>, the `refids` attribute doesn't do us any good because it may contain any number of `ID`s. All is not lost, however. What we did previously was use the `id` attribute of each node returned by the `id()` function—a minor inconvenience, but another difference in processing an attribute of type `IDREFS` instead of `IDREF`.

The final difference is that we want to add commas after all items except the last. The `<xsl:if>` element shown previously does just this. If the `position()` of the current item is the last, we don't output the comma and space (defined here with the `<xsl:text>` element). We formatted all references here as a sentence; as an exercise, feel free to process the items in a more sophisticated way. For example, you could generate an HTML list from the `IDREFS`, or maybe format things differently if the `refids` attribute only contains a single `ID`.

We've done several useful things with the `id()` function. We've been able to use attributes of type `ID` to discover the links between related pieces of information, and we've converted the XML into HTML links, renderable in an ordinary household browser. If this is the only kind of linking and referencing you need to do, that's great. Unfortunately, there are times when we need to do more, and on those occasions, the `id()` function doesn't quite cut it. We'll mention the limitations of the `id()` function briefly, then we'll discuss XSLT functions that let us overcome them.

Limitations of IDs

To this point, we've been able to generate cross-references easily. There are some limitations of the `ID` datatype and the `id()` function, though:

- If you want to use the `ID` datatype, you have to declare the attributes that use that datatype in your DTD or schema. Unfortunately, if your DTD is defined externally to your XML document, the XML parser isn't required to read it. If the DTD isn't read, then the parser has no idea that a given attribute is of type `ID`.
- You must define the `ID` and `IDREF` relationship in the XML document. It would be nice to have the XML document define the data only, with the relationships between parts of the document defined externally (say, in a stylesheet). That way, if you needed to define a new relationship between parts of the document, you could do it by creating a new stylesheet, and you wouldn't have to modify your XML document. Requiring the XML document structure to change every time you need to define a new relationship between parts of the document will become unwieldy quickly.
- An element can have at most one attribute of type `ID`. If you'd like to refer to the same element in more than one way, you can't use the `id()` function.
- Any given `ID` value can be found on at most one element. If you'd like to refer to more than one element with a single value, you can't use the `id()` function for that, either.
- Only one set of `ID`s exists for the entire document. In other words, if you declare the attributes `customer_number`, `part_number`, and `order_number` to be of type `ID`, the value of a `customer_number` must be unique across all the attributes of type `ID`. It is illegal in this case for a `customer_number` to be the same as a `part_number`, even though those attributes might belong to different elements.

- An `ID` can only be an attribute of an XML element. The only way you can use the `id()` function to refer to another element is through its attribute of type `ID`. If you want to find another element based on an attribute that isn't an `ID`, based on the element's content, based on the element's children, etc., the `id()` function is of no use whatsoever.
- The value of an `ID` must be an XML name. In other words, it can't contain spaces, it can't start with a number, and it's subject to the other restrictions of XML names. (Section 2.3 of the XML Recommendation defines these restrictions; see *http://www.w3.org/TR/REC-xml* if you'd like more information.)

To get around all of these limitations, XSLT defines the `key()` function. We'll discuss that function in the next section.

Generating Links with the key() Function

Now that we've covered the `id()` function in great detail, we'll move on to XSLT's `key()` function. Each `key()` function effectively creates an index of the document. You can then use that index to find all elements that have a particular property. Conceptually, `key()` works like a database index. If you have a database of (U.S. postal) addresses, you might want to index that database by the people's last names, by the states in which they live, by their Zip Codes, etc. Each index takes a certain amount of time to build, but it saves processing time later. If you want to find all the people who live in the state of Idaho, you can use the index to find all those people directly; you don't have to search the entire database.

We'll discuss the details of how the `key()` function works, then we'll compare it to the `id()` function.

Defining a key()

You define a `key()` function with the `<xsl:key>` element:

```
<xsl:key name="language-index" match="defn" use="@language"/>
```

The key has three elements:

- A `name`, used to refer to this particular key. When you want to find parts of your XML document, use the `name` to indicate the key you want to use.
- A `match` attribute containing an XPath expression. This specifies what part of the document you want to index. The previous example created an index on all of the `<defn>` elements. When we call the `key()` function, it will return a `<defn>` element. Note: according to Section 12.2 of the XSLT specification, the value of the `match` attribute can't contain a variable.

- A `use` attribute containing another XPath expression. This attribute is interpreted in the context of the `match` attribute. In other words, the previous `<xsl:key>` element created an index of all the `<defn>` elements, and used the `language` attribute to retrieve them. Note: according to Section 12.2 of the XSLT specification, the value of the `use` attribute can't contain a variable.

A Slightly More Complicated XML Document in Need of Links

To illustrate the full power of the `key()` function, we'll modify our original glossary slightly. Here's an excerpt:

```
<glentry>
  <term id="DMZlong" xreftext="demilitarized zone">demilitarized
    zone (DMZ)</term>
  <defn topic="security" language="en">
    In network security, a network that is isolated from, and
    serves as a neutral zone between, a trusted network (for example,
    a private intranet) and an untrusted network (for example, the
    Internet). One or more secure gateways usually control access
    to the DMZ from the trusted or the untrusted network.
  </defn>
  <defn topic="security" language="it">
    [Pretend this is an Italian definition of DMZ.]
  </defn>
  <defn topic="security" language="es">
    [Pretend this is a Spanish definition of DMZ.]
  </defn>
  <defn topic="security" language="jp">
    [Pretend this is a Japanese definition of DMZ.]
  </defn>
  <defn topic="security" language="de">
    [Pretend this is a German definition of DMZ.]
  </defn>
</glentry>

<glentry>
  <term id="DMZ" acronym="yes">DMZ</term>
  <defn topic="security" language="en">
    See <xref refid="DMZlong"/>.
  </defn>
</glentry>
```

In our modified document, we've added two new attributes to `<defn>`: `topic` and `language`. We also added the `acronym` attribute to the `<term>` element. We've modified our DTD to add these attributes and enumerate their valid values:

```
<!--The word being defined-->
<!ELEMENT term  (#PCDATA) >
```

```
<!--The id is used for cross-referencing, and the
    xreftext is the text used by cross-references.-->
<!ATTLIST term
              id        ID       #REQUIRED
              xreftext  CDATA    #IMPLIED
              acronym   (yes|no) "no">

<!--The definition of the term-->
<!ELEMENT defn  (#PCDATA | xref | seealso)* >

<!--The topic defines the subject of the definition, the
    language code defines the language of this definition,
    and the acronym is yes or no (default is no).-->
<!ATTLIST defn
               topic    (Java|general|security) "general"
               language (en|de|es|it|jp)        "en">
```

The `topic` attribute defines the computing topic to which this definition applies, and the `language` attribute defines the language in which this definition is written. The `acronym` attribute defines whether or not this term is an acronym.

Now that we've created a more flexible XML document, we can use the `key()` function to do several useful things:

- We can find all `<defn>` elements that are written in a particular language (as long as it's one of the five languages we defined).
- We can find all `<defn>` elements that apply to a particular topic.
- We can find all `<term>` elements that are acronyms.

Thinking back to our earlier discussion, these are all things we can't do with the `id()` function. If the `language`, `topic`, and `acronym` attributes were defined to be of type `ID`, only one definition could be written in English, only one definition could apply to the security topic, and only one term could be an acronym. Clearly, that's an unacceptable limitation on our document.

Stylesheets That Use the key() Function

We've mentioned some useful things we can do with the `key()` function, so now we'll build some stylesheets that use it. Our first stylesheet will list all definitions written in a particular language. We'll go through the various parts of the stylesheet, explaining all the things we had to add to make everything work. The first thing we'll do, of course, is define the `key()` function:

```
<xsl:key name="language-index" match="defn" use="@language"/>
```

Notice that the `match` attribute we used was the simple element name `defn`. This tells the XSLT processor to match all `<defn>` elements at all levels of the document. Because of the structure of our document, we could have written `match="/glossary/glentry/defn"`, as well. Although this XPath expression is more restrictive, it matches the same elements because all <defn> elements must appear inside <glentry> elements, which in turn appear inside the <glossary> element.

Next, we set up our stylesheet to determine what value of the `language` attribute we're searching for. We'll do this with a global <xsl:param> element:

```
<xsl:param name="targetLanguage"/>
```

Recall from our earlier discussion of the <xsl:param> element that any top-level <xsl:param> is a global parameter to the stylesheet and may be set or initialized from outside the stylesheet. The way to do this varies from one XSLT processor to another. Here's how it's done with Xalan. (The command should be on one line.)

```
java org.apache.xalan.xslt.Process -in moreterms.xml -xsl crossref2.xsl
-param targetLanguage it
```

If you use Michael Kay's Saxon processor, the syntax looks like this:

```
java com.icl.saxon.StyleSheet moreterms.xml crossref2.xsl targetLanguage=it
```

Now that we've defined our `key()` function and defined a parameter to specify which language we're looking for, we need to generate our output. Here's the modified template that generates the HTML <title> and <h1> tags:

```
<xsl:template match="glossary">
  <html>
    <head>
      <title>
        <xsl:text>Glossary Listing: </xsl:text>
        <xsl:value-of select="key('language-index',
          $targetLanguage)[1]/preceding-sibling::term"/>
        <xsl:text> - </xsl:text>
        <xsl:value-of select="key('language-index',
          $targetLanguage)[last()]/preceding-sibling::term"/>
      </title>
    </head>
    <body>
      <h1>
        <xsl:text>Glossary Listing: </xsl:text>
        <xsl:value-of select="key('language-index',
          $targetLanguage)[1]/ancestor::glentry/term"/>
        <xsl:text> - </xsl:text>
        <xsl:value-of select="key('language-index',
          $targetLanguage)[last()]/ancestor::glentry/term"/>
      </h1>
      <xsl:for-each select="key('language-index', $targetLanguage)">
        <xsl:apply-templates select="ancestor::glentry"/>
      </xsl:for-each>
    </body>
  </html>
</xsl:template>
```

There are a couple of significant changes here. When we were using the id() function, it was easy to find the first and last terms in the document. Because we're now trying to list only the definitions that are written in a particular language, that won't work. Reading the XPath expressions in the <xsl:value-of> elements from left to right, we find the first and last <defn> elements returned by the key() function, then use the preceding-sibling axis to reference the <term> element that preceded it. We could also have written our XPath expressions using the ancestor axis:

```
<h1>
  <xsl:text>Glossary Listing: </xsl:text>
  <xsl:value-of select="key('language-index',
    $targetLanguage)[1]/ancestor::glentry/term"/>
  <xsl:text> - </xsl:text>
  <xsl:value-of select="key('language-index',
    $targetLanguage)[last()]/ancestor::glentry/term"/>
</h1>
```

Now that we've successfully generated the HTML <title> and <h1> elements, we need to process the actual definitions for the chosen language. To do this, we'll use the targetLanguage parameter. Here's how the rest of the template looks:

```
<xsl:for-each select="key('language-index', $targetLanguage)">
  <xsl:apply-templates select="ancestor::glentry"/>
</xsl:for-each>
```

In this code, we've selected all the values from the language-index key that match the targetLanguage parameter. For each one, we use the ancestor axis to select the <glentry> element. We've already written the templates that process these elements correctly, so we can just reuse them.

The final change we make is to select only those <defn> elements whose language attributes match the targetLanguage parameter. We do this with a simple XPath expression:

```
<xsl:apply-templates select="defn[@language=$targetLanguage]"/>
```

Here's the complete stylesheet:

```
<?xml version="1.0"?>
<xsl:stylesheet version="1.0" xmlns:xsl="http://www.w3.org/1999/XSL/Transform">
<xsl:output method="html" indent="yes"/>
<xsl:strip-space elements="*"/>

  <xsl:key name="language-index" match="defn" use="@language"/>

  <xsl:param name="targetLanguage"/>

  <xsl:template match="/">
    <xsl:apply-templates select="glossary"/>
  </xsl:template>
```

```
<xsl:template match="glossary">
  <html>
    <head>
      <title>
        <xsl:text>Glossary Listing: </xsl:text>
        <xsl:value-of select="key('language-index',
          $targetLanguage)[1]/preceding-sibling::term"/>
        <xsl:text> - </xsl:text>
        <xsl:value-of select="key('language-index',
          $targetLanguage)[last()]/preceding-sibling::term"/>
      </title>
    </head>
    <body>
      <h1>
        <xsl:text>Glossary Listing: </xsl:text>
        <xsl:value-of select="key('language-index',
          $targetLanguage)[1]/ancestor::glentry/term"/>
        <xsl:text> - </xsl:text>
        <xsl:value-of select="key('language-index',
          $targetLanguage)[last()]/ancestor::glentry/term"/>
      </h1>
      <xsl:for-each select="key('language-index', $targetLanguage)">
        <xsl:apply-templates select="ancestor::glentry"/>
      </xsl:for-each>
    </body>
  </html>
</xsl:template>

<xsl:template match="glentry">
  <p>
    <b>
      <a name="{term/@id}"/>
      <xsl:value-of select="term"/>
      <xsl:text>: </xsl:text>
    </b>
    <xsl:apply-templates select="defn[@language=$targetLanguage]"/>
  </p>
</xsl:template>

<xsl:template match="defn">
  <xsl:apply-templates
   select="*|comment()|processing-instruction()|text()"/>
</xsl:template>

<xsl:template match="xref">
  <a href="#{@refid}">
    <xsl:choose>
      <xsl:when test="id(@refid)/@xreftext">
        <xsl:value-of select="id(@refid)/@xreftext"/>
      </xsl:when>
      <xsl:otherwise>
        <xsl:value-of select="id(@refid)"/>
      </xsl:otherwise>
```

```
      </xsl:choose>
    </a>
  </xsl:template>

  <xsl:template match="seealso">
    <b>
      <xsl:text>See also: </xsl:text>
    </b>
    <xsl:for-each select="id(@refids)">
      <a href="#{@id}">
        <xsl:choose>
          <xsl:when test="@xreftext">
            <xsl:value-of select="@xreftext"/>
          </xsl:when>
          <xsl:otherwise>
            <xsl:value-of select="."/>
          </xsl:otherwise>
        </xsl:choose>
      </a>
      <xsl:if test="not(position()=last())">
        <xsl:text>, </xsl:text>
      </xsl:if>
    </xsl:for-each>
    <xsl:text>.  </xsl:text>
  </xsl:template>

</xsl:stylesheet>
```

Given our sample document and a `targetLanguage` of `en`, we get these results:

```
<html>
  <head>
    <title>Glossary Listing: applet - wildcard character</title>
  </head>
  <body>
    <h1>Glossary Listing: applet - wildcard character</h1>
    <p>
      <b><a name="applet"></a>applet: </b>
      An application program,
      written in the Java programming language, that can be
      retrieved from a web server and executed by a web browser.
      A reference to an applet appears in the markup for a web
      page, in the same way that a reference to a graphics
      file appears; a browser retrieves an applet in the same
      way that it retrieves a graphics file.
      For security reasons, an applet's access rights are limited
      in two ways: the applet cannot access the file system of the
      client upon which it is executing, and the applet's
      communication across the network is limited to the server
      from which it was downloaded.
      Contrast with <a href="#servlet">servlet</a>.
      ...
```

Changing the targetLanguage to it, the results are now different:

```
<html>
  <head>
    <title>Glossary Listing: applet - servlet</title>
  </head>
  <body>
    <h1>Glossary Listing: applet - servlet</h1>
    <p>
      <b><a name="applet"></a>applet: </b>
      [Pretend this is an Italian definition of applet.]
    </p>
    <p>
      <b><a name="DMZlong"></a>demilitarized
      zone (DMZ): </b>
      [Pretend this is an Italian definition of DMZ.]
    </p>
    <p>
      <b><a name="servlet"></a>servlet: </b>
      [Pretend this is an Italian definition of servlet.]
    </p>
  </body>
</html>
```

With this stylesheet, we have a way to create a useful subset of our glossary. Notice that we're still using our original technique of ID, IDREF, and IDREFS to process the <xref> and <seealso> elements. If you want, you could redefine the processing to use the key() function instead. Here's how you'd define a key() function to mimic our earlier use of ID and IDREF:

```
<xsl:template match="xref">
  <a href="#{@refid}">
    <xsl:choose>
      <xsl:when test="key('term-ids', @refid)[1]/@xreftext">
        <xsl:value-of select="key('term-ids', @refid)[1]/@xreftext"/>
      </xsl:when>
      <xsl:otherwise>
        <xsl:value-of select="key('term-ids', @refid)[1]"/>
      </xsl:otherwise>
    </xsl:choose>
  </a>
</xsl:template>
```

As an exercise for the reader, you can modify this stylesheet so that it lists only definitions that apply to a particular topic, or only terms that are acronyms.

The key() function and the IDREFS datatype

For all its flexibility, the `key()` function doesn't support anything like the `IDREFS` datatype. We can try to use the `key()` function the same way we used `id()`:

```
<xsl:template match="seealso">
  <b>
    <xsl:text>See also: </xsl:text>
  </b>
  <xsl:for-each select="key('term-ids', @refids)">
    <a>
  ...
```

But the `<xsl:for-each>` doesn't have anything to work with. That's because the key value we're looking for is `"wildcard-char DMZlong pattern-matching"`. When we were dealing with the `id()` function, this string was broken into three tokens because anything with a datatype of `ID` can't contain a space. With the `key()` function, we can search on anything, including the contents of an element. (See the section "Generating Links in Unstructured Documents" for an example of this.) For this reason, our call to the `key()` function asking for all the `<term>` elements with an `id` attribute equal to `"wildcard-char DMZlong pattern-matching"` returns nothing. Any attribute with a datatype of `ID` can't contain spaces, so we get no results.

There are several ways to deal with this problem; we'll go through our choices next.

Solution #1: Replace the IDREFS datatype

If you consider this a problem and refuse to use the `id()` function, there are several approaches you can take. The most drastic (but probably the simplest to implement) is to not use the `IDREFS` datatype at all. You could change the `<seealso>` element so that it contains a list of references to other elements:

```
<seealso>
  <item refid="wildcard-character"/>
  <item refid="DMZlong"/>
  <item refid="pattern-matching"/>
</seealso>
```

This approach has the advantage that we can use the value of all the `refid` attributes of all `<item>` elements with the `key()` function. That means we can search on anything, not just values of attributes. The disadvantage, of course, is that we had to change the structure of our XML document to make this approach work. If you have control of the structure of your XML document, that's possible;

it's entirely likely, of course, that you can't change the XML document at all. A variation on this approach would be to use a stylesheet to transform the `IDREFS` datatype into the previous structure.

Solution #2: Use the XPath contains() function

A second approach is to leave the structure of the XML document unchanged, then use the XPath `contains()` function to find all `<term>` elements whose `id` attributes are contained in the value of the `refids` attribute of the `<seealso>` element. Here's how that would work:

```
<xsl:template match="seealso">
  <b>
    <xsl:text>See also: </xsl:text>
  </b>
  <xsl:variable name="id_list" select="@refids"/>
  <xsl:for-each select="//term">
    <xsl:if test="contains($id_list, @id)">
      <a href="#{@id}">
        <xsl:choose>
          <xsl:when test="@xreftext">
            <xsl:value-of select="@xreftext"/>
          </xsl:when>
          <xsl:otherwise>
            <xsl:value-of select="."/>
          </xsl:otherwise>
        </xsl:choose>
      </a>
      <xsl:if test="not(position()=last())">
        <xsl:text>, </xsl:text>
      </xsl:if>
    </xsl:if>
  </xsl:for-each>
  <xsl:text>.  </xsl:text>
</xsl:template>
```

We've done a couple of things here: First, we've saved the value of the `refids` attribute of the `<seealso>` element in the variable `id_list`. That's because we can't access it within the `<for-each>` element. We can find a given `<seealso>` element from within a given `<term>` element, but it's too difficult to find that element generically from every `<term>` element. The simplest way to find the element is to save the value in a variable.

Second, we look at all of the `<term>` elements in the document. For each one, if our variable (containing the `refids` attribute of the `<seealso>` element) contains the value of the current `<term>` element's `id` attribute, then we process that `<term>` element.

Here are the results our stylesheet generates:

```
<html>
  <head>
    <title>Glossary Listing: applet - wildcard character</title>
  </head>
  <body>
    <h1>Glossary Listing: applet - wildcard character</h1>
    <p>
      <b><a name="applet"></a>applet: </b>
      An application program,
      written in the Java programming language, that can be
      retrieved from a web server and executed by a web browser.
      A reference to an applet appears in the markup for a web
      page, in the same way that a reference to a graphics
      file appears; a browser retrieves an applet in the same
      way that it retrieves a graphics file.
      For security reasons, an applet's access rights are limited
      in two ways: the applet cannot access the file system of the
      client upon which it is executing, and the applet's
      communication across the network is limited to the server
      from which it was downloaded.
      Contrast with <a href="#servlet">servlet</a>.
      <b>See also: </b><a
      href="#DMZlong">demilitarized zone</a>, <a href="#DMZ">
      DMZ</a>, <a href="#pattern-matching">pattern-matching
      character</a>, <a href="#wildcard-char">wildcard
      character</a>.
    </p>
      ...
```

There are a couple of problems here. The most mundane is that in our stylesheet, we don't know how many `<term>` elements have `id` attributes contained in our variable. That means it's difficult to insert commas correctly between the matching `<term>`s. In the output here, we were lucky that the last match was in fact the last term, so the results here are correct. For any `<seealso>` element whose `refid` attribute doesn't contain the `id` attribute of the last `<term>` element in the document, this stylesheet won't work.

The more serious problem is that one of the matches is, in fact, wrong. If you look closely at the output, we get a match for the term `DMZ`, even though there isn't an exact match for its `id` in our variable. That's because the XPath `contains()` function says (correctly) that the value `DMZlong` contains the `id`s `DMZlong` and `DMZ`.

So our second attempt at solving this problem doesn't require us to change the structure of the XML document, but in this case, we have to change some of our `ID`s so that the problem we just mentioned doesn't occur. That's probably going to be a maintenance nightmare and a serious drawback to this approach.

Solution #3: Use recursion to process the IDREFS datatype

Here we use a recursive template to tokenize the `refids` attribute into individual IDs, then process each one individually. This style of programming takes a while to get used to, but it can be fairly simple. Here's the crux of our stylesheet:

```
<xsl:template match="seealso">
  <b>
    <xsl:text>See also: </xsl:text>
  </b>
  <xsl:call-template name="resolveIDREFS">
    <xsl:with-param name="stringToTokenize" select="@refids"/>
  </xsl:call-template>
</xsl:template>

<xsl:template name="resolveIDREFS">
  <xsl:param name="stringToTokenize"/>
  <xsl:variable name="normalizedString">
    <xsl:value-of
      select="concat(normalize-space($stringToTokenize), ' ')"/>
  </xsl:variable>
  <xsl:choose>
    <xsl:when test="$normalizedString!=' '">
      <xsl:variable name="firstOfString"
        select="substring-before($normalizedString, ' ')"/>
      <xsl:variable name="restOfString"
        select="substring-after($normalizedString, ' ')"/>
      <a href="#{$firstOfString}">
        <xsl:choose>
          <xsl:when
            test="key('term-ids', $firstOfString)[1]/@xreftext">
            <xsl:value-of
              select="key('term-ids', $firstOfString)[1]/@xreftext"/>
          </xsl:when>
          <xsl:otherwise>
            <xsl:value-of
              select="key('term-ids', $firstOfString)[1]"/>
          </xsl:otherwise>
        </xsl:choose>
      </a>
      <xsl:if test="$restOfString!=''">
        <xsl:text>, </xsl:text>
      </xsl:if>
      <xsl:call-template name="resolveIDREFS">
        <xsl:with-param name="stringToTokenize"
          select="$restOfString"/>
      </xsl:call-template>
    </xsl:when>
    <xsl:otherwise>
      <xsl:text>.</xsl:text>
    </xsl:otherwise>
  </xsl:choose>
</xsl:template>
```

The first thing we did was invoke the named template `resolveIDREFS` in the template for the <seealso> element. While invoking the template, we pass in the value of the `refids` attribute and let recursion work its magic.

The `resolveIDREFS` template works like this:

- Break the string into two parts: the first ID and the rest of the string. If there is no first ID (i.e., the string contains only whitespace), we're done.
- Resolve the cross-reference for the first ID.
- Invoke the template with the rest of the string.

One technique in particular is worth mentioning here: the way we handled whitespace in the attribute value. We pass the string we want to tokenize as a parameter to the template, but we need to normalize the whitespace. We use two XPath functions to do this: `normalize-space()` and `concat()`. The call looks like this:

```
<xsl:template name="resolveIDREFS">
  <xsl:param name="stringToTokenize"/>
  <xsl:variable name="normalizedString">
    <xsl:value-of
      select="concat(normalize-space($stringToTokenize), ' ')"/>
  </xsl:variable>
```

The `normalize-space()` function removes all leading and trailing whitespace from a string and replaces internal whitespace characters with a single space. Remember that whitespace inside an attribute isn't significant; our <seealso> element could be written like this:

```
  <seealso refids="  wildcard-char





DMZlong
pattern-matching        "/>
```

When we pass this attribute to `normalizeSpace()`, the returned value is `wildcard-char DMZlong pattern-matching`. All whitespace at the start and end of the value has been removed and all the whitespace between characters has been replaced with a single space.

Because we're using the `substring-before()` and `substring-after()` functions to find the first token and the rest of the string, it's important that there be at least one space in the string. (It's possible, of course, that an `IDREFS` attribute contains only one `ID`.) We use the `concat()` function to add a space to the end of the string. When the string contains only that space, we know we're done.

Although this approach is more tedious, it does everything we need it to do. We don't have to change our XML document, and we correctly resolve all the `IDs` in the `IDREFS` datatype.

Solution #4: Use an extension function

The final approach is to write an extension function that tokenizes the `refids` attribute and returns a node-set containing all `id` values we need to search for. Xalan ships with an extension that does just that. We invoke the extension function on the value of the `refids` attribute, then use a `<xsl:for-each>` element to process all items in the node-set. We'll cover extension functions in Chapter 8, but for now, here's what the stylesheet looks like:

```
<?xml version="1.0"?>
<xsl:stylesheet version="1.0" xmlns:xsl="http://www.w3.org/1999/XSL/Transform"
  xmlns:java="http://xml.apache.org/xslt/java"
  exclude-result-prefixes="java">

<xsl:output method="html" indent="yes"/>
<xsl:strip-space elements="*"/>

  <xsl:key name="term-ids" match="term" use="@id"/>

  <xsl:template match="/">
    <xsl:apply-templates select="glossary"/>
  </xsl:template>

  <xsl:template match="glossary">
    <html>
      <head>
        <title>
          <xsl:text>Glossary Listing: </xsl:text>
          <xsl:value-of select="glentry[1]/term"/>
          <xsl:text> - </xsl:text>
          <xsl:value-of select="glentry[last()]/term"/>
        </title>
      </head>
      <body>
        <h1>
          <xsl:text>Glossary Listing: </xsl:text>
          <xsl:value-of select="glentry[1]/term"/>
          <xsl:text> - </xsl:text>
          <xsl:value-of select="glentry[last()]/term"/>
        </h1>
        <xsl:apply-templates select="glentry"/>
      </body>
    </html>
  </xsl:template>

  <xsl:template match="glentry">
    <p>
      <b>
```

```
        <a name="{term/@id}"/>
        <xsl:value-of select="term"/>
        <xsl:text>: </xsl:text>
      </b>
      <xsl:apply-templates select="defn"/>
    </p>
  </xsl:template>

  <xsl:template match="defn">
    <xsl:apply-templates
     select="*|comment()|processing-instruction()|text()"/>
  </xsl:template>

  <xsl:template match="xref">
    <a href="#{@refid}">
      <xsl:choose>
        <xsl:when test="key('term-ids', @refid)[1]/@xreftext">
          <xsl:value-of select="key('term-ids', @refid)[1]/@xreftext"/>
        </xsl:when>
        <xsl:otherwise>
          <xsl:value-of select="key('term-ids', @refid)[1]"/>
        </xsl:otherwise>
      </xsl:choose>
    </a>
  </xsl:template>

  <xsl:template match="seealso">
    <b>
      <xsl:text>See also: </xsl:text>
    </b>
    <xsl:for-each
      select="java:org.apache.xalan.lib.Extensions.tokenize(@refids)">
      <a href="{key('term-ids', .)/@id}">
        <xsl:choose>
          <xsl:when test="key('term-ids', .)/@xreftext">
            <xsl:value-of select="key('term-ids', .)/@xreftext"/>
          </xsl:when>
          <xsl:otherwise>
            <xsl:value-of select="key('term-ids', .)"/>
          </xsl:otherwise>
        </xsl:choose>
      </a>
      <xsl:if test="not(position()=last())">
        <xsl:text>, </xsl:text>
      </xsl:if>
    </xsl:for-each>
    <xsl:text>.</xsl:text>
  </xsl:template>

</xsl:stylesheet>
```

In this case, the `tokenize` function (defined in the Java class `org.apache.xalan.lib.Extensions`) takes a string as input, then converts the string into a node-set in which each token in the original string becomes a node.

Be aware that using extension functions limits the portability of your stylesheets. The extension function here does what we want, but we couldn't use this extension function with Saxon, XT, or the XSLT tools from Oracle or Microsoft. They may or may not supply similar functions, and if they do, you'll have to modify your stylesheet slightly to use them. If it's important to you that you be able to switch XSLT processors at some point in the future, using extensions will limit your ability to do that.

Hopefully at this point you're convinced of at least one of the following two things:

- If you have an attribute with a datatype of `IDREFS`, you should use the `id()` function to resolve cross-references.
- The `IDREFS` datatype is pretty limited, so you should avoid using it.

Advantages of the key() Function

Now that we've taken the `key()` function through its paces, you can see that it has several advantages:

- The `key()` function is defined in a stylesheet. That means I can define any number of relationships between parts of an XML document at any time. If I need to define a new relationship tomorrow, I don't have to change my XML documents.
- Any number of `key()` functions can be defined for a given element. In our glossary example, we could define `key()` functions for the values of the `language`, `topic`, and `acronym` attributes. We could also create `key()` functions based on the text of various elements or their children. If we used `ID`s instead of the `key()` function, we would be limited to a single index based on the value of the single attribute of the `ID` datatype.

  To sum up the advantages for this point, an element can have more than one `key()` defined against it, and that key doesn't have to be based on an attribute. The key can be based on the element's text, the text of child elements, or other constructs.
- Any number of elements can match a given value. Taking another look at our glossary example, when we use the `key()` function to find all `<defn>` elements that are written in a particular language, the function returns a node-set that can have any number of nodes. If we use an `ID` instead, legally there can be only one element that matches a given `ID` value.
- The value we use to look up elements in the key function isn't constrained to be an XML name. If we use the `ID` datatype, its value can't contain spaces, among other constraints.

Generating Links in Unstructured Documents

Before we leave the topic of linking, we'll discuss one more useful technique. So far, all of this chapter's examples have been structured nicely. When there was a relationship between two pieces of information, we had an `id` and `refid` pair to match them. What happens if the XML document you're transforming isn't written that way? Fortunately, we can use the `key()` function and a new function, `generate-id()`, to create structure where there isn't any.

An Unstructured XML Document in Need of Links

For our example here, we'll take out all of the `id` and `refid` attributes that have served us well so far. This may be a contrived example, but it demonstrates how we can use the `key()` and `generate-id()` functions to generate links between parts of our document.

In our new sample document, we've stripped out the references that neatly tied things together before:

```
<?xml version="1.0" ?>
<!DOCTYPE glossary SYSTEM "unstructuredglossary.dtd">
<glossary>
  <glentry>
    <term>applet</term>
    <defn>
      An application program,
      written in the Java programming language, that can be
      retrieved from a web server and executed by a web browser.
      A reference to an applet appears in the markup for a web
      page, in the same way that a reference to a graphics
      file appears; a browser retrieves an applet in the same
      way that it retrieves a graphics file.
      For security reasons, an applet's access rights are limited
      in two ways: the applet cannot access the file system of the
      client upon which it is executing, and the applet's
      communication across the network is limited to the server
      from which it was downloaded.
      Contrast with <refterm>servlet</refterm>.
    </defn>
  </glentry>

  <glentry>
    <term>demilitarized zone</term>
    <defn>
      In network security, a network that is isolated from, and
      serves as a neutral zone between, a trusted network (for example,
      a private intranet) and an untrusted network (for example, the
```

```
      Internet). One or more secure gateways usually control access
      to the DMZ from the trusted or the untrusted network.
    </defn>
  </glentry>

  <glentry>
    <term>DMZ</term>
    <defn>
      See <refterm>delimitarized zone</refterm>.
    </defn>
  </glentry>

  <glentry>
    <term>pattern-matching character</term>
    <defn>
      A special character such as an asterisk (*) or a question mark
      (?) that can be used to represent zero or more characters.
      Any character or set of characters can replace a pattern-matching
      character.
    </defn>
  </glentry>

  <glentry>
    <term>servlet</term>
    <defn>
      An application program, written in the Java programming language,
      that is executed on a web server. A reference to a servlet
      appears in the markup for a web page, in the same way that a
      reference to a graphics file appears. The web server executes
      the servlet and sends the results of the execution (if there are
      any) to the web browser. Contrast with <refterm>applet</refterm>.
    </defn>
  </glentry>

  <glentry>
    <term>wildcard character</term>
    <defn>
      See <refterm>pattern-matching character</refterm>.
    </defn>
  </glentry>
</glossary>
```

To generate cross-references between the `<refterm>` elements and the associated `<term>` elements, we'll need to do three things:

1. Define a `key` for all terms. We'll use this `key` to find terms that match the text of the `<refterm>` element.
2. Generate a new ID for each `<term>` we find.
3. For each `<refterm>`, use the `key()` function to find the `<term>` element that matches the text of `<refterm>`. Once we've found the matching `<term>`, we call `generate-id()` to find the newly created ID.

We'll go through the relevant parts of the stylesheet. First, we define the key:

```
<xsl:key name="terms" match="term" use="."/>
```

Notice that we use the value of the <term> element itself as the lookup value for the key. Given a string, we can find all <term> elements with that same text.

Second, we need to generate a named anchor point for each <term> element:

```
<xsl:template match="glentry">
  <p>
    <b>
      <a name="{generate-id(term)}">
        <xsl:value-of select="term"/>
        <xsl:text>: </xsl:text>
      </a>
    </b>
    <xsl:apply-templates select="defn"/>
  </p>
</xsl:template>
```

Third, we find the appropriate reference for a given <refterm>. Given the text of a <refterm>, we can use the key() function to find the <term> that matches. Passing the <term> to the generate-id() function returns the same ID generated when we created the named anchor for that <term>:

```
<xsl:template match="refterm">
  <a href="#{generate-id(key('terms', .))}">
    <xsl:value-of select="."/>
  </a>
</xsl:template>
```

Our generated HTML output creates cross-references similar to those in our earlier stylesheets:

```
    <h1>Glossary Listing: applet - wildcard character</h1>
    <p>
        <b><a name="N11">applet: </a></b>
  An application program,
  written in the Java programming language, that can be
  retrieved from a web server and executed by a web browser.
  A reference to an applet appears in the markup for a web
  page, in the same way that a reference to a graphics
  file appears; a browser retrieves an applet in the same
  way that it retrieves a graphics file.
  For security reasons, an applet's access rights are limited
  in two ways: the applet cannot access the file system of the
  client upon which it is executing, and the applet's
  communication across the network is limited to the server
  from which it was downloaded.
  Contrast with <a href="#N53">servlet</a>.
</p>
...
```

```
    <p>
      <b><a name="N53">servlet: </a></b>
  An application program, written in the Java programming language,
  that is executed on a web server. A reference to a servlet
  appears in the markup for a web page, in the same way that a
  reference to a graphics file appears. The web server executes
  the servlet and sends the results of the execution (if there are
  any) to the web browser. Contrast with <a href="#N11">applet</a>.
</p>
```

Using the `key()` and `generate-id()` functions, we've been able to create IDs and references automatically. This approach isn't perfect; we have to make sure the text of the `<refterm>` element matches the text of the `<term>` exactly.

This example, like all of the examples we've shown so far, uses a single input file. A more likely scenario is that we have one XML document that contains terms, and we want to reference definitions in a second XML document that contains definitions, but no IDs. We can combine the technique we've described here with the `document()` function to import a second XML document and generate links between the two. We'll talk about the `document()` function in a later chapter; for now, just remember that there are ways to use more than one XML input document in your transformations.

The generate-id() Function

Before we leave the topic of linking, we'll go over the details of the `generate-id()` function. This function takes a node-set as its argument, and works as follows:

- For a given transformation, every time `generate-id()` is invoked against a given node, it returns the same ID. The ID doesn't change while you're doing a given transformation. If you run the transformation again, there's no guarantee `generate-id()` will generate the same ID the second time around. All calls to `generate-id()` in the second transformation will return the same ID, but that ID might not be the same as in the first transformation.

The `generate-id()` function is not required to check if an ID it generates duplicates an ID that's already in the document. In other words, if your document has an attribute of type `ID` with a value of `sdk3829a`, there's a possibility that an ID returned by `generate-id()` will also be `sdk3829a`. It's not likely, but be aware that it could happen.

- If you invoke `generate-id()` against two different nodes, the two generated IDs will be different.
- Given a node-set, `generate-id()` returns an ID for the node in the node-set that occurs first in document order.
- If the node-set you pass to the function is empty (you invoke `generate-id(fleeber)`, and there are no `<fleeber>` elements in the current context), `generate-id()` returns an empty string.
- If no node-set is passed in (you invoke `generate-id()`), the function generates an ID for the context node.

Summary

In this chapter, we've examined a several ways to generate links and cross-references between different parts of a document. If your XML document has a reasonable amount of structure, you can use the `id()` and `key()` functions to define many different relationships between the parts of a document. Even if your XML document isn't structured, you may be able to use `key()` and `generate-id()` to create simple references. In the next chapter, we'll look at sorting and grouping, two more ways to organize the information in our XML documents.

6

Sorting and Grouping Elements

By now, I hope you're convinced that you can use XSLT to convert big piles of XML data into other useful things. Our examples to this point have pretty much gone through the XML source in what's referred to as *document order*. We'd like to go through our XML documents in a couple of other common ways, though:

- We could sort some or all of the XML elements, then generate output based on the sorted elements.
- We could group the data, selecting all elements that have some property in common, then sorting the groups of elements.

We'll give several examples of these operations in this chapter.

Sorting Data with <xsl:sort>

The simplest way to rearrange our XML elements is to use the `<xsl:sort>` element. This element temporarily rearranges a collection of elements based on criteria we define in our stylesheet.

Our First Example

For our first example, we'll have a set of U.S. postal addresses that we want to sort. (No chauvinism is intended here; obviously every country has different conventions for mailing addresses. We just needed a short sample document that can be sorted in many useful ways.) Here's our original document:

```
<?xml version="1.0"?>
<addressbook>
  <address>
    <name>
      <title>Mr.</title>
```

```
      <first-name>Chester Hasbrouck</first-name>
      <last-name>Frisby</last-name>
    </name>
    <street>1234 Main Street</street>
    <city>Sheboygan</city>
    <state>WI</state>
    <zip>48392</zip>
  </address>
  <address>
    <name>
      <first-name>Mary</first-name>
      <last-name>Backstayge</last-name>
    </name>
    <street>283 First Avenue</street>
    <city>Skunk Haven</city>
    <state>MA</state>
    <zip>02718</zip>
  </address>
  <address>
    <name>
      <title>Ms.</title>
      <first-name>Natalie</first-name>
      <last-name>Attired</last-name>
    </name>
    <street>707 Breitling Way</street>
    <city>Winter Harbor</city>
    <state>ME</state>
    <zip>00218</zip>
  </address>
  <address>
    <name>
      <first-name>Harry</first-name>
      <last-name>Backstayge</last-name>
    </name>
    <street>283 First Avenue</street>
    <city>Skunk Haven</city>
    <state>MA</state>
    <zip>02718</zip>
  </address>
  <address>
    <name>
      <first-name>Mary</first-name>
      <last-name>McGoon</last-name>
    </name>
    <street>103 Bryant Street</street>
    <city>Boylston</city>
    <state>VA</state>
    <zip>27318</zip>
  </address>
  <address>
    <name>
```

```
      <title>Ms.</title>
      <first-name>Amanda</first-name>
      <last-name>Reckonwith</last-name>
    </name>
    <street>930-A Chestnut Street</street>
    <city>Lynn</city>
    <state>MA</state>
    <zip>02930</zip>
  </address>
</addressbook>
```

We'd like to generate a list of these addresses, sorted by `<last-name>`. We'll use the magical `<xsl:sort>` element to do the work. Our stylesheet looks like this:

```
<?xml version="1.0"?>
<xsl:stylesheet version="1.0" xmlns:xsl="http://www.w3.org/1999/XSL/Transform">

  <xsl:output method="text" indent="no"/>
  <xsl:strip-space elements="*"/>

  <xsl:variable name="newline">
<xsl:text>
</xsl:text>
  </xsl:variable>

  <xsl:template match="/">
    <xsl:for-each select="addressbook/address">
      <xsl:sort select="name/last-name"/>
      <xsl:value-of select="name/title"/>
      <xsl:text> </xsl:text>
      <xsl:value-of select="name/first-name"/>
      <xsl:text> </xsl:text>
      <xsl:value-of select="name/last-name"/>
      <xsl:value-of select="$newline"/>
      <xsl:value-of select="street"/>
      <xsl:value-of select="$newline"/>
      <xsl:value-of select="city"/>
      <xsl:text>, </xsl:text>
      <xsl:value-of select="state"/>
      <xsl:text>  </xsl:text>
      <xsl:value-of select="zip"/>
      <xsl:value-of select="$newline"/>
      <xsl:value-of select="$newline"/>
    </xsl:for-each>
  </xsl:template>
</xsl:stylesheet>
```

The heart of our stylesheet are the `<xsl:for-each>` and `<xsl:sort>` elements. The `<xsl:for-each>` element selects the items with which we'll work, and the `<xsl:sort>` element rearranges them before we write them out.

Notice that we're generating a text file (`<xsl:output method="text"/>`). (You could generate an HTML file or something more complicated if you want.) To invoke the stylesheet engine, we run this command:

```
java org.apache.xalan.xslt.Process -in names.xml -xsl namesorter1.xsl
  -out names.text
```

Here are the results we get from our first attempt at sorting:

```
Ms. Natalie Attired
707 Breitling Way
Winter Harbor, ME  00218

 Mary Backstayge
283 First Avenue
Skunk Haven, MA  02718

 Harry Backstayge
283 First Avenue
Skunk Haven, MA  02718

Mr. Chester Hasbrouck Frisby
1234 Main Street
Sheboygan, WI  48392

 Mary McGoon
103 Bryant Street
Boylston, VA  27318

Ms. Amanda Reckonwith
930-A Chestnut Street
Lynn, MA  02930
```

As you can see from the output, the addresses in our original document were sorted by last name. All we had to do was add `xsl:sort` to our stylesheet, and all the elements were magically reordered. If you aren't convinced that XSLT can increase your programmer productivity, try writing the Java code and DOM method calls to do the same thing.

We can do a couple of things to improve our original stylesheet, however. For one thing, there's an annoying blank space at the start of every name that doesn't have a `<title>` element. A more significant improvement is that we'd like to sort addresses by `<first-name>` within `<last-name>`. In our last example, Mary Backstayge should appear after Harry Backstayge. Here's how we can modify our stylesheet to use more than one sort key:

```
<xsl:template match="/">
  <xsl:for-each select="addressbook/address">
    <xsl:sort select="name/last-name"/>
    <xsl:sort select="name/first-name"/>
    ...
```

We've simply added a second `<xsl:sort>` element to our stylesheet. This element does what we want; it sorts the `<address>` elements by `<first-name>` within `<last-name>`. To be thoroughly obsessive about our output, we can use an `<xsl:if>` element to get rid of that annoying blank space in front of names with no `<title>` element:

```
<xsl:if test="name/title">
  <xsl:value-of select="name/title"/>
  <xsl:text> </xsl:text>
</xsl:if>
```

Now our output is perfect:

```
Ms. Natalie Attired
707 Breitling Way
Winter Harbor, ME  00218

Harry Backstayge
283 First Avenue
Skunk Haven, MA  02718

Mary Backstayge
283 First Avenue
Skunk Haven, MA  02718

Mr. Chester Hasbrouck Frisby
1234 Main Street
Sheboygan, WI  48392

Mary McGoon
103 Bryant Street
Boylston, VA  27318

Ms. Amanda Reckonwith
930-A Chestnut Street
Lynn, MA  02930
```

The Details on the <xsl:sort> Element

Now that we've seen a couple of examples of how `<xsl:sort>` works, we'll go over its syntax, its attributes, and where you can use it.

What's the deal with that syntax?

I'm so glad you asked that question. One thing the XSLT working group could have done is something like this:

```
<xsl:for-each select="addressbook/address" sort-key-1="name/last-name"
  sort-key-2="name/first-name"/>
```

The problem with this approach is that no matter how many `sort-key-x` attributes you define, out of sheer perverseness, someone will cry out that they really need the `sort-key-8293` attribute. To avoid this messy problem, the XSLT designers decided to let you specify the sort keys by using a number of `<xsl:sort>` elements. The first is the primary sort key, the second is the secondary sort key, the 8293rd one is the eight-thousand-two-hundred-and-ninety-third sort key, etc.

Well, that's why the syntax looks the way it does, but how does it actually work? When I first saw this syntax:

```
<xsl:for-each select="addressbook/address">
  <xsl:sort select="name/last-name"/>
  <xsl:sort select="name/first-name"/>
  <xsl:apply-templates select="."/>
</xsl:for-each>
```

I thought it meant that all the nodes were sorted during each iteration through the `<xsl:for-each>` element. That seemed incredibly inefficient; if you've sorted all the nodes, why resort them each time through the `<xsl:for-each>` element? Actually, the XSLT processor handles all `<xsl:sort>` elements before it does anything, then it processes the `<xsl:for-each>` element as if the `<xsl:sort>` elements weren't there.

It's less efficient, but if it makes you feel better about the syntax, you could write the stylesheet like this:

```
<xsl:template match="/">
  <xsl:for-each select="addressbook/address">
    <xsl:sort select="name/last-name"/>
    <xsl:sort select="name/first-name"/>
    <xsl:for-each select=".">  <!-- This is slower, but it works -->
      <xsl:apply-templates select="."/>
    </xsl:for-each>
  </xsl:for-each>
</xsl:template>
```

(Don't actually do this. I'm only trying to make a point.) This stylesheet generates the same results as our earlier stylesheet.

Attributes

The `<xsl:sort>` element has several attributes, all of which are discussed here.

`select`
: The `select` attribute defines the characteristic we'll use for sorting. Its contents are an XPath expression, so you can select elements, text, attributes, comments, ancestors, etc. As always, the XPath expression defined in `select` is evaluated in terms of the current context.

`data-type`

The `data-type` attribute can have three values:

- `data-type="text"`
- `data-type="number"`
- A `data-type="QName"` that identifies a particular datatype. The stated goal of the XSLT working group is that the datatypes defined in the XML Schema specification will eventually be supported here.

The XSLT specification defines the behavior for `data-type="text"` and `data-type="number"`. Consider this XML document:

```
<?xml version="1.0"?>
<numberlist>
  <number>127</number>
  <number>23</number>
  <number>10</number>
</numberlist>
```

We'll sort these values using the default value (`data-type="text"`):

```
<?xml version="1.0"?>
<xsl:stylesheet version="1.0"
  xmlns:xsl="http://www.w3.org/1999/XSL/Transform">

  <xsl:output method="text" indent="no"/>
  <xsl:strip-space elements="*"/>

  <xsl:variable name="newline">
<xsl:text>
</xsl:text>
  </xsl:variable>

  <xsl:template match="/">
    <xsl:for-each select="numberlist/number">
      <xsl:sort select="."/>
      <xsl:value-of select="."/>
      <xsl:value-of select="$newline"/>
    </xsl:for-each>
  </xsl:template>
</xsl:stylesheet>
```

When we sort these elements using `data-type="text"`, here's what we get:

```
10
127
23
```

We get this result because a text-based sort puts anything that starts with a "1" before anything that starts with a "2." If we change the `<xsl:sort>` element to be `<xsl:sort select="." data-type="number"/>`, we get these results:

```
10
27
123
```

If you use something else here (`data-type="floating-point"`, for example), what the XSLT processor does is anybody's guess. The XSLT specification allows for other values here, but it's up to the XSLT processor to decide how (or if) it wants to process those values. Check your processor's documentation to see if it does anything relevant or useful for values other than `data-type="text"` or `data-type="number"`.

A final note: if you're using `data-type="number"`, and any of the values aren't numbers, those non-numeric values will sort before the numeric values. That means if you're using `order="ascending"`, the non-numeric values appear first; if you use `order="descending"`, the non-numeric values appear last.

```
<?xml version="1.0"?>
<numberlist>
  <number>127</number>
  <number>23</number>
  <number>zzz</number>
  <number>10</number>
  <number>yyy</number>
</numberlist>
```

Given this less-than-perfect data, here are the correctly sorted results:

```
zzz
yyy
10
23
127
```

Notice that the non-numeric values were not sorted; they simply appear in the output document in the order in which they were encountered.

`order`
: You can order the sort as `order="ascending"` or `order="descending"`. The default is `order="ascending"`.

`case-order`
: This attribute can have two values. `case-order="upper-first"` means that uppercase letters sort before lowercase letters, and `case-order="lower-first"` means that lowercase letters sort first. The `case-order` attribute is used only when the `data-type` attribute is `text`. The default value depends on the value of the soon-to-be-discussed `lang` attribute.

`lang`

This attribute defines the language of the sort keys. The valid values for this attribute are the same as those for the `xml:lang` attribute defined in Section 2.12 of the XML 1.0 specification. The language codes are those commonly used in Java programming, UNIX locales, and other places ISO language and country namings are defined. For example, `lang="en"` means "English," `lang="en-US"` means "U.S. English," and `lang="en-GB"` means "U.K. English." Without the `lang` attribute (it's rarely used in practice), the XSLT processor determines the default language from the system environment.

Where can you use <xsl:sort>?

The `<xsl:sort>` element can appear inside two elements:

- `<xsl:apply-templates>`
- `<xsl:for-each>`

If you use an `<xsl:sort>` element inside `<xsl:for-each>`, the `<xsl:sort>` element(s) must appear first. If you tried something like this, you'd get an exception from the XSLT processor:

```
<xsl:for-each select="addressbook/address">
  <xsl:sort select="name/last-name"/>
  <xsl:value-of select="name/title"/>
  <xsl:sort select="name/first-name"/> <!-- NOT LEGAL! -->
  ...
```

Another Example

We've pretty much covered the `<xsl:sort>` element at this point. To add another wrinkle to our example, we'll change the stylesheet so the `xsl:sort` element acts upon a subset of the addresses, then sorts that subset. We'll sort only the addresses from states that start with the letter `M`. As you'd expect, we'll do this magic with an XPath expression that limits the elements to be sorted:

```
<?xml version="1.0"?>
<xsl:stylesheet version="1.0" xmlns:xsl="http://www.w3.org/1999/XSL/Transform">
  <xsl:output method="text" indent="no"/>
  <xsl:strip-space elements="*"/>
  <xsl:variable name="newline">
<xsl:text>
</xsl:text>
  </xsl:variable>

  <xsl:template match="/">
    <xsl:for-each select="addressbook/address/[starts-with(state, 'M')]">
      <xsl:sort select="name/last-name"/>
      <xsl:sort select="name/first-name"/>
```

```
        <xsl:if test="name/title">
          <xsl:value-of select="name/title"/>
          <xsl:text> </xsl:text>
        </xsl:if>
        <xsl:value-of select="name/first-name"/>
        <xsl:text> </xsl:text>
        <xsl:value-of select="name/last-name"/>
        <xsl:value-of select="$newline"/>
        <xsl:value-of select="street"/>
        <xsl:value-of select="$newline"/>
        <xsl:value-of select="city"/>
        <xsl:text>, </xsl:text>
        <xsl:value-of select="state"/>
        <xsl:text>  </xsl:text>
        <xsl:value-of select="zip"/>
        <xsl:value-of select="$newline"/>
        <xsl:value-of select="$newline"/>
      </xsl:for-each>
    </xsl:template>
  </xsl:stylesheet>
```

Here are the results, only those addresses from states beginning with the letter `M`, sorted by first name within last name:

```
Ms. Natalie Attired
707 Breitling Way
Winter Harbor, ME  00218

Harry Backstayge
283 First Avenue
Skunk Haven, MA  02718

Mary Backstayge
283 First Avenue
Skunk Haven, MA  02718

Ms. Amanda Reckonwith
930-A Chestnut Street
Lynn, MA  02930
```

Notice that in the `xsl:for-each` element, we used a predicate in our XPath expression so that only addresses containing `<state>` elements whose contents begin with `M` are selected. This example starts us on the path to grouping nodes. We could do lots of other things here:

- We could generate output that prints all the unique Zip Codes, along with the number of addresses that have those Zip Codes.
- For each unique Zip Code (or state, or last name, etc.) we could sort on a field and list all addresses with that Zip Code.

We'll discuss these topics in the next section.

Grouping Nodes

When grouping nodes, we sort things to get them into a certain order, then we group all items that have the same value for the sort key (or keys). We'll use `xsl:sort` for this grouping, then use variables or functions like `key()` or `generate-id()` to finish the job.

Our First Attempt

For our first example, we'll take our list of addresses and group them. We'll look for all unique values of the <zip> element and list the addresses that match each one. What we'll do is sort the list by Zip Code, then go through the list. If a given item doesn't match the previous Zip Code, we'll print out a heading; if it does match, we'll just print out the address. Here's our first attempt:

```
<?xml version="1.0"?>
<xsl:stylesheet version="1.0" xmlns:xsl="http://www.w3.org/1999/XSL/Transform">
  <xsl:output method="text" indent="no"/>
  <xsl:variable name="newline">
<xsl:text>
</xsl:text>
  </xsl:variable>

  <xsl:template match="/">
    <xsl:text>Addresses sorted by Zip Code</xsl:text>
    <xsl:value-of select="$newline"/>
    <xsl:for-each select="addressbook/address">
      <xsl:sort select="zip"/>
      <xsl:if test="zip!=preceding-sibling::address[1]/zip">
        <xsl:value-of select="$newline"/>
        <xsl:text>Zip code </xsl:text>
        <xsl:value-of select="zip"/>
        <xsl:text> (</xsl:text>
        <xsl:value-of select="city"/>
        <xsl:text>, </xsl:text>
        <xsl:value-of select="state"/>
        <xsl:text>): </xsl:text>
        <xsl:value-of select="$newline"/>
      </xsl:if>
      <xsl:if test="name/title">
        <xsl:value-of select="name/title"/>
        <xsl:text> </xsl:text>
      </xsl:if>
      <xsl:value-of select="name/first-name"/>
      <xsl:text> </xsl:text>
      <xsl:value-of select="name/last-name"/>
      <xsl:value-of select="$newline"/>
      <xsl:value-of select="street"/>
      <xsl:value-of select="$newline"/>
      <xsl:value-of select="$newline"/>
```

```
    </xsl:for-each>
  </xsl:template>
</xsl:stylesheet>
```

Our approach in this stylesheet consists of two steps:

1. Sort the addresses by Zip Code.

   ```
   <xsl:sort select="zip"/>
   ```

2. For each Zip Code, if it doesn't match the previous Zip Code, print out a heading, then print out the addresses that match it.

   ```
   <xsl:if test="zip!=preceding-sibling::address[1]/zip">
     <xsl:value-of select="$newline"/>
     <xsl:text>Zip code </xsl:text>
     ...
   ```

   (Remember that `preceding-sibling` returns a `NodeSet`, so `preceding-sibling::address[1]` represents the first preceding sibling.)

That sounds reasonable, doesn't it? Let's take a look at the results:

```
Addresses sorted by Zip Code

Zip code 00218 (Winter Harbor, ME):
Ms. Natalie Attired
707 Breitling Way


Zip code 02718 (Skunk Haven, MA):
Mary Backstayge
283 First Avenue

Harry Backstayge
283 First Avenue


Zip code 02930 (Lynn, MA):
Ms. Amanda Reckonwith
930-A Chestnut Street


Zip code 27318 (Boylston, VA):
Mary McGoon
103 Bryant Street

Mr. Chester Hasbrouck Frisby
1234 Main Street
```

Yes, that certainly seemed like a good approach, but there's one minor problem: it doesn't work.

Looking at our results, there seems to be only one problem: one of the addresses (Mr. Chester Hasbrouck Frisby) is grouped under the heading for Boylston, Virginia, but he actually lives in Sheboygan, Wisconsin, Zip Code 48392. The problem here is that the axes work with the document order, not the sorted order we've created inside the `xsl:for-each` element.

As straightforward as our logic seemed, we'll have to find another way.

A Brute-Force Approach

One thing we could do is make the transformation in two passes; we could write an intermediate stylesheet to sort the names and generate a new XML document, then use the stylesheet we've already written, because document order and sorted order will be the same. Here's how that intermediate stylesheet would look:

```
<?xml version="1.0"?>
<xsl:stylesheet version="1.0" xmlns:xsl="http://www.w3.org/1999/XSL/Transform">

  <xsl:output method="xml" indent="no"/>
  <xsl:strip-space elements="*"/>

  <xsl:template match="/">
    <addressbook>
      <xsl:for-each select="addressbook/address">
        <xsl:sort select="name/last-name"/>
        <xsl:sort select="name/first-name"/>
        <xsl:copy-of select="."/>
      </xsl:for-each>
    </addressbook>
  </xsl:template>
</xsl:stylesheet>
```

This stylesheet generates a new `<addressbook>` document that has all of the `<address>` elements sorted correctly. We can then run our original stylesheet against the sorted document and get the results we want. This works, but it's not very elegant. Even worse, it's really slow because we have to stop in the middle and write a file out to disk, then read that data back in. We'll find a way to group elements in a single stylesheet, but we'll have to do it with a different technique.

Grouping with <xsl:variable>

We mentioned earlier that sometimes `<xsl:variable>` is useful for grouping, so let's try that approach. We'll save the value of the `<zip>` element each time through the `<xsl:for-each>` element and use `preceding-sibling` in a slightly different way. Here's how attempt number three looks:

```
<?xml version="1.0"?>
<xsl:stylesheet version="1.0" xmlns:xsl="http://www.w3.org/1999/XSL/Transform">

  <xsl:output method="text" indent="no"/>

  <xsl:variable name="newline">
<xsl:text>
</xsl:text>
  </xsl:variable>

  <xsl:template match="/">
    <xsl:text>Addresses sorted by Zip Code</xsl:text>
    <xsl:value-of select="$newline"/>
    <xsl:for-each select="addressbook/address">
      <xsl:sort select="zip"/>
      <xsl:sort select="name/last-name"/>
      <xsl:sort select="name/first-name"/>
      <xsl:variable name="lastZip" select="zip"/>
      <xsl:if test="not(preceding-sibling::address[zip=$lastZip])">
        <xsl:text>Zip code </xsl:text>
        <xsl:value-of select="zip"/>
        <xsl:text>: </xsl:text>
        <xsl:value-of select="$newline"/>
        <xsl:for-each select="/addressbook/address[zip=$lastZip]">
          <xsl:sort select="name/last-name"/>
          <xsl:sort select="name/first-name"/>
          <xsl:if test="name/title">
            <xsl:value-of select="name/title"/>
            <xsl:text> </xsl:text>
          </xsl:if>
          <xsl:value-of select="name/first-name"/>
          <xsl:text> </xsl:text>
          <xsl:value-of select="name/last-name"/>
          <xsl:value-of select="$newline"/>
          <xsl:value-of select="street"/>
          <xsl:value-of select="$newline"/>
          <xsl:value-of select="$newline"/>
        </xsl:for-each>
      </xsl:if>
    </xsl:for-each>
  </xsl:template>
</xsl:stylesheet>
```

This stylesheet generates what we want:

```
Addresses sorted by Zip Code
Zip code 00218:
Ms. Natalie Attired
707 Breitling Way

Zip code 02718:
Harry Backstayge
283 First Avenue
```

```
Mary Backstayge
283 First Avenue

Zip code 02930:
Ms. Amanda Reckonwith
930-A Chestnut Street

Zip code 27318:
Mary McGoon
103 Bryant Street

Zip code 48392:
Mr. Chester Hasbrouck Frisby
1234 Main Street
```

So why does this approach work when our first attempt didn't? The answer is: we don't count on the sorted order of the elements to generate the output. The downside of this approach is that we go through several steps to get the results we want:

1. We sort all the addresses by Zip Code:

   ```
   <xsl:sort select="zip"/>
   ```

2. We store the current <zip> element's value in the variable `lastZip`:

   ```
   <xsl:variable name="lastZip" select="zip"/>
   ```

3. For each <zip> element, we look at all of its preceding siblings to see if this is the first time we've encountered this particular value (stored in `lastZip`). If it is, there won't be any preceding siblings that match.

   ```
   <xsl:if test="not(preceding-sibling::address[zip=$lastZip])">
   ```

4. If this is the first time we've encountered this value in the <zip> element, we go back and reselect all <address> elements with <zip> children that match this value. Once we have that group, we sort them by first name within last name and print each address.

   ```
   <xsl:for-each select="/addressbook/address[zip=$lastZip]">
     <xsl:sort select="name/last-name"/>
     <xsl:sort select="name/first-name"/>
   ```

So, we've found a way to get the results we want, but it's really inefficient. We sort the data, then we look at each Zip Code in sorted order, then see if we've encountered that value before in document order, then we reselect all the items that match the current Zip Code and resort them before we write them out. Whew! There's got to be a better way, right? Well, since we're not at the end of the chapter, it's a safe bet we'll find a better way in the next section. Read on . . . .

The <xsl:key> Approach

In this section, we'll look at using <xsl:key> to group items in an XML document. This approach is commonly referred to as the "Muench method," after Oracle XML Evangelist (and O'Reilly author) Steve Muench, who first suggested this technique. The Muench method has three steps:

1. Define a key for the property we want to use for grouping.
2. Select all of the nodes we want to group. We'll do some tricks with the key() and generate-id() functions to find the unique grouping values.
3. For each unique grouping value, use the key() function to retrieve all nodes that match it. Because the key() function returns a node-set, we can do further sorts on the set of nodes that match any given grouping value.

Well, that's how the technique works—let's start building the stylesheet that makes the magic happen. The first step, creating a key function, is easy. Here's how it looks:

```
<xsl:key name="zipcodes" match="address" use="zip"/>
```

This <xsl:key> element defines a new index called zipcodes. It indexes <address> elements based on the value of the <zip> element they contain.

Now that we've defined our key, we're ready for the complicated part. We use the key() and generate-id() functions together. Here's the syntax, which we'll discuss extensively in a minute:

```
<xsl:for-each select="//address[generate-id(.)=
  generate-id(key('zipcodes', zip)[1])]">
```

Okay, let's take a deep, cleansing breath and start digging through this syntax. What we're selecting here is all <address> elements in which the automatically generated id matches the automatically generated id of the first node returned by the key() function when we ask for all <address> elements that match the current <zip> element.

Well, that's clear as crystal, isn't it? Let me try to explain that again from a slightly different perspective.

For each <address>, we use the key() function to retrieve all <address>es that have the same <zip>. We then take the first node from that node-set. Finally, we use the generate-id() function to generate an id for both nodes. If the two generated ids are identical, then the two nodes are the same.

Whew. Let me catch my breath.

If this <address> matches the first node returned by the `key()` function, then we know we've found the first <address> that matches this grouping value. Selecting all of the first values (remember, our previous predicate ends with `[1]`) gives us a node-set of some number of <address> elements, each of which contains one of the unique grouping values we need.

Well, that's how this technique works. At this point, we've got a way to generate a node-set that contains all of the unique grouping values; now we need to process those nodes. From this point, we'll do several things, all of which are comparatively simple:

- Sort all nodes based on the grouping property. In this example, the property is the <zip> element. We start by selecting the first occurrence of every unique <zip> element in the document, then we sort those <zip> elements. Here's how it looks in the stylesheet:

```
<xsl:for-each
  select="//address[generate-id(.)=generate-id(key('zipcodes', zip)[1])]">
  <xsl:sort select="zip"/>
```

- The outer <xsl:for-each> element selects all the unique values of the <zip> element. Next, we use the `key()` function to retrieve all <address> elements that match the current <zip> element:

```
<xsl:for-each select="key('zipcodes', zip)">
```

- The `key()` function gives us a node-set of all matching <address> elements. We sort that node-set based on the <last-name> and <first-name> elements, then process them in turn:

```
<xsl:sort select="name/last-name"/>
<xsl:sort select="name/first-name"/>
<tr>
  <xsl:if test="position() = 1">
    <td valign="center" bgcolor="#999999">
      <xsl:attribute name="rowspan">
        <xsl:value-of select="count(key('zipcodes', zip))"/>
      </xsl:attribute>
      <b>
        <xsl:text>Zip code </xsl:text><xsl:value-of select="zip"/>
      </b>
    </td>
  </xsl:if>
  <td align="right">
    <xsl:value-of select="name/first-name"/>
    <xsl:text> </xsl:text>
    <b><xsl:value-of select="name/last-name"/></b>
  </td>
  <td>
    <xsl:value-of select="street"/>
    <xsl:text>, </xsl:text>
```

```
            <xsl:value-of select="city"/>
            <xsl:text>, </xsl:text>
            <xsl:value-of select="state"/>
            <xsl:text> </xsl:text>
            <xsl:value-of select="zip"/>
          </td>
        </tr>
      </xsl:for-each>
    </xsl:for-each>
```

We generate a table cell that contains the Zip Code common to all addresses, creating a `rowspan` attribute based on the number of matches for the current Zip Code. From there, we write the other data items into table cells.

Here's our complete stylesheet:

```
<?xml version="1.0"?>

<xsl:stylesheet version="1.0" xmlns:xsl="http://www.w3.org/1999/XSL/Transform">

  <xsl:output method="html" indent="no"/>

  <xsl:key name="zipcodes" match="address" use="zip"/>

  <xsl:template match="/">
    <table border="1">
      <xsl:for-each select="//address[generate-id(.)=
        generate-id(key('zipcodes', zip)[1])]">
        <xsl:sort select="zip"/>
        <xsl:for-each select="key('zipcodes', zip)">
          <xsl:sort select="name/last-name"/>
          <xsl:sort select="name/first-name"/>
          <tr>
            <xsl:if test="position() = 1">
              <td valign="center" bgcolor="#999999">
                <xsl:attribute name="rowspan">
                  <xsl:value-of select="count(key('zipcodes', zip))"/>
                </xsl:attribute>
                <b>
                  <xsl:text>Zip code </xsl:text><xsl:value-of select="zip"/>
                </b>
              </td>
            </xsl:if>
            <td align="right">
              <xsl:value-of select="name/first-name"/>
              <xsl:text> </xsl:text>
              <b><xsl:value-of select="name/last-name"/></b>
            </td>
            <td>
              <xsl:value-of select="street"/>
              <xsl:text>, </xsl:text>
              <xsl:value-of select="city"/>
              <xsl:text>, </xsl:text>
              <xsl:value-of select="state"/>
```

```
              <xsl:text> </xsl:text>
              <xsl:value-of select="zip"/>
            </td>
          </tr>
        </xsl:for-each>
      </xsl:for-each>
    </table>
  </xsl:template>

</xsl:stylesheet>
```

When we view the generated HTML document in a browser, it looks like Figure 6-1.

Zip code 00218	Natalie **Attired**	707 Breitling Way, Winter Harbor, ME 00218
Zip code 02718	Harry **Backstayge**	283 First Avenue, Skunk Haven, MA 02718
	Mary **Backstayge**	283 First Avenue, Skunk Haven, MA 02718
Zip code 02930	Amanda **Reckonwith**	930-A Chestnut Street, Lynn, MA 02930
Zip code 27318	Mary **McGoon**	103 Bryant Street, Boylston, VA 27318
Zip code 48392	Chester Hasbrouck **Frisby**	1234 Main Street, Sheboygan, WI 48392

Figure 6-1. HTML document with grouped items

Notice how the two <xsl:for-each> and the various <xsl:sort> elements work together. The outer <xsl:for-each> element selects the unique values of the <zip> element and sorts them; the inner <xsl:for-each> element selects all <address> elements that match the current <zip> element, and then sorts them by <last-name> and <first-name>.

Summary

In this chapter, we've gone over all of the common techniques used for sorting and grouping elements. Regardless of the kinds of stylesheets you'll need to write in your XML projects, you'll probably use these techniques in everything you do. Now that we've covered how to sort and group elements, we'll talk about how to combine multiple input documents next; this subject will build on the topics we've covered here.

7

Combining XML Documents

One of XSLT's most powerful features is the `document()` function. `document()` lets you use part of an XML document (identified with an XPath expression, of course) as a URI. In other words, you can look in a document, use parts of that document as URLs (or filenames), open and parse those files, then perform stylesheet functions on the combination of all those documents. In this chapter, we'll cover the `document()` function in all its glory.

Overview

The `document()` function is very useful for defining views of multiple XML documents. In this chapter, we'll use XML-tagged purchase orders that look like this:

```
<purchase-order id="38292">
  <customer id="4738" level="Platinum">
    <address type="business">
      <name>
        <title>Mr.</title>
        <first-name>Chester Hasbrouck</first-name>
        <last-name>Frisby</last-name>
      </name>
      <street>1234 Main Street</street>
      <city>Sheboygan</city>
      <state>WI</state>
      <zip>48392</zip>
    </address>
    <address type="ship-to"/>
  </customer>
  <items>
    <item part_no="28392-33-TT">
      <name>Turnip Twaddler</name>
```

```
      <qty>3</qty>
      <price>9.95</price>
    </item>
    <item part_no="28813-70-PG">
      <name>Prawn Goader</name>
      <qty>1</qty>
      <price>18.95</price>
    </item>
  </items>
</purchase-order>
```

If we had a few dozen documents like this, we might want to view the collection of purchase orders in a number of ways. We could view them sorted (or even grouped) by customer, by part number, by the amount of the total order, by the state to which they were shipped, etc. One way to do this would be to write code that worked directly with the Document Object Model. We could parse each document, retrieve its DOM tree, then use DOM functions to order and group the various DOM trees, display certain parts of the DOM trees, etc. Because this is an XSLT book, though, you probably won't be surprised to learn that XSLT provides a function to handle most of the heavy lifting for us.

The document() Function

We'll start with a couple of simple examples that use the `document()` function. We'll assume that we have several purchase orders and that we want to combine them into a single report document. One thing we can do is create a *master document* that references all the purchase orders we want to include in the report. Here's what that master document might look like:

```
<report>
  <title>Purchase Orders</title>
  <po filename="po38292.xml"/>
  <po filename="po38293.xml"/>
  <po filename="po38294.xml"/>
  <po filename="po38295.xml"/>
</report>
```

We'll fill in the details of our stylesheet as we go along, but here's what the shell of our stylesheet looks like:

```
<xsl:template match="/">
  <xsl:for-each select="/report/po">
    <xsl:apply-templates select="document(@filename)"/>
  </xsl:for-each>
</xsl:template>
```

In this template, we use the filename attribute as the argument to the document() function. The simplest thing we can do is open each purchase order, then write its details to the output stream. Here's a stylesheet that does this:

```
<?xml version="1.0">
<xsl:stylesheet version="1.0" xmlns:xsl="http://www.w3.org/1999/XSL/Transform">

  <xsl:output method="html" indent="no">
  <xsl:strip-space elements="*">

  <xsl:template match="/">
    <html>
      <head>
        <title><xsl:value-of select="/report/title"></title>
      </head>
      <body>
        <xsl:for-each select="/report/po">
          <xsl:apply-templates select="document(@filename)/purchase-order">
        </xsl:for-each>
      </body>
    </html>
  </xsl:template>

  <xsl:template match="purchase-order">
    <h1>
      <xsl:value-of select="customer/address[@type='business']/name/title">
      <xsl:text> </xsl:text>
      <xsl:value-of select="customer/address[@type='business']/name/first-name">
      <xsl:text> </xsl:text>
      <xsl:value-of select="customer/address[@type='business']/name/last-name">
    </h1>
    <p>
      <xsl:text>Ordered on </xsl:text>
      <xsl:value-of select="date/@month">
      <xsl:text>/</xsl:text>
      <xsl:value-of select="date/@day">
      <xsl:text>/</xsl:text>
      <xsl:value-of select="date/@year">
    </p>
    <h2>Items:</h2>
    <table width="100%" border="1" cols="55% 15% 15% 15%">
      <tr bgcolor="lightgreen">
        <th>Item</th>
        <th>Quantity</th>
        <th>Price Each</th>
        <th>Total</th>
      </tr>
      <xsl:for-each select="items/item">
        <tr>
          <xsl:attribute name="bgcolor">
            <xsl:choose>
              <xsl:when test="position() mod 2">
                <xsl:text>white</xsl:text>
```

```
              </xsl:when>
              <xsl:otherwise>
                <xsl:text>lightgreen</xsl:text>
              </xsl:otherwise>
            </xsl:choose>
          </xsl:attribute>
          <td>
            <b><xsl:value-of select="name"></b>
            <xsl:text> (part #</xsl:text>
            <xsl:value-of select="@part_no">
            <xsl:text>)</xsl:text>
          </td>
          <td align="center">
            <xsl:value-of select="qty">
          </td>
          <td align="right">
            <xsl:value-of select="price">
          </td>
          <td align="right">
            <xsl:choose>
              <xsl:when test="position()=1">
                <xsl:value-of select="format-number(price * qty, '$#,###.00')">
              </xsl:when>
              <xsl:otherwise>
                <xsl:value-of select="format-number(price * qty, '#,###.00')">
              </xsl:otherwise>
            </xsl:choose>
          </td>
        </tr>
      </xsl:for-each>
      <tr>
        <td colspan="3" align="right">
          <b>Total:</b>
        </td>
        <td align="right">
          <xsl:variable name="orderTotal">
            <xsl:call-template name="sumItems">
              <xsl:with-param name="index" select="'1'">
              <xsl:with-param name="items" select="items">
              <xsl:with-param name="runningTotal" select="'0'">
            </xsl:call-template>
          </xsl:variable>
          <xsl:value-of select="format-number($orderTotal, '$#,###.00')">
        </td>
      </tr>
    </table>
  </xsl:template>

  <xsl:template name="sumItems">
    <xsl:param name="index" select="'1'">
    <xsl:param name="items">
    <xsl:param name="runningTotal" select="'0'">
    <xsl:variable name="currentItem">
      <xsl:value-of select="$items/item[$index]/qty *
```

```
    $items/item[$index]/price">
      </xsl:variable>
      <xsl:variable name="remainingItems">
        <xsl:choose>
          <xsl:when test="$index=count($items/item)">
            <xsl:text>0</xsl:text>
          </xsl:when>
          <xsl:otherwise>
            <xsl:call-template name="sumItems">
              <xsl:with-param name="index" select="$index+1">
              <xsl:with-param name="items" select="$items">
              <xsl:with-param name="runningTotal"
                select="$runningTotal+$currentItem">
            </xsl:call-template>
          </xsl:otherwise>
        </xsl:choose>
      </xsl:variable>
      <xsl:value-of select="$currentItem+$remainingItems">
    </xsl:template>

  </xsl:stylesheet>
```

When we process our master document with this stylesheet, the results look like Figure 7-1.

The most notable thing about our results is that we've been able to generate a document that contains the contents of several other documents. To keep our example short, we've only combined four purchase orders, but there's no limit (beyond the physical limits of our machine) to the number of documents we could combine. Best of all, we didn't have to modify any of the individual purchase orders to generate our report.

An Aside: Doing Math with Recursion

While we're here, we'll also mention the recursive technique we used to calculate the total for each purchase order. At first glance, this seems like a perfect opportunity to use the `sum()` function. We want to add the total of the price of each item multiplied by its quantity. We could try to invoke the `sum()` function like this:

```
<xsl:value-of select="sum(item/qty*item/price)"/>
```

Unfortunately, the `sum()` function simply takes the node-set passed to it, converts each item in the node-set to a number, then returns the sum of all of those numbers. The expression `item/qty*item/price`, while a perfectly valid XPath expression, isn't a valid node-set. With that in mind, we have to create a recursive `<xsl:template>` to do the work for us. There are a couple of techniques worth mentioning here; we'll go through them in the order we used them in our stylesheet.

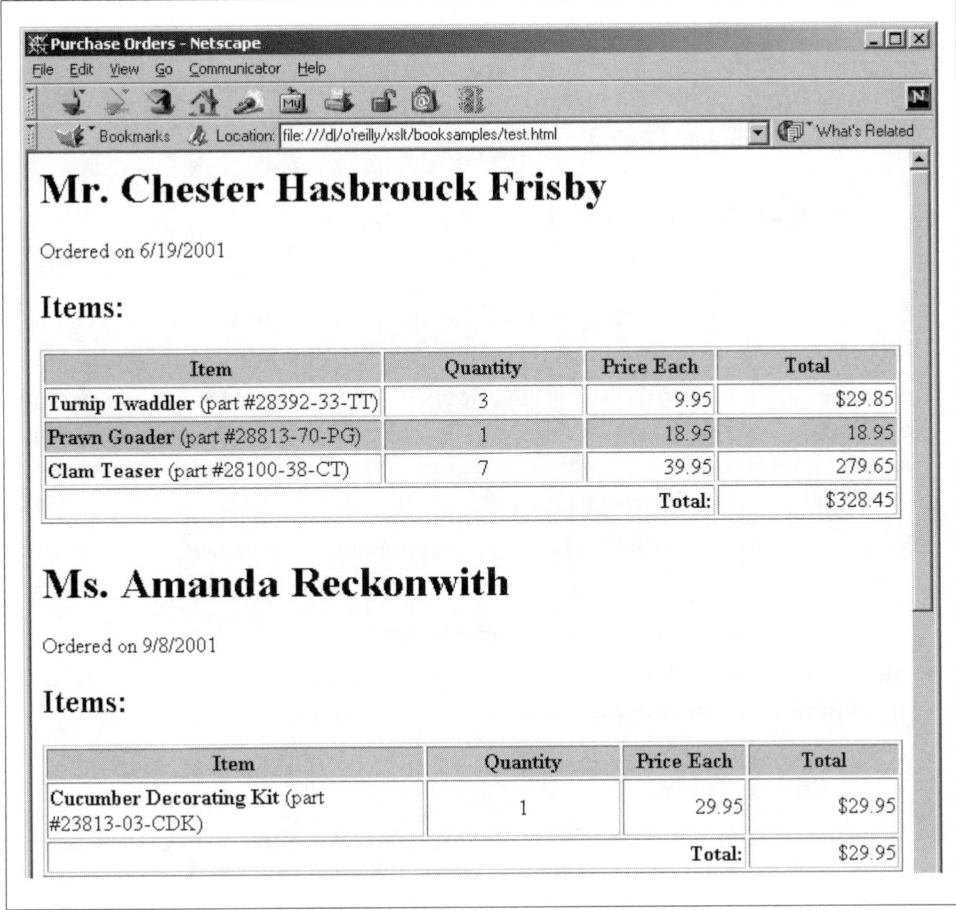

Figure 7-1. Document generated from multiple input files

Recursive design

First, we pass three parameters to the template:

`items`
: The node-set of all `<item>` elements in the current `<items>` element.

`index`
: The position in that node-set of the `<item>` we're currently processing.

`runningTotal`
: The total of all the `<item>`s we've processed so far.

Our basic design is as follows:

- Calculate the total for the current <item>. This total is the value of the <qty> element multiplied by the value of the <price> element. We store this value in the variable currentItem:

  ```
  <xsl:variable name="currentItem">
    <xsl:value-of select="$items/item[$index]/qty *
      $items/item[$index]/price"/>
  </xsl:variable>
  ```

  Notice how the XPath expression in the select attribute uses the $items and $index parameters to find the exact items we're looking for.

- Calculate the total for the remaining items. If this is the last item (the parameter $index is equal to the number of <item> elements), then the total for the remaining items is zero. Otherwise, the total for the remaining items is returned by calling the template again.

  When we call the template again, we increment the position of the current item:

  ```
  <xsl:with-param name="index" select="$index+1"/>
  ```

  We also update the parameter $runningTotal, which is equal to the value of the current item plus the previous value of $runningTotal:

  ```
  <xsl:with-param name="runningTotal"
    select="$runningTotal+$currentItem"/>
  ```

This recursive design lets us generate the totals we need for our purchase order. Our approach is equivalent to invoking a function against each node in a node-set, only this approach doesn't require us to use extensions. As a result, we can use this stylesheet with any standards-compliant stylesheet processor, without having to worry about porting any extension functions or extension elements.

Generating output to initialize a variable

When we needed to set the value of the variable runningTotal, we simply called the template named sumItems. The sumItems template uses the <xsl:value-of> element to output some text; everything output by the template is concatenated to form the value of the variable runningTotal. The advantage of this technique is that it allows us to completely control the value of the variable, and it allows us to avoid converting the variable to a number until we're ready. Once the sumItems template finishes its work, we can pass the variable's value to the format-number() function to print the invoice total exactly how we want.

Using format-number() to control output

The final nicety in our stylesheet is that we use the XSLT `format-number()` function to display the total for the current purchase order. We've already discussed how we set the value of the variable `$orderTotal` to be the output of the template named `sumItems`; once the variable is set, we use `format-number` to display it with a currency sign, commas, and two decimal places:

```
<xsl:value-of select="format-number($order-total, '$#,###.00')"/>
```

Invoking the document() Function

In our previous stylesheet, we used the `document()` function to select some number of nodes from the original source document (our list of purchase orders), then open those files. There are a number of ways to invoke the `document()` function; we'll discuss them briefly here.

The most common way to use the `document()` function is as we just did. We use an XPath expression to describe a node-set; the `document()` function takes each node in the node-set, converts it to a string, then uses that string as a URI. So, when we passed a node-set containing the `filename` attributes in the list of purchase orders, each one is used as a URI. If those URIs are relative references (i.e., they don't begin with a protocol like `http`), the base URI of the stylesheet is used as the base URI for the reference.

If the `document()` function has two arguments, the second must be a node-set. The first argument is processed as just described, with the difference that the base URI of the first node in the node-set is used as the base URI for any relative URIs. That combination isn't used often, but it's there if you need it.

Every node in the XPath source tree is associated with a *base URI*. When using the `document()` function, the base URI is important for resolving references to various resources (typically specified with relative links in a file opened with the `document()` function.

If a given node is an element or processing instruction node, and that node occurs in an external entity, then the base URI for that node is the base URI of the external entity. If an element or processing instruction node does not occur in an external entity, then its base URI is the base URI of the document in which it appears. The base URI of a document node is the base URI of the document itself, and the base URI of an attribute, comment, namespace, or text node is the base URI of that node's parent.

You can also pass a string or any other XPath datatype to the `document()` function. If we wanted to open a particular resource, we could simply pass the name of the resource:

```
document('http://www.ibm.com/pricelist.xml')
```

This action would open this particular resource and process it. Be aware that XSLT processors are required to return an empty node-set if a resource can't be found, but they aren't required to signal an error. XSLT processors also don't have to support any particular protocols (`http`, `ftp`, etc.); you have to check the documentation of your XSLT processor to see what protocols are and aren't supported.

A special case occurs when you pass an empty string to the `document()` function. As we've discussed the various combinations of arguments that can be passed to the function, we've gone over the rules for resolving URIs. When we call `document('')`, the XSLT processor parses the current stylesheet and returns a single node, the root node of the stylesheet itself. This technique is very useful for processing lookup tables in a stylesheet, something we'll discuss later in this chapter.

More Sophisticated Techniques

Up to now, we've written a simple XML document that contains references to other XML documents, then we created a stylesheet that combines all those referenced XML documents into a single output document. That's all well and good, but we'll probably want to do more advanced things. For example, it might be useful to generate a document that lists all items ordered by all the customers. It might be useful to sort all the purchase orders by the state to which they were shipped, by the last name of the customer, or to group them by the state to which they were shipped. We'll go through some of these scenarios to illustrate the design challenges we face when generating documents from multiple input files.

The document() Function and Sorting

Our first challenge will be to generate a listing of all purchase orders and sort them by state. This isn't terribly difficult; we'll simply use the `<xsl:sort>` element in conjunction with the `document()` function. Here's the heart of our new stylesheet:

```
<body>
  <h3>Selected Purchase Orders - <i>Sorted by state</i></h3>
  <xsl:for-each
  select="document(/report/po/@filename)/purchase-order/customer/address/state">
    <xsl:sort select="."/>
    <xsl:apply-templates select="ancestor::purchase-order"/>
  </xsl:for-each>
</body>
```

What makes this process slightly challenging is the fact that we're sorting on one thing (the value of the `<state>` element), then invoking `<xsl:apply-templates>` against the `<purchase-order>` ancestor of the `<state>` element. We simply used the `ancestor::` axis to do this. Figure 7-2 shows our output document, sorted by the value of the `<state>` element in each purchase order.

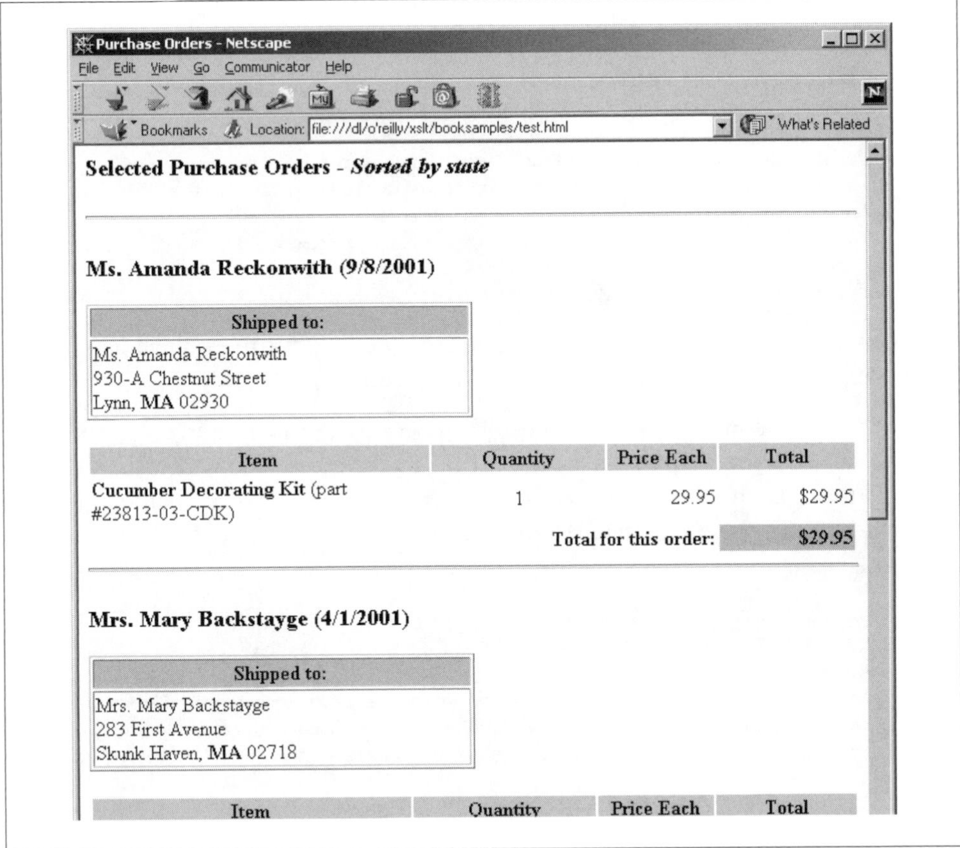

Figure 7-2. Another document generated from multiple input files

Implementing Lookup Tables

We mentioned earlier that calling the `document()` function with an empty string enabled us to access the nodes in the stylesheet itself. We can use this behavior to implement a lookup table. As an example, we'll create a lookup table that replaces an abbreviation such as `ME` with `Maine`. We can then use the value from the lookup table as the sort key. More attentive readers might have noticed in our previous example that although the abbreviation `MA` does indeed sort before the abbreviation `ME`, a sorted list of the state names themselves would put `Maine` (abbreviation `ME`) before `Massachusetts` (abbreviation `MA`).

First, we'll create our lookup table. We'll use the fact that a stylesheet can have any element as a top-level element, provided that element is namespace-qualified to distinguish it from the `xsl:` namespace reserved for stylesheets. Here's the namespace prefix definition and part of the lookup table that uses it:

```
<?xml version="1.0"?>
<xsl:stylesheet version="1.0" xmlns:xsl="http://www.w3.org/1999/XSL/Transform"
  xmlns:states="http://new.usps.com/cgi-bin/uspsbv/scripts/content.jsp?D=10090">

  <states:name abbrev="AL">Alabama</states:name>
  <states:name abbrev="AL">Alabama</states:name>
  <states:name abbrev="AK">Alaska</states:name>
  <states:name abbrev="AS">American Samoa</states:name>
  <!-- Most state abbreviations removed to keep this listing brief... -->
  <states:name abbrev="ME">Maine</states:name>
  <states:name abbrev="MH">Marshall Islands</states:name>
  <states:name abbrev="MD">Maryland</states:name>
  <states:name abbrev="MA">Massachusetts</states:name>
```

(The namespace mapped to the `states` prefix is the URL for the official list of state abbreviations from the United States Postal Service.)

To look up values in our table, we'll use the `document()` function to return the root node of our stylesheet, then we'll look for a `<states:name>` element with a `abbrev` attribute that matches the value of the current `<state>` element in the purchase order we're currently processing. Here's the somewhat convoluted syntax that performs this magic:

```
<body>
  <h3>Selected Purchase Orders - <i>Sorted by state</i></h3>
  <xsl:for-each
  select="document(/report/po/@filename)/purchase-order/customer/address/state">
    <xsl:sort select="document('')/*/states:name[@abbrev=current()]"/>
    <xsl:apply-templates select="ancestor::purchase-order"/>
  </xsl:for-each>
</body>
```

Notice that we use the `document()` function twice; once to open the document referred to by the `filename` element, and once to open the stylesheet itself. We also need to discuss the XPath expression in the `select` attribute of the `<xsl:sort>` element. There are four significant parts to this expression:

`document('')`
: Returns the root node of the current stylesheet.

`/*/`
: Indicates that what follows must be a top-level element of the stylesheet. This syntax starts at the root of the document, then has a single element. The

element's name can be anything. For our current stylesheet, we could have written the XPath expression like this:

```
select="document('')/xsl:stylesheet/states:name[@abbrev=current()]"
```

Because the root element of a stylesheet can be either `xsl:stylesheet` or `xsl:transform`, it's better to use the asterisk.

`states:name`
: Indicates a `name` element combined with a namespace prefix that maps to `http://new.usps.com/cgi-bin/uspsbv/scripts/content.jsp?D=10090`. If we were referencing elements in another document, the prefix wouldn't have to be `states`; it could be anything, as long as it mapped to the same string.

`[@abbrev=current()]`
: Means that the `abbrev` attribute of the current `<states:name>` element has the same value as the current node. We have to use the XSLT `current()` function here because we want the current node, not the context node. Inside the predicate expression, the current node is the `<state>` element we process, while the context node is the `<states:name>` element that contains the `abbrev` attribute we evaluate.

Figure 7-3 shows the output from the stylesheet with a lookup table.

Notice that now the purchase orders have been sorted by the actual name of the state referenced in the address, not by the state's abbreviation. Lookup tables are an extremely useful side effect of the way the `document('')` function works. You could place a lookup table in another file and you could use the `document('')` function for other purposes, but the technique we've covered here is the most common way to implement lookup tables.

Grouping Across Multiple Documents

Our final task will be to group our collection of purchase orders. We'll create a new listing that groups all the purchase orders by the state to which they were shipped. We'll start by attempting the grouping technique we used earlier.

The most efficient grouping technique we used before was to use the XSLT `key()` function along with the XPath `generate-id()` function. We create a key for the nodes we want to index (in this case, the `<state>` elements), then compare each address we find to the first value returned by the `key()` function. Here's how we define the key:

```
<xsl:key name="states"
  match="document(/report/po/@filename)/purchase-order/customer/address"
  use="state"/>
```

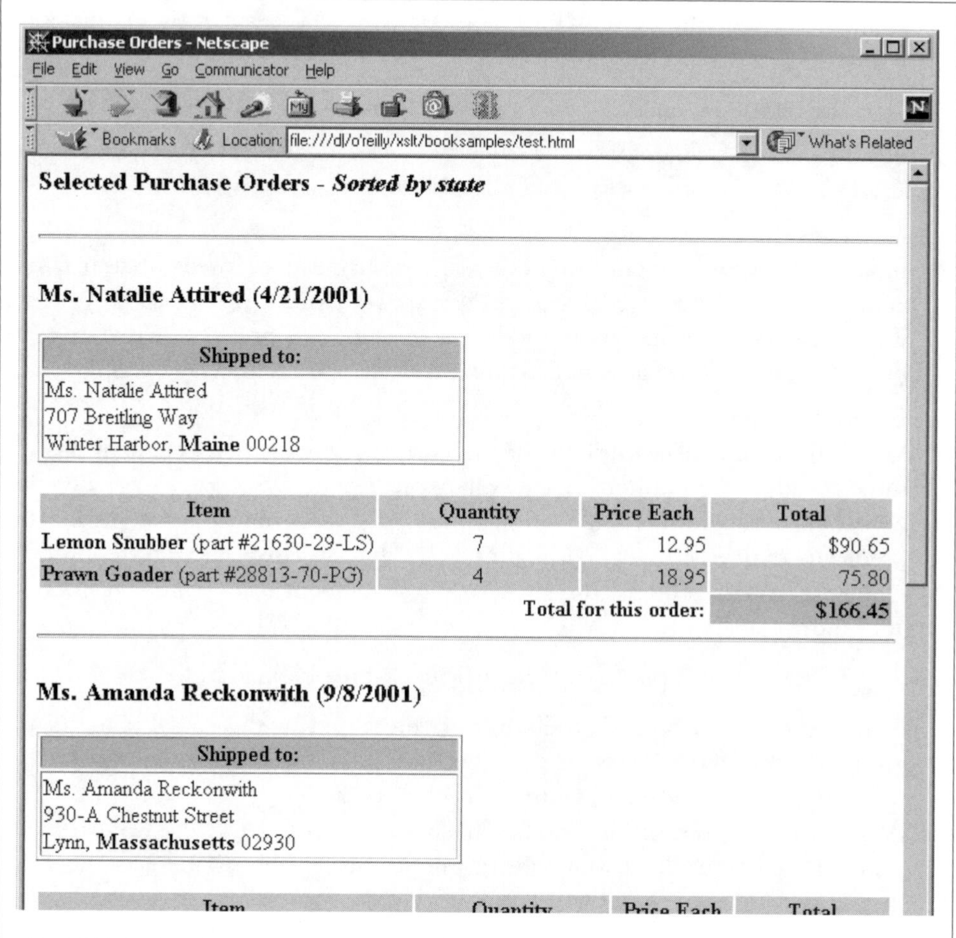

Figure 7-3. Document generated with a lookup table

Unfortunately, the `match` attribute of the `<xsl:key>` element can't begin with a call to the `document()` function. Maybe we could try creating a variable that contains all the nodes we want to use, then use that node-set to create the key:

```
<xsl:variable name="addresses"
  select="document(/report/po/@filename)/purchase-order/customer/address"/>
<xsl:key name="states" match="$addresses" use="state"/>
```

This doesn't work either; you can't use a variable in the `match` attribute. Our hopes for a quick solution to this problem are fading quickly. Complicating the problem is the fact that axes won't help, either. Trying to use the `preceding::` axis to see if a previous purchase order came from the current state also doesn't work. Consider this example:

```
<xsl:if test="not(preceding::address[state=$state])">
```

When we were working with a single document, the `preceding::` axis gave us useful information. Because all of the nodes we're working with are now in separate documents, the various axes defined in XPath won't help. When I ask for any nodes in the `preceding::` axis, I only get nodes from the current document. We're going to have to roll up our sleeves and do this the hard way.

Now that we're resigned to grouping nodes with brute force, we'll try to make the process as efficient as possible. For performance reasons, we want to avoid having to call the `document()` function any more than we have to. This won't be pretty, but here's our approach:

- Use the `document()` function to retrieve the values of all of the `<state>` elements. To keep things simple, we'll write these values out to a string, separating them with spaces. We'll also use the `<xsl:sort>` element to sort the `<state>` elements; that will save us some time later.
- Take our string of sorted, space-separated state names (to be precise, they're the values of all the `<state>` elements) and remove the duplicates. Because things are sorted, I only have to compare two adjacent values. We'll use recursion to handle this.
- For each item in our string of sorted, space-separated, unique state names, use the `document()` function to see which purchase orders match the current state.

This certainly isn't efficient; for each unique state, we'll have to call the `document()` function once for every `filename` attribute. In other words, if we had 500 purchase orders from 50 unique states, we would have to open each of those 500 documents 51 times, invoking the `document()` 25,500 times! It's not pretty, but it works.

Retrieving the values of all `<state>` elements is relatively straightforward. We'll use the technique of creating a variable whose value contains output from an `<xsl:for-each>` element:

```
    <xsl:variable name="list-of-states">
      <xsl:for-each
select="document(/report/po/@filename)/purchase-order/customer/address/state">
        <xsl:sort select="document('')/*/states:name[@abbrev=current()]"/>
        <xsl:value-of select="."/><xsl:text> </xsl:text>
      </xsl:for-each>
    </xsl:variable>
```

This code produces the string "ME MA MA WI" for our current set of purchase orders. Our next step will remove any duplicate values from the list. We'll do this with recursion, using the following algorithm:

- Call our recursive template with two arguments: the list of states and the name of the last state we found. the first time we invoke this template, the name of the last state will be blank.
- Break the list of states into two parts: The first state in the list, followed by the remaining states in the list.
- If the list of states is empty, exit.

  If the first state in the list is different from the last state we found, output the first state and invoke the template on the remaining states on the list.

  If the first state in the list is the same as the last state we found, simply invoke the template on the remaining states on the list.

Again, we use our technique of calling this template inside an `<xsl:variable>` element to save the list of unique states for later. Here is the `<xsl:variable>` element, along with the recursive template that removes duplicate state names from the string:

```
<xsl:variable name="list-of-unique-states">
  <xsl:call-template name="remove-duplicates">
    <xsl:with-param name="list-of-states" select="$list-of-states"/>
    <xsl:with-param name="last-state" select="''"/>
  </xsl:call-template>
</xsl:variable>

<xsl:template name="remove-duplicates">
  <xsl:param name="list-of-states"/>
  <xsl:param name="last-state" select="''"/>
  <xsl:variable name="next-state">
    <xsl:value-of select="substring-before($list-of-states, ' ')"/>
  </xsl:variable>
  <xsl:variable name="remaining-states">
    <xsl:value-of select="substring-after($list-of-states, ' ')"/>
  </xsl:variable>
  <xsl:choose>
    <xsl:when test="not(string-length(normalize-space($list-of-states)))">
      <!-- If the list of states is empty, do nothing -->
    </xsl:when>
    <xsl:when test="not($last-state=$next-state)">
      <xsl:value-of select="$next-state"/>
      <xsl:text> </xsl:text>
      <xsl:call-template name="remove-duplicates">
        <xsl:with-param name="list-of-states" select="$remaining-states"/>
        <xsl:with-param name="last-state" select="$next-state"/>
      </xsl:call-template>
    </xsl:when>
    <xsl:when test="$last-state=$next-state">
      <xsl:call-template name="remove-duplicates">
        <xsl:with-param name="list-of-states" select="$remaining-states"/>
```

```
        <xsl:with-param name="last-state" select="$next-state"/>
      </xsl:call-template>
    </xsl:when>
  </xsl:choose>
</xsl:template>
```

At this point, we have a variable named `list-of-unique-states` that contains the value `ME MA WI`. Now all we have to do is get each value and output all the purchase orders from each state. We'll use recursion yet again to make this happen. We'll pass our list of unique states to our recursive template, which does the following:

- Breaks the string into two parts: the first state in the list and the remaining states.
- Outputs a heading for the first state in the list.
- Invokes the `document()` function against each purchase order. If a given purchase order is from the first state in the list, use `<xsl:apply-templates>` to transform it.
- Invokes the template again for the remaining states. If no states remain (the value of `normalize-space($remaining-states)` is an empty string), we're done.

Here is the root template and the recursive template we use to group our data. The result of our hard work looks like Figure 7-4.

```
<xsl:template match="/">
  <html>
    <head>
      <title><xsl:value-of select="/report/title"/></title>
    </head>
    <body>
      <h3>Selected Purchase Orders - <i><b>Grouped</b> by state</i></h3>
      <xsl:call-template name="group-by-state">
        <xsl:with-param name="list-of-unique-states"
          select="$list-of-unique-states"/>
      </xsl:call-template>
    </body>
  </html>
</xsl:template>

<xsl:template name="group-by-state">
  <xsl:param name="list-of-unique-states"/>
  <xsl:variable name="next-state">
    <xsl:value-of select="substring-before($list-of-unique-states, ' ')"/>
  </xsl:variable>
  <xsl:variable name="remaining-states">
    <xsl:value-of select="substring-after($list-of-unique-states, ' ')"/>
  </xsl:variable>
  <hr/>
  <h1>Purchase Orders from
  <xsl:value-of select="document('')/*/states:name[@abbrev=$next-state]"/>
```

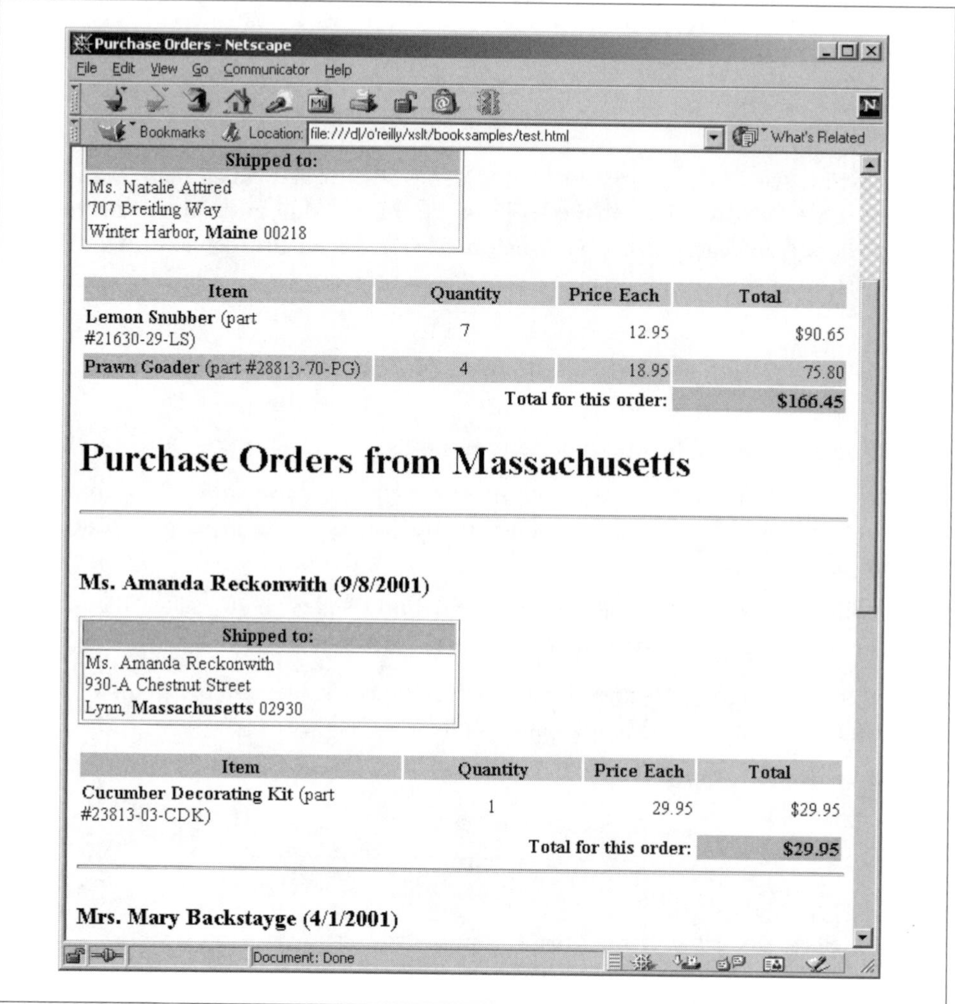

Figure 7-4. Document featuring grouped items from multiple input files

```
    </h1>
    <xsl:for-each
      select="document(/report/po/@filename)/purchase-order/customer/address">
      <xsl:if test="state=$next-state">
        <xsl:apply-templates select="ancestor::purchase-order"/>
      </xsl:if>
    </xsl:for-each>
    <xsl:if test="normalize-space($remaining-states)">
      <xsl:call-template name="group-by-state">
        <xsl:with-param name="list-of-unique-states"
          select="$remaining-states"/>
      </xsl:call-template>
    </xsl:if>
  </xsl:template>
```

Summary

This chapter completes our tour of the `document()` function. This powerful function allows us to generate an output document containing elements from many different input documents. In our examples here, we generated several views of those input documents, but many more combinations might be useful. The biggest benefit of the `document()` function is that it allows us to define views of multiple documents that are separate from those documents themselves. As we need to define other views, we don't have to change our input documents. The `document()` function can save you a tremendous amount of development time in generating reports and other summarizing documents.

8

Extending XSLT

To this point, we've spent a lot of time learning how to use the built-in features of XSLT and XPath to get things done. We've also talked about the somewhat unusual processing model that makes life challenging for programmers from the world of procedural languages (a.k.a. Earth). But what do you do if you still can't do everything with XSLT and XPath?

In this section, we'll discuss the XSLT extension mechanism that allows you to add new functions and elements to the language. Unfortunately, Version 1.0 of the XSLT standard doesn't define all of the details about how these things should work, so there are some inconsistencies between processors. The good news is that if you write an extension function or element that works with your favorite processor, another vendor can't do something sinister to prevent your functions or elements from working. On the other hand, if you decide to change XSLT processors, you'll probably have to change your code.

Most examples in this chapter are written for the Xalan processor. We'll discuss how to write stylesheets that can work with multiple processors, and we'll briefly look at the differences between the various APIs supported by those processors. In addition, Xalan comes with extensions written in Java, but you can use other languages, as well. We'll look at extensions written in Jython (formerly JPython), JavaScript, and Jacl.

Extension Elements, Extension Functions, and Fallback Processing

Section 14 of the XSLT standard defines two kinds of extensions: extension elements and extension functions. Section 15 of the specification defines fallback processing, a way for stylesheets to respond gracefully when extension elements and functions aren't available. We'll talk about these items briefly, then we'll move on to some examples that illustrate the full range of extensions.

Extension Elements

An extension element is an element that should be processed by a piece of code external to the XSLT processor. In the case of the Java version of Xalan, our stylesheet defines the Java class that should be loaded and invoked to process the extension element. Although the implementation details vary from one XSLT processor to the next, we'll discuss how an extension element can access the XPath representation of our source document, how it can generate output, and how it can move through the XPath tree to manipulate the source document.

Example: Generating multiple output files

The whole point of extensions is to allow you to add new capabilities to the XSLT processor. One of the most common needs is the ability to generate multiple output documents. As we saw earlier, the `document()` function allows you to have multiple input documents—but XSLT doesn't give us any way to create multiple output documents. Xalan, Saxon, and XT all ship with extensions that allow you to create such documents. Here's an XML document that we'll use for several of our examples in this chapter:

```
<?xml version="1.0"?>
<book>
  <title>XSLT</title>
  <chapter>
    <title>Getting Started</title>
    <para>If this chapter had any text, it would appear here.</para>
  </chapter>
  <chapter>
    <title>The Hello World Example</title>
    <para>If this chapter had any text, it would appear here.</para>
  </chapter>
  <chapter>
    <title>XPath</title>
    <para>If this chapter had any text, it would appear here.</para>
  </chapter>
  <chapter>
    <title>Stylesheet Basics</title>
    <para>If this chapter had any text, it would appear here.</para>
  </chapter>
  <chapter>
    <title>Branching and Control Elements</title>
    <para>If this chapter had any text, it would appear here.</para>
  </chapter>
  <chapter>
    <title>Functions</title>
    <para>If this chapter had any text, it would appear here.</para>
```

```
  </chapter>
  <chapter>
    <title>Creating Links and Cross-References</title>
    <para>If this chapter had any text, it would appear here.</para>
  </chapter>
  <chapter>
    <title>Sorting and Grouping Elements</title>
    <para>If this chapter had any text, it would appear here.</para>
  </chapter>
  <chapter>
    <title>Combining XML Documents</title>
    <para>If this chapter had any text, it would appear here.</para>
  </chapter>
</book>
```

For our first example, we want to create a stylesheet that converts the document to HTML, writing the contents of each <chapter> element to a separate HTML file. Here's what that stylesheet looks like:

```
<?xml version="1.0"?>
<xsl:stylesheet version="1.0" xmlns:xsl="http://www.w3.org/1999/XSL/Transform"
  xmlns:redirect="org.apache.xalan.xslt.extensions.Redirect"
  extension-element-prefixes="redirect">

  <xsl:output method="html"/>

  <xsl:template match="/">
    <xsl:choose>
      <xsl:when test="element-available('redirect:write')">
        <xsl:for-each select="/book/chapter">
          <redirect:write select="concat('chapter', position(), '.html')">
            <html>
              <head>
                <title><xsl:value-of select="title"/></title>
              </head>
              <body>
                <h1><xsl:value-of select="title"/></h1>
                <xsl:apply-templates select="para"/>
                <xsl:if test="not(position()=1)">
                  <p><a href="chapter{position()-1}.html">Previous</a></p>
                </xsl:if>
                <xsl:if test="not(position()=last())">
                  <p><a href="chapter{position()+1}.html">Next</a></p>
                </xsl:if>
              </body>
            </html>
          </redirect:write>
        </xsl:for-each>
      </xsl:when>
      <xsl:otherwise>
        <html>
          <head>
            <title><xsl:value-of select="/book/title"/></title>
          </head>
```

```
        <xsl:for-each select="/book/chapter">
          <h1><xsl:value-of select="title"/></h1>
          <xsl:apply-templates select="para"/>
        </xsl:for-each>
      </html>
    </xsl:otherwise>
  </xsl:choose>
</xsl:template>

<xsl:template match="para">
  <p><xsl:apply-templates select="*|text()"/></p>
</xsl:template>

</xsl:stylesheet>
```

Let's go through the relevant parts of this example. To begin with, our `<xsl:stylesheet>` element defines the `redirect` namespace prefix and tells the XSLT engine that the prefix will be used to refer to an extension element.

```
<xsl:stylesheet version="1.0" xmlns:xsl="http://www.w3.org/1999/XSL/Transform"
  xmlns:redirect="org.apache.xalan.xslt.extensions.Redirect"
  extension-element-prefixes="redirect">
```

The syntax of everything we've done so far is according to the standard, although there's a fair amount of latitude in what the XSLT engines do with the information we've defined. For example, when defining the `redirect` namespace, Xalan uses the value here as a Java class name. In other words, Xalan attempts to load the class `org.apache.xalan.xslt.extensions.Redirect` when it encounters an extension element or function defined with this namespace. The way other XSLT processors use the namespace URI can vary.

To this point, we've simply defined our extension class so Xalan can find our code, load it, and invoke it. Our next step is to actually use it:

```
<xsl:when test="element-available('redirect:write')">
  <xsl:for-each select="/book/chapter">
    <redirect:write select="concat('chapter', position(), '.html')">
      <html>
        <head>
          <title><xsl:value-of select="title"/></title>
        </head>
        <body>
          <h1><xsl:value-of select="title"/></h1>
          <xsl:apply-templates select="para"/>
          <xsl:if test="not(position()=1)">
            <p><a href="chapter{position()-1}.html">Previous</a></p>
          </xsl:if>
          <xsl:if test="not(position()=last())">
            <p><a href="chapter{position()+1}.html">Next</a></p>
          </xsl:if>
        </body>
      </html>
```

```
    </redirect:write>
  </xsl:for-each>
</xsl:when>
```

This code does several things:

- It checks to see if our extension element is available. If it is, we'll use it; if not, the `<xsl:otherwise>` element will be evaluated instead.
- For each `<chapter>` in our XML document, it calls an extension element from our `Redirect` class. In the example here, we're calling the `<redirect:write>` element, which opens a file and directs all the output generated by Xalan into that file. Notice that the filename here is generated automatically; the filename for the first `<chapter>` is *chapter1.html*, the filename for the second is *chapter2.html*, etc. This convenient naming convention creates a unique filename for each chapter and makes it easy to figure out which filename contains the output from each chapter.
- It creates the HTML tags to define the document and its `<title>`. After creating the `<head>` section, it creates an `<h1>` for the chapter title, followed by a `<p>` generated from each `<para>` element in the XML source.
- It generates hyperlinks between the different documents. If a given document is any chapter other than the first (`not(position()=1)`), it creates a link to the previous chapter. The filename for the previous chapter is generated with the expression `chapter{position()-1}.html`. If the document is any chapter other than the last (`not(position()=last())`), it creates a link to the next chapter. The filename for the next chapter is generated with the function call `concat('chapter', position()+1, '.html')`.

  In this example, we used both the curly brace notation and the `<xsl:attribute>` element. Both work the same way; for the rest of this chapter, we'll use the curly brace notation to save space. (For more information, see the discussion of the section "Attribute Value Templates" in Chapter 3.)
- After any required hyperlinks have been generated, it writes the closing HTML tags and ends the `<redirect:write>` element. Ending the `<redirect:write>` element closes the file.

An individual output file looks like Figure 8-1.

This particular chapter contains both a `Previous` and a `Next` link. The first chapter won't have a `Previous` link, and the last chapter won't have a `Next`; other than that, all individual chapters are formatted the same way.

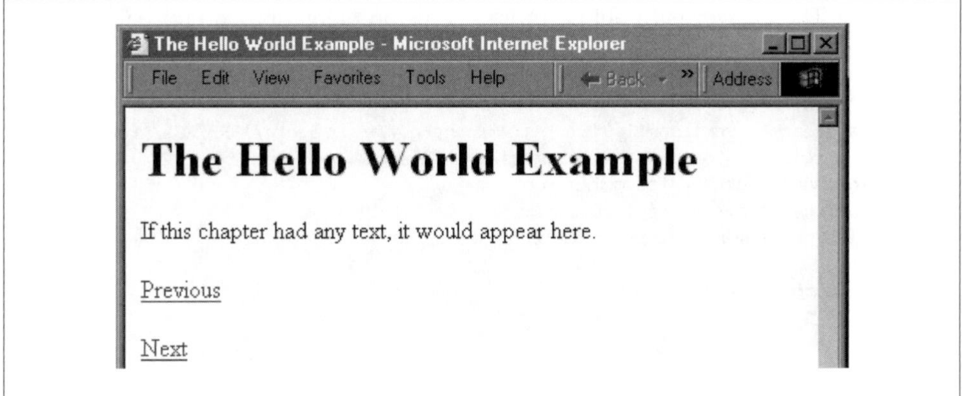

Figure 8-1. An individual output file

That code covers how we generate multiple output files when the extension element is available. When it isn't available, we simply generate a single HTML file that contains the text of all the chapters:

```
<xsl:otherwise>
  <html>
    <head>
      <title><xsl:value-of select="/book/title"/></title>
    </head>
    <xsl:for-each select="/book/chapter">
      <h1><xsl:value-of select="title"/></h1>
      <xsl:apply-templates select="para"/>
    </xsl:for-each>
  </html>
</xsl:otherwise>
```

In the `<xsl:otherwise>` element, we create a single HTML element, then process each `<chapter>` in turn. The output is a single large file; not ideal for a really large document, but an acceptable alternative when our extension element isn't available.

In this relatively simple example, we've broken a single XML document into multiple HTML files, we've generated useful filenames for all of them, and we've automatically built hyperlinks between the different HTML files. If we add, delete, or move a chapter, we can simply rerun our stylesheet and all the files and links between them will be updated. For now, we've simply discussed how to use an extension; we'll talk about how to write your own extension later in this chapter.

Example: Using extension functions from multiple processors

So far, we've used an extension function to convert a single XML document into multiple HTML files. Unfortunately, our stylesheet only works with the Xalan XSLT processor. How can we write a stylesheet that will work with multiple XSLT processors? The answer is to define more extension elements, one for each processor. Here's a stylesheet that works with Xalan, Saxon, and XT:

```
<?xml version="1.0"?>
<xsl:stylesheet version="1.0" xmlns:xsl="http://www.w3.org/1999/XSL/Transform"
  xmlns:redirect="org.apache.xalan.xslt.extensions.Redirect"
  xmlns:saxon="http://icl.com/saxon"
  xmlns:xt="http://www.jclark.com/xt"
  extension-element-prefixes="redirect saxon xt">

  <xsl:output method="html"/>

  <xsl:template match="/">
    <xsl:choose>
      <xsl:when test="contains(system-property('xsl:vendor'), 'James Clark')">
        <xsl:for-each select="/book/chapter">
          <xt:document method="xml"
            href="chapter{position()}.html">
            <html>
              <head>
                <title><xsl:value-of select="title"/></title>
              </head>
              <body>
                <h1><xsl:value-of select="title"/></h1>
                <xsl:apply-templates select="para"/>
                <xsl:if test="not(position()=1)">
                  <p><a href="chapter{position()-1}.html">Previous</a></p>
                </xsl:if>
                <xsl:if test="not(position()=last())">
                  <p><a href="chapter{position()+1}.html">Next</a></p>
                </xsl:if>
              </body>
            </html>
          </xt:document>
        </xsl:for-each>
      </xsl:when>
      <xsl:when test="contains(system-property('xsl:vendor'), 'Apache')">
        <xsl:for-each select="/book/chapter">
          <redirect:write select="concat('chapter', position(), '.html')">
            <html>
              <head>
                <title><xsl:value-of select="title"/></title>
              </head>
              <body>
                <h1><xsl:value-of select="title"/></h1>
                <xsl:apply-templates select="para"/>
                <xsl:if test="not(position()=1)">
                  <p><a href="chapter{position()-1}.html">Previous</a></p>
                </xsl:if>
                <xsl:if test="not(position()=last())">
                  <p><a href="chapter{position()+1}.html">Next</a></p>
                </xsl:if>
              </body>
            </html>
```

```
          </redirect:write>
        </xsl:for-each>
      </xsl:when>
      <xsl:when test="contains(system-property('xsl:vendor'), 'SAXON')">
        <xsl:for-each select="/book/chapter">
          <saxon:output href="chapter{position()}.html">
            <html>
              <head>
                <title><xsl:value-of select="title"/></title>
              </head>
              <body>
                <h1><xsl:value-of select="title"/></h1>
                <xsl:apply-templates select="para"/>
                <xsl:if test="not(position()=1)">
                  <p><a href="chapter{position()-1}.html">Previous</a></p>
                </xsl:if>
                <xsl:if test="not(position()=last())">
                  <p><a href="chapter{position()+1}.html">Next</a></p>
                </xsl:if>
              </body>
            </html>
          </saxon:output>
        </xsl:for-each>
      </xsl:when>
      <xsl:otherwise>
        <html>
          <head>
            <title><xsl:value-of select="/book/title"/></title>
          </head>
          <xsl:for-each select="/book/chapter">
            <h1><xsl:value-of select="title"/></h1>
            <xsl:apply-templates select="para"/>
          </xsl:for-each>
        </html>
      </xsl:otherwise>
    </xsl:choose>
  </xsl:template>

  <xsl:template match="para">
    <p><xsl:apply-templates select="*|text()"/></p>
  </xsl:template>

</xsl:stylesheet>
```

All we've done here is add more `<xsl:when>` elements, each of which tries to figure out which XSLT processor we're using. The difference here is that the XT processor doesn't implement the `element-available()` function, so we can't use it in any stylesheet that will be processed by XT. To get around this problem, we use the `system-property()` function to get the `vendor` property. If the vendor contains the string "James Clark," we know that we're using XT. We test the other processors similarly. If we find that we're using an XSLT processor we recognize, we use its extension functions to split the output into multiple HTML files; otherwise, we write all the output to a single file. Obviously, maintenance of this stylesheet is more involved, but it does give us the freedom to switch XSLT processors. (The other downside is that we depend on the value of the `vendor` system property; if the next release of Saxon identifies the vendor as `Saxon` instead of `SAXON`, our stylesheet won't work properly.)

Extension Functions

As you might guess, an extension function is defined in a piece of code external to the XSLT processor. You can pass values to the function, and the function can return a result. That result can be any of the datatypes supported by XPath. In addition, various XSLT processors are free to allow extension functions to return other datatypes, although those other datatypes must be handled by some other function that does return one of XPath's datatypes.

Example: A library of trigonometric functions

As we outlined the functions and operators available in XPath and XSLT, you probably noticed that the mathematical functions at your disposal are rather limited. In this example, we'll write an extension that provides a variety of trignometric functions.

Our scenario here is that we want to generate a Scalable Vector Graphics (SVG) pie chart from an XML document. Our XML document contains the sales figures for various regions of a company; we need to calculate the dimensions of the various slices of the pie graph for our SVG document. Here's the XML source we'll be working with:

```
<?xml version="1.0" ?>
<sales>
  <caption>
    <heading>3Q 2001 Sales Figures</heading>
    <subheading>($ millions)</subheading>
  </caption>
  <region>
    <name>Southeast</name>
    <product name="Heron">38.3</product>
    <product name="Kingfisher">12.7</product>
    <product name="Pelican">6.1</product>
    <product name="Sandpiper">29.9</product>
    <product name="Crane">57.2</product>
  </region>
  <region>
    <name>Northeast</name>
    <product name="Heron">49.7</product>
    <product name="Kingfisher">2.8</product>
    <product name="Pelican">4.8</product>
    <product name="Sandpiper">31.5</product>
```

```
    <product name="Crane">60.0</product>
  </region>
  <region>
    <name>Southwest</name>
    <product name="Heron">31.1</product>
    <product name="Kingfisher">9.8</product>
    <product name="Pelican">8.7</product>
    <product name="Sandpiper">34.3</product>
    <product name="Crane">50.4</product>
  </region>
  <region>
    <name>Midwest</name>
    <product name="Heron">44.5</product>
    <product name="Kingfisher">9.3</product>
    <product name="Pelican">5.7</product>
    <product name="Sandpiper">28.8</product>
    <product name="Crane">54.6</product>
  </region>
  <region>
    <name>Northwest</name>
    <product name="Heron">36.6</product>
    <product name="Kingfisher">5.4</product>
    <product name="Pelican">9.1</product>
    <product name="Sandpiper">39.1</product>
    <product name="Crane">58.2</product>
  </region>
</sales>
```

Our goal is to create an SVG file that looks like that in Figure 8-2.

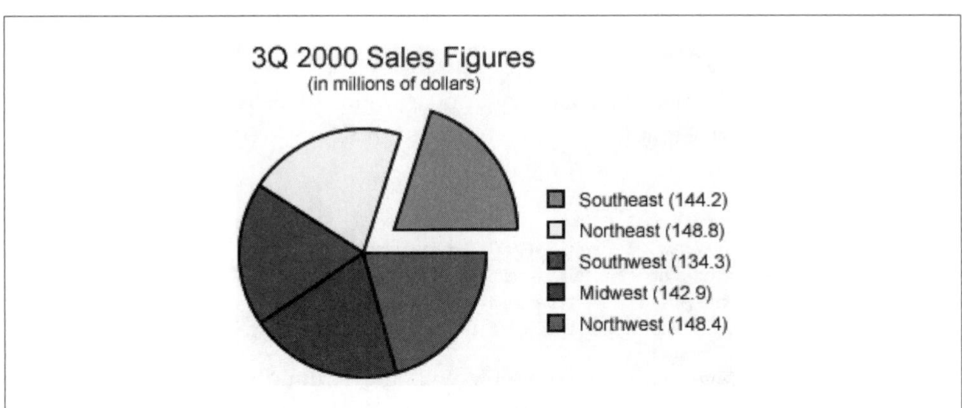

Figure 8-2. Target SVG file format

To make things really interesting, we'll generate an HTML page that embeds the SVG file. We'll use the `Redirect` extension we used earlier to generate an HTML file and an SVG file in a single transformation. If we view the HTML page in a web browser, we can use Adobe's SVG plug-in to make the graphic interactive. If we move the mouse over a given slice of the pie, the legend will change to show the sales details for that region of the company. Thus, we'll also have to create all the different legends and generate the JavaScript code to make the various SVG elements visible or hidden in response to mouse events. Figure 8-3 shows how the graphic looks if we move the mouse over the pie slice for the Southwest region.

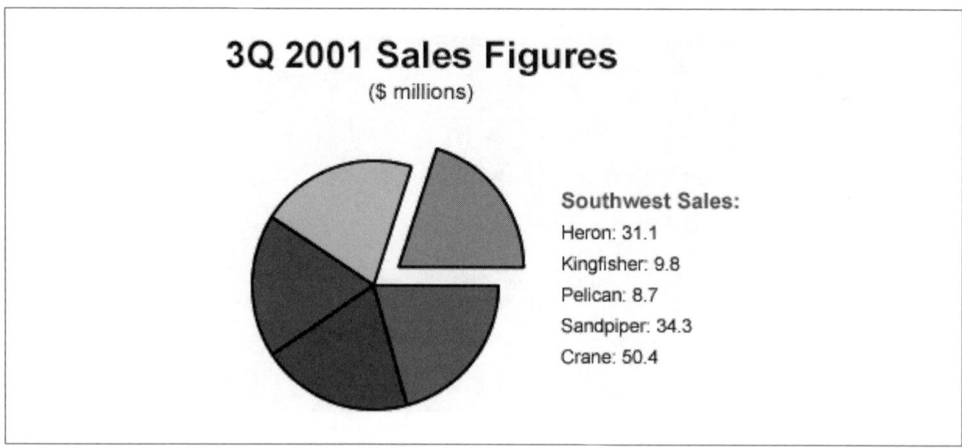

Figure 8-3. SVG chart changes in response to mouse events

XPath's limited math functions won't allow us to calculate the dimensions of the various arcs that make up the pie chart, so we'll use extension functions to solve this problem. Fortunately for us, Java provides all the basic trigonometric functions we need in the `java.lang.Math` class. Even better, Xalan makes it easy for us to load this class and execute its methods (such as `sin()`, `cos()`, and `toRadians()`).

We'll go over the relevant details as they appear in the stylesheet. First, we have to declare our namespace prefixes, just as we did when we used an extension element:

```
<xsl:stylesheet version="1.0"
  xmlns:xsl="http://www.w3.org/1999/XSL/Transform"
  xmlns:redirect="org.apache.xalan.xslt.extensions.Redirect"
  extension-element-prefixes="java redirect"
  xmlns:java="http://xml.apache.org/xslt/java">
```

We associated the `java` namespace prefix with the string "http://xml.apache.org/xslt/java"; Xalan uses this string to support extension functions and elements written in Java. Before we use the extension functions to generate the SVG file, we'll take care of the HTML. First, we generate the <head> section of the HTML document, including the JavaScript code we need to make the pie chart interactive:

```
<xsl:template match="sales">
  <html>
    <head>
      <title>
```

```
          <xsl:value-of select="caption/heading"/>
        </title>
        <script language="JavaScript1.2">
          <xsl:comment>
            <xsl:call-template name="js"/>
            <xsl:text>// </xsl:text></xsl:comment>
        </script>
      </head>
      <body>
        <center>
          <embed name="pie" width="650" height="500" src="saleschart.svg"/>
        </center>
      </body>
    </html>
```

The HTML file we create generates an HTML <title> element from the XML document, calls the named template that generates the JavaScript code, then embeds the SVG file that we'll generate in a minute. The template we use to generate the JavaScript code is worth a closer look. Here's the code:

```
<xsl:template name="js">
  <xsl:text>
      function suppress_errors ()
      {
        return true;
      }

      function does_element_exist (svg_name, element_name)
      {
        // First, redirect the error handler so that if the SVG plug-in has
        // not yet loaded or is not present, it doesn't cause the browser to
        // issue a JavaScript error.
        var old_error = window.onerror;
        window.onerror = suppress_errors;

        // Now attempt to get the SVG object.
        var svgobj = document.embeds[svg_name].
            getSVGDocument().getElementById(element_name);

        // Reset the error handler to the browser's default handler.
        window.onerror = old_error;

        // Return appropriate value.
        if (svgobj == null)
          return false;
        else
          return true;
      }

      function mouse_over (target_id)
      {
        var svgdoc = document.pie.getSVGDocument();
        var svgobj;
        var svgstyle;
```

```
        var detail_name = 'details' + target_id;
        svgobj = svgdoc.getElementById(detail_name);
        if (svgobj != null)
        {
          svgstyle = svgobj.getStyle();
          svgstyle.setProperty ('visibility', 'visible');
        }
</xsl:text>
<xsl:for-each select="/sales/region">
  <xsl:text>svgobj = svgdoc.getElementById('legend</xsl:text>
  <xsl:value-of select="position()"/><xsl:text>');</xsl:text>
  <xsl:text>
        if (svgobj != null)
        {
          svgstyle = svgobj.getStyle();
          svgstyle.setProperty ('visibility', 'hidden');
        }
  </xsl:text>
</xsl:for-each>
<xsl:text>
        // Propagate the event to other handlers.
        return true;
      }

      function mouse_out ()
      {
        var svgdoc = document.pie.getSVGDocument();
        var svgobj;
        var svgstyle;

</xsl:text>
<xsl:for-each select="/sales/region">
  <xsl:text>svgobj = svgdoc.getElementById('legend</xsl:text>
  <xsl:value-of select="position()"/><xsl:text>');</xsl:text>
  <xsl:text>
        if (svgobj != null)
        {
          svgstyle = svgobj.getStyle();
          svgstyle.setProperty ('visibility', 'visible');
        }
  </xsl:text>
  <xsl:text>svgobj = svgdoc.getElementById('details</xsl:text>
  <xsl:value-of select="position()"/><xsl:text>');</xsl:text>
  <xsl:text>
        if (svgobj != null)
        {
          svgstyle = svgobj.getStyle();
          svgstyle.setProperty ('visibility', 'hidden');
        }
  </xsl:text>
</xsl:for-each>
<xsl:text>
```

```
          // Propagate the event to other handlers.
            return true;
        }
      </xsl:text>
    </xsl:template>
```

We begin with the functions (`suppress_errors()` and `does_element_exist()`) that we'll need for error checking and handling. The `mouse_over()` function is more complicated. When the user moves the mouse over a particular section of the pie, we need to make some SVG elements visible and others invisible. We'll use a naming convention here; for each <region> in our original document, we'll generate a legend entry and a set of details. Originally, the legend is visible and all details are hidden. When our `mouse_over()` function is called, it makes all the legend elements hidden and makes the appropriate details element visible. Here's how the generated code looks:

```
function mouse_over (target_id)
{
  var svgdoc = document.pie.getSVGDocument();
  var svgobj;
  var svgstyle;

  var detail_name = 'details' + target_id;
  svgobj = svgdoc.getElementById(detail_name);
  if (svgobj != null)
  {
  svgstyle = svgobj.getStyle();
  svgstyle.setProperty ('visibility', 'visible');
  }
  svgobj = svgdoc.getElementById('legend1');
  if (svgobj != null)
  {
    svgstyle = svgobj.getStyle();
    svgstyle.setProperty ('visibility', 'hidden');
  }

  ...

  // Propagate the event to other handlers.
  return true;
}
```

The section that begins `svgdoc.getElementById('legend1')` repeats for each <region> in the XML source document. The repeated code ensures that all legend elements are hidden. This code handles the mouse over event; our final task is to handle the mouse out event. The generated `mouse_out()` function looks like:

```
function mouse_out ()
{
  var svgdoc = document.pie.getSVGDocument();
  var svgobj;
```

```
    var svgstyle;

    svgobj = svgdoc.getElementById('legend1');
    if (svgobj != null)
    {
      svgstyle = svgobj.getStyle();
      svgstyle.setProperty ('visibility', 'visible');
    }
    svgobj = svgdoc.getElementById('details1');
    if (svgobj != null)
    {
      svgstyle = svgobj.getStyle();
      svgstyle.setProperty ('visibility', 'hidden');
    }

    ...

    // Propagate the event to other handlers.
      return true;
  }
```

The `mouse_out()` function makes sure that all legend elements are visible and that all details elements are hidden. Although these two functions are relatively simple, they work together to make our pie chart interactive and dynamic.

One final note about our generated JavaScript code; notice how we invoked the named template inside an `<xsl:comment>` element:

```
<script language="JavaScript1.2">
  <xsl:comment>
    <xsl:call-template name="js"/>
    <xsl:text>// </xsl:text></xsl:comment>
</script>
```

Scripting code is typically written inside a comment in an HTML file, allowing browsers that don't support scripting to safely ignore the code. The end of the generated JavaScript code looks like this:

```
  // Propagate the event to other handlers.
    return true;
}
    // --></script>
```

We used an `<xsl:text>` element to draw the double slash at the end of the script. The double slash is a JavaScript comment, which tells the JavaScript processor to ignore the `-->` at the end of the script. Without this slash, some JavaScript processors attempt to process the end of the comment and issue an error message. Keep this in mind when you're generating JavaScript code with your stylesheets; if you don't, you'll have trouble tracking down the occasional errors that occur in some browsers.

Now that we've built the HTML file, here's how we draw each wedge of the pie:

1. Calculate the total sales for the entire company and store it in a variable. Calculating total sales is relatively expensive because the XSLT processor has to navigate the entire tree. We'll need to use this value many times, so we calculate it once and store it away. Here's the calculation for total sales:

   ```
   <xsl:variable name="totalSales" select="sum(//product)"/>
   ```

2. For each slice of the pie, we calculate certain values and pass them as parameters to the `region` template. First, we determine the color of the slice and the total sales for this particular region of the company. We use the `position()` function and the `mod` operator to calculate the color, and we use the `sum()` function to calculate the sales for this region of the company.

3. If this is the first slice of the pie, we'll explode it. That means that the first slice will be offset from the rest of the pie. We will set the variable `$explode` as follows:

   ```
   <xsl:variable name="explode" select="position()=1"/>
   ```

4. The last value we calculate is the total sales of all previous regions. When we draw each slice of the pie, we rotate the coordinate axis a certain number of degrees. The amount of the rotation depends on how much of the total sales have been drawn so far. In other words, if we've drawn exactly 50 percent of the total sales so far, we'll rotate the axis 180 degrees (50 percent of 360). Rotating the axis simplifies the trigonometry we have to do. To calculate the total sales we've drawn so far, we use the `preceding-sibling` axis:

   ```
   <xsl:with-param name="runningTotal"
     select="sum(preceding-sibling::region/product)"/>
   ```

5. Inside the template itself, our first step is to calculate the angle in radians of the current slice of the pie. This is the first time we use one of our extension functions:

   ```
   <xsl:variable name="currentAngle"
     select="java:java.lang.Math.toRadians(($regionSales div
                                               $totalSales) * 360.0)"/>
   ```

   We store this value in the variable `currentAngle`; we'll use this value later with the `sin()` and `cos()` functions.

6. Now we're finally ready to draw the pie slice. We'll do this with an SVG `<path>` element. Here's what one looks like; we'll discuss what the attributes mean in a minute:

   ```
   <path onclick="return false;" onmouseout="mouse_out();" style="fill:orange;
   stroke:black; stroke-width:2; fillrule:evenodd; stroke-linejoin:bevel;"
   transform="translate(100,160)  rotate(-72.24046757584189)"
   ```

```
onmouseover="return mouse_over(2);"
d="M 80 0 A 80 80 0 0 0 21.318586104178774 -77.10718440274366 L 0 0 Z ">
</path>
```

The following stylesheet fragment generated this intimidating element:

```
<path style="fill:{$color}; stroke:black; stroke-width:2;
  fillrule:evenodd; stroke-linejoin:bevel;"
  onmouseout="mouse_out();" onclick="return false;">
  <xsl:attribute name="transform">
    <xsl:choose>
      <xsl:when test="$explode">
        <xsl:text>translate(</xsl:text>
        <xsl:value-of
          select="(java:java.lang.Math.cos($currentAngle div 2) * 20) +
                  100"/>
        <xsl:text>,</xsl:text>
        <xsl:value-of
          select="(java:java.lang.Math.sin($currentAngle div 2) * -20) +
                  160"/>
          <xsl:text>) </xsl:text>
      </xsl:when>
      <xsl:otherwise>
        <xsl:text>translate(100,160) </xsl:text>
      </xsl:otherwise>
    </xsl:choose>
    <xsl:text> rotate(</xsl:text>
    <xsl:value-of
      select="-1 * (($runningTotal div $totalSales) * 360.0)"/>
    <xsl:text>)</xsl:text>
  </xsl:attribute>
  <xsl:attribute name="onmouseover">
    <xsl:text>return mouse_over(</xsl:text>
    <xsl:value-of select="$position"/><xsl:text>);</xsl:text>
  </xsl:attribute>
  <xsl:attribute name="d">
    <xsl:text>M 80 0 A 80 80 0 </xsl:text>
    <xsl:choose>
      <xsl:when test="$currentAngle > 3.14">
        <xsl:text>1 </xsl:text>
      </xsl:when>
      <xsl:otherwise>
        <xsl:text>0 </xsl:text>
      </xsl:otherwise>
    </xsl:choose>
    <xsl:text>0 </xsl:text>
    <xsl:value-of
      select="java:java.lang.Math.cos($currentAngle) * 80"/>
    <xsl:text> </xsl:text>
    <xsl:value-of
      select="java:java.lang.Math.sin($currentAngle) * -80"/>
    <xsl:text> L 0 0 Z </xsl:text>
  </xsl:attribute>
</path>
```

The `style` attribute defines various properties of the path, including the color in which the path should be drawn, with which the path should be filled, etc. With the exception of the color, everything in the `style` attribute is the same for all slices of the pie. The `transform` attribute does two things: it moves the center of the coordinate space to a particular point, then it rotates the axes some number of degrees. The center of the coordinate space is moved to a slightly different location if the `$explode` variable is true. The extent to which the axes are rotated depends on the percentage of total sales represented by the previous regions of the company. Moving the center of the coordinate space and rotating the axes simplifies the math we have to do later.

That brings us to the gloriously cryptic `d` attribute. This attribute contains a number of drawing commands; in our previous example, we move the current point to `(80,0)` (`M` stands for move), then we draw an elliptical arc (`A` stands for arc) with various properties. Finally, we draw a line (`L` stands for line) from the current point (the end of our arc) to the origin, then we use the `Z` command, which closes the path by drawing a line from wherever we are to wherever we started.

If you really must know what the properties of the `A` command are, they are the two radii of the ellipse, the degrees by which the x-axis should be rotated, two parameters called the large-arc-flag and the sweep-flag that determine how the arc is drawn, and the x- and y-coordinates of the end of the arc. In our example here, the two radii of the ellipse are the same (we want the pie to be round, not elliptical). Next is the x-axis rotation, which is `0`. After that is the large-arc-flag, which is `1` if this particular slice of the pie is greater than 180 degrees, `0` otherwise. The sweep-flag is `0`, and the last two parameters, the x- and y-coordinates of the end point, are calculated. See the SVG specification for more details on the `path` and `shape` elements.

7. Our next task is to draw all of the legends. We'll draw one legend to identify each slice of the pie; after that, we'll create a separate legend for each slice of the pie. Initially, all of the separate legends will be invisible (`<g style="visibility:hidden">`, in SVG parlance), and the basic legend for the pie will be visible. As we mouse over the various slices of the pie, different legends will become visible or invisible. First, we'll draw the basic legend, using the `mode` attribute of the `<apply-templates>` element:

```
<xsl:apply-templates select="." mode="legend">
  <xsl:with-param name="color" select="$color"/>
  <xsl:with-param name="regionSales" select="$regionSales"/>
  <xsl:with-param name="y-legend-offset"
    select="90 + (position() * 20)"/>
  <xsl:with-param name="position" select="position()"/>
</xsl:apply-templates>
```

When we apply our template, we pass in several parameters, including the color of the box in the legend entry and the y-coordinate offset where the legend entry should be drawn. We call this template once for each <region> element, ensuring that our legend identifies each slice of the pie, regardless of how many slices there are. For each slice, we draw a box filled with the appropriate color, with the name of the region next to it.

8. Our final task is to draw the details for this region of the company. We'll draw the name of the region in the same color we used for the pie slice, then list all sales figures for the region. Here's what the template looks like:

```
<xsl:template match="region" mode="details">
  <xsl:param name="color" select="black"/>
  <xsl:param name="position" select="'0'"/>
  <xsl:param name="y-legend-offset"/>

  <g style="visibility:hidden">
    <xsl:attribute name="id">
      <xsl:text>details</xsl:text><xsl:value-of select="$position"/>
    </xsl:attribute>
    <text style="font-size:14; font-weight:bold;
      text-anchor:start; fill: {$color}" x="220">
      <xsl:attribute name="y">
        <xsl:value-of select="$y-legend-offset"/>
      </xsl:attribute>
      <xsl:value-of select="name"/><xsl:text> Sales:</xsl:text>
    </text>
    <xsl:for-each select="product">
      <text style="font-size:12; text-anchor:start" x="220">
        <xsl:attribute name="y">
          <xsl:value-of select="$y-legend-offset + (position() * 20)"/>
        </xsl:attribute>
        <xsl:value-of select="@name"/>
        <xsl:text>: </xsl:text><xsl:value-of select="."/>
      </text>
    </xsl:for-each>
  </g>
</xsl:template>
```

Notice that we draw this item to be invisible (`style="visibility:hidden"`); we'll use our JavaScript effects to make the various legends and details visible or hidden. In our stylesheet, we draw the title of the current region using the same color we used for the slice of the pie, followed by the sales figures for each product sold in this region.

Here's the complete stylesheet:

```
<?xml version="1.0" encoding="ISO-8859-1"?>
<xsl:stylesheet version="1.0"
  xmlns:xsl="http://www.w3.org/1999/XSL/Transform"
  xmlns:redirect="org.apache.xalan.xslt.extensions.Redirect"
  extension-element-prefixes="java redirect"
```

```
xmlns:java="http://xml.apache.org/xslt/java">

<xsl:output method="html"/>

<xsl:strip-space elements="*"/>

<xsl:template name="js">
  <xsl:text>
      function suppress_errors ()
      {
        return true;
      }

      function does_element_exist (svg_name, element_name)
      {
        // First, redirect the error handler so that if the SVG plug-in has
        // not yet loaded or is not present, it doesn't cause the browser to
        // issue a JavaScript error.
        var old_error = window.onerror;
        window.onerror = suppress_errors;

        // Now attempt to get the SVG object.
        var svgobj = document.embeds[svg_name].
            getSVGDocument().getElementById(element_name);

        // Reset the error handler to the browser's default handler.
        window.onerror = old_error;

        // Return appropriate value.
        if (svgobj == null)
          return false;
        else
          return true;
      }

      function mouse_over (target_id)
      {
        var svgdoc = document.pie.getSVGDocument();
        var svgobj;
        var svgstyle;

        var detail_name = 'details' + target_id;
        svgobj = svgdoc.getElementById(detail_name);
        if (svgobj != null)
        {
          svgstyle = svgobj.getStyle();
          svgstyle.setProperty ('visibility', 'visible');
        }
    </xsl:text>
    <xsl:for-each select="/sales/region">
      <xsl:text>svgobj = svgdoc.getElementById('legend</xsl:text>
      <xsl:value-of select="position()"/><xsl:text>');</xsl:text>
      <xsl:text>
        if (svgobj != null)
```

```
          {
            svgstyle = svgobj.getStyle();
            svgstyle.setProperty ('visibility', 'hidden');
          }
      </xsl:text>
    </xsl:for-each>
    <xsl:text>
          // Propagate the event to other handlers.
          return true;
        }

        function mouse_out ()
        {
          var svgdoc = document.pie.getSVGDocument();
          var svgobj;
          var svgstyle;

    </xsl:text>
    <xsl:for-each select="/sales/region">
      <xsl:text>svgobj = svgdoc.getElementById('legend</xsl:text>
      <xsl:value-of select="position()"/><xsl:text>');</xsl:text>
      <xsl:text>
          if (svgobj != null)
          {
            svgstyle = svgobj.getStyle();
            svgstyle.setProperty ('visibility', 'visible');
          }
      </xsl:text>
      <xsl:text>svgobj = svgdoc.getElementById('details</xsl:text>
      <xsl:value-of select="position()"/><xsl:text>');</xsl:text>
      <xsl:text>
          if (svgobj != null)
          {
            svgstyle = svgobj.getStyle();
            svgstyle.setProperty ('visibility', 'hidden');
          }
      </xsl:text>
    </xsl:for-each>
    <xsl:text>
          // Propagate the event to other handlers.
            return true;
        }
    </xsl:text>
  </xsl:template>

  <xsl:template match="/">
    <xsl:apply-templates select="sales"/>
  </xsl:template>

  <xsl:template match="sales">
    <html>
      <head>
        <title>
          <xsl:value-of select="caption/heading"/>
```

```
        </title>
        <script language="JavaScript1.2">
          <xsl:comment>
            <xsl:call-template name="js"/>
            <xsl:text>// </xsl:text></xsl:comment>
        </script>
      </head>
      <body>
        <center>
          <embed name="pie" width="650" height="500" src="saleschart.svg"/>
        </center>
      </body>
    </html>
    <redirect:write select="concat('sales', 'chart', '.svg')">
      <svg width="450" height="300">
        <text style="font-size:24; text-anchor:middle;
          font-weight:bold" x="130" y="20">
          <xsl:value-of select="caption/heading"/>
        </text>
        <text style="font-size:14; text-anchor:middle" y="40" x="130">
          <xsl:value-of select="caption/subheading"/>
        </text>

        <xsl:variable name="totalSales" select="sum(//product)"/>

        <xsl:for-each select="region">
          <xsl:variable name="regionSales" select="sum(product)"/>
          <xsl:variable name="color">
            <xsl:choose>
              <xsl:when test="(position() mod 6) = 1">
                <xsl:text>red</xsl:text>
              </xsl:when>
              <xsl:when test="(position() mod 6) = 2">
                <xsl:text>orange</xsl:text>
              </xsl:when>
              <xsl:when test="(position() mod 6) = 3">
                <xsl:text>purple</xsl:text>
              </xsl:when>
              <xsl:when test="(position() mod 6) = 4">
                <xsl:text>blue</xsl:text>
              </xsl:when>
              <xsl:when test="(position() mod 6) = 5">
                <xsl:text>green</xsl:text>
              </xsl:when>
              <xsl:otherwise>
                <xsl:text>orange</xsl:text>
              </xsl:otherwise>
            </xsl:choose>
          </xsl:variable>
          <xsl:variable name="explode" select="position()=1"/>

          <xsl:apply-templates select=".">
            <xsl:with-param name="color" select="$color"/>
            <xsl:with-param name="regionSales" select="$regionSales"/>
```

```
          <xsl:with-param name="totalSales" select="$totalSales"/>
          <xsl:with-param name="runningTotal"
            select="sum(preceding-sibling::region/product)"/>
          <xsl:with-param name="explode" select="$explode"/>
          <xsl:with-param name="position" select="position()"/>
        </xsl:apply-templates>

        <xsl:apply-templates select="." mode="legend">
          <xsl:with-param name="color" select="$color"/>
          <xsl:with-param name="regionSales" select="$regionSales"/>
          <xsl:with-param name="y-legend-offset"
            select="90 + (position() * 20)"/>
          <xsl:with-param name="position" select="position()"/>
        </xsl:apply-templates>

        <xsl:apply-templates select="." mode="details">
          <xsl:with-param name="color" select="$color"/>
          <xsl:with-param name="position" select="position()"/>
          <xsl:with-param name="y-legend-offset" select="110"/>
        </xsl:apply-templates>

      </xsl:for-each>
    </svg>
  </redirect:write>
</xsl:template>

<xsl:template match="region">
  <xsl:param name="color" select="'red'"/>
  <xsl:param name="runningTotal" select="'0'"/>
  <xsl:param name="totalSales" select="'0'"/>
  <xsl:param name="regionSales" select="'0'"/>
  <xsl:param name="explode"/>
  <xsl:param name="position" select="'1'"/>

  <xsl:variable name="currentAngle"
    select="java:java.lang.Math.toRadians(($regionSales div
                                       $totalSales) * 360.0)"/>

  <path style="fill:{$color}; stroke:black; stroke-width:2;
    fillrule:evenodd; stroke-linejoin:bevel;"
    onmouseout="mouse_out();" onclick="return false;">
    <xsl:attribute name="transform">
      <xsl:choose>
        <xsl:when test="$explode">
          <xsl:text>translate(</xsl:text>
          <xsl:value-of
            select="(java:java.lang.Math.cos($currentAngle div 2) * 20) +
                    100"/>
          <xsl:text>,</xsl:text>
          <xsl:value-of
            select="(java:java.lang.Math.sin($currentAngle div 2) * -20) +
                    160"/>
            <xsl:text>) </xsl:text>
        </xsl:when>
```

```
          <xsl:otherwise>
            <xsl:text>translate(100,160) </xsl:text>
          </xsl:otherwise>
        </xsl:choose>
        <xsl:text> rotate(</xsl:text>
        <xsl:value-of select="-1 * (($runningTotal div $totalSales) * 360.0)"/>
        <xsl:text>)</xsl:text>
      </xsl:attribute>
      <xsl:attribute name="onmouseover">
        <xsl:text>return mouse_over(</xsl:text>
        <xsl:value-of select="$position"/><xsl:text>);</xsl:text>
      </xsl:attribute>
      <xsl:attribute name="d">
        <xsl:text>M 80 0 A 80 80 0 </xsl:text>
        <xsl:choose>
          <xsl:when test="$currentAngle > 3.14">
            <xsl:text>1 </xsl:text>
          </xsl:when>
          <xsl:otherwise>
            <xsl:text>0 </xsl:text>
          </xsl:otherwise>
        </xsl:choose>
        <xsl:text>0 </xsl:text>
        <xsl:value-of select="java:java.lang.Math.cos($currentAngle) * 80"/>
        <xsl:text> </xsl:text>
        <xsl:value-of select="java:java.lang.Math.sin($currentAngle) * -80"/>
        <xsl:text> L 0 0 Z </xsl:text>
      </xsl:attribute>
    </path>
  </xsl:template>

  <xsl:template match="region" mode="legend">
    <xsl:param name="color" select="'red'"/>
    <xsl:param name="regionSales" select="'0'"/>
    <xsl:param name="y-legend-offset" select="'0'"/>
    <xsl:param name="position" select="'1'"/>

    <g>
      <xsl:attribute name="id">
        <xsl:text>legend</xsl:text><xsl:value-of select="$position"/>
      </xsl:attribute>

      <text>
        <xsl:attribute name="style">
          <xsl:text>font-size:12; text-anchor:start</xsl:text>
        </xsl:attribute>
        <xsl:attribute name="x">
          <xsl:text>240</xsl:text>
        </xsl:attribute>
        <xsl:attribute name="y">
          <xsl:value-of select="$y-legend-offset"/>
        </xsl:attribute>
        <xsl:value-of select="name"/>
        <xsl:text> (</xsl:text>
```

```
          <xsl:value-of select="$regionSales"/>
          <xsl:text>) </xsl:text>
        </text>

        <path>
          <xsl:attribute name="style">
            <xsl:text>stroke:black; stroke-width:2; fill:</xsl:text>
            <xsl:value-of select="$color"/>
          </xsl:attribute>
          <xsl:attribute name="d">
            <xsl:text>M 220 </xsl:text>
            <xsl:value-of select="$y-legend-offset - 10"/>
            <xsl:text> L 220 </xsl:text>
            <xsl:value-of select="$y-legend-offset"/>
            <xsl:text> L 230 </xsl:text>
            <xsl:value-of select="$y-legend-offset"/>
            <xsl:text> L 230 </xsl:text>
            <xsl:value-of select="$y-legend-offset - 10"/>
            <xsl:text> Z</xsl:text>
          </xsl:attribute>
        </path>
      </g>
    </xsl:template>

    <xsl:template match="region" mode="details">
      <xsl:param name="color" select="black"/>
      <xsl:param name="position" select="'0'"/>
      <xsl:param name="y-legend-offset"/>

      <g style="visibility:hidden">
        <xsl:attribute name="id">
          <xsl:text>details</xsl:text><xsl:value-of select="$position"/>
        </xsl:attribute>
        <text style="font-size:14; font-weight:bold;
          text-anchor:start; fill: {$color}" x="220">
          <xsl:attribute name="y">
            <xsl:value-of select="$y-legend-offset"/>
          </xsl:attribute>
          <xsl:value-of select="name"/><xsl:text> Sales:</xsl:text>
        </text>
        <xsl:for-each select="product">
          <text style="font-size:12; text-anchor:start" x="220">
            <xsl:attribute name="y">
              <xsl:value-of select="$y-legend-offset + (position() * 20)"/>
            </xsl:attribute>
            <xsl:value-of select="@name"/>
            <xsl:text>: </xsl:text><xsl:value-of select="."/>
          </text>
        </xsl:for-each>
      </g>
    </xsl:template>

  </xsl:stylesheet>
```

In this example, we've used XSLT extension functions to add new capabilities to the XSLT processor. We needed a couple of simple trigonometric functions, and Xalan's ability to use existing Java classes made adding new capabilities simple. You can use this technique to invoke methods of Java classes anywhere you need them. Best of all, we didn't have to write any Java code to make this happen.

Example: Writing extensions in other languages

One of the nice features of Xalan's extension mechanism is that it uses the Bean Scripting Framework (BSF), an open source library from IBM that allows you to execute code written in a variety of scripting languages. We'll take the HTML/SVG stylesheet we just discussed and implement it again, writing the extension functions in Jython.

Other languages supported by the Bean Scripting Framework include NetRexx, PerlScript, Jacl, Tcl, VBScript, and pnuts. If you're using a Microsoft platform, BSF also supports Windows Script Technologies, so you may have even more choices if you're running some flavor of Windows.

As you would expect, we must do several things to identify our extension code to Xalan. We'll cover them, and then look at the source of the various extension functions. First we need to define the namespace prefixes we'll use:

```
<xsl:stylesheet version="1.0" xmlns:xsl="http://www.w3.org/1999/XSL/Transform"
  xmlns:jython-extension="http://www.jython.org/"
  xmlns:redirect="org.apache.xalan.xslt.extensions.Redirect"
  extension-element-prefixes="redirect"
  xmlns:lxslt="http://xml.apache.org/xslt"
  exclude-result-prefixes="lxslt">
```

We still need the `Redirect` class, so that prefix is still with us. The other two prefixes are `jython-extension`, associated with the URL of the Jython home page (though the value could be anything), and `lxslt`. Xalan uses this prefix to implement scripting languages. Our next step is to actually write the Jython code. With Xalan, this code goes inside an `<lxslt:component>` element:

```
  <lxslt:component prefix="jython-extension" functions="cos sin toRadians">
    <lxslt:script lang="jpython">
import math

def cos(d):
  return math.cos(d)

def sin(d):
  return math.sin(d)
```

```
def toRadians(d):
  return d / 180 * math.pi
    </lxslt:script>
  </lxslt:component>
```

The `prefix` attribute associates this `<lxslt:component>` with the `jython-extension` prefix, and the `functions` attribute lists all of the functions supported by this script. The `<lxslt:script lang="jpython">` tells Xalan to use the Jython interpreter (the current version of BSF requires us to use `lang="jpython"`, the language's former name) whenever these functions are invoked. Now that we've set everything up, all we have to do is invoke the extension functions:

```
<xsl:variable name="currentAngle"
  select="jython-extension:toRadians(($regionSales div
                                    $totalSales) * 360.0)"/>
```

Other than the `jython-extension` extension before the function call, the rest of our stylesheet is exactly the same. Notice that the Python `math` library does not define a `toRadians` function, so we had to define that function ourselves. The other two functions are part of the library, so all we had to do was invoke them.

One final point: when we invoke these extension functions written in other languages, the Java `CLASSPATH` must be set up correctly. If the class libraries for Jython or Javascript or whatever scripting language you're using can't be found, the extension functions will fail. Our example here uses *jython.jar*, available at *http://www.jython.org*.

We promised we'd look at extensions in JavaScript, as well. Here's how the `<lxslt:component>` element looks when we write the extension functions in JavaScript:

```
<lxslt:component prefix="javascript-extension" functions="cos sin toRadians">
  <lxslt:script lang="javascript">
    function cos(d)
    {
      return Math.cos(d);
    }

    function sin(d)
    {
      return Math.sin(d);
    }

    function toRadians(d)
    {
      return d * Math.PI / 180;
    }
  </lxslt:script>
</lxslt:component>
```

Here is the `<lxslt:component>` element with the extension functions written in Jacl:

```
<lxslt:component prefix="jacl-extension"
 functions="cosine sine toRadians">
 <lxslt:script lang="jacl">
  proc cosine {d} {expr cos($d)}
  proc sine {d} {expr sin($d)}
  proc toRadians {d} {expr $d * 3.14159265358979323846264338327950 / 180.0}
 </lxslt:script>
</lxslt:component>
```

Again, most of our task is to use existing features of the language. In the JavaScript and Jacl code, the `cos()` and `sin()` functions are part of the language, and we wrote our own versions of the `toRadians()` function. Jacl doesn't define a constant for `pi`, so we hardcoded the first 32 digits into the Jacl version of `toRadians()`.

Fallback Processing

If the code that implements a given extension element can't be found, we need some relatively graceful way for the stylesheet to handle the situation. XSLT defines the `<xsl:fallback>` element to handle this case. In an earlier stylesheet, we used the `element-available()` function to determine whether a given function is available. In this case, we'll use the `<xsl:fallback>` to transform our document if the `Redirect` extension can't be found:

```
<?xml version="1.0"?>
<xsl:stylesheet version="1.0" xmlns:xsl="http://www.w3.org/1999/XSL/Transform"
  xmlns:redirect="org.apache.xalan.xslt.extensions.Redirect"
  extension-element-prefixes="redirect">

  <xsl:output method="html"/>

  <xsl:template match="/">
    <xsl:for-each select="/book/chapter">
      <redirect:write
        select="concat('chapter', position(), '.html')">
        <html>
          <head>
            <title><xsl:value-of select="title"/></title>
          </head>
          <body>
            <h1><xsl:value-of select="title"/></h1>
            <xsl:apply-templates select="para"/>
            <xsl:if test="not(position()=1)">
              <p><a href="chapter{position()-1}.html">Previous</a></p>
            </xsl:if>
            <xsl:if test="not(position()=last())">
              <p>
                <a>
                  <xsl:attribute name="href">
```

```
                    <xsl:value-of
                      select="concat('chapter', position()+1, '.html')"/>
                  </xsl:attribute>
                  Next
                </a>
              </p>
            </xsl:if>
          </body>
        </html>
        <xsl:fallback>
          <xsl:if test="position()=1">
            <html>
              <head>
                <title><xsl:value-of select="/book/title"/></title>
              </head>
              <body>
                <xsl:for-each select="/book/chapter">
                  <h1><xsl:value-of select="title"/></h1>
                  <xsl:apply-templates select="para"/>
                </xsl:for-each>
              </body>
            </html>
          </xsl:if>
        </xsl:fallback>
      </redirect:write>
    </xsl:for-each>
  </xsl:template>

  <xsl:template match="para">
    <p><xsl:apply-templates select="*|text()"/></p>
  </xsl:template>

</xsl:stylesheet>
```

In our example, we only invoke the fallback processing once. This approach assumes that if something's wrong with the extension, it will fail the first time and be completely inaccessible. Using `<xsl:fallback>`, we know that the contents of the `<xsl:fallback>` element will be invoked if anything goes wrong when the stylesheet processor attempts to use an extension element. If you'd like more complete control over fallback processing, you can use the `element-available()` and `function-available()` functions as we did in our earlier example.

Extending the Saxon Processor

Michael Kay's excellent Saxon processor also provides an extension mechanism. One of the nice features of Saxon's extensibility mechanism is that you can implement your own sort functions. When we discussed the `<xsl:sort>` element a couple of chapters ago, we mentioned that it has a `lang` attribute that defines the language of the things being sorted. While Xalan doesn't currently support this attribute (although by the time you're reading this, it might), Saxon lets you create your own extension function to handle the sorting. Your extension function must extend the `com.icl.saxon.sort.TextComparer` class. Here's a sample XML document we'll use to illustrate this function:

```
<?xml version="1.0"?>
<wordlist>
  <word>campo</word>
  <word>luna</word>
  <word>ciudad</word>
  <word>llaves</word>
  <word>chihuahua</word>
  <word>arroz</word>
  <word>limonada</word>
</wordlist>
```

This document contains Spanish words that are sorted differently than they would be in English. (In Spanish, "ch" and "ll" are separate letters that sort after "c" and "l," respectively.) We'll write a stylesheet that uses three `<xsl:template>`s to illustrate how our extension function works. Here's the stylesheet:

```
<?xml version="1.0"?>
<xsl:stylesheet version="1.0" xmlns:xsl="http://www.w3.org/1999/XSL/Transform">

  <xsl:output method="text" indent="no"/>
  <xsl:strip-space elements="*"/>

  <xsl:variable name="newline">
<xsl:text>
</xsl:text>
  </xsl:variable>

  <xsl:template match="/">
    <xsl:value-of select="$newline"/>
    <xsl:apply-templates select="wordlist" mode="unsorted"/>
    <xsl:apply-templates select="wordlist" mode="default"/>
    <xsl:apply-templates select="wordlist" mode="Spanish"/>
  </xsl:template>

  <xsl:template match="wordlist" mode="unsorted">
    <xsl:text>Word list - unsorted:</xsl:text>
    <xsl:value-of select="$newline"/>
    <xsl:for-each select="word">
      <xsl:value-of select="."/>
      <xsl:value-of select="$newline"/>
    </xsl:for-each>
    <xsl:value-of select="$newline"/>
  </xsl:template>
```

```
  <xsl:template match="wordlist" mode="default">
    <xsl:text>Word list - sorted with default rules:</xsl:text>
    <xsl:value-of select="$newline"/>
    <xsl:for-each select="word">
      <xsl:sort select="."/>
      <xsl:value-of select="."/>
      <xsl:value-of select="$newline"/>
    </xsl:for-each>
    <xsl:value-of select="$newline"/>
  </xsl:template>

  <xsl:template match="wordlist" mode="Spanish">
    <xsl:text>Word list - sorted with Spanish rules:</xsl:text>
    <xsl:value-of select="$newline"/>
    <xsl:for-each select="word">
      <xsl:sort select="." lang="es"/>
      <xsl:value-of select="."/>
      <xsl:value-of select="$newline"/>
    </xsl:for-each>
    <xsl:value-of select="$newline"/>
  </xsl:template>
</xsl:stylesheet>
```

When we run the stylesheet against our document, it invokes the three templates with three different modes. One template simply lists the <word> elements as they appear in the original document, the second sorts the <word> elements using the default sorting sequence, and the third sorts the <word> elements using the traditional rules of Spanish sorting. Refreshingly enough, the code that implements the sorting function is simple. Here's the entire listing:

```
package com.icl.saxon.sort;

import java.text.ParseException;
import java.text.RuleBasedCollator;
import java.util.Locale;

public class Compare_es extends TextComparer
{
  private static String smallnTilde  = new String("\u00F1");
  private static String capitalNTilde = new String("\u00D1");

  private static String traditionalSpanishRules =
    ("< a,A < b,B < c,C " +
     "< ch, cH, Ch, CH "  +
     "< d,D < e,E < f,F " +
     "< g,G < h,H < i,I < j,J < k,K < l,L " +
     "< ll, lL, Ll, LL "  +
     "< m,M < n,N " +
     "< " + smallnTilde + "," + capitalNTilde + " " +
     "< o,O < p,P < q,Q < r,R " +
     "< s,S < t,T < u,U < v,V < w,W < x,X " +
     "< y,Y < z,Z");
```

```
  private static RuleBasedCollator rbc = null;

  static
  {
    try
    {
      rbc = new RuleBasedCollator(traditionalSpanishRules);
    }
    catch (ParseException pe)
    {
      System.err.println("Error creating RuleBasedCollator: " + rbc);
    }
  }

  public int compare(Object a, Object b)
  {
    if (rbc != null)
      return rbc.compare((String)a, (String)b);
    else
      return 0;
  }
}
```

(See the documentation for the `java.text.RuleBasedCollator` class for an explanation of the `traditionalSpanishRules` string.)

When Saxon sees an `<xsl:sort>` element with a `lang` attribute of `es`, it attempts to load a Java class named `com.icl.saxon.sort.Compare_es`. If that class can be loaded, Saxon calls that class's `compare` method as it sorts the `<word>` elements. When we run the stylesheet against our earlier example document, here are the results:

```
Word list - unsorted:
campo
luna
ciudad
llaves
chihuahua
arroz
limonada

Word list - sorted with default rules:
arroz
campo
chihuahua
ciudad
limonada
llaves
luna

Word list - sorted with Spanish rules:
arroz
campo
```

```
ciudad
chihuahua
limonada
luna
llaves
```

In the output, our Spanish sorting routine puts `chihuahua` after `ciudad`, and `llaves` after `luna`. With less than 20 lines of code, we've been able to add a new sorting function to our stylesheet. Most of the work is done for us by the Saxon processor and the methods of the `java.text.RuleBasedCollator` class.

The Saxon documentation has more information on extending Saxon with your own code. As you'll see in the examples in this chapter, most of the Java extensions you'll need to write will be simple pieces of code that simply make Java library methods and classes available to the XSLT processor.

More Examples

You can use XSLT extension mechanisms to push XSLT processing beyond text or markup generation and to read information from non-XML sources.

Generating JPEG Files from XML Content

When converting XML content into HTML files for a web site, there are times when you want to have complete control over the look of a piece of text. In this example, we'll use an extension function to convert the text of an XML element into a JPEG graphic. Our code will load a JPEG background graphic, draw the text from the XML document on top of it, and then write the graphic out to a new JPEG file. We'll reuse the XML file from our first example to demonstrate the extension function.

Our stylesheet passes each `<title>` element to the extension function. When we invoke the extension, we'll also pass in the name of the background JPEG, the name of the output file (which we'll call *title1.jpg*, *title2.jpg*, etc.), and various information about the font name, font size, and other parameters. Here's what our stylesheet looks like:

```
<?xml version="1.0"?>
<xsl:stylesheet version="1.0" xmlns:xsl="http://www.w3.org/1999/XSL/Transform"
  xmlns:jpeg="xalan://JPEGWriter"
  extension-element-prefixes="jpeg">

  <xsl:output method="html"/>

  <xsl:template match="/">
    <html>
      <head>
        <title>
```

```
          <xsl:value-of select="/book/title"/>
        </title>
      </head>
      <body>
        <xsl:for-each select="/book/chapter">
          <xsl:choose>
            <xsl:when test="function-available('jpeg:createJPEG')">
              <xsl:value-of
                select="jpeg:createJPEG(title, 'bg.jpg',
                concat('title', position(), '.jpg'),
                'Swiss 721 Bold Condensed', 'BOLD', 22, 52, 35)"/>
              <img>
                <xsl:attribute name="src">
                  <xsl:value-of select="concat('title', position(), '.jpg')"/>
                </xsl:attribute>
              </img>
              <br />
            </xsl:when>
            <xsl:otherwise>
              <h1><xsl:value-of select="title"/></h1>
            </xsl:otherwise>
          </xsl:choose>
        </xsl:for-each>
      </body>
    </html>
  </xsl:template>

</xsl:stylesheet>
```

Our background JPEG looks like Figure 8-4.

Figure 8-4. Background JPEG image

Figure 8-5 shows a couple of graphics created by the combination of our XML sample document, our stylesheet, and the extension function.

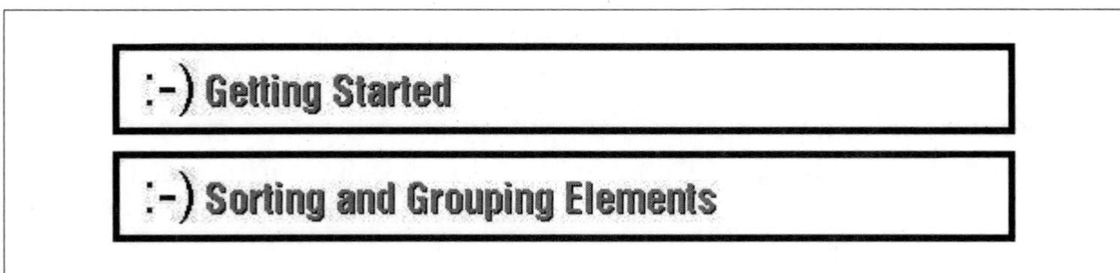

Figure 8-5. Generated JPEG files for XML <title> elements

These files are *title1.jpg* and *title8.jpg*, respectively. Our extension function has taken the text of the appropriate `<title>` elements, drawn it on top of the background graphic, then written the new image out as a JPEG graphic.

Let's take a look at the call to our extension function:

```
<xsl:value-of
  select="jpeg:createJPEG(title, 'bg.jpg',
  concat('title', position(), '.jpg'),
  'Swiss 721 Bold Condensed', 'BOLD', 22, 52, 35)"/>
```

First of all, look at the call itself. What we've written here is `jpeg:createJPEG` as the name of the function. The namespace prefix `jpeg` is defined in the stylesheet. We associated this prefix with the string `xalan://JPEGWriter`; this string tells Xalan that any function invoked with this prefix should be treated as a method of the named class `JPEGWriter`. If you use an XSLT processor other than Xalan, the way you define and invoke an extension function will probably vary.

Next, let's look at the parameters to the function. We're passing eight different parameters:

- The text that should be written in the JPEG image. This text is passed in as a `NodeList`, one of the datatypes available to us in the Xalan API. In our previous example, we're selecting all `<title>` elements contained in the current node.
- The filename of the background image that should be used. This filename is passed in as a `String`.
- The filename of the created JPEG image. The image will be created, then written out to this filename. Notice that in our example, we generate the filename by concatenating the string "title", the position of the current node, and the string ".jpg". This procedure ensures that all our title graphics have unique filenames. It also makes it easy to determine which JPEG matches a given `<title>` element.
- The name of the font we want to use. This name is a `String`.
- The font style we want to use. We've written our function to accept three different values: `BOLD`, `ITALIC`, and `BOLDITALIC`. These values mirror the three values used by the Java `Font` class.
- The point size of the font. Notice that this font size is passed to our extension function as a Java `Double`; XPath and XSLT do not define an `Integer` type. The first thing our function does is convert the `Double` values into `ints` to simplify our arithmetic instructions.

- The x-offset where the text should begin. We're using a Java `Canvas` object, whose coordinate system begins in the upper left corner. The value of x-offset determines where we should start drawing the text on the background JPEG. As with the font size, this value is a `Double` that we convert to an `int`.
- The y-offset where the text should begin.

You could certainly modify this function to support other options, such as the color of the text, the depth of the shadow effects on the text, the location of the shadow, etc. You could also create different versions of the function with different method signatures, allowing some calls to the `createJPEG` function to default certain parameters. The benefit of this approach is that you can access a wide range of behaviors in your extension function by changing your XSLT stylesheet.

Here's the code for the extension function itself:

```
import com.sun.image.codec.jpeg.ImageFormatException;
import com.sun.image.codec.jpeg.JPEGCodec;
import com.sun.image.codec.jpeg.JPEGImageDecoder;
import com.sun.image.codec.jpeg.JPEGImageEncoder;
import java.awt.Color;
import java.awt.Font;
import java.awt.FontMetrics;
import java.awt.Graphics2D;
import java.awt.GraphicsEnvironment;
import java.awt.image.BufferedImage;
import java.io.FileInputStream;
import java.io.FileNotFoundException;
import java.io.FileOutputStream;
import java.io.IOException;
import org.apache.xpath.objects.XNodeSet;
import org.w3c.dom.NodeList;

public class JPEGWriter
{
  public static void createJPEG(NodeList nodes, String backgroundFilename,
                               String outputFilename, String fontName,
                               String fontAttributes, Double dFontSize,
                               Double dXOffset, Double dYOffset)
    throws IOException, FileNotFoundException, ImageFormatException
  {
    try
    {
      int fontSize = dFontSize.intValue();
      int xOffset = dXOffset.intValue();
      int yOffset = dYOffset.intValue();

      String jpegText = (new XNodeSet(nodes.item(1))).str();
      FileInputStream fis = new FileInputStream(backgroundFilename);
      JPEGImageDecoder northDecoder = JPEGCodec.createJPEGDecoder(fis);
      BufferedImage bi = northDecoder.decodeAsBufferedImage();
```

```
int fa = Font.PLAIN;
if (fontAttributes.equalsIgnoreCase("BOLD"))
  fa = Font.BOLD;
else if (fontAttributes.equalsIgnoreCase("ITALIC"))
   fa = Font.ITALIC;
else if (fontAttributes.equalsIgnoreCase("BOLDITALIC"))
  fa = Font.BOLD & Font.ITALIC;

Graphics2D g = bi.createGraphics();

int maxTextWidth = bi.getWidth() - xOffset - 5;
GraphicsEnvironment ge = GraphicsEnvironment.
                         getLocalGraphicsEnvironment();
Font allFonts[] = ge.getAllFonts();
Font chosenFont = new Font("Arial", fa, fontSize);
int i = 0;
boolean fontNotFound = true;
while (fontNotFound && (i < allFonts.length))
{
  if (allFonts[i].getFontName().equalsIgnoreCase(fontName))
  {
    chosenFont = allFonts[i].deriveFont(fa, fontSize);
    if (!chosenFont.getFontName().equalsIgnoreCase(fontName))
    {
      fa = Font.PLAIN;
      chosenFont = allFonts[i].deriveFont(fa, fontSize);
    }
    g.setFont(chosenFont);
    FontMetrics fm = g.getFontMetrics();
    int textWidth = fm.stringWidth(jpegText);
    while (textWidth > maxTextWidth && fontSize > 1)
    {
      fontSize -= 2;
      chosenFont = allFonts[i].deriveFont(fa, fontSize);
      g.setFont(chosenFont);
      fm = g.getFontMetrics();
      textWidth = fm.stringWidth(jpegText);
    }
    if (fontSize < 1)
      chosenFont = allFonts[i].deriveFont(fa, 12);

    g.setFont(chosenFont);
    fontNotFound = false;
  }
  else
    i++;
}

g.setColor(Color.black);
g.drawString(jpegText, xOffset, yOffset);
g.setColor(Color.gray);
g.drawString(jpegText, xOffset - 1, yOffset - 1);
FileOutputStream fos = new FileOutputStream(outputFilename);
JPEGImageEncoder encoder = JPEGCodec.createJPEGEncoder(fos);
```

```
          encoder.encode(bi);
          fos.flush();
          fos.close();
        }
        catch (FileNotFoundException fnfe)
        {
          System.err.println(fnfe);
        }
        catch (IOException ioe)
        {
          System.err.println(ioe);
        }
      }
    }
```

Notice that we use a `while` loop to check the font size. If drawing the text string in the current font size won't fit inside the graphic, we'll try to reduce the font size until it does. Given this <chapter> element:

```
<chapter>
  <title>A chapter in which the title is so very long, most people
    don't bother reading it</title>
  <para>If this chapter had any text, it would appear here.</para>
</chapter>
```

Our extension generates the JPEG shown in Figure 8-6.

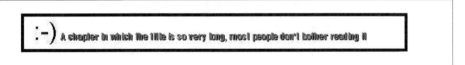

Figure 8-6. Generated image with too much text

Accessing a Database with an Extension Element

In this example, we're going to build an extension element rather than an extension function. When we wrote our extension functions, all we had to worry about was the data passed to us on the function call. We weren't concerned with the document tree, the context, or anything else. With an extension element, though, we have to be much more aware of the document as a whole. Our code will use the attributes of the extension element to connect to a database, run a query, and then return the result set as a node set (specifically, a Xalan `XNodeSet`). That node-set will be inserted into the output tree, giving us the capability to build a document dynamically. Our XML document defines the parameters for the database access and the query, then the extension element does the work in the background magically. Here's how the XML document looks:

```
<?xml version="1.0"?>
<report>
  <title>HR employee listing</title>
  <section>
    <title>Employees by department</title>
    <dbaccess driver="COM.ibm.db2.jdbc.app.DB2Driver"
      database="jdbc:db2:sample" tablename="employee" where="*"
      fieldnames='workdept as "Department", lastname as "Last Name",
                  firstnme as "First Name"'
      order-by="workdept" group-by="workdept, lastname, firstnme"/>
  </section>
</report>
```

Notice that all of the vendor-specific information about our database connection is contained in the attributes of our XML document. That means we can use our extension element with any JDBC-compliant database. The following documents work just as well:

```
<?xml version="1.0"?>
<report>
  <title>Sales Results</title>
  <section>
    <title>Top sales people - 3Q 2001</title>
    <dbaccess driver="com.sybase.jdbc2.jdbc.SybDriver""
      database="jdbc:sybase:Tds:localhost:5000/sales"
      tablename="results" where="*"
      fieldnames='lastname as "Last Name",
      firstnme as "First Name", sum(order) as "Totals"'
      order-by="sum(order)" />
  </section>
</report>

<?xml version="1.0"?>
<report>
  <title>Pets We Own</title>
  <section>
    <title>Our pets</title>
    <dbaccess driver="org.gjt.mm.mysql.Driver"
      database="jdbc:mysql://localhost/test" tablename="pet" where="*"
      fieldnames='name as "Pet Name", species as "Species", sex as "M/F"'/>
  </section>
</report>
```

The first listing uses DB2, the second uses Sybase, and the final listing uses MySQL. Our stylesheet uses our database-accessing extension element to replace the <dbaccess> elements with HTML tables filled with the results of our database query. In our sample document, the XML input closely mirrors the SQL statements we'll use to interact with the database. Our extension element takes the elements and attributes of the <dbaccess> element, gets data out of the database, then formats it accordingly.

The stylesheet that invokes our extension element looks like this:

```
<?xml version="1.0"?>
<xsl:stylesheet version="1.0" xmlns:xsl="http://www.w3.org/1999/XSL/Transform"
  xmlns:db="DatabaseExtension"
  extension-element-prefixes="db">

  <xsl:output method="html"/>

  <xsl:template match="/">
    <html>
      <head>
        <title>
          <xsl:value-of select="report/title"/>
        </title>
      </head>
      <body>
        <h1>
          <xsl:value-of select="report/title"/>
        </h1>
        <xsl:for-each select="report/section">
          <h2>
            <xsl:value-of select="title"/>
          </h2>
          <xsl:for-each select="dbaccess">
            <db:accessDatabase/>
          </xsl:for-each>
        </xsl:for-each>
      </body>
    </html>
  </xsl:template>

</xsl:stylesheet>
```

The stylesheet is pretty straightforward. The namespace declaration `xmlns:db="xalan://DatabaseExtension"` associates the Java class `DatabaseExtension` with the namespace prefix `db`. Whenever our stylesheet processes an XML element with a namespace prefix of `db`, our code is invoked to do the processing. Notice that in our stylesheet, we used the extension element <db:accessDatabase>; this tells Xalan to invoke the `accessDatabase()` method of the `DatabaseExtension` class.

In this example, we want our extension element to look at the various attributes of the <dbaccess> element, build a SQL query from the information it finds there, connect to the requested database, and put in the result tree elements that represent the database query results. To keep our example simple, we'll have our extension element return those results in an HTML <table> element; you could write the extension element to generate other types of output, if you wanted. Our extension element returns an `XNodeSet`; the nodes in the returned `XNodeSet` are added to the result tree.

For our extension element to work, it has to do several things:

- Find the <dbaccess> element we need to process.
- Use the `driver` attribute of the <dbaccess> element to determine what JDBC driver to use. Once we have this value, we need to load the driver. Specifying the database driver allows us to use different databases in the same XML document. In our previous sample XML files, the three queries specify databases managed by DB2, Sybase, and MySQL; because JDBC itself is vendor-neutral, we can use our extension element with any JDBC-compliant database.
- Examine the `tablename`, `where`, `fieldnames`, `group-by`, and `order-by` attributes of the <dbaccess> element to build the SQL query statement.
- Connect to the database specified by the `tablename` attribute of the <dbaccess> element.
- Execute the query statement.
- Build the table based on the items in the JDBC `ResultSet` object. To build the table, we have to get a DOM `Document` object; we'll use that object as a factory method to create all the nodes in the node-set our extension element returns. We'll create a `<table>` element, then for each row in the result set, we'll create a `<tr>` element (with the appropriate `<td>` elements as its children) and append it to the table. For Xalan, we use the `DOMHelper` class to get the `Document` object that we'll use to create all nodes.
- Return the result set. We create an `XNodeSet`, attach our `<table>` element (with all its children) to it, then return it. This result is added automatically to the output document.

Now that we've said what we're going to do, let's take a look at the code:

```
import java.sql.Connection;
import java.sql.DriverManager;
import java.sql.ResultSet;
import java.sql.ResultSetMetaData;
import java.sql.Statement;
import org.apache.xalan.extensions.XSLProcessorContext;
import org.apache.xalan.templates.ElemExtensionCall;
import org.apache.xpath.DOMHelper;
import org.apache.xpath.objects.XNodeSet;
import org.w3c.dom.Document;
import org.w3c.dom.Element;
```

```
public class DatabaseExtension
{
  private static boolean getDriver(String driverName)
  {
    boolean gotTheDriver = false;
    try
    {
      Class.forName(driverName);
      gotTheDriver = true;
    }
    catch (Exception e)
    {
      System.out.println("Can't load the database driver " + driverName);
      e.printStackTrace();
    }
    return gotTheDriver;
  }

  public static XNodeSet accessDatabase(XSLProcessorContext context,
                                        ElemExtensionCall elem)
  {
    XNodeSet dbResult = null;
    DOMHelper dh = new DOMHelper();
    Document doc = dh.getDOMFactory();
    Element table = null, header = null, tr = null, td = null, th = null;

    Element contextNode = (Element) context.getContextNode();
    if (getDriver(contextNode.getAttribute("driver")))
    {
      try
      {
        StringBuffer query = new StringBuffer("select ");
        query.append(contextNode.getAttribute("fieldnames") + " ");
        query.append("from " + contextNode.getAttribute("tablename") + " ");
        String nextAttr = contextNode.getAttribute("group-by");
        if (nextAttr != null)
          query.append(" group by " + nextAttr);
        nextAttr = contextNode.getAttribute("order-by");
        if (nextAttr != null)
          query.append(" order by " + nextAttr);

        Connection con = DriverManager.
          getConnection(contextNode.getAttribute("database"));
        Statement stmt = con.createStatement();
        ResultSet rs = stmt.executeQuery(query.toString());

        ResultSetMetaData rsmd = rs.getMetaData();
        int columnCount = rsmd.getColumnCount();
        table = doc.createElement("table");
        table.setAttribute("border", "1");

        header = doc.createElement("tr");
        for (int i = 1; i <= columnCount; i++)
```

```
          {
            th = doc.createElement("th");
            th.appendChild(doc.createTextNode(rsmd.getColumnName(i)));
            header.appendChild(th);
          }
          table.appendChild(header);

          while (rs.next())
          {
            tr = doc.createElement("tr");
            for (int i = 1; i <= columnCount; i++)
            {
              td = doc.createElement("td");
              td.appendChild(doc.createTextNode(rs.getString(i)));
              tr.appendChild(td);
            }
            table.appendChild(tr);
          }
          dbResult = new XNodeSet(table);
          rs.close();
          stmt.close();
          con.close();
        }
        catch (java.sql.SQLException sqle)
        {
          System.out.println("Exception: " + sqle);
        }
      }
      else
        System.out.println("Couldn't load the driver!");

      return dbResult;
    }
  }
```

Extension elements in Xalan are called with two arguments: an `XSLProcessorContext` object and an `ElemExtensionCall` object. In our code here, we'll use the `XSLProcessorContext` object to get the context node. Once we have the context node (the <dbaccess> element), we can get the values of the various <dbaccess> element attributes in the source tree.

The first thing we do in our extension element is declare the `XNodeSet` we're going to return to Xalan. After that, we create a `DOMHelper` object and use the `getDOMFactory` method to create the `DOM Document` object we'll use as a factory for creating new nodes:

```
XNodeSet dbResult = null;
DOMHelper dh = new DOMHelper();
Document doc = dh.getDOMFactory();
```

Our next task is to instantiate the JDBC driver. To make our code more flexible, we specify the driver in the `driver` attribute of the <dbaccess> element. In the previous XML examples, we used drivers for MySQL, Sybase, and DB2. Assuming everything to this point has succeeded, we'll build the query string. To simplify things, our example assumes we're going to build an `SQL SELECT` statement; feel free to extend this code to do more sophisticated things. The query is built from various attributes of the <dbaccess> element.

Once the query has been built, we connect to the appropriate database. The database is specified with the `database` attribute of the <dbaccess> element. (In our previous XML samples, notice that DB2, Sybase, and MySQL specify databases in different ways. Specifying this in an attribute makes our extension element more flexible.) We connect to the database, execute the query statement, and get a JDBC `ResultSet` object in return.

Once we have the `ResultSet`, our job is relatively simple. We need to create an HTML table, with each row in the table containing a row from the `ResultSet`. In the previous code, we call our `Document` object to create each new node. Here are some examples:

```
while (rs.next())
{
  tr = doc.createElement("tr");
  for (int i = 1; i <= columnCount; i++)
  {
    td = doc.createElement("td");
    td.appendChild(doc.createTextNode(rs.getString(i)));
    tr.appendChild(td);
  }
  table.appendChild(tr);
}
dbResult = new XNodeSet(table);
```

In this sample, we create the <tr> element with the DOM `createElement` method. Notice that when we want to add text to a node, we use the `createTextNode` method to create a text node and append it as a child. In the loop just shown, we take each row of the `ResultSet` and create a <tr> element for it. We create a <td> element for each column in the `ResultSet`, then append it to the <tr> element. When we're done with the row, we append the <tr> element to the <table>.

Once we've processed the entire `ResultSet`, we create a new `XNodeSet` by passing our <table> element to the `XNodeSet` constructor. This technique can be used to create any number of nodes, including elements, attributes, text, and comments.

For example, here's how we created the HTML <table> element and added the `border="1"` attribute to it:

```
Element table = doc.createElement("table");
table.setAttribute("border", "1");
```

Our final step is simply to clean up all of the JDBC stuff and return the `XNodeSet` to Xalan:

```
rs.close();
stmt.close();
con.close();

...

return dbResult;
```

The nodes in our `XNodeSet` are sent straight to the output document, where they appear as ordinary HTML nodes, as shown in Figure 8-7.

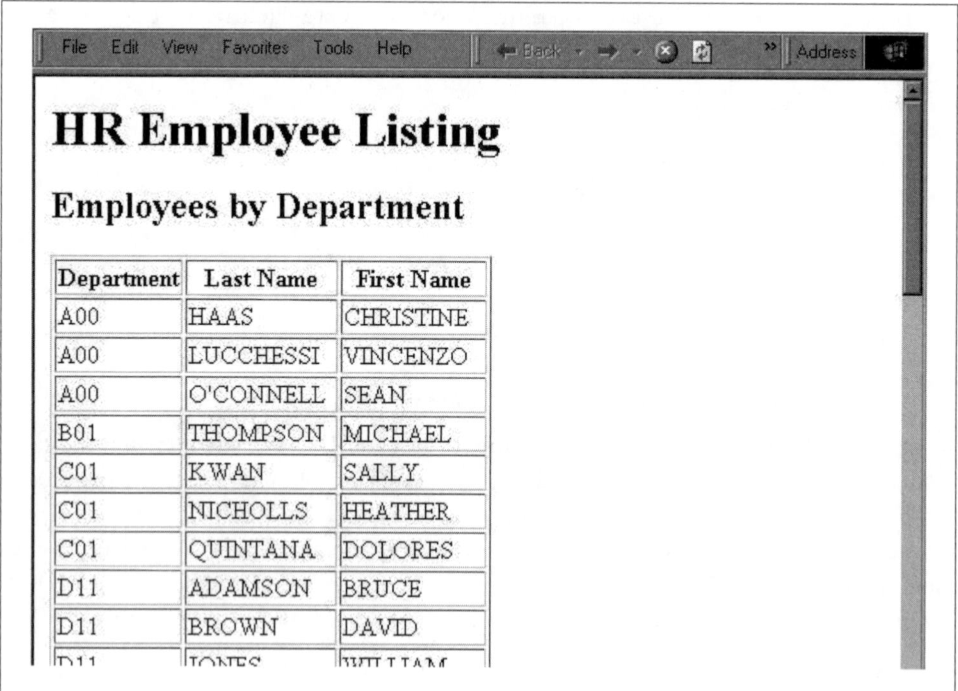

Department	Last Name	First Name
A00	HAAS	CHRISTINE
A00	LUCCHESSI	VINCENZO
A00	O'CONNELL	SEAN
B01	THOMPSON	MICHAEL
C01	KWAN	SALLY
C01	NICHOLLS	HEATHER
C01	QUINTANA	DOLORES
D11	ADAMSON	BRUCE
D11	BROWN	DAVID

Figure 8-7. HTML file with output from an extension element

With this extension, we've been able to generate nodes dynamically, then add them to the output document. Every time this stylesheet is processed, the extension adds the latest data from various databases to the output. You could improve this extension element by adding caching, connection pooling, and other features for performance and scalability; the point of this example was to show you how extension elements work. Whatever its limitations, the best feature of our extension element is that we can use it with any JDBC-compliant database. You can use this code to generate HTML (or XML) from any database, whether the database vendor supports it or not.

As of this writing, efforts are underway to standardize extension functions and exension elements across XSLT processors. The EXSLT project is one such effort. Visit their web site (*http://www.exslt.org*) for more information on the EXSLT library of extensions.

Summary

In this chapter, we've run the gamut of extension functions and extension elements, demonstrating how to add sophisticated processing power to our stylesheets. All examples have been self-contained; you could combine these functions and elements to do something really sophisticated. For example, you could use the database extension to extract live sales data from a database, and then convert it into an interactive graphic.

At this point, we've covered just about everything in the XSLT and XPath specifications. In the next chapter, we'll go through a real-world example that illustrates the full power and flexibility of using stylesheets to manipulate structured data.

9

Case Study: The Toot-O-Matic

In this chapter, we'll examine a tutorial-building tool called the Toot-O-Matic. Developed by yours truly for IBM's developerWorks web site (*http://www.ibm.com/developerWorks*, check your local listings), it's a good example of how stylesheets can drive a sophisticated publishing system for structured information. Our tool is built around the Xalan XSLT processor, the Apache XML Project's FOP tool, and various Java facilities (such as the `JPEGCodec` class).

About the Toot-O-Matic

Tutorials are the most popular kind of content at developerWorks. Unfortunately, in the early days of the site, we didn't have good tools for creating tutorials. We often started with a document written in a word processor, then we printed it as a PDF file, then we converted it to an HTML file, then we broke the single HTML file into smaller pieces to represent the various panels of the tutorial. Much of this was a tedious, error-prone process that cried out for automation. The Toot-O-Matic handles most of the work necessary to generate files, allowing the tutorial author and production staff to focus on more important things.

To publish a tutorial, we need to create several kinds of output:

- A web of interlinked HTML files. There should be an introductory panel for the tutorial. It should contain links to all sections of the tutorial. From each panel, there are links to the previous and next panels, as well as links to the Main menu and a section index. All these links are separate HTML files that refer to one another.
- A pair of PDF files. We produce two PDF files, one with letter-sized pages and one with A4-sized pages. Each PDF file contains a table of contents that lists the different sections of the tutorial. Whenever possible, the graphics used in

the tutorial should be part of the PDF file, and any hyperlinks in the tutorial (links between panels, or links to web resources) should be part of the PDF file, as well.

- A zip file. Many of our customers told us that Internet access was too slow or too expensive for them to read our tutorials online. With a zip file, customers can download everything they need to run the tutorial on their machines without being connected to the Web.

Design Goals

We had several design goals in mind when we started to design the Toot-O-Matic tag set:

- Make it easier to create tutorials.
- Show our audience that we use the technologies we advocate.
- See just how much we can accomplish through stylesheets.

We'll discuss each of these goals in detail before we move on to the design of the tutorials themselves.

Make It Easier to Create Tutorials

Our first tutorials were incredibly tedious to create. Authors and editors wrote and edited the content in a tool such as Microsoft Word, then we started the publishing process. Our first step was typically to create a PDF version of the tutorial. High-quality printable versions of our tutorials are popular, and it's easy to create them from a single formatted document in Microsoft Word.

Once that was done, we would convert the tutorial document into a single HTML file. We would then take the file, break it into small pieces, and add the standard IBM header and footer to each small piece. This step gave us a number of HTML files (usually 50 to 100) that we needed to link together. In other words, if you look at the third panel in a section, clicking Next should take you to the fourth panel, and clicking Previous should take you to the second panel. We also needed to create a menu panel; from the menu panel, you can link directly to the first panel of any particular section. Finally, each panel had mouseover effects that had to be tested.

While the writer and editor worked on the actual content, our graphic designers created artwork for the titles of the sections and for the tutorial itself. It was important that the heading text look a particular way, so our designers created graphics that contained that text, drawn on the appropriate background. For some titles, both plain and highlighted versions were created for the mouseover effects.

Clearly, much of the tutorial-building process was hand-coded and error-prone (particularly when we were feverishly finishing a tutorial at 5:30 in the morning so it would be on the site by sunrise). We wanted to automate as many of these steps as we could, to save us time and minimize the chance of errors.

Show Our Audience That We Use the Technologies We Advocate

Another goal was to actually use the technologies we espouse. We were certainly aware of the irony of a site that promotes open, standards-based computing creating content with a closed-source, proprietary tool, such as Microsoft Word. One attraction of building tools from XML documents and XSLT stylesheets was that it enabled us to show the world that XML and XSLT can do useful work today. Choosing these technologies to manipulate structured data was a no-brainer for us.

See Just How Much We Could Accomplish Through Stylesheets

Our final goal was to see how much we could do with XSLT. As you'll see, we exercise all the advanced capabilities of XSLT in the Toot-O-Matic, including multiple input files, multiple output files, and extension functions. Through our stylesheets, we convert an XML document into:

- A web of interlinked HTML documents
- A menu for the entire tutorial
- A table of contents for each section of the tutorial
- JPEG graphics containing the title of the tutorial and each of the individual sections
- A letter-sized PDF file
- An A4-sized PDF file
- A zip file containing everything users need to run the tutorial on their machine

As we'll discuss, creating all of these things through stylesheets required us to push XSLT to its limits. The design of the XML document allows us to manipulate the information for a tutorial in a variety of sophisticated ways, and the structure of our stylesheets makes it easy for us to change the look and feel of our tutorials without having to modify the original XML content.

In addition to these goals, we decided to make the XSLT stylesheets and the necessary extensions open source. We did this so our readers could see what we were doing to "eat our own dog food," and to see if tight integration with a standards-compliant stylesheet processor would allow us to use existing tools to generate tutorials in a semi-WYSIWYG environment.

Tutorial Layout

Before we talk about the details of the XML document design and the XSLT source code, we'll review the actual HTML, zip, and PDF files we need to create. One advantage we had in this project is that we didn't have any existing XML documents to contend with; this advantage gave us complete freedom over the XML document design.

Menu Panel

The menu panel is the first HTML document a user sees. It looks like Figure 9-1.

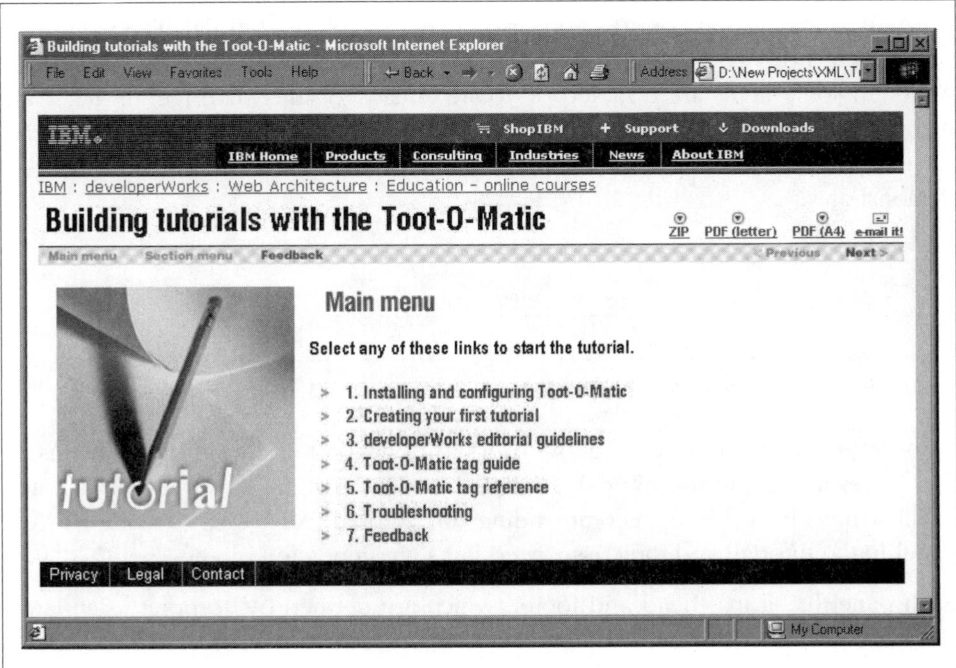

Figure 9-1. Toot-O-Matic menu panel

In this example, the string "Building tutorials with the Toot-O-Matic" and all section titles are JPEG graphics created with our stylesheets and extensions. If you mouseover a section title, its background color changes, as shown in Figure 9-2.

Main menu

Select any of these links to start the tutorial.

>> 1. Installing and configuring Toot-O-Matic
> 2. Creating your first tutorial
> 3. developer 1. Installing and configuring Toot-O-Matic

Figure 9-2. Mouseover effect for section titles

In this sample, notice that the text of the menu item appears as a tooltip. This appearance is useful for sight-impaired users, and is consistent with the Web Accessibility Guidelines defined by the W3C.

A variety of navigation controls appear on every panel in a tutorial. The navigation bar contains items such as "Main menu," "Section menu," and "Feedback." Although some items are disabled (if you're already on the Main menu, the "Main menu" item isn't active, for example), they appear on every panel of the tutorial. There are also icons for viewing the tutorial in alternate formats, as Figure 9-3 demonstrates.

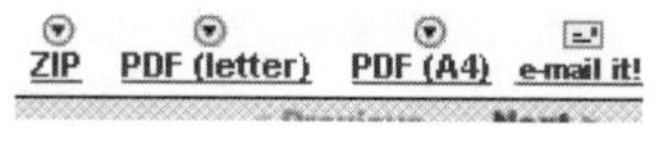

Figure 9-3. Icons for alternate tutorial forms

From left to right, these icons allow users to download a zip file that contains all files necessary to run the tutorial, a letter-sized PDF file, an A4-sized PDF file, and email a note to a friend, recommending this tutorial. All icons appear on every panel in the tutorial, and their associated links are generated by the Toot-O-Matic.

Each panel has a masthead and footer, which are defined by corporate standards. They are generated by named templates cleverly named `masthead` and `footer`. As corporate standards are updated, we simply change those templates to change the look and feel of the tutorial panel.

Individual Panels

Most HTML files that make up a complete tutorial use this format. Notice that the panel contains the text `page 1 of 6`; we generate this text with XPath expressions. The `1` is generated by the `position()` function, and the `6` is generated by the `count()` function. Each panel's navigation bar also contains links to the Main menu panel and the Section menu panel. An individual panel looks like Figure 9-4.

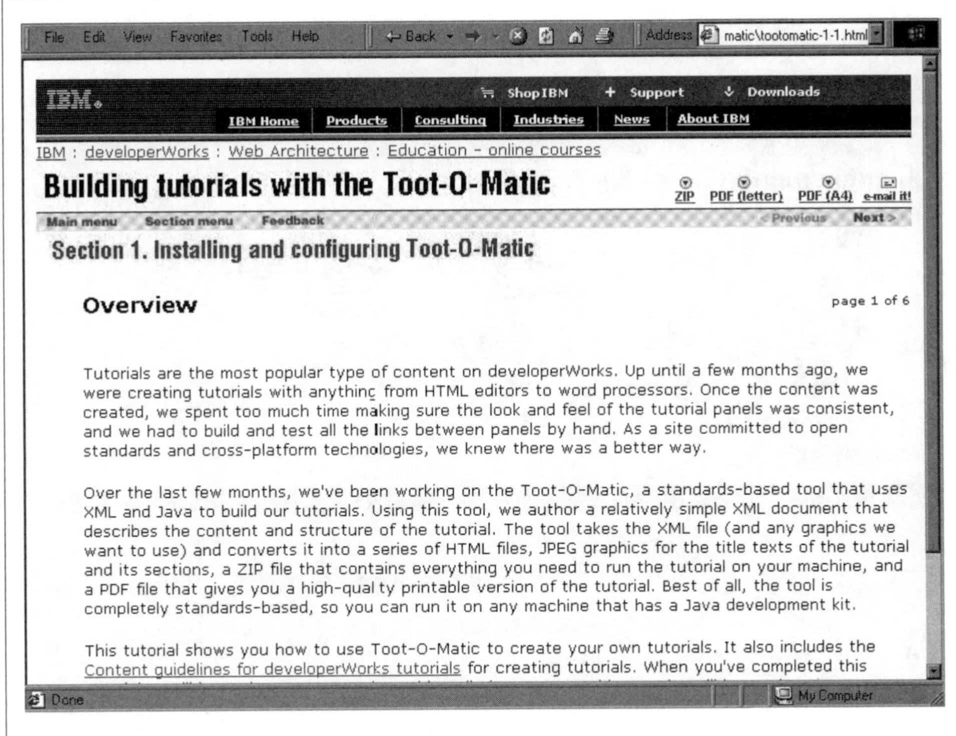

Figure 9-4. An individual tutorial panel

Section Menu

If you click on the "Section menu" item while on any panel in a tutorial, you'll see a listing similar to Figure 9-5.

You can click on the title of any panel to go directly to it. We generate the panel titles with a <xsl:for-each select="panel/title"> element. We'll discuss how we generate the links between panels soon.

Feedback Panel

The Toot-O-Matic generates a Feedback panel automatically. The Feedback panel contains an HTML form that lets readers send in their comments on the tutorial. Code on the server takes reader comments and stores them in a database automatically. Figure 9-6 shows what the generated Feedback panel looks like.

The XML document identifies one panel as the Feedback panel. The Feedback button on the navigation bar of every HTML file points to the HTML file with the feedback form. Again, all of these cross-references are generated automatically through the magic of XSLT and XPath.

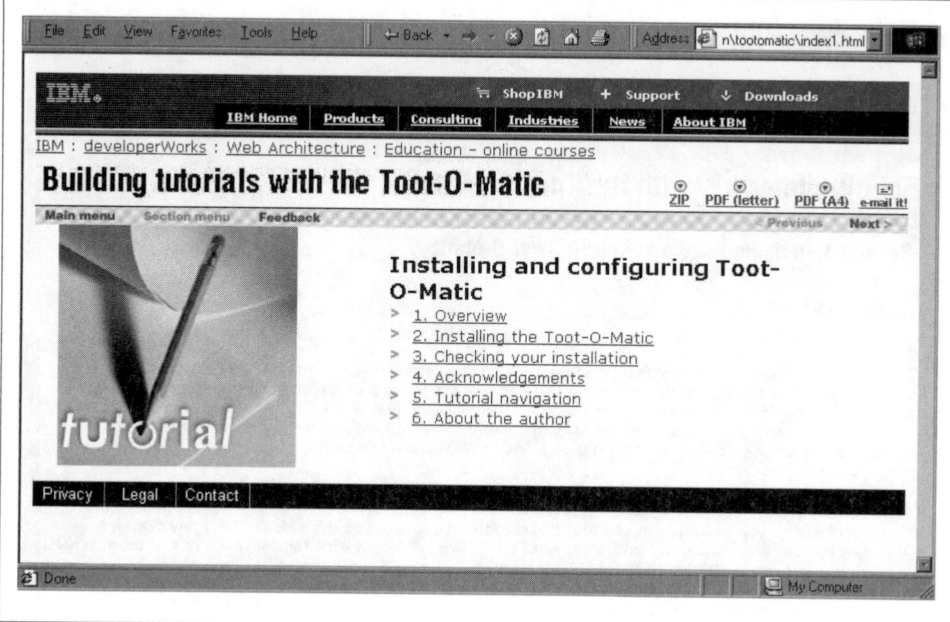

Figure 9-5. A section menu

Email Panel

Another feature of our tutorials is that you can email the URL of the tutorial to a friend. Clicking the "e-mail it!" icon on any panel displays a new browser window as shown in Figure 9-7.

In this example, the text beneath the title of the tutorial is derived from the `abstract` attribute of the `<tutorial>` element.

Zip File

To help readers who have either occasional or expensive web access, we build a zip file that contains everything they need to use the tutorial on their machines. The contents include all generated HTML files, all of the standard graphics used in the header and footer, and any referenced graphics from the tutorial itself.

PDF Files

For readers who want to print out the tutorial and read it offline, we produce two PDF versions of the tutorial, one for letter-sized paper, and one for A4-sized paper. Although we could provide an HTML file that simply contains the HTML rendering

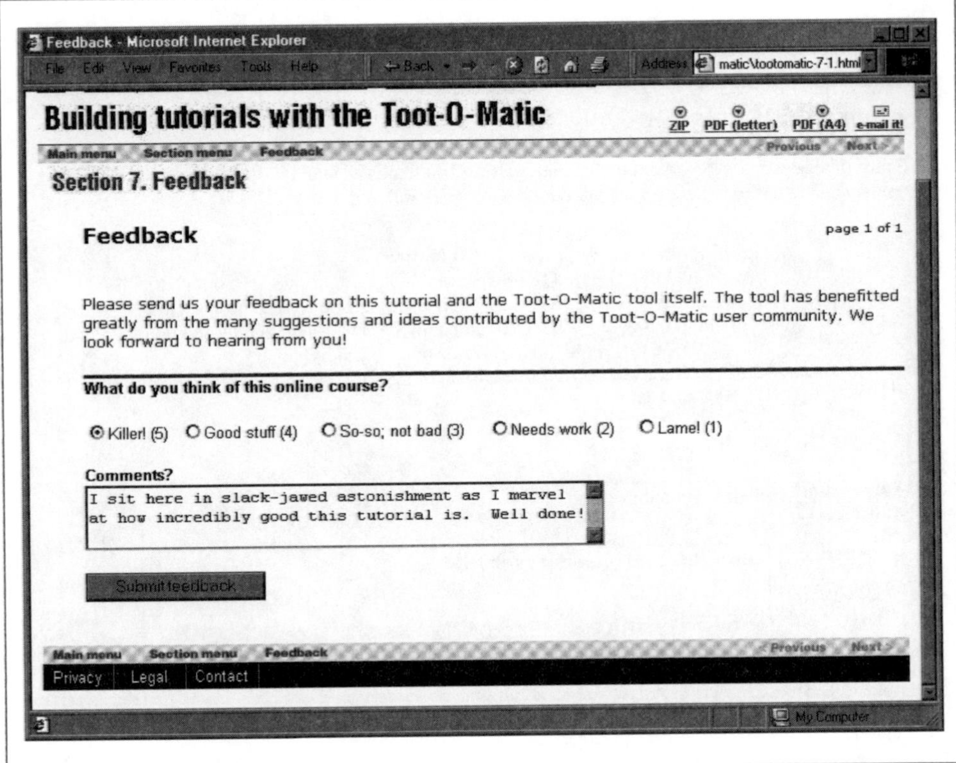

Figure 9-6. A typical Feedback panel

of all the pages of the tutorial, we want higher-quality printable output. The first page of the tutorial, shown in Figure 9-8, features the title of the tutorial and a table of contents.

In the table of contents, both the section titles and the page numbers are hyperlinks. If you view the PDF file online, you can click on those items and go directly to the various parts of the tutorial. Even if you read a printout of the PDF file, the page numbers are still an important navigational tool. Cross-references between panels in the tutorial are similarly converted to hyperlinks and printable page numbers. Best of all, any hyperlinks to web sites are also converted to hyperlinks. If your machine is connected, and you have a recent version of the Adobe Acrobat Reader, you can click on the web site and go directly to it.

Pages in the body of the tutorial feature the text and illustrations of each panel, with a horizontal line between panels. The first panel of each section starts on a new page. Figure 9-9 shows the layout of an individual panel in the PDF file.

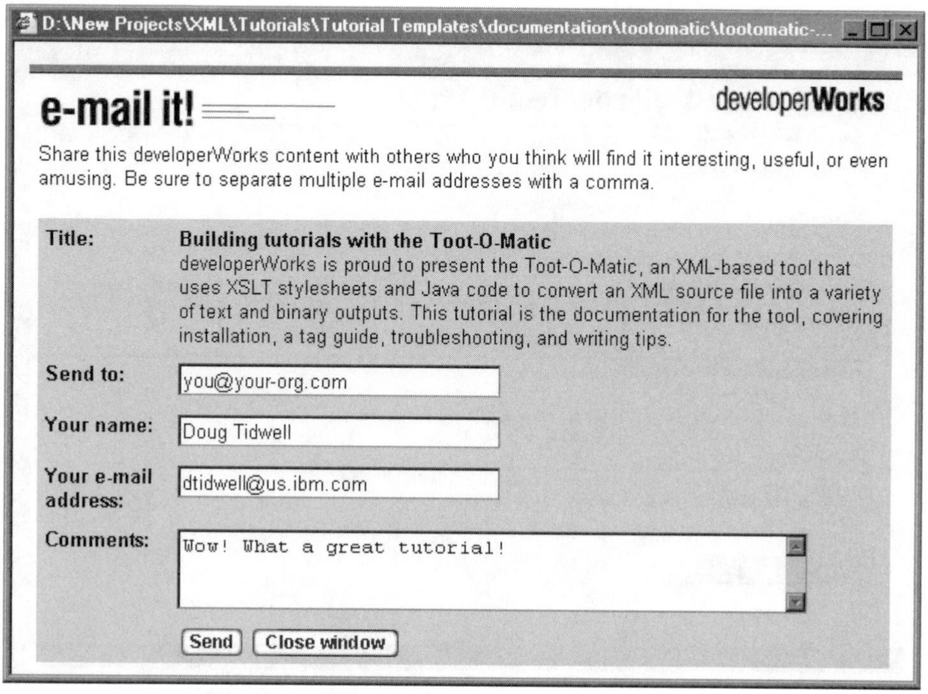

Figure 9-7. The email panel

To accommodate our worldwide audience, we create letter-sized and A4-sized versions of the PDF file. We use the same stylesheet for each PDF file; we simply change the page dimensions and let the Formatting Objects to PDF (FOP) tool generate the line, column, and page breaks for us. We are responsible for creating the formatting objects the FOP tool needs to do its work.

XML Document Design

Now that we've covered how our tutorials appear in all their various forms, we'll discuss the structure of the XML documents that become our tutorials. To start with, we used some obvious structural principles:

- A `<tutorial>` should contain a single `<title>` and one or more `<section>`s.
- A `<section>` should contain a single `<title>` and one or more `<panel>`s.
- A `<panel>` should contain a single `<title>` and a `<body>`, which in turn contains the markup for the panel's contents.

This foundation creates an XML structure identical to the layout of our tutorials, so it was an obvious place to start.

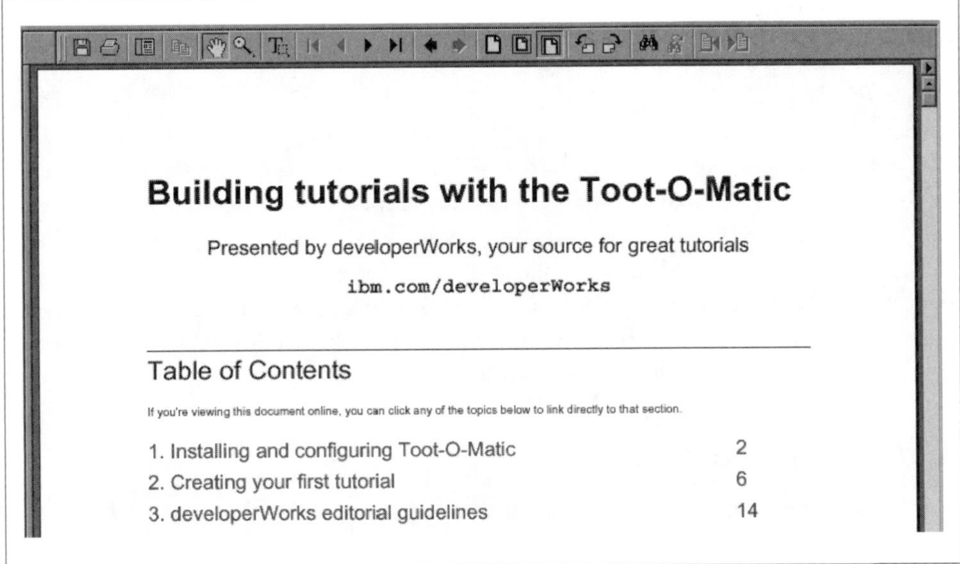

Building tutorials with the Toot-O-Matic

Presented by developerWorks, your source for great tutorials

ibm.com/developerWorks

Table of Contents

If you're viewing this document online, you can click any of the topics below to link directly to that section.

Figure 9-8. First page of the tutorial PDF file

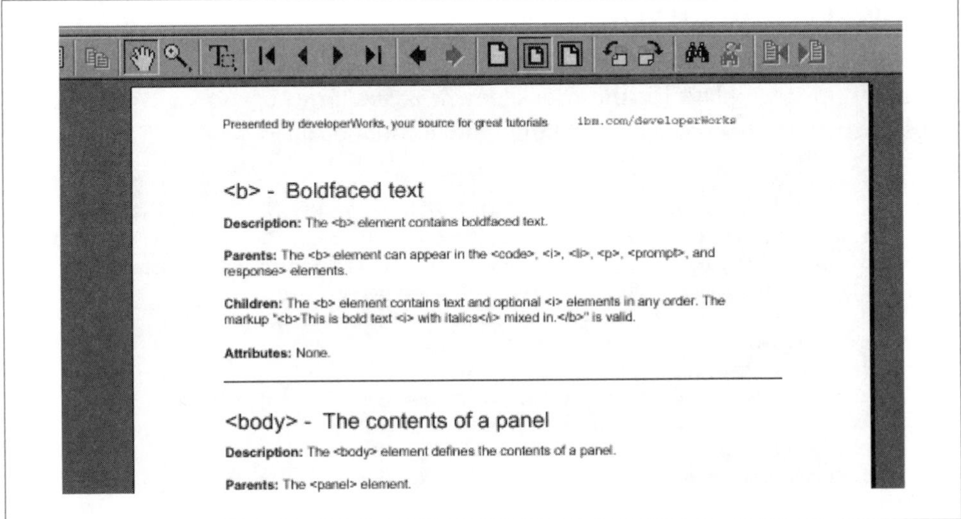

Presented by developerWorks, your source for great tutorials ibm.com/developerWorks

<b> - Boldfaced text

Description: The <b> element contains boldfaced text.

Parents: The <b> element can appear in the <code>, <i>, <li>, <p>, <prompt>, and response> elements.

Children: The <b> element contains text and optional <i> elements in any order. The markup "<b>This is bold text <i> with italics</i> mixed in.</b>" is valid.

Attributes: None.

<body> - The contents of a panel

Description: The <body> element defines the contents of a panel.

Parents: The <panel> element.

Figure 9-9. PDF layout for an individual panel

Individual Panels

An individual panel has the following structure:

```
<panel>
  <title>Title of the panel</title>
  <body>
    <image-column>
```

```
    <text-column>
      Basic HTML markup (<p>, <ol>, <li>, <b>, <i>, <u>, <a>, etc.)
    </text-column>
  </body>
</panel>
```

The <image-column> element is optional; it's used to define the image that appears on the left side of the panel. We intentionally kept our markup design simple so that rendering the tutorials would be relatively straightforward. Although this approach is heavy-handed, it does allow us to enforce a certain amount of consistency in the layout of our tutorials. Reusing common HTML tags inside the <text-column> element allows authors to use the tags they already know and love, and it simplifies the XML-to-HTML transformation.

XSLT Source Code

Now that we've discussed the design issues we went through as we defined our XML document structure, we'll talk about how our XSLT stylesheets transform XML-tagged tutorials into the files we want.

Stylesheets and Modes

To start with, we use the XSLT `mode` attribute to process the same set of nodes several times. Our template for the root element is similar to a Java or C++ program whose `main()` method contains nothing but subroutine calls:

```
<xsl:template match="/">
  <xsl:apply-templates select="tutorial" mode="build-main-index"/>
  <xsl:apply-templates select="tutorial" mode="build-section-indexes"/>
  <xsl:apply-templates select="tutorial" mode="build-individual-panels"/>
  <xsl:apply-templates select="tutorial" mode="generate-graphics"/>
  <xsl:apply-templates select="tutorial" mode="generate-pdf-file">
    <xsl:with-param name="page-size" select="'letter'"/>
  </xsl:apply-templates>
  <xsl:apply-templates select="tutorial" mode="generate-pdf-file">
    <xsl:with-param name="page-size" select="'a4'"/>
  </xsl:apply-templates>
  <xsl:apply-templates select="tutorial" mode="generate-zip-file"/>
</xsl:template>
```

If this were a Java program, we might create a `main()` method that looks like this:

```
public static void main(String[] argv)
{
  buildMainIndex();
  buildSectionIndexes();
  buildIndividualPanels();
  generateGraphics();
  generatePDFFile("letter");
```

```
    generatePDFFile("a4");
    generateZipFile();
  }
```

This style of coding facilitates maintenance; if the PDF files aren't generated correctly, the templates with `mode="generate-pdf-file"` are the obvious place to start debugging. In addition, we structured the files so that all the templates for a given `mode` are in a single file that can be included into our main stylesheet:

```
<xsl:include href="toot-o-matic-variables.xsl"/>

<xsl:include href="xslt-utilities.xsl"/>
<xsl:include href="dw-style.xsl"/>

<xsl:include href="build-main-index.xsl"/>
<xsl:include href="build-section-indexes.xsl"/>
<xsl:include href="build-individual-panels.xsl"/>
<xsl:include href="build-graphics.xsl"/>
<xsl:include href="build-pdf-file.xsl"/>
<xsl:include href="build-zip-file.xsl"/>
```

In addition to the obviously named files, the file *toot-o-matic-variables.xsl* defines several global variables used throughout the stylesheets, *xslt-utilities.xsl* is a library of generic routines (substring replacement, for example) we use, and *dw-style.xsl* defines the look and feel of our HTML pages.

Initializing Global Variables

It's worth discussing the global variables initialized in *toot-o-matic-variables.xsl*. All of these variables are used throughout our various stylesheets, and initializing them saves us a significant amount of processing time. The most significant variable is `$mouse-effects`. This variable is an automatically generated segment of JavaScript code used to process mouseover effects on all the HTML pages we generate. Here's how the generated code looks:

```
<!-- var emailAbstract="developerWorks is proud to present the Toot-O-Matic,...";
var justTitle="Building tutorials with the Toot-O-Matic";
var tutorialPrereqs="http://www-4.ibm.com/education/tootomatic";
var menu1blurb="Installing and configuring Toot-O-Matic";
var menu2blurb="Creating your first tutorial";
var menu3blurb="developerWorks editorial guidelines";
var menu4blurb="Toot-O-Matic tag guide";
var menu5blurb="Toot-O-Matic tag reference";
var menu6blurb="Troubleshooting";
var menu7blurb="Feedback";

var browser = "x";
if (navigator.userAgent.indexOf("Mozilla/4") != -1) browser = "N3";
else if (navigator.userAgent.indexOf("Mozilla/3") != -1) browser = "N3";
else browser = "x";
```

```
if (browser=="N3")
{
  var menu1over=new Image(108,68);
  var menu1out=new Image(108,68);
  var menu2over=new Image(108,68);
  var menu2out=new Image(108,68);
  var menu3over=new Image(108,68);
  var menu3out=new Image(108,68);
  ...
  var topmainover=new Image(77,15);
  var topmainout=new Image(77,15);
  var bottommainover=new Image(77,15);
  var bottommainout=new Image(77,15);
  var topsectionover=new Image(98,15);
  var topsectionout=new Image(98,15);
  var bottomsectionover=new Image(98,15);
  var bottomsectionout=new Image(98,15);
  var topfeedbackover=new Image(80,15);
  var topfeedbackout=new Image(80,15);
  var bottomfeedbackover=new Image(80,15);
  var bottomfeedbackout=new Image(80,15);
  var toppreviousover=new Image(77,15);
  var toppreviousout=new Image(77,15);
  var bottompreviousover=new Image(77,15);
  var bottompreviousout=new Image(77,15);
  var topnextover=new Image(60,15);
  var topnextout=new Image(60,15);
  var bottomnextover=new Image(60,15);
  var bottomnextout=new Image(60,15);
  var topnextsectionover=new Image(108,15);
  var topnextsectionout=new Image(108,15);
  var bottomnextsectionover=new Image(108,15);
  var bottomnextsectionout=new Image(108,15);

  menu1over.src="imagemaster/himenu1.jpg";
  menu1out.src="imagemaster/menu1.jpg";
  menu2over.src="imagemaster/himenu2.jpg";
  menu2out.src="imagemaster/menu2.jpg";
  menu3over.src="imagemaster/himenu3.jpg";
  menu3out.src="imagemaster/menu3.jpg";
  ...
  var mainblurb="Main menu";
  var sectionblurb="Section menu";
  var feedbackblurb="Give feedback on this tutorial";
  var previousblurb="Go to previous panel";
  var nextblurb="Go to next panel";
  var nextsectionblurb="Go to next section";

  topmainover.src="../i/h-main.gif";
  topmainout.src="../i/main.gif";
...
}
function iOut(image)
{
```

```
  if (browser=="N3")document[image].src=eval(image + "out.src");
}
function iOver(image)
{
  if (browser=="N3")document[image].src=eval(image + "over.src");
}
// -->
```

This JavaScript code is used for the mouseover effects on the HTML panels. To streamline processing, we generate this code as a variable. (We've removed roughly half the code here to keep the listing short; most of this code deals with initializing a number of variables.) Whenever we create a new HTML page, we simply insert this variable into the output document:

```
<script language="javascript">
  <xsl:value-of select="$mouse-effects"/>
</script>
```

As in traditional programming, storing frequently used values in a variable instead of calculating them each time simplifies the code and improves performance. Notice in the code listing that a significant amount of JavaScript code is generated from the XML source document. This fragment is the XSLT that generates a set of JavaScript variables that contain the titles of all the sections:

```
<xsl:for-each select="/tutorial/section">
  <xsl:text>var menu</xsl:text>
  <xsl:value-of select="position()"/>
  <xsl:text>blurb="</xsl:text>
  <xsl:value-of select="title"/>
  <xsl:text>"; </xsl:text>
  <xsl:value-of select="$newline"/>
</xsl:for-each>
```

The code generates seven new variables, one for each <section> element in our tutorial:

```
var menu1blurb="Installing and configuring Toot-O-Matic";
var menu2blurb="Creating your first tutorial";
var menu3blurb="developerWorks editorial guidelines";
var menu4blurb="Toot-O-Matic tag guide";
var menu5blurb="Toot-O-Matic tag reference";
var menu6blurb="Troubleshooting";
var menu7blurb="Feedback";
```

This is one of many cases when a naming convention is invaluable. If we want the JavaScript variable that contains the title of the fifth section, we know that variable is named `menu5blurb`. This technique is useful in many other places, as well. If we're creating HTML files for the third `<section>`, and we're currently processing the fourth `<panel>` in that `<section>`, and the root filename we're using is *tootomatic*, the newly created HTML file will be named *tootomatic-3-4.html*. Similarly, if we want to create a link to the previous and next HTML files, those files are named *tootomatic-3-3.html* and *tootomatic-3-5.html*, respectively. You'll see this technique used throughout this case study.

Generating the Main Menu Panel

The Main menu panel consists of a standard header and footer, with a list of all sections of the tutorial in between. Clicking on any of the section titles takes you to the first panel in that section. To enhance the visual appeal of the panel, generated graphics and mouseover effects are used to display the panel title.

The stylesheet that generates the list of sections is straightforward. The header and footer are generated from boilerplate text; the list of sections is generated with an `<xsl:for-each>` element:

```
<xsl:for-each select="section">
  <a border="0">
    <xsl:attribute name="href">
      <xsl:value-of select="$fn"/>
      <xsl:text>-</xsl:text>
      <xsl:value-of select="position()"/>
      <xsl:text>-1.html</xsl:text>
    </xsl:attribute>
    <xsl:attribute name="onMouseOver">
      <xsl:text>iOver('menu</xsl:text>
      <xsl:value-of select="position()"/>
      <xsl:text>'); self.status=menu</xsl:text>
      <xsl:value-of select="position()"/>
      <xsl:text>blurb; return true;</xsl:text>
    </xsl:attribute>
    <xsl:attribute name="onMouseOut">
      <xsl:text>iOut('menu</xsl:text>
      <xsl:value-of select="position()"/>
      <xsl:text>'); self.status=''; return true;</xsl:text>
    </xsl:attribute>
    <img width="380" height="20" border="0">
      <xsl:attribute name="name">
        <xsl:text>menu</xsl:text>
        <xsl:value-of select="position()"/>
      </xsl:attribute>
```

```
        <xsl:attribute name="src">
          <xsl:text>imagemaster/</xsl:text>
          <xsl:text>menu</xsl:text>
          <xsl:value-of select="position()"/>
          <xsl:text>.jpg</xsl:text>
        </xsl:attribute>
        <xsl:attribute name="alt">
          <xsl:value-of select="position()"/>
          <xsl:text>. </xsl:text>
          <xsl:value-of select="title"/>
        </xsl:attribute>
      </img>
    </a>
    <br/>
  </xsl:for-each>
```

This XSLT produces the following HTML code for our example XML file:

```
<a border="0" href="tootomatic-1-1.html"
  onMouseOver="iOver('menu1'); self.status=menu1blurb; return true;"
  onMouseOut="iOut('menu1'); self.status=''; return true;">
  <img border="0" height="20" width="380" name="menu1"
    src="imagemaster/menu1.jpg"
    alt="1. Installing and configuring Toot-O-Matic">
</a>
<br>
<a border="0" href="tootomatic-2-1.html"
  onMouseOver="iOver('menu2'); self.status=menu2blurb; return true;"
  onMouseOut="iOut('menu2'); self.status=''; return true;">
  <img border="0" height="20" width="380" name="menu2"
    src="imagemaster/menu2.jpg"
    alt="2. Creating your first tutorial">
</a>
<br>
<a border="0" href="tootomatic-3-1.html"
  onMouseOver="iOver('menu3'); self.status=menu3blurb; return true;"
  onMouseOut="iOut('menu3'); self.status=''; return true;">
  <img border="0" height="20" width="380" name="menu3"
    src="imagemaster/menu3.jpg"
    alt="3. developerWorks editorial guidelines">
</a>
<br>
<a border="0" href="tootomatic-4-1.html"
  onMouseOver="iOver('menu4'); self.status=menu4blurb; return true;"
  onMouseOut="iOut('menu4'); self.status=''; return true;">
  <img border="0" height="20" width="380" name="menu4"
    src="imagemaster/menu4.jpg"
    alt="4. Toot-O-Matic tag guide">
</a>
<br>
<a border="0" href="tootomatic-5-1.html"
  onMouseOver="iOver('menu5'); self.status=menu5blurb; return true;"
  onMouseOut="iOut('menu5'); self.status=''; return true;">
  <img border="0" height="20" width="380" name="menu5"
```

```
      src="imagemaster/menu5.jpg"
      alt="5. Toot-O-Matic tag reference">
  </a>
  <br>
  <a border="0" href="tootomatic-6-1.html"
    onMouseOver="iOver('menu6'); self.status=menu6blurb; return true;"
    onMouseOut="iOut('menu6'); self.status=''; return true;">
    <img border="0" height="20" width="380" name="menu6"
      src="imagemaster/menu6.jpg"
      alt="6. Troubleshooting">
  </a>
  <br>
  <a border="0" href="tootomatic-7-1.html"
    onMouseOver="iOver('menu7'); self.status=menu7blurb; return true;"
    onMouseOut="iOut('menu7'); self.status=''; return true;">
    <img border="0" height="20" width="380" name="menu7"
      src="imagemaster/menu7.jpg"
      alt="7. Feedback">
  </a>
```

Notice the number of things that are automatically generated in this list of sections. We know the filename of any given section, thanks to our filenaming convention. The first panel in the fifth section of the tutorial is *tootomatic-5-1.html*, for example. For the JavaScript mouseover effects we mentioned previously, we name the <img> elements in the list menu1, menu2, etc. Similarly, the name of each graphic is *imagemaster/menu1.jpg*, *imagemaster/menu2.jpg*, etc. The onMouseOver attribute uses variables such as menu1blurb and menu2blurb. Generating these items removes the chance for human error (once the stylesheets are correct) and allows us to control the look and feel of the HTML pages in the tutorial.

Generating the Section Indexes

To generate a section index, we create an HTML file with an ordered list of all of the <panel> elements in the current <section>. Retrieving the titles of all the panels can be done with a <xsl:for-each> element in the stylesheet:

```
<xsl:for-each select="panel">
  <img border="0" src="../i/arrow.gif"/>
  <a>
    <xsl:attribute name="href">
      <xsl:value-of select="$fn"/><xsl:text>-</xsl:text>
      <xsl:value-of select="$sectionNumber"/><xsl:text>-</xsl:text>
      <xsl:value-of select="position()"/><xsl:text>.html</xsl:text>
    </xsl:attribute>
    <xsl:value-of select="position()"/><xsl:text>. </xsl:text>
    <xsl:value-of select="title"/>
  </a>
  <br/>
</xsl:for-each>
```

In this listing, the variable `$fn` is defined as the root filename used to generate all HTML filenames for this tutorial. The filename convention used for section indexes is *index1.html* for the first section index, *index2.html* for the second section index, etc. This convention makes it easy to generate the section index when we need it, and it makes it easy for the individual panels in a given section to reference the proper section index on each panel.

We use the Xalan `Redirect` extension to write output to multiple files. Here's how we invoke that extension to begin writing output to another file:

```
<xsl:for-each select="section">
  <redirect:write select="concat($curDir, $fileSep, 'index', position(),
    '.html')">
```

The `select` attribute of the `<redirect:write>` element defines the name of the output file. To generate this filename, we concatenate the current directory to which we're writing files (a global variable), the file separator character (another global variable), the text `index`, the position of this section, and the text `.html`. If we use the *tootomatic* directory on a Windows machine, the index for the second `<section>` will be written to the file *tootomatic\index2.html*. We use the *Redirect* extension whenever we need to generate an HTML file for a section index or an individual panel.

Generating the Individual Panels

The masthead and footer of each panel are fairly straightforward; both use a predefined format and a series of links common to all pages on IBM sites. This is a perfect use for named templates. We need to create certain HTML markup for the masthead of each HTML page, and we need to create more markup for the footer of each page. In addition, we need to create the title bar at the top of each page and a navigation bar (an area with Previous and Next links, among other things) at the top and bottom of most pages. We use four templates, cleverly named `dw-masthead`, `dw-title-bar`, `dw-nav-bar`, and `dw-footer`, to do this:

```
<xsl:call-template name="dw-masthead"/>
<xsl:call-template name="dw-title-bar"/>
<xsl:call-template name="dw-nav-bar">
  <xsl:with-param name="includeMain" select="'youBetcha'"/>
  <xsl:with-param name="sectionNumber" select="$sectionNumber"/>
  <xsl:with-param name="position" select="$pos"/>
  <xsl:with-param name="last" select="$last"/>
  <xsl:with-param name="topOrBottom" select="'top'"/>
  <xsl:with-param name="oneOrTwo" select="'two'"/>
</xsl:call-template>
```

```
<!-- Processing for the main body of the page goes here -->

<xsl:call-template name="dw-nav-bar">
  <xsl:with-param name="includeMain" select="'youBetcha'"/>
  <xsl:with-param name="sectionNumber" select="$sectionNumber"/>
  <xsl:with-param name="position" select="$pos"/>
  <xsl:with-param name="last" select="$last"/>
  <xsl:with-param name="topOrBottom" select="'bottom'"/>
  <xsl:with-param name="oneOrTwo" select="'two'"/>
</xsl:call-template>
<xsl:call-template name="dw-footer"/>
```

Of the four templates, only `dw-nav-bar` takes any parameters. Depending on the page we're currently generating, we may or may not need the Main menu button (we don't include this button on the Main menu panel). We need the current section number so the navigation bar can create filenames for the links to the section menu, the previous panel, and the next panel. The `position` parameter defines the position of this particular panel; `last` defines the position of the last panel. If `position` is 1, then the Previous button will be disabled. If `position` is equal to `last`, then the Next button will be disabled. The parameter `topOrBottom` defines whether this navigation bar is being created at the top or bottom of the panel (we have to name the images differently so the JavaScript mouseover effects work correctly). Finally, the `oneOrTwo` parameter determines whether this panel will have two navigation bars or just one. This is also necessary for the mouseover effects.

Now that we've built all these parts of the page, building the actual content of the panel is somewhat anticlimactic. We support a limited set of HTML tags (the 20 or so most-used tags, added sparingly as we've needed to add new functions to the tool), most of which are converted directly into their HTML equivalents.

Generating the PDF Files

Converting the XML document to an XSL Formatting Objects (XSL-FO) stream is fairly straightforward, as well. Our printed layout consists of the graphics and text from the tutorial, combined with page numbers, headers, and footers to create high-quality printed output. We use the Apache XML Project's FOP (Formatting Objects to PDF) tool to do this.

When we invoke the PDF-generating templates with the `mode=generate-pdf` attribute, we pass in the `page-size` parameter to set the dimensions of the printed page. We generate PDFs with both letter-sized and A4-sized pages to support our customers around the world.

To create the PDF, we first create the output file of formatting objects, converting the various XML tags from our source document into the various formatting objects we need:

```
<fo:block font-size="16pt" line-height="19pt" font-weight="bold"
  space-after.optimum="12pt">
  Introduction to JavaServer Pages
</fo:block>
<fo:block space-after.optimum="6pt">
  In today's environment, most web sites want to display dynamic
  content based on the user and the session. Most content, such
  as images, text, and banner ads, is most easily built with
  HTML editors. So we need to mix the "static" content of HTML
  files with "directives" for accessing or generating dynamic
  content.
</fo:block>
<fo:block space-after.optimum="6pt">
  JavaServer Pages meet this need. They provide server-side
  scripting support for generating web pages with combined
  static and dynamic content.
</fo:block>
```

Currently, the XSL:FO specification is a candidate recommendation at the World Wide Web Consortium (W3C). Because future changes are likely, we won't discuss the formatting objects themselves. It suffices to say that our stylesheet defines page layouts (margins, running headers and footers, etc.) and then creates a number of formatting objects inside those page layouts. The FOP tool handles the details of calculating line, page, and column breaks, page references, and hyperlinks.

Once the file of formatting objects is created, we call an extension function to convert the formatting objects file into a PDF. Here's the exension's main code:

```
public static void buildPDFFile(String foFilename, String pdfFilename)
{
  try
  {
    XMLReader parser =
      (XMLReader) Class.forName("org.apache.xerces.parsers.SAXParser")
                       .newInstance();
    Driver driver = new Driver();
    driver.setRenderer("org.apache.fop.render.pdf.PDFRenderer",
                       Version.getVersion());
    driver.addElementMapping("org.apache.fop.fo.StandardElementMapping");
    driver.addElementMapping("org.apache.fop.svg.SVGElementMapping");
    driver.addPropertyList("org.apache.fop.fo.StandardPropertyListMapping");
    driver.addPropertyList("org.apache.fop.svg.SVGPropertyListMapping");
    driver.setOutputStream(new FileOutputStream(pdfFilename));
    driver.buildFOTree(parser, new InputSource(foFilename));
    driver.format();
    driver.render();
  }
```

The code merely creates the FOP `Driver` object, sets its various properties, and then tells it to render the formatting objects in a PDF file. The main difficulty here is in determining how the various XML elements should be converted to formatting objects; once the conversion is done, we have a tool that generates high-quality printable output from our XML source files. Best of all, this code uses open source tools exclusively.

Generating the JPEG Files

Another thing we need to produce for the tutorial is a series of JPEG files. To have precise control over the appearance of the titles in the tutorial, we create a JPEG file in which the title text is written in a particular font. We discussed this code in Chapter 8, so we won't go over it here. Here's the first significant section of the *build-graphics.xsl* file:

```
<xsl:template match="tutorial" mode="generate-graphics">
  <xsl:choose>
    <xsl:when test="function-available('jpeg:buildJPEGFile')">
      <xsl:value-of
        select="jpeg:buildJPEGFile(title,
        concat('master', $fileSep, 'masthead.jpg'),
        concat($curDir, $fileSep, 'imagemaster', $fileSep, 'masthead.jpg'),
        $baseFont, 27, 5, 30, 0, 0, 0)"/>
    </xsl:when>
    <xsl:otherwise>
      <xsl:message terminate="yes">
        Error! JPEG library not available!
      </xsl:message>
    </xsl:otherwise>
  </xsl:choose>
```

The `buildJPEGFile` function takes several parameters, including the title text (in the example, our XPath expression passes in the value of the `title` element), the name of the background JPEG file (we load this file, draw the text on top of it, and then save the new JPEG), the name of the new JPEG file, the name of the font, and other details about the font size, the x- and y-coordinates where the text should start, and the color in which to draw it.

Although neither this extension nor the stylesheet that calls it are rocket science, they save us a tremendous amount of time in the tutorial development process. Before we had the Toot-O-Matic, we had to ask our highly trained, highly talented, and highly overworked graphics staff to create these graphics for us; now we do it automatically and the graphics staff can focus their talents on more important things.

Generating the Zip File

Our last task is to generate a zip file that contains all the files needed to view the tutorial locally. This includes all HTML files, all standard graphics, all JPEGs we generate, and any graphics referenced in the XML source (anything in an `<img>` tag). We call another Java extension to build the zip file. Determining which files should be loaded into the zip file relies heavily on our naming conventions.

When we invoke the `buildZipFile` function, we pass in several arguments. The first three are the root filename, the directory to which we write the output files, and the file separator for this platform. The next argument is the `<tutorial>` node itself; the extension uses DOM functions to determine what files should be added to the zip file. The final argument is a `node-set` of all the things that reference graphics files in the XML source. That includes the `img` attribute of any tag and the `src` attribute of the `<img>` element. Here's what the function call looks like:

```
<xsl:template match="tutorial" mode="generate-zip-file">
  <xsl:choose>
    <xsl:when test="function-available('zip:buildZipFile')">
      <xsl:variable name="referencedGraphics"
        select="./@img|//image-column/@img|//img/@src"/>
      <xsl:value-of
        select="zip:buildZipFile($fn, $curDir,
                                 $fileSep, ., $referencedGraphics)"/>
    </xsl:when>
    <xsl:otherwise>
      <xsl:message terminate="yes">
        Error! Zip file library not available!
      </xsl:message>
    </xsl:otherwise>
  </xsl:choose>
</xsl:template>
```

In the extension function code itself, we start by creating the `ZipOutputStream` itself:

```
ZipOutputStream zipOut =
  new ZipOutputStream(new FileOutputStream(currentDirectory +
                                           fileSeparator +
                                           baseFilename + ".zip"));
```

Once we've created our `ZipOutputStream`, we'll see if there's a comment for the zip file in the `zip-file-comment` attribute of the `<tutorial>` element:

```
Node currentNode = tutorialElement.nextNode();

while (currentNode != null)
{
  if (currentNode.getLocalName().equals("tutorial"))
  {
    ElementImpl currentElement = (ElementImpl)currentNode;
```

```
    String zipFileComment = currentElement.getAttribute("zip-file-comment");
    if (zipFileComment != null)
      zipOut.setComment(zipFileComment);
    else
    {
      zipFileComment = currentElement.getAttribute("alt");
      if (zipFileComment != null)
        zipOut.setComment(zipFileComment);
    }
```

With everything we do with the DOM nodes, we'll need to make sure we actually work with the appropriate nodes; that's why we use the function call `getLocalName().equals("tutorial")`. Once we've found the `<tutorial>` element, we can work with its children to figure out the names of all the HTML and JPEG files we need to add to the zip file. If the `<tutorial>` element has five `<section>` children, and the first `<section>` contains eleven `<panel>`s, then we'll need to write the files *tootomatic-1-1.html* through *tootomatic-1-11.html* to the zip file. (This assumes that the base filename we use is *tootomatic.*) Here's an excerpt from the code:

```
int numKids = currentElement.getChildCount();
int numSections = 0;
for (int i = 0; i < numKids; i++)
{
  Node currentChild = currentElement.getChild(i);
  if (currentChild.getLocalName().equals("section"))
  {
    ElementImpl currentChildElement = (ElementImpl)currentChild
    fileToZip = new File(currentDirectory + fileSeparator + "index" +
                         ++numSections + ".html");
    fis = new FileInputStream(fileToZip);
    entry = new ZipEntry(currentDirectory + fileSeparator +
                              fileToZip.getName());
    if (zipOut != null)
    {
      zipOut.putNextEntry(entry);
      while((bytes_read = fis.read(buffer)) != -1)
        zipOut.write(buffer, 0, bytes_read);
    }
    fis.close();

    int numGrandkids = currentChildElement.getChildCount();
    int numPanels = 0;
    for (int j = 0; j < numGrandkids; j++)
    {
      Node currentGrandchildElement = currentChildElement.getChild(j);
      if (currentGrandchildElement.getLocalName().equals("panel"))
      {
        fileToZip = new File(currentDirectory + fileSeparator +
                             baseFilename + "-" + numSections + "-" +
                             ++numPanels + ".html");
        fis = new FileInputStream(fileToZip);
        entry = new ZipEntry(currentDirectory + fileSeparator +
```

```
                              fileToZip.getName());
          if (zipOut != null)
          {
            zipOut.putNextEntry(entry);
            while((bytes_read = fis.read(buffer)) != -1)
              zipOut.write(buffer, 0, bytes_read);
          }
          fis.close();
        }
      }
    }
  }
```

Now that we know how many <section> elements are in our <tutorial>, we can write all the generated JPEG graphics to the zip file. Our extension function also contains a static array of the filenames of all standard files used by every tutorial:

```
static String standardFiles[] = {"c.gif", "sw-gold.gif",
                                 "main.gif", "xmain.gif",
                                 "section.gif", "xsection.gif",
                                 "feedback.gif", "xfeedback.gif",
                                 "previous.gif", "xprevious.gif",
                                 "next.gif", "xnext.gif",
                                 "icon-discuss.gif", "icon-email.gif",
                                 "icon-pdf-ltr.gif", "icon-zip.gif",
                                 "icon-pdf-a4.gif",
                                 "mast_logo.gif", "shopibm.gif",
                                 "support.gif", "downloads.gif",
                                 "mast_lnav_sp.gif", "about.gif",
                                 "h-menu.gif", "h-main.gif",
                                 "h-section.gif", "h-feedback.gif",
                                 "h-previous.gif", "h-next.gif",
                                 "nextsection.gif", "h-nextsection.gif",
                                 "arrow.gif", "mgradient.gif",
                                 "email.gif", "dw-logo2.gif",
                                 "btn-send.gif", "btn-close.gif",
                                 "emailfriend.js"};
```

We store each of these standard files in the zip file for each tutorial. Storing the names of the files in an array makes it easy to add or delete new files from the list. If this list of files changed frequently, we would consider writing an XML-based configuration file that listed all standard files. We could then parse that file, extract the filenames from it, and add those files to the zip file.

Our next task is to use our `node-set` of graphics elements to add all referenced graphics to the zip file:

```
currentNode = graphicsElements.nextNode();

HashMap zipEntries = new HashMap();
while (currentNode != null)
```

```
{
  String nextGraphicsFile = currentNode.getNodeValue();
  if (!zipEntries.containsKey(nextGraphicsFile))
  {
    fileToZip = new File(currentNode.getNodeValue());
    fis = new FileInputStream(fileToZip);
    entry = new ZipEntry(currentDirectory + fileSeparator +
                         currentNode.getNodeValue());
    zipOut.putNextEntry(entry);
    while ((bytes_read = fis.read(buffer)) != -1)
      zipOut.write(buffer, 0, bytes_read);
    zipEntries.put(nextGraphicsFile, nextGraphicsFile);
  }
  currentNode = graphicsElements.nextNode();
}
```

As we add a referenced graphics file to the zip file, we put the name of the file into a `HashMap`. If we attempt to add a file to the zip archive and that file is already in the archive, we'll get an exception. To avoid that problem, we check each filename before we add it to the zip file.

Our last task is to close the `ZipOutputStream`:

```
zipOut.flush();
zipOut.close();
```

Summary

The stylesheets and extensions that make up the Toot-O-Matic exercise almost everything in XSLT and XPath. Best of all, it allows us to take the structured content of an XML document and transform it into dozens of HTML, JPEG, PDF, and zip files, all of which are extensively cross-referenced and hyperlinked. Even though developerWorks doesn't actually publish the XML file itself (the XML file never leaves our server), using XML for this purpose saves us a tremendous amount of time and money. If you've got a project that needs to convert structured data into several different kinds of documents, an XSLT-based solution can be a winner.

If you'd like to look at the source code for the Toot-O-Matic, it's available at *http://www6.software.ibm.com/dl/devworks/dw-tootomatic-p*. Even if you're not writing tutorials, there are a number of useful techniques in the code that you're welcome to use in your own projects. The developerWorks site also has articles and a discussion forum related to the Toot-O-Matic code.

XSLT Reference

This chapter is a complete reference to all the elements defined in the XSLT specification.

<xsl:apply-imports> — Allows you to apply any overridden templates to the current node. It is comparable to the `super()` method in Java.

Category

Instruction

Required Attributes

None.

Optional Attributes

None.

Content

None. `<xsl:apply-imports>` is an empty element.

Appears in

`<xsl:apply-imports>` appears inside a template.

Defined in

XSLT section 5.6, Overriding Template Rules.

Example

Here is a short XML file we'll use to illustrate `<xsl:apply-imports>`:

```
<?xml version="1.0"?>
<test>
```

```
  <p>This is a test XML document used by several
  of our sample stylesheets.</p>
  <question>
    <text>When completed, the Eiffel Tower was the
    tallest building in the world.</text>
    <true correct="yes">You're correct!  The Eiffel
    Tower was the world's tallest building until 1930.</true>
    <false>No, the Eiffel Tower was the world's tallest
    building for over 30 years.</false>
  </question>
  <question>
    <text>New York's Empire State Building knocked the
    Eiffel Tower from its pedestal.</text>
    <true>No, that's not correct.</true>
    <false correct="yes">Correct!  New York's Chrysler
    Building, completed in 1930, became the world's tallest.</false>
  </question>
</test>
```

Here's the stylesheet we'll import:

```
<?xml version="1.0"?>
<xsl:stylesheet version="1.0" xmlns:xsl="http://www.w3.org/1999/XSL/Transform">

  <xsl:output method="html"/>

  <xsl:template match="/">
    <html>
      <body>
        <xsl:for-each select="//text|//true|//false">
          <p>
            <xsl:apply-templates select="."/>
          </p>
        </xsl:for-each>
      </body>
    </html>
  </xsl:template>

  <xsl:template match="text">
    <xsl:text>True or False: </xsl:text><xsl:value-of select="."/>
  </xsl:template>

  <xsl:template match="true|false">
    <b><xsl:value-of select="name()"/>:</b>
    <br/>
    <xsl:value-of select="."/>
  </xsl:template>

</xsl:stylesheet>
```

This template provides basic formatting for the `<true>` and `<false>` elements, as shown in Figure A-1.

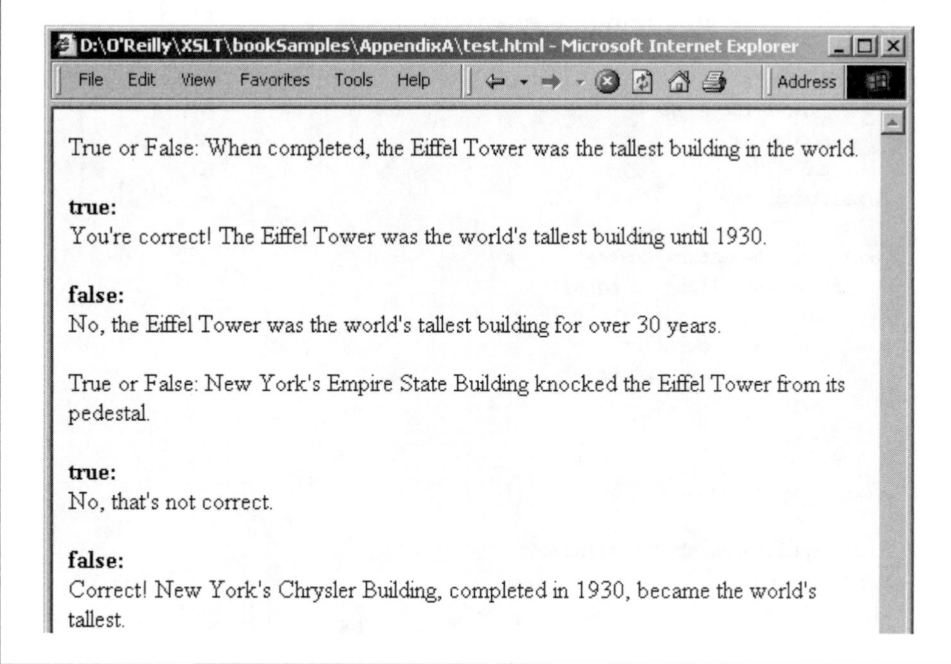

Figure A-1. Document generated with basic formatting

We'll illustrate `<xsl:apply-imports>` with this stylesheet, which imports the other stylesheet:

```
<?xml version="1.0"?>
<xsl:stylesheet version="1.0" xmlns:xsl="http://www.w3.org/1999/XSL/Transform">

  <xsl:import href="imported.xsl"/>
  <xsl:output method="html"/>

  <xsl:template match="/">
    <html>
      <head>
        <title>A Brief Test</title>
        <style>
          <xsl:comment>
            p.question {font-size: 125%; font-weight: bold}
            p.right    {color: green}
            p.wrong    {color: red}
          </xsl:comment>
        </style>
      </head>
      <body>
        <h1>A Brief Test</h1>
```

```
        <xsl:for-each select="//question">
          <table border="1">
            <xsl:apply-templates select="text"/>
            <xsl:apply-templates select="true|false"/>
          </table>
          <br/>
        </xsl:for-each>
      </body>
    </html>
  </xsl:template>

  <xsl:template match="text">
    <tr bgcolor="lightslategray">
      <td>
        <p class="question">
          <xsl:apply-imports/>
        </p>
      </td>
    </tr>
  </xsl:template>

  <xsl:template match="true|false">
    <tr>
      <td>
        <xsl:choose>
          <xsl:when test="@correct='yes'">
            <p class="right">
              <xsl:apply-imports/>
            </p>
          </xsl:when>
          <xsl:otherwise>
            <p class="wrong">
              <xsl:apply-imports/>
            </p>
          </xsl:otherwise>
        </xsl:choose>
      </td>
    </tr>
  </xsl:template>

</xsl:stylesheet>
```

Using <xsl:apply-imports> allows us to augment the behavior of the imported templates. Our new stylesheet produces this document:

```
<html>
<head>
<META http-equiv="Content-Type" content="text/html; charset=UTF-8">
<title>A Brief Test</title>
<style>
```

```
<!--
            p.question {font-size: 125%; font-weight: bold}
            p.right    {color: green}
            p.wrong    {color: red}
          -->
</style>
</head>
<body>
<h1>A Brief Test</h1>
<table border="1">
<tr bgcolor="lightslategray">
<td>
<p class="question">True or False: When completed, the Eiffel
Tower was the tallest building in the world.</p>
</td>
</tr>
<tr>
<td>
<p class="right">
<b>true:</b>
<br>You're correct!  The Eiffel Tower was the world's tallest
building until 1930.</p>
</td>
</tr>
<tr>
<td>
<p class="wrong">
<b>false:</b>
<br>No, the Eiffel Tower was the world's tallest building for
over 30 years.</p>
</td>
</tr>
</table>
<br>
<table border="1">
<tr bgcolor="lightslategray">
<td>
<p class="question">True or False: New York's Empire State Building
knocked the Eiffel Tower from its pedestal.</p>
</td>
</tr>
<tr>
<td>
<p class="wrong">
<b>true:</b>
<br>No, that's not correct.</p>
</td>
</tr>
```

```
<tr>
<td>
<p class="right">
<b>false:</b>
<br>Correct!  New York's Chrysler Building, completed in 1930,
became the world's tallest.</p>
</td>
</tr>
</table>
<br>
</body>
</html>
```

When rendered, this stylesheet looks like Figure A-2.

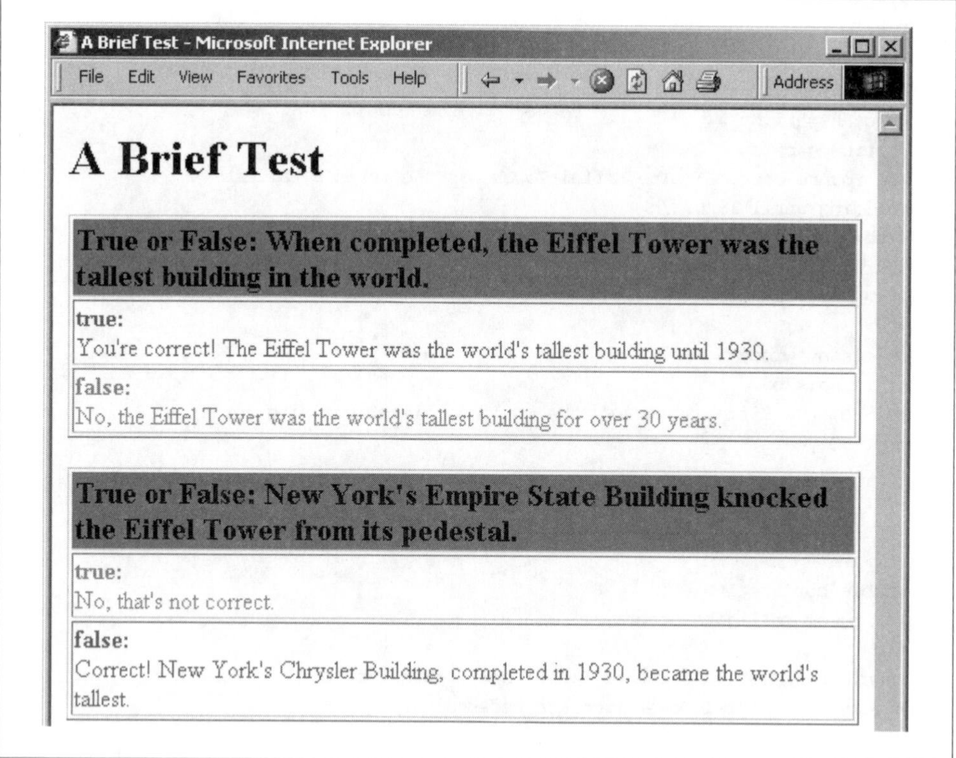

Figure A-2. Document generated with <xsl:apply-imports>

<xsl:apply-templates> — Instructs the XSLT processor to apply the appropriate templates to a node-set.

Category

Instruction

Required Attributes

None.

Optional Attributes

select
: Contains an XPath expression that selects the nodes to which templates should be applied. Valid values include `*` to select the entire node-set. Without this attribute, all element children of the current node are selected.

mode
: Defines a processing mode, a convenient syntax that lets you write specific templates for specific purposes. For example, I could write an `<xsl:template>` with `mode="toc"` to process a node for the table of contents of a document, and other `<xsl:template>`s with `mode="print"`, `mode="online"`, `mode="index"`, etc. to process the same information for different purposes.

Content

The `<xsl:apply-templates>` element can contain any number of `<xsl:sort>` and `<xsl:with-param>` elements. In most cases, `<xsl:apply-templates>` is empty.

Appears in

`<xsl:apply-templates>` appears inside a template.

Defined in

XSLT section 5.4, Applying Template Rules.

Example

In our case study (see Chapter 9), we needed to create several different outputs from the same data. We addressed this need with the `mode` attribute of the `<xsl:apply-templates>` element. Here's the main template (`match="/"`):

```
<xsl:template match="/">
  <xsl:apply-templates select="tutorial" mode="build-main-index"/>
  <redirect:write select="concat($curDir, $fileSep, 'index.html')">
    <xsl:apply-templates select="tutorial" mode="build-main-index"/>
  </redirect:write>
  <xsl:apply-templates select="tutorial" mode="build-section-indexes"/>
  <xsl:apply-templates select="tutorial" mode="build-individual-panels"/>
  <xsl:apply-templates select="tutorial" mode="generate-graphics"/>
  <xsl:apply-templates select="tutorial" mode="generate-pdf-file">
    <xsl:with-param name="page-size" select="'ltr'"/>
  </xsl:apply-templates>
```

```
    <xsl:apply-templates select="tutorial" mode="generate-pdf-file">
      <xsl:with-param name="page-size" select="'a4'"/>
    </xsl:apply-templates>
    <xsl:apply-templates select="tutorial" mode="generate-zip-file"/>
  </xsl:template>
```

Notice that this example selects the <tutorial> element eight times, but applies templates with a different mode (or different parameters for the same mode) each time.

<xsl:attribute> — Allows you to create an attribute in the output document. The advantage of <xsl:attribute> is that it allows you to build the attribute's value from parts of the input document, hardcoded text, values returned by functions, and any other value you can access from your stylesheet.

Category

Instruction

Required Attributes

name

The name attribute defines the name of the attribute created by the <xsl:attribute> element. (No matter how you try to say this, talking about the attributes of the <xsl:attribute> element is confusing, isn't it?)

Optional Attributes

namespace

The namespace attribute defines the namespace URI that should be used for this attribute in the output document. You don't have control over the namespace prefix used; the only thing you specify with the namespace attribute is the URI of the namespace.

Content

An XSLT template. In other words, you can build the contents of an attribute with <xsl:choose> elements, <xsl:text>, and <xsl:value-of> elements.

Appears in

<xsl:attribute> appears inside a template.

Defined in

XSLT section 7.1.3, Creating Attributes with xsl:attribute.

Example

For this example, we want to create an HTML table from the following XML document:

```
<?xml version="1.0"?>
<list xml:lang="en">
  <title>Albums I've bought recently:</title>
  <listitem>The Sacred Art of Dub</listitem>
  <listitem>Only the Poor Man Feel It</listitem>
```

```
    <listitem>Excitable Boy</listitem>
    <listitem xml:lang="sw">Aki Special</listitem>
    <listitem xml:lang="en-gb">Combat Rock</listitem>
    <listitem xml:lang="zu">Talking Timbuktu</listitem>
    <listitem xml:lang="jz">The Birth of the Cool</listitem>
  </list>
```

We'll create a table that has each `<listitem>` in a separate row in the right column of the table, and a single cell with `rowspan` equal to the number of `<listitem>` elements in the XML document on the left. Clearly we can't hardcode a value for the `rowspan` attribute because the number of `<listitem>`s can change. This stylesheet uses `<xsl:attribute>` to do what we want:

```
<?xml version="1.0"?>
<xsl:stylesheet version="1.0" xmlns:xsl="http://www.w3.org/1999/XSL/Transform">

  <xsl:output method="html"/>

  <xsl:template match="/">
    <html>
      <head>
        <title><xsl:value-of select="list/title"/></title>
      </head>
      <body>
        <xsl:apply-templates select="list"/>
      </body>
    </html>
  </xsl:template>

  <xsl:template match="list">
    <table border="1" width="75%">
      <tr>
        <td bgcolor="lightslategray" width="100" align="right">
          <xsl:attribute name="rowspan">
            <xsl:value-of select="count(listitem)"/>
          </xsl:attribute>
          <p style="font-size: 125%">
            <xsl:value-of select="title"/>
          </p>
        </td>
        <td>
          <xsl:value-of select="listitem[1]"/>
        </td>
      </tr>
      <xsl:for-each select="listitem">
        <xsl:if test="position() > 1">
          <tr>
            <td>
              <xsl:value-of select="."/>
            </td>
```

```
        </tr>
      </xsl:if>
    </xsl:for-each>
  </table>
</xsl:template>

</xsl:stylesheet>
```

Here is the generated HTML document:

```
<html>
<head>
<META http-equiv="Content-Type" content="text/html; charset=UTF-8">
<title>Albums I've bought recently:</title>
</head>
<body>
<table width="75%" border="1">
<tr>
<td align="right" width="100" rowspan="7" bgcolor="lightslategray">
<p style="font-size: 125%">Albums I've bought recently:</p>
</td><td>The Sacred Art of Dub</td>
</tr>
<tr>
<td>Only the Poor Man Feel It</td>
</tr>
<tr>
<td>Excitable Boy</td>
</tr>
<tr>
<td>Aki Special</td>
</tr>
<tr>
<td>Combat Rock</td>
</tr>
<tr>
<td>Talking Timbuktu</td>
</tr>
<tr>
<td>The Birth of the Cool</td>
</tr>
</table>
</body>
</html>
```

Notice that the <td> element had several attributes hardcoded on it; those attributes are combined with the attribute we created with <xsl:attribute>. You can have as many <xsl:attribute> elements as you want, but they must appear together as the first thing inside the element to which you add attributes. Figure A-3 shows how our generated HTML document looks.

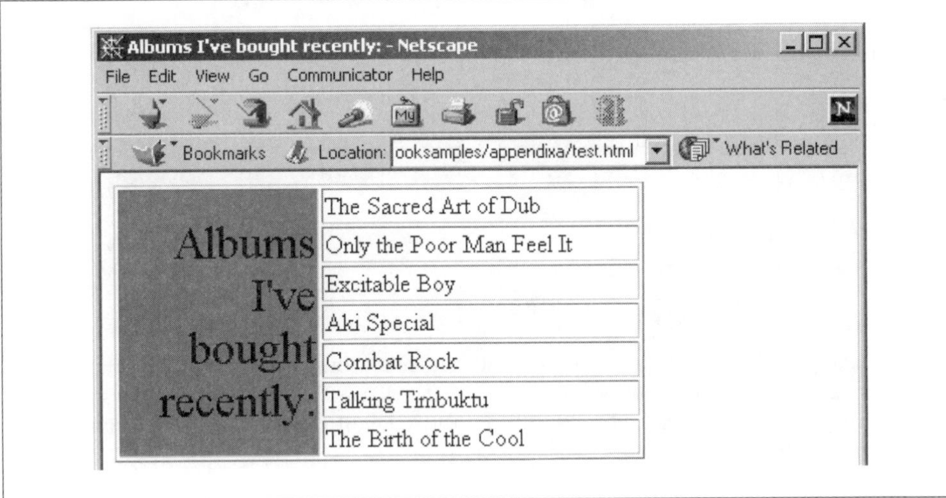

Figure A-3. Document with generated Attributes

Be aware that in this instance, we could have used an attribute-value template. You could generate the value of the `rowspan` attribute like this:

```
<td bgcolor="lightslategray" rowspan="{count(listitem)}"
  width="100" align="right">
```

The expression in curly braces (`{}`) is evaluated and replaced with whatever its value happens to be. In this case, `count(listitem)` returns the number `7`, which becomes the value of the `rowspan` attribute.

<xsl:attribute-set> — Allows you to define a group of attributes for the output document. You can then reference the entire attribute set with its name, rather than create all attributes individually.

Category

Top-level element

Required Attributes

name
: Defines the name of this attribute set.

Optional Attributes

use-attribute-sets
: Lists one or more attribute sets that should be used by this attribute set. If you specify more than one set, separate their names with whitespace characters. You can use this attribute to embed other `<xsl:attribute-set>`s in this one, but be aware that an `<xsl:attribute-set>` that directly or indirectly embeds itself results in an error. In other words, if attribute set `A` embeds attribute set `B`, which in turn embeds attribute set `C`, which in turn embeds attribute set `A`, the XSLT processor will signal an error.

Content

One or more <xsl:attribute> elements.

Appears in

<xsl:stylesheet>. <xsl:attribute-set> is a top-level element and can only appear as a child of <xsl:stylesheet>.

Defined in

XSLT section 7.1.4, Named Attribute Sets.

Example

For this example, we'll create a stylesheet that defines attribute sets for regular text, emphasized text, and large text. Just for variety's sake, we'll use the Extensible Stylesheet Language Formatting Objects (XSL-FO) specification to convert our XML document into a PDF file. Here's our stylesheet:

```
<?xml version="1.0"?>
<xsl:stylesheet version="1.0"
  xmlns:xsl="http://www.w3.org/1999/XSL/Transform"
  xmlns:fo="http://www.w3.org/1999/XSL/Format">

  <xsl:output method="html"/>

  <xsl:attribute-set name="regular-text">
    <xsl:attribute name="font-size">12pt</xsl:attribute>
    <xsl:attribute name="font-family">sans-serif</xsl:attribute>
  </xsl:attribute-set>

  <xsl:attribute-set name="emphasized-text" use-attribute-sets="regular-text">
    <xsl:attribute name="font-style">italic</xsl:attribute>
  </xsl:attribute-set>

  <xsl:attribute-set name="large-text" use-attribute-sets="regular-text">
    <xsl:attribute name="font-size">18pt</xsl:attribute>
    <xsl:attribute name="font-weight">bold</xsl:attribute>
    <xsl:attribute name="space-after.optimum">21pt</xsl:attribute>
  </xsl:attribute-set>

  <xsl:template match="/">
    <fo:root xmlns:fo="http://www.w3.org/1999/XSL/Format">
      <fo:layout-master-set>
        <fo:simple-page-master margin-right="75pt" margin-left="75pt"
          page-height="11in" page-width="8.5in"
          margin-bottom="25pt" margin-top="25pt" master-name="main">
          <fo:region-before extent="25pt"/>
          <fo:region-body margin-top="50pt" margin-bottom="50pt"/>
          <fo:region-after extent="25pt"/>
        </fo:simple-page-master>
        <fo:page-sequence-master master-name="standard">
```

```
        <fo:repeatable-page-master-alternatives>
          <fo:conditional-page-master-reference master-name="main"
            odd-or-even="any"/>
        </fo:repeatable-page-master-alternatives>
      </fo:page-sequence-master>
    </fo:layout-master-set>

    <fo:page-sequence master-name="standard">
      <fo:flow flow-name="xsl-region-body">
        <xsl:apply-templates select="list"/>
      </fo:flow>
    </fo:page-sequence>
  </fo:root>
</xsl:template>

<xsl:template match="list">
  <fo:block xsl:use-attribute-sets="large-text">
    <xsl:value-of select="title"/>
  </fo:block>
  <fo:list-block provisional-distance-between-starts="0.4cm"
    provisional-label-separation="0.15cm">
    <xsl:for-each select="listitem">
      <fo:list-item start-indent="0.5cm" space-after.optimum="17pt">
        <fo:list-item-label>
          <fo:block xsl:use-attribute-sets="regular-text">*</fo:block>
        </fo:list-item-label>
        <fo:list-item-body>
          <fo:block xsl:use-attribute-sets="emphasized-text">
            <xsl:value-of select="."/>
          </fo:block>
        </fo:list-item-body>
      </fo:list-item>
    </xsl:for-each>
  </fo:list-block>
</xsl:template>

</xsl:stylesheet>
```

Notice that both the `emphasized-text` and `large-text` attribute sets use the `regular-text` attribute set as a base. In the case of `large-text`, the `font-size` attribute defined in the `large-text` attribute set overrides the `font-size` attribute included from the `regular-text` attribute set. We'll apply our stylesheet to the following XML document:

```
<?xml version="1.0"?>
<list>
  <title>A few of my favorite albums</title>
  <listitem>A Love Supreme</listitem>
  <listitem>Beat Crazy</listitem>
  <listitem>Here Come the Warm Jets</listitem>
  <listitem>Kind of Blue</listitem>
```

```
    <listitem>London Calling</listitem>
    <listitem>Remain in Light</listitem>
    <listitem>The Joshua Tree</listitem>
    <listitem>The Indestructible Beat of Soweto</listitem>
  </list>
```

The stylesheet generates this messy-looking file of formatting objects, which describe how the text of our XML source document should be rendered:

```
<fo:root xmlns:fo="http://www.w3.org/1999/XSL/Format">
<fo:layout-master-set>
<fo:simple-page-master master-name="main" margin-top="25pt"
margin-bottom="25pt" page-width="8.5in" page-height="11in"
margin-left="75pt" margin-right="75pt">
<fo:region-before extent="25pt"/>
<fo:region-body margin-bottom="50pt" margin-top="50pt"/>
<fo:region-after extent="25pt"/>
</fo:simple-page-master>
<fo:page-sequence-master master-name="standard">
<fo:repeatable-page-master-alternatives>
<fo:conditional-page-master-reference odd-or-even="any" master-name="main"/>
</fo:repeatable-page-master-alternatives>
</fo:page-sequence-master>
</fo:layout-master-set>
<fo:page-sequence master-name="standard">
<fo:flow flow-name="xsl-region-body">
<fo:block font-size="18pt" font-family="sans-serif"
font-weight="bold" space-after.optimum="21pt">A few of my
favorite albums</fo:block>
<fo:list-block provisional-label-separation="0.15cm"
provisional-distance-between-starts="0.4cm">
<fo:list-item space-after.optimum="17pt" start-indent="0.5cm">
<fo:list-item-label>
<fo:block font-size="12pt" font-family="sans-serif">*</fo:block>
</fo:list-item-label>
<fo:list-item-body>
<fo:block font-size="12pt" font-family="sans-serif"
font-style="italic">A Love Supreme</fo:block>
</fo:list-item-body>
</fo:list-item>
<fo:list-item space-after.optimum="17pt" start-indent="0.5cm">
<fo:list-item-label>
<fo:block font-size="12pt" font-family="sans-serif">*</fo:block>
</fo:list-item-label>
<fo:list-item-body>
<fo:block font-size="12pt" font-family="sans-serif"
font-style="italic">Beat Crazy</fo:block>
</fo:list-item-body>
</fo:list-item>
<fo:list-item space-after.optimum="17pt" start-indent="0.5cm">
```

```
<fo:list-item-label>
<fo:block font-size="12pt" font-family="sans-serif">*</fo:block>
</fo:list-item-label>
<fo:list-item-body>
<fo:block font-size="12pt" font-family="sans-serif"
font-style="italic">Here Come the Warm Jets</fo:block>
</fo:list-item-body>
</fo:list-item>
<fo:list-item space-after.optimum="17pt" start-indent="0.5cm">
<fo:list-item-label>
<fo:block font-size="12pt" font-family="sans-serif">*</fo:block>
</fo:list-item-label>
<fo:list-item-body>
<fo:block font-size="12pt" font-family="sans-serif"
font-style="italic">Kind of Blue</fo:block>
</fo:list-item-body>
</fo:list-item>
<fo:list-item space-after.optimum="17pt" start-indent="0.5cm">
<fo:list-item-label>
<fo:block font-size="12pt" font-family="sans-serif">*</fo:block>
</fo:list-item-label>
<fo:list-item-body>
<fo:block font-size="12pt" font-family="sans-serif"
font-style="italic">London Calling</fo:block>
</fo:list-item-body>
</fo:list-item>
<fo:list-item space-after.optimum="17pt" start-indent="0.5cm">
<fo:list-item-label>
<fo:block font-size="12pt" font-family="sans-serif">*</fo:block>
</fo:list-item-label>
<fo:list-item-body>
<fo:block font-size="12pt" font-family="sans-serif"
font-style="italic">Remain in Light</fo:block>
</fo:list-item-body>
</fo:list-item>
<fo:list-item space-after.optimum="17pt" start-indent="0.5cm">
<fo:list-item-label>
<fo:block font-size="12pt" font-family="sans-serif">*</fo:block>
</fo:list-item-label>
<fo:list-item-body>
<fo:block font-size="12pt" font-family="sans-serif"
font-style="italic">The Joshua Tree</fo:block>
</fo:list-item-body>
</fo:list-item>
<fo:list-item space-after.optimum="17pt" start-indent="0.5cm">
<fo:list-item-label>
<fo:block font-size="12pt" font-family="sans-serif">*</fo:block>
</fo:list-item-label>
<fo:list-item-body>
<fo:block font-size="12pt" font-family="sans-serif"
```

```
font-style="italic">The Indestructible Beat of Soweto</fo:block>
</fo:list-item-body>
</fo:list-item>
</fo:list-block>
</fo:flow>
</fo:page-sequence>
</fo:root>
```

Be aware that as of this writing (May 2001), the XSL-FO specification isn't final, so there's no guarantee that these formatting objects will work correctly with future XSL-FO tools. Here's how we invoke the Apache XML Project's FOP (Formatting Objects to PDF translator) tool to create a PDF:

```
java org.apache.fop.apps.CommandLine test.fo test.pdf
```

The FOP tool creates a PDF that looks like Figure A-4.

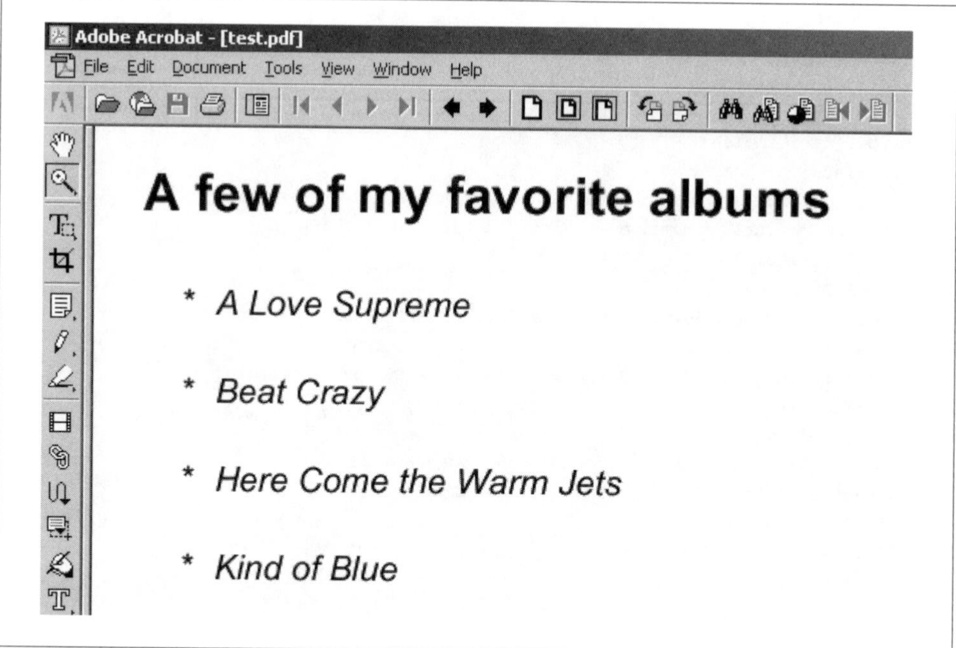

Figure A-4. PDF generated from an XSL-FO file

<xsl:call-template> — Lets you invoke a particular template by name.

Lets you invoke a particular template by name. This invocation is a convenient way to create commonly used output. For example, if you create an HTML page and all your HTML pages have the same masthead and footer, you could define templates named `masthead` and `footer`, then use `<xsl:call-template>` to invoke those templates as needed.

Category

Instruction

Required Attributes

name
: The name of the template you're invoking.

Optional Attributes

None.

Content

This element can contain any number of optional <xsl:with-param> elements.

Appears in

<xsl:call-template> appears inside a template.

Defined in

XSLT section 6, Named Templates.

Example

The <xsl:call-template> element gives you an excellent way to create modular stylesheets. In our case study (see Chapter 9), we need to generate common items at the top and bottom of every HTML page we generate. We build a navigation bar and title bar at the top of each panel in a similar way. Rather than intermingle these templates with the rest of our stylesheets, we put the templates for the common sections of the HTML pages in a separate stylesheet, then reference them when needed.

```
<xsl:call-template name="dw-masthead"/>
<xsl:call-template name="dw-title-bar"/>
<xsl:call-template name="dw-nav-bar">
  <xsl:with-param name="includeMain" select="'youBetcha'"/>
  <xsl:with-param name="sectionNumber" select="$sectionNumber"/>
  <xsl:with-param name="position" select="$pos"/>
  <xsl:with-param name="last" select="$last"/>
  <xsl:with-param name="topOrBottom" select="'top'"/>
  <xsl:with-param name="oneOrTwo" select="'two'"/>
</xsl:call-template>

<!-- Processing for the main body of the page goes here -->

<xsl:call-template name="dw-nav-bar">
  <xsl:with-param name="includeMain" select="'youBetcha'"/>
  <xsl:with-param name="sectionNumber" select="$sectionNumber"/>
  <xsl:with-param name="position" select="$pos"/>
  <xsl:with-param name="last" select="$last"/>
  <xsl:with-param name="topOrBottom" select="'bottom'"/>
  <xsl:with-param name="oneOrTwo" select="'two'"/>
</xsl:call-template>
<xsl:call-template name="dw-footer"/>
```

In this code fragment, we've invoked four templates to generate the look and feel we want our HTML pages to have. If we decide to change the look and feel of our tutorials, changing those four named templates lets us change the look and feel by simply transforming the XML document again. See the section "Generating the Individual Panels" in Chapter 9 for details on how this works.

<xsl:choose> — The <xsl:choose> element is XSLT's version of the switch or case statement found in many procedural programming languages.

Category

Instruction

Required Attributes

None.

Optional Attributes

None.

Content

Contains one or more <xsl:when> elements and might contain a single <xsl:otherwise> element. Any <xsl:otherwise> elements must be the last element inside <xsl:choose>.

Appears in

<xsl:choose> appears inside a template.

Defined in

XSLT section 9.2, Conditional Processing with xsl:choose.

Example

Here's an example that uses <xsl:choose> to select the background color for the rows of an HTML table. We cycle among four different values, using <xsl:choose> to determine the value of the bgcolor attribute in the generated HTML document. Here's the XML document we'll use:

```
<?xml version="1.0"?>
<list xml:lang="en">
  <title>Albums I've bought recently:</title>
  <listitem>The Sacred Art of Dub</listitem>
  <listitem>Only the Poor Man Feel It</listitem>
  <listitem>Excitable Boy</listitem>
  <listitem xml:lang="sw">Aki Special</listitem>
  <listitem xml:lang="en-gb">Combat Rock</listitem>
  <listitem xml:lang="zu">Talking Timbuktu</listitem>
  <listitem xml:lang="jz">The Birth of the Cool</listitem>
</list>
```

And here's our stylesheet:

```
<?xml version="1.0"?>
<xsl:stylesheet version="1.0" xmlns:xsl="http://www.w3.org/1999/XSL/Transform">

  <xsl:output method="html"/>

  <xsl:template match="/">
    <html>
      <head>
        <title>
          <xsl:value-of select="list/title"/>
        </title>
      </head>
      <body>
        <h1><xsl:value-of select="list/title"/></h1>
        <table border="1">
          <xsl:for-each select="list/listitem">
            <tr>
              <td>
                <xsl:attribute name="bgcolor">
                  <xsl:choose>
                    <xsl:when test="position() mod 4 = 0">
                      <xsl:text>papayawhip</xsl:text>
                    </xsl:when>
                    <xsl:when test="position() mod 4 = 1">
                      <xsl:text>mintcream</xsl:text>
                    </xsl:when>
                    <xsl:when test="position() mod 4 = 2">
                      <xsl:text>lavender</xsl:text>
                    </xsl:when>
                    <xsl:otherwise>
                      <xsl:text>whitesmoke</xsl:text>
                    </xsl:otherwise>
                  </xsl:choose>
                </xsl:attribute>
                <xsl:value-of select="."/>
              </td>
            </tr>
          </xsl:for-each>
        </table>
      </body>
    </html>
  </xsl:template>

</xsl:stylesheet>
```

We use <xsl:choose> to determine the background color of each generated <td> element. Here's the generated HTML document, which cycles through the various background colors:

```
<html>
<head>
<META http-equiv="Content-Type" content="text/html; charset=UTF-8">
<title>Albums I've bought recently:</title>
</head>
<body>
<h1>Albums I've bought recently:</h1>
<table border="1">
<tr>
<td bgcolor="mintcream">The Sacred Art of Dub</td>
</tr>
<tr>
<td bgcolor="lavender">Only the Poor Man Feel It</td>
</tr>
<tr>
<td bgcolor="whitesmoke">Excitable Boy</td>
</tr>
<tr>
<td bgcolor="papayawhip">Aki Special</td>
</tr>
<tr>
<td bgcolor="mintcream">Combat Rock</td>
</tr>
<tr>
<td bgcolor="lavender">Talking Timbuktu</td>
</tr>
<tr>
<td bgcolor="whitesmoke">The Birth of the Cool</td>
</tr>
</table>
</body>
</html>
```

When rendered, our HTML document looks like Figure A-5.

<xsl:comment> — Allows you to create a comment in the output document. Comments are sometimes used to add legal notices, disclaimers, or information about when the output document was created. Another useful application of the <xsl:comment> element is the generation of CSS definitions

The stylesheet will apply one CSS style to the <title> element and will alternate between two CSS styles for the <listitem>s. Here's the generated HTML:

```
<html>
<head>
<META http-equiv="Content-Type" content="text/html; charset=UTF-8">
<title>XSLT and CSS Demo</title>
<style>
<!--
            p.big       {font-size: 125%; font-weight: bold}
            p.green     {color: green; font-weight: bold}
            p.red       {color: red; font-style: italic}
          -->
</style>
</head>
<body>
<p class="big">Albums I've bought recently:</p>
<p class="green">The Sacred Art of Dub</p>
<p class="red">Only the Poor Man Feel It</p>
<p class="green">Excitable Boy</p>
<p class="red">Aki Special</p>
<p class="green">Combat Rock</p>
<p class="red">Talking Timbuktu</p>
<p class="green">The Birth of the Cool</p>
</body>
</html>
```

When rendered, the document looks like Figure A-6.

<xsl:copy> — Makes a shallow copy of an element to the result tree. This element only copies the current node and its namespace nodes. The children of the current node and any attributes it has are not copied.

Category

Instruction

Required Attributes

None.

Optional Attributes

use-attribute-sets

Lists one or more attribute sets that should be used by this element. If you specify more than one attribute set, separate their names with whitespace characters. See the description of the <xsl:attribute-set> element for more information.

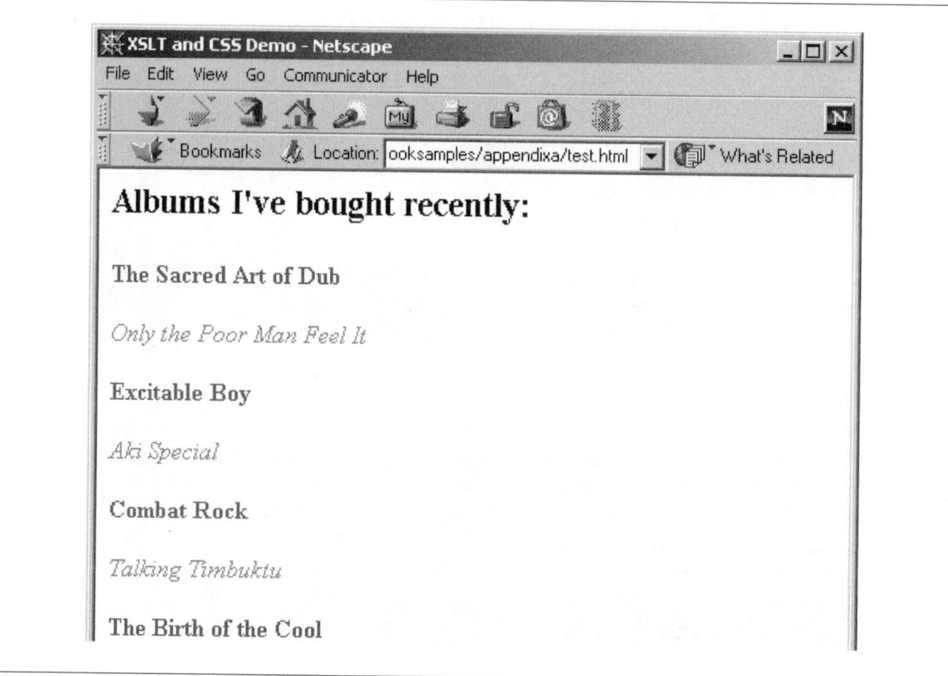

Figure A-6. Document with generated comment nodes

Content

An XSLT template.

Appears in

<xsl:copy> appears in a template.

Defined in

XSLT section 7.5, Copying.

Example

We'll demonstrate <xsl:copy> with an example that copies an element to the result tree. Notice that we do not specifically request that the attribute nodes of the source document be processed, so the result tree will not contain any attributes. Here is our stylesheet:

```
<?xml version="1.0"?>
<xsl:stylesheet xmlns:xsl="http://www.w3.org/1999/XSL/Transform" version="1.0">
  <xsl:output method="xml"/>

  <xsl:template match="*">
    <xsl:copy>
      <xsl:apply-templates/>
```

```
    </xsl:copy>
  </xsl:template>

</xsl:stylesheet>
```

We'll test our stylesheet with the following XML document:

```
<?xml version="1.0"?>
<report>
  <title>Miles Flown in 2001</title>
  <month sequence="01">
    <miles-flown>12379</miles-flown>
    <miles-earned>35215</miles-earned>
  </month>
  <month sequence="02">
    <miles-flown>32857</miles-flown>
    <miles-earned>92731</miles-earned>
  </month>
  <month sequence="03">
    <miles-flown>19920</miles-flown>
    <miles-earned>76725</miles-earned>
  </month>
  <month sequence="04">
    <miles-flown>18903</miles-flown>
    <miles-earned>31781</miles-earned>
  </month>
</report>
```

Here are the results:

```
<?xml version="1.0" encoding="UTF-8"?>
<report>
  <title>Miles Flown in 2001</title>
  <month>
    <miles-flown>12379</miles-flown>
    <miles-earned>35215</miles-earned>
  </month>
  <month>
    <miles-flown>32857</miles-flown>
    <miles-earned>92731</miles-earned>
  </month>
  <month>
    <miles-flown>19920</miles-flown>
    <miles-earned>76725</miles-earned>
  </month>
  <month>
    <miles-flown>18903</miles-flown>
    <miles-earned>31781</miles-earned>
  </month>
</report>
```

The <xsl:copy> does a shallow copy, which gives you more control over the output than the <xsl:copy-of> element does. However, you must explicitly specify any child nodes or attribute nodes you would like copied to the result tree. The <xsl:apply-templates> element selects all text, element, comment, and processing-instruction children of the current element; without this element, the result tree would contain only a single, empty <report> element. Compare this approach with the example in the <xsl:copy-of> element.

<xsl:copy-of>

— Copies things to the result tree. The `select` attribute defines the content to be copied. If the `select` attribute identifies a result-tree fragment, the complete fragment is copied to the result tree. If `select` identifies a node-set, all nodes in the node-set are copied to the result tree in document order; unlike <xsl:copy>, the node is copied in its entirety, including any namespace nodes, attribute nodes, and child nodes. If the `select` attribute identifies something other than a result-tree fragment or a node-set, it is converted to a string and inserted into the result tree.

Category

Instruction

Required Attributes

select

Contains an XPath expression that defines the nodes to be copied to the output document.

Optional Attributes

None.

Content

None. <xsl:copy-of> is an empty element.

Appears in

<xsl:copy-of> appears inside a template.

Defined in

XSLT section 11.3, Using Values of Variables and Parameters with `xsl:copy-of`.

Example

We'll demonstrate <xsl:copy-of> with a simple stylesheet that copies the input document to the result tree. Here is our stylesheet:

```
<?xml version="1.0"?>
<xsl:stylesheet xmlns:xsl="http://www.w3.org/1999/XSL/Transform" version="1.0">
  <xsl:output method="xml"/>
```

```
  <xsl:template match="/">
    <xsl:copy-of select="."/>
  </xsl:template>

</xsl:stylesheet>
```

We'll test our stylesheet with the following document:

```
<?xml version="1.0"?>
<list>
  <title>A few of my favorite albums</title>
  <listitem>A Love Supreme</listitem>
  <listitem>Beat Crazy</listitem>
  <listitem>Here Come the Warm Jets</listitem>
  <listitem>Kind of Blue</listitem>
  <listitem>London Calling</listitem>
  <listitem>Remain in Light</listitem>
  <listitem>The Joshua Tree</listitem>
  <listitem>The Indestructible Beat of Soweto</listitem>
</list>
```

When we transform the XML document, the results are strikingly similar to the input document:

```
<?xml version="1.0" encoding="UTF-8"?>
<list>
  <title>A few of my favorite albums</title>
  <listitem>A Love Supreme</listitem>
  <listitem>Beat Crazy</listitem>
  <listitem>Here Come the Warm Jets</listitem>
  <listitem>Kind of Blue</listitem>
  <listitem>London Calling</listitem>
  <listitem>Remain in Light</listitem>
  <listitem>The Joshua Tree</listitem>
  <listitem>The Indestructible Beat of Soweto</listitem>
</list>
```

The only difference between the two documents is that the stylesheet engine has added an `encoding` to the XML declaration. Compare this to the example in the `<xsl:copy>` element.

<xsl:decimal-format> — Defines a number format to be used when writing numeric values to the output document. If the `<decimal-format>` does not have a `name`, it is assumed to be the default number format used for all output. On the other hand, if a number format is named, it can be referenced from the `format-number()` function.

Category

Top-level element

Required Attributes

None.

Optional Attributes

name

Gives a name to this format.

decimal-separator

Defines the character (usually either a period or comma) used as the decimal point. This character is used both in the format string and in the output. The default value is the period character (`.`).

grouping-separator

Defines the character (usually either a period or comma) used as the thousands separator. This character is used both in the format string and in the output. The default value is the comma (`,`).

infinity

Defines the string used to represent infinity. Be aware that XSLT's number facilities support both positive and negative infinity. This string is used only in the output. The default value is the string "Infinity".

minus-sign

Defines the character used as the minus sign. This character is used only in the output. The default value is the hyphen character (-, #x2D).

NaN

Defines the string displayed when the value to be formatted is not a number. This string is used only in the output; the default value is the string "NaN".

percent

Defines the character used as the percent sign. This character is used both in the format string and in the output. The default value is the percent sign (`%`).

per-mille

Defines the character used as the per-mille sign. This character is used both in the format string and in the output. The default value is the Unicode per-mille character (#x2030).

zero-digit

Defines the character used for the digit zero. This character is used both in the format string and in the output. The default is the digit zero (`0`).

digit

Defines the character used in the format string to stand for a digit. The default is the number sign character (`#`).

pattern-separator

Defines the character used to separate the positive and negative subpatterns in a pattern. The default value is the semicolon (`;`). This character is used only in the format string.

Content

None. <xsl:decimal-format> is an empty element.

Appears in

<xsl:decimal-format> is a top-level element and can only appear as a child of <xsl:stylesheet>.

Defined in

XSLT section 12.3, Number Formatting.

Example

Here is a stylesheet that defines two <decimal-format>s:

```
<?xml version="1.0" encoding="ISO-8859-1" ?>
<xsl:stylesheet version="1.0"
  xmlns:xsl="http://www.w3.org/1999/XSL/Transform"
  xmlns:months="Lookup table for month names">

  <xsl:output method="text"/>

  <months:name sequence="01">January</months:name>
  <months:name sequence="02">February</months:name>
  <months:name sequence="03">March</months:name>
  <months:name sequence="04">April</months:name>

  <xsl:variable name="newline">
<xsl:text>
</xsl:text>
  </xsl:variable>

  <xsl:decimal-format name="f1"
    decimal-separator=":"
    grouping-separator="/"/>

  <xsl:decimal-format name="f2"
    infinity="Really, really big"
    NaN="[not a number]"/>

  <xsl:template match="/">
    <xsl:value-of select="$newline"/>
    <xsl:text>Tests of the <decimal-format> element:</xsl:text>

    <xsl:value-of select="$newline"/>
    <xsl:value-of select="$newline"/>
    <xsl:text>   format-number(1528.3, '#/###:00', 'f1')=</xsl:text>
    <xsl:value-of select="format-number(1528.3, '#/###:00;-#/###:00', 'f1')"/>
    <xsl:value-of select="$newline"/>
    <xsl:text>   format-number(1 div 0, '###,###.00', 'f2')=</xsl:text>
    <xsl:value-of select="format-number(1 div 0, '###,###.00', 'f2')"/>
```

```
    <xsl:value-of select="$newline"/>
    <xsl:text>   format-number(blue div orange, '#.##', 'f2')=</xsl:text>
    <xsl:value-of select="format-number(blue div orange, '#.##', 'f2')"/>
    <xsl:value-of select="$newline"/>
    <xsl:value-of select="$newline"/>
    <xsl:for-each select="report/month">
      <xsl:text>   </xsl:text>
      <xsl:value-of
        select="document('')/*/months:name[@sequence=current()/@sequence]"/>
      <xsl:text> - </xsl:text>
      <xsl:value-of select="format-number(miles-flown, '##,###')"/>
      <xsl:text> miles flown, </xsl:text>
      <xsl:value-of select="format-number(miles-earned, '##,###')"/>
      <xsl:text> miles earned.</xsl:text>
      <xsl:value-of select="$newline"/>
      <xsl:text>     (</xsl:text>
      <xsl:value-of
        select="format-number(miles-flown div sum(//miles-flown), '##%')"/>
      <xsl:text> of all miles flown, </xsl:text>
      <xsl:value-of
        select="format-number(miles-earned div sum(//miles-earned), '##%')"/>
      <xsl:text> of all miles earned.)</xsl:text>
      <xsl:value-of select="$newline"/>
      <xsl:value-of select="$newline"/>
    </xsl:for-each>
    <xsl:text>   Total miles flown: </xsl:text>
    <xsl:value-of select="format-number(sum(//miles-flown), '##,###')"/>
    <xsl:text>, total miles earned: </xsl:text>
    <xsl:value-of select="format-number(sum(//miles-earned), '##,###')"/>
  </xsl:template>

</xsl:stylesheet>
```

We'll use this stylesheet against the following document:

```
<?xml version="1.0"?>
<report>
  <title>Miles Flown in 2001</title>
  <month sequence="01">
    <miles-flown>12379</miles-flown>
    <miles-earned>35215</miles-earned>
  </month>
  <month sequence="02">
    <miles-flown>32857</miles-flown>
    <miles-earned>92731</miles-earned>
  </month>
  <month sequence="03">
    <miles-flown>19920</miles-flown>
    <miles-earned>76725</miles-earned>
  </month>
```

```
    <month sequence="04">
      <miles-flown>18903</miles-flown>
      <miles-earned>31781</miles-earned>
    </month>
  </report>
```

When we process this document with the stylesheet, here are the results:

```
Tests of the <decimal-format> element:

   format-number(1528.3, '#/###:00', 'f1')=1/528:30
   format-number(1 div 0, '###,###.00', 'f2')=Really, really big
   format-number(blue div orange, '#.##', 'f2')=[not a number]

   January - 12,379 miles flown, 35,215 miles earned.
     (15% of all miles flown, 15% of all miles earned.)

   February - 32,857 miles flown, 92,731 miles earned.
     (39% of all miles flown, 39% of all miles earned.)

   March - 19,920 miles flown, 76,725 miles earned.
     (24% of all miles flown, 32% of all miles earned.)

   April - 18,903 miles flown, 31,781 miles earned.
     (22% of all miles flown, 13% of all miles earned.)

   Total miles flown: 84,059, total miles earned: 236,452
```

<xsl:element> — Allows you to create an element in the output document. It works similarly to the `<xsl:attribute>` element.

Category

Instruction

Required Attributes

name

Defines the name of this element. A value of `name="fred"` will produce a `<fred>` element in the output document.

Optional Attributes

namespace

Defines the namespace used for this attribute.

use-attribute-sets

Lists one or more attribute sets that should be used by this element. If you specify more than one attribute set, separate their names with whitespace characters.

Content

An XSLT template.

Appears in

<xsl:element> appears inside a template.

Defined in

XSLT section 7.1.2, Creating Elements with xsl:element.

Example

We'll use a generic stylesheet that copies the input document to the result tree, with one exception: all attributes in the original documents are converted to child elements in the result tree. The name of the new element will be the name of the format attribute, and its text will be the value of the attribute. Because we don't know the name of the attribute until we process the XML source document, we must use the <xsl:element> element to create the result tree. Here's how our stylesheet looks:

```
<?xml version="1.0"?>
<xsl:stylesheet xmlns:xsl="http://www.w3.org/1999/XSL/Transform" version="1.0">
  <xsl:output method="xml"/>

  <xsl:template match="*">
    <xsl:element name="{name()}">
      <xsl:for-each select="@*">
        <xsl:element name="{name()}">
          <xsl:value-of select="."/>
        </xsl:element>
      </xsl:for-each>
      <xsl:apply-templates select="*|text()"/>
    </xsl:element>
  </xsl:template>

</xsl:stylesheet>
```

This stylesheet uses the <xsl:element> element in two places: first to create a new element with the same name as the original element, and second to create a new element with the same name as each attribute. We'll apply the stylesheet to this document:

```
<?xml version="1.0"?>
<report>
  <title>Miles Flown in 2001</title>
  <month sequence="01">
    <miles-flown>12379</miles-flown>
    <miles-earned>35215</miles-earned>
  </month>
  <month sequence="02">
    <miles-flown>32857</miles-flown>
    <miles-earned>92731</miles-earned>
  </month>
  <month sequence="03">
```

```
      <miles-flown>19920</miles-flown>
      <miles-earned>76725</miles-earned>
    </month>
    <month sequence="04">
      <miles-flown>18903</miles-flown>
      <miles-earned>31781</miles-earned>
    </month>
  </report>
```

Here are our results:

```
  <?xml version="1.0" encoding="UTF-8"?>
  <report>
    <title>Miles Flown in 2001</title>
    <month><sequence>01</sequence>
      <miles-flown>12379</miles-flown>
      <miles-earned>35215</miles-earned>
    </month>
    <month><sequence>02</sequence>
      <miles-flown>32857</miles-flown>
      <miles-earned>92731</miles-earned>
    </month>
    <month><sequence>03</sequence>
      <miles-flown>19920</miles-flown>
      <miles-earned>76725</miles-earned>
    </month>
    <month><sequence>04</sequence>
      <miles-flown>18903</miles-flown>
      <miles-earned>31781</miles-earned>
    </month>
  </report>
```

The `<xsl:element>` element created all the elements in the output document, including the `<sequence>` elements that were created from the `sequence` attributes in the original document.

<xsl:fallback> — Defines a template that should be used when an extension element can't be found.

Category

Instruction

Required Attributes

None.

Optional Attributes

None.

Content

An XSLT template.

Appears in

<xsl:fallback> appears inside a template.

Defined in

XSLT section 15, Fallback.

Example

Here is a stylesheet that uses <xsl:fallback> to terminate the transformation if an extension element can't be found:

```
<?xml version="1.0"?>
<xsl:stylesheet version="1.0"
  xmlns:xsl="http://www.w3.org/1999/XSL/Transform"
  xmlns:db="xalan://DatabaseExtension"
  extension-element-prefixes="db">

  <xsl:output method="html"/>

  <xsl:template match="/">
    <html>
      <head>
        <title><xsl:value-of select="report/title"/></title>
      </head>
      <body>
        <h1><xsl:value-of select="report/title"/></h1>
        <xsl:for-each select="report/section">
          <h2><xsl:value-of select="title"/></h2>
          <xsl:for-each select="dbaccess">
            <db:accessDatabase>
              <xsl:fallback>
                <xsl:message terminate="yes">
                  Database library not available!
                </xsl:message>
              </xsl:fallback>
            </db:accessDatabase>
          </xsl:for-each>
        </xsl:for-each>
      </body>
    </html>
  </xsl:template>

</xsl:stylesheet>
```

When we use this stylesheet to transform a document, the `<xsl:fallback>` element is processed if the extension element can't be found:

```
Database library not available!

Processing terminated using xsl:message
```

In this case, the extension element is the Java class `DatabaseExtension`. If, for whatever reason, that class can't be loaded, the `<xsl:fallback>` element is processed. Note that the `<xsl:fallback>` element is processed only when the extension element can't be found; if the code that implements that extension element is found, but fails, it must be handled some other way. Also be aware that the exact format of the message and the gracefulness of stylesheet termination will vary from one XSLT processor to the next.

<xsl:for-each> — Acts as XSLT's iteration operator. This element has a `select` attribute that selects some nodes from the current context.

Category

Instruction

Required Attributes

select
: Contains an XPath expression that selects nodes from the current context.

Optional Attributes

None.

Content

`<xsl:for-each>` contains a template that is evaluated against each of the selected nodes. The `<xsl:for-each>` element can contain one or more `<xsl:sort>` elements to order the selected nodes before they are processed. All `<xsl:sort>` elements must appear first, before the template begins.

Appears in

`<xsl:for-each>` appears inside a template.

Defined in

XSLT section 8, Repetition.

Example

We'll demonstrate the `<xsl:for-each>` element with the following stylesheet:

```
<?xml version="1.0"?>
<xsl:stylesheet version="1.0" xmlns:xsl="http://www.w3.org/1999/XSL/Transform">

  <xsl:output method="text"/>

  <xsl:variable name="newline">
<xsl:text>
```

```
</xsl:text>
  </xsl:variable>

  <xsl:variable name="complicatedVariable">
    <xsl:choose>
      <xsl:when test="count(//listitem) > 10">
        <xsl:text>really long list</xsl:text>
      </xsl:when>
      <xsl:when test="count(//listitem) > 5">
        <xsl:text>moderately long list</xsl:text>
      </xsl:when>
      <xsl:otherwise>
        <xsl:text>fairly short list</xsl:text>
      </xsl:otherwise>
    </xsl:choose>
  </xsl:variable>

  <xsl:template match="/">
    <xsl:value-of select="$newline"/>
    <xsl:text>Here is a </xsl:text>
    <xsl:value-of select="$complicatedVariable"/>
    <xsl:text>:</xsl:text>
    <xsl:value-of select="$newline"/>
    <xsl:variable name="listitems" select="list/listitem"/>
    <xsl:call-template name="processListitems">
      <xsl:with-param name="items" select="$listitems"/>
    </xsl:call-template>
  </xsl:template>

  <xsl:template name="processListitems">
    <xsl:param name="items"/>
    <xsl:for-each select="$items">
      <xsl:value-of select="position()"/>
      <xsl:text>.  </xsl:text>
      <xsl:value-of select="."/>
      <xsl:value-of select="$newline"/>
    </xsl:for-each>
  </xsl:template>

</xsl:stylesheet>
```

In this stylesheet, we use an `<xsl:param>` named `items` to illustrate the `<xsl:for-each>` element. The `items` parameter contains some number of `<listitem>` elements from the XML source document; the `<xsl:for-each>` element iterates through all those elements and processes each one. We'll use our stylesheet with the following XML document:

```
<?xml version="1.0"?>
<list>
  <title>A few of my favorite albums</title>
  <listitem>A Love Supreme</listitem>
```

```
    <listitem>Beat Crazy</listitem>
    <listitem>Here Come the Warm Jets</listitem>
    <listitem>Kind of Blue</listitem>
    <listitem>London Calling</listitem>
    <listitem>Remain in Light</listitem>
    <listitem>The Joshua Tree</listitem>
    <listitem>The Indestructible Beat of Soweto</listitem>
</list>
```

When we run the transformation, here are the results:

```
Here is a moderately long list:
1.  A Love Supreme
2.  Beat Crazy
3.  Here Come the Warm Jets
4.  Kind of Blue
5.  London Calling
6.  Remain in Light
7.  The Joshua Tree
8.  The Indestructible Beat of Soweto
```

The `<xsl:for-each>` element has iterated through all the `<listitem>` elements from the XML source document and has processed each one.

— Implements an `if` statement. It contains a `test` attribute and an XSLT template. If the `test` attribute evaluates to the boolean value `true`, the XSLT template is processed. This element implements an `if` statement only; if you need an `if-then-else` statement, use the `<xsl:choose>` element with a single `<xsl:when>` and a single `<xsl:otherwise>`.

Category

Instruction

Required Attributes

test

The `test` attribute contains a boolean expression. If it evaluates to the boolean value `true`, then the XSLT template inside the `<xsl:if>` element is processed.

Optional Attributes

None.

Content

An XSLT template.

Appears in

`<xsl:if>` appears inside a template.

Defined in

XSLT section 9.1, Conditional Processing with `xsl:if`.

Example

We'll illustrate the `<xsl:if>` element with the following stylesheet:

```
<?xml version="1.0"?>
<xsl:stylesheet version="1.0" xmlns:xsl="http://www.w3.org/1999/XSL/Transform">

  <xsl:output method="text"/>

  <xsl:variable name="newline">
<xsl:text>
</xsl:text>
  </xsl:variable>

  <xsl:template match="/">
    <xsl:value-of select="$newline"/>
    <xsl:text>Here are the odd-numbered items from the list:</xsl:text>
    <xsl:value-of select="$newline"/>
    <xsl:for-each select="list/listitem">
      <xsl:if test="(position() mod 2) = 1">
        <xsl:number format="1. "/>
        <xsl:value-of select="."/>
        <xsl:value-of select="$newline"/>
      </xsl:if>
    </xsl:for-each>
  </xsl:template>

</xsl:stylesheet>
```

This stylesheet uses the `<xsl:if>` element to see if a given `<listitem>`'s position is an odd number. If it is, we write it to the result tree. We'll test our stylesheet with this XML document:

```
<?xml version="1.0"?>
<list>
  <title>A few of my favorite albums</title>
  <listitem>A Love Supreme</listitem>
  <listitem>Beat Crazy</listitem>
  <listitem>Here Come the Warm Jets</listitem>
  <listitem>Kind of Blue</listitem>
  <listitem>London Calling</listitem>
  <listitem>Remain in Light</listitem>
  <listitem>The Joshua Tree</listitem>
  <listitem>The Indestructible Beat of Soweto</listitem>
</list>
```

When we run this transformation, here are the results:

```
Here are the odd-numbered items from the list:
1. A Love Supreme
3. Here Come the Warm Jets
5. London Calling
7. The Joshua Tree
```

<xsl:import> — Allows you to import the templates found in another XSLT stylesheet. Unlike `<xsl:include>`, all templates imported with `<xsl:import>` have a lower priority than those in the including stylesheet. Another difference between `<xsl:include>` and `<xsl:import>` is that `<xsl:include>` can appear anywhere in a stylesheet, while `<xsl:import>` can appear only at the beginning.

Category

Top-level element

Required Attributes

href
: Defines the URI of the imported stylesheet.

Optional Attributes

None.

Content

None. `<xsl:import>` is an empty element.

Appears in

`<xsl:import>` is a top-level element and can appear only as a child of `<xsl:stylesheet>`.

Defined in

XSLT section 2.6.2, Stylesheet Import.

Example

Here is a simple stylesheet that we'll import:

```
<?xml version="1.0"?>
<xsl:stylesheet version="1.0" xmlns:xsl="http://www.w3.org/1999/XSL/Transform">

  <xsl:output method="text"/>

  <xsl:variable name="newline">
<xsl:text>
</xsl:text>
  </xsl:variable>
```

```
  <xsl:template match="/">
    <xsl:value-of select="$newline"/>
    <xsl:apply-templates select="list/title"/>
    <xsl:apply-templates select="list/listitem"/>
  </xsl:template>

  <xsl:template match="title">
    <xsl:value-of select="."/>
    <xsl:text>: </xsl:text>
    <xsl:value-of select="$newline"/>
    <xsl:value-of select="$newline"/>
  </xsl:template>

  <xsl:template match="listitem">
    <xsl:text>HERE IS LISTITEM NUMBER </xsl:text>
    <xsl:value-of select="position()"/>
    <xsl:text>:  </xsl:text>
    <xsl:value-of select="."/>
    <xsl:value-of select="$newline"/>
  </xsl:template>

</xsl:stylesheet>
```

We'll test both this stylesheet and the one that imports it with this XML document:

```
<?xml version="1.0"?>
<list>
  <title>A few of my favorite albums</title>
  <listitem>A Love Supreme</listitem>
  <listitem>Beat Crazy</listitem>
  <listitem>Here Come the Warm Jets</listitem>
  <listitem>Kind of Blue</listitem>
  <listitem>London Calling</listitem>
  <listitem>Remain in Light</listitem>
  <listitem>The Joshua Tree</listitem>
  <listitem>The Indestructible Beat of Soweto</listitem>
</list>
```

When we process our XML source document with this stylesheet, here are the results:

```
A few of my favorite albums:

HERE IS LISTITEM NUMBER 1:  A Love Supreme
HERE IS LISTITEM NUMBER 2:  Beat Crazy
HERE IS LISTITEM NUMBER 3:  Here Come the Warm Jets
HERE IS LISTITEM NUMBER 4:  Kind of Blue
HERE IS LISTITEM NUMBER 5:  London Calling
HERE IS LISTITEM NUMBER 6:  Remain in Light
HERE IS LISTITEM NUMBER 7:  The Joshua Tree
HERE IS LISTITEM NUMBER 8:  The Indestructible Beat of Soweto
```

Now we'll use `<xsl:import>` in another stylesheet:

```
<?xml version="1.0"?>
<xsl:stylesheet version="1.0" xmlns:xsl="http://www.w3.org/1999/XSL/Transform">

  <xsl:import href="listitem.xsl"/>

  <xsl:output method="text"/>

  <xsl:variable name="newline">
<xsl:text>
</xsl:text>
  </xsl:variable>

  <xsl:template match="/">
    <xsl:value-of select="$newline"/>
    <xsl:apply-templates select="list/title"/>
    <xsl:apply-templates select="list/listitem"/>
  </xsl:template>

  <xsl:template match="listitem">
    <xsl:value-of select="position()"/>
    <xsl:text>.  </xsl:text>
    <xsl:value-of select="."/>
    <xsl:value-of select="$newline"/>
  </xsl:template>

</xsl:stylesheet>
```

Here are the results created by our second stylesheet:

```
A few of my favorite albums:

1.  A Love Supreme
2.  Beat Crazy
3.  Here Come the Warm Jets
4.  Kind of Blue
5.  London Calling
6.  Remain in Light
7.  The Joshua Tree
8.  The Indestructible Beat of Soweto
```

Notice that both stylesheets had a template with `match="listitem"`. The template in the imported stylesheet has a lower priority, so it is not used. Only the imported stylesheet has a template with `match="title"`, so the imported template is used for the `<title>` element.

<xsl:include> — Allows you to include another XSLT stylesheet. This element allows you to put common transformations in a separate stylesheet, then include the templates from that stylesheet at any time. Unlike <xsl:import>, all templates included with <xsl:include> have the same priority as those in the including stylesheet. Another difference is that <xsl:include> can appear anywhere in a stylesheet, while <xsl:import> must appear at the beginning.

Category

Top-level element

Required Attributes

href
    Defines the URI of the included stylesheet.

Optional Attributes

None.

Content

None. <xsl:include> is an empty element.

Appears in

<xsl:include> is a top-level element and can appear only as a child of <xsl:stylesheet>.

Defined in

XSLT section 2.6.1, Stylesheet Inclusion.

Example

The <xsl:include> element is a good way to break your stylesheets into smaller pieces. (Those smaller pieces are often easier to reuse.) In our case study (see Chapter 9), we had a number of different stylesheets, each of which contained templates for a particular purpose. Here's how our <xsl:include> elements look:

```
<xsl:include href="toot-o-matic-variables.xsl"/>

<xsl:include href="xslt-utilities.xsl"/>
<xsl:include href="dw-style.xsl"/>

<xsl:include href="build-main-index.xsl"/>
<xsl:include href="build-section-indexes.xsl"/>
<xsl:include href="build-individual-panels.xsl"/>
<xsl:include href="build-graphics.xsl"/>
<xsl:include href="build-pdf-file.xsl"/>
<xsl:include href="build-zip-file.xsl"/>
```

Segmenting your stylesheets this way can make debugging simpler, as well. In our example here, all the rules for creating a PDF file are in the stylesheet *build-pdf-file.xsl*. If the PDF files are not built correctly, *build-pdf-file.xsl* is most likely the source of the problem. All visual elements of our generated HTML pages are created in the stylesheet *dw-style.xsl*. If we need to change the look of all the HTML pages, changing the templates in *dw-style.xsl* will do the trick.

<xsl:key>

— Defines an index against the current document. The element is defined with three attributes: a `name`, which names this index; a `match`, an XPath expression that describes the nodes to be indexed; and a `use` attribute, an XPath expression that defines the property used to create the index.

Category

Top-level element

Required Attributes

name
: Defines a name for this key.

match
: Represents an XPath expression that defines the nodes to be indexed by this key.

use
: Represents an XPath expression that defines the property of the indexed nodes that will be used to retrieve nodes from the index.

Optional Attributes

None.

Content

None. `<xsl:key>` is an empty element.

Appears in

`<xsl:key>` is a top-level element and can only appear as a child of `<xsl:stylesheet>`.

Defined in

XSLT section 12.2, Keys.

Example

Here is a stylesheet that defines two `<xsl:key>` relations against an XML document:

```
<?xml version="1.0"?>
<xsl:stylesheet version="1.0" xmlns:xsl="http://www.w3.org/1999/XSL/Transform">
<xsl:output method="html" indent="yes"/>
<xsl:strip-space elements="*"/>

  <xsl:key name="language-index" match="defn" use="@language"/>
  <xsl:key name="term-ids"       match="term" use="@id"/>

  <xsl:param name="targetLanguage"/>
```

```
  <xsl:template match="/">
    <xsl:apply-templates select="glossary"/>
  </xsl:template>

  <xsl:template match="glossary">
    <html>
      <head>
        <title>
          <xsl:text>Glossary Listing: </xsl:text>
          <xsl:value-of select="key('language-index',
        $targetLanguage)[1]/preceding-sibling::term"/>
          <xsl:text> - </xsl:text>
          <xsl:value-of select="key('language-index',
        $targetLanguage)[last()]/preceding-sibling::term"/>
        </title>
      </head>
      <body>
        <h1>
          <xsl:text>Glossary Listing: </xsl:text>
          <xsl:value-of select="key('language-index',
        $targetLanguage)[1]/ancestor::glentry/term"/>
          <xsl:text> - </xsl:text>
          <xsl:value-of select="key('language-index',
        $targetLanguage)[last()]/ancestor::glentry/term"/>
        </h1>
        <xsl:for-each select="key('language-index', $targetLanguage)">
          <xsl:apply-templates select="ancestor::glentry"/>
        </xsl:for-each>
      </body>
    </html>
  </xsl:template>

  ...

</xsl:stylesheet>
```

For a complete discussion of this stylesheet, illustrating how the <xsl:key> relations are used, see the section "Stylesheets That Use the key() Function" in Chapter 5.

<xsl:message> — Sends a message. How the message is sent can vary from one XSLT processor to the next, but it's typically written to the standard output device. This element is useful for debugging stylesheets.

Category

Instruction

Required Attributes

None.

Optional Attributes

terminate="yes" | "no"

If this attribute has the value `yes`, the XSLT processor stops execution after issuing this message. The default value for this attribute is `no`; if the `<xsl:message>` doesn't terminate the processor, the message is sent and processing continues.

Content

An XSLT template.

Appears in

`<xsl:message>` appears inside a template.

Defined in

XSLT section 13, Messages.

Example

Here's a stylesheet that uses the `<xsl:message>` element to trace the transformation of an XML document. We'll use our list of recently purchased albums again:

```
<?xml version="1.0"?>
<list xml:lang="en">
  <title>Albums I've bought recently:</title>
  <listitem>The Sacred Art of Dub</listitem>
  <listitem>Only the Poor Man Feel It</listitem>
  <listitem>Excitable Boy</listitem>
  <listitem xml:lang="sw">Aki Special</listitem>
  <listitem xml:lang="en-gb">Combat Rock</listitem>
  <listitem xml:lang="zu">Talking Timbuktu</listitem>
  <listitem xml:lang="jz">The Birth of the Cool</listitem>
</list>
```

We'll list all of the purchased albums in an HTML table, with the background color of each row alternating through various colors. Our stylesheet uses an `<xsl:choose>` element inside an `<xsl:attribute>` element to determine the value of the `bgcolor` attribute. If a given `<listitem>` is converted to an HTML `<tr>` with a background color of `lavender`, we'll issue a celebratory message:

```
<?xml version="1.0"?>
<xsl:stylesheet version="1.0" xmlns:xsl="http://www.w3.org/1999/XSL/Transform">

  <xsl:output method="html"/>

  <xsl:template match="/">
    <html>
      <head>
        <title>
```

```
        <xsl:value-of select="list/title"/>
      </title>
    </head>
    <body>
      <h1><xsl:value-of select="list/title"/></h1>
      <table border="1">
        <xsl:for-each select="list/listitem">
          <tr>
            <td>
              <xsl:attribute name="bgcolor">
                <xsl:choose>
                  <xsl:when test="position() mod 4 = 0">
                    <xsl:text>papayawhip</xsl:text>
                  </xsl:when>
                  <xsl:when test="position() mod 4 = 1">
                    <xsl:text>mintcream</xsl:text>
                  </xsl:when>
                  <xsl:when test="position() mod 4 = 2">
                    <xsl:text>lavender</xsl:text>
                    <xsl:message terminate="no">
                      <xsl:text>Table row #</xsl:text>
                      <xsl:value-of select="position()"/>
                      <xsl:text> is lavender!</xsl:text>
                    </xsl:message>
                  </xsl:when>
                  <xsl:otherwise>
                    <xsl:text>whitesmoke</xsl:text>
                  </xsl:otherwise>
                </xsl:choose>
              </xsl:attribute>
              <xsl:value-of select="."/>
            </td>
          </tr>
        </xsl:for-each>
      </table>
    </body>
  </html>
</xsl:template>

</xsl:stylesheet>
```

Note that the XSLT specification doesn't define how the message is issued. When we use this stylesheet with Xalan 2.0.1, we get these results:

```
file:///D:/O'Reilly/XSLT/bookSamples/AppendixA/message.xsl; Line 32; Column 51;
Table row #2 is lavender!
file:///D:/O'Reilly/XSLT/bookSamples/AppendixA/message.xsl; Line 32; Column 51;
Table row #6 is lavender!
```

Xalan gives us feedback on the part of the stylesheet that generated each message. Saxon, on the other hand, keeps things short and sweet:

```
Table row #2 is lavender!
Table row #6 is lavender!
```

For variety's sake, here's how XT processes the `<xsl:message>` element:

```
file:/D:/O'Reilly/XSLT/bookSamples/AppendixA/test4.xml:5: Table row #2 is lavender!
file:/D:/O'Reilly/XSLT/bookSamples/AppendixA/test4.xml:9: Table row #6 is lavender!
```

XT gives information about the line in the XML source document that generated the message.

<xsl:namespace-alias> — Allows you to define an alias for a namespace when using the namespace directly would complicate processing. This seldom-used element is the simplest way to write a stylesheet that generates another stylesheet.

Category

Top-level element

Required Attributes

stylesheet-prefix
: Defines the prefix used in the stylesheet to refer to the namespace.

result-prefix
: Defines the prefix for the namespace referred to by the alias. This prefix must be declared in the stylesheet, regardless of whether any elements in the stylesheet use it.

Optional Attributes

None.

Content

None. `<xsl:namespace-alias>` is an empty element.

Appears in

`<xsl:stylesheet>`. `<xsl:namespace-alias>` is a top-level element and can appear only as a child of `<xsl:stylesheet>`.

Defined in

XSLT section 7.1.1, Literal Result Elements.

Example

This element is not used frequently, and the reasons for its existence are based on the somewhat obscure case of an XSLT stylesheet that needs to generate another XSLT stylesheet. Our test case here creates a stylesheet that generates the identity transform, a stylesheet that simply copies any input document to the result tree. Here's our original stylesheet that uses the namespace alias:

```
<xsl:stylesheet version="1.0"
  xmlns:xsl="http://www.w3.org/1999/XSL/Transform"
  xmlns:xslout="(the namespace URI doesn't matter here)">

  <xsl:output method="xml" indent="yes"/>

  <xsl:namespace-alias stylesheet-prefix="xslout"
    result-prefix="xsl"/>

  <xsl:template match="/">
    <xslout:stylesheet version="1.0">
      <xslout:output method="xml"/>
      <xslout:template match="/">
        <xslout:copy-of select="."/>
      </xslout:template>
    </xslout:stylesheet>
  </xsl:template>

</xsl:stylesheet>
```

When we run this stylesheet with any XML document at all, we get a new stylesheet:

```
<?xml version="1.0" encoding="UTF-8"?>
<xslout:stylesheet xmlns:xslout="http://www.w3.org/1999/XSL/Transform"
  version="1.0">
<xslout:output method="xml"/>
<xslout:template match="/">
<xslout:copy-of select="."/>
</xslout:template>
</xslout:stylesheet>
```

You can take this generated stylesheet and use it to copy any XML document. In our original stylesheet, we use an `<xsl:namespace-alias>` because we have no other way of identifying to the XSLT processor with which XSLT elements should be processed and which ones should be treated as literals passed to the output. Using the namespace alias lets us generate the XSLT elements we need in our output. Notice in the result document that the correct namespace value was declared automatically on the `<xslout:stylesheet>` element.

<xsl:number> — Counts something. It is most often used to number parts of a document, although it can also be used to format a numeric value.

Category

Instruction

Required Attributes

None.

Optional Attributes

count
: The `count` attribute is an XPath expression that defines what should be counted.

level
: This attribute defines what levels of the source tree should be considered when numbering elements. The three valid values for this attribute are `single`, `multiple`, and `any`:

  `single`
  : Counts items at one level only. The XSLT processor goes to the first node in the `ancestor-or-self` axis that matches the `count` attribute, then counts that node plus all its preceding siblings that also match the `count` attribute.

  `multiple`
  : Counts items at multiple levels. The XSLT processor looks at all ancestors of the current node and the current node itself, then it selects all of those nodes that match the `count` attribute.

  `any`
  : Includes all of the current node's ancestors (as `level="multiple"` does) as well as all elements in the `preceding` axis.

  In all of these cases, if the `from` attribute is used, the only ancestors that are examined are descendants of the nearest ancestor that matches the `from` attribute. In other words, with `from="h1"`, the only nodes considered for counting are those that appear under the nearest `<h1>` attribute.

from
: The `from` attribute is an XPath expression that defines where counting starts. For example, you can use the `from` attribute to say that counting should begin at the previous `<h1>` element.

value
: An expression that is converted to a number. Using this attribute is a quick way to format a number; the element `<xsl:number value="7" format="i:"/>` returns the string "vii:".

format
: The `format` attribute defines the format of the generated number:

`format="1"`
: Formats a sequence of numbers as `1 2 3 4 5 6 7 8 9 10 11 ....`

`format="01"`
: Formats a sequence of numbers as `01 02 03 04 ... 09 10 11 ... 99 100 101 ....`

`format="a"`
: Formats a sequence of numbers as `a b c d e f ... x y z aa ab ac ....`

`format="A"`
: Formats a sequence of numbers as `A B C D E F ... X Y Z AA AB AC ....`

`format="i"`
: Formats a sequence of numbers as `i ii iii iv v vi vii viii ix x ....`

`format="I"`
: Formats a sequence of numbers as `I II III IV V VI VII VIII IX X ....`

`format="anything else"`
: How this works is depends on the XSLT processor you're using. The XSLT specification lists several other numbering schemes (Thai digits, Katakana numbering, traditional Hebrew numbering, etc.); check your XSLT processor's documentation to see which formats it supports. If the XSLT processor doesn't support the numbering scheme you requested, the XSLT spec requires that it use `format="1"` as the default.

lang
: The `lang` attribute defines the language whose alphabet should be used. Different XSLT processors support different language values, so check the documentation of your favorite XSLT processor for more information.

letter-value
: This attribute has the value `alphabetic` or `traditional`. There are a number of languages in which two letter-based numbering schemes are used; one assigns numeric values in alphabetic sequence, while the other uses a tradition native to that language. (Roman numerals—a letter-based numbering scheme that doesn't use an alphabetic order—are one example.) The default for this attribute is `alphabetic`.

grouping-separator
: This attribute is the character that should be used between groups of digits in a generated number. The default is the comma (`,`).

grouping-size
: This attribute defines the number of digits that appear in each group; the default is `3`.

Content

None. `<xsl:number>` is an empty element.

Appears in

`<xsl:number>` appears inside a template.

Defined in

XSLT section 7.7, Numbering.

Example

To fully illustrate how `<xsl:number>` works, we'll need an XML document with many things to count. Here's the document we'll use:

```
<?xml version="1.0"?>
<book>
  <chapter>
    <title>Alfa Romeo</title>
    <sect1>
      <title>Bentley</title>
    </sect1>
    <sect1>
      <title>Chevrolet</title>
      <sect2>
        <title>Dodge</title>
        <sect3>
          <title>Eagle</title>
        </sect3>
      </sect2>
    </sect1>
  </chapter>
  <chapter>
    <title>Ford</title>
    <sect1>
      <title>GMC</title>
      <sect2>
        <title>Honda</title>
        <sect3>
          <title>Isuzu</title>
        </sect3>
        <sect3>
          <title>Javelin</title>
        </sect3>
        <sect3>
          <title>K-Car</title>
        </sect3>
        <sect3>
          <title>Lincoln</title>
        </sect3>
      </sect2>
      <sect2>
        <title>Mercedes</title>
      </sect2>
      <sect2>
        <title>Nash</title>
        <sect3>
          <title>Opel</title>
```

```
          </sect3>
          <sect3>
            <title>Pontiac</title>
          </sect3>
        </sect2>
        <sect2>
          <title>Quantum</title>
          <sect3>
            <title>Rambler</title>
          </sect3>
          <sect3>
            <title>Studebaker</title>
          </sect3>
        </sect2>
      </sect1>
      <sect1>
        <title>Toyota</title>
        <sect2>
          <title>Um, is there a car that starts with "U"?</title>
        </sect2>
      </sect1>
      <sect1>
        <title>Volkswagen</title>
      </sect1>
    </chapter>
  </book>
```

We'll use <xsl:number> in several different ways to illustrate the various options we have in numbering things. We'll look at the stylesheet and the results, then we'll discuss them. Here's the stylesheet:

```
<?xml version="1.0"?>
<xsl:stylesheet version="1.0" xmlns:xsl="http://www.w3.org/1999/XSL/Transform">

  <xsl:output method="text"/>

  <xsl:variable name="newline">
<xsl:text>
</xsl:text>
  </xsl:variable>

  <xsl:template match="/">
    <xsl:value-of select="$newline"/>
    <xsl:apply-templates select="book" mode="number-1"/>
    <xsl:apply-templates select="book" mode="number-2"/>
    <xsl:apply-templates select="book" mode="number-3"/>
    <xsl:apply-templates select="book" mode="number-4"/>
    <xsl:apply-templates select="book" mode="number-5"/>
    <xsl:apply-templates select="book" mode="number-6"/>
```

```
  <xsl:apply-templates select="book" mode="number-7"/>
</xsl:template>

<xsl:template match="book" mode="number-1">
  <xsl:text>Test #1: level="multiple",
       count="chapter|sect1|sect2|sect3",
       format="1.1.1.1. "</xsl:text>
  <xsl:value-of select="$newline"/>
  <xsl:value-of select="$newline"/>
  <xsl:for-each select="chapter|.//sect1|.//sect2|.//sect3">
    <xsl:number level="multiple" count="chapter|sect1|sect2|sect3"
      format="1.1.1.1. "/>
      <xsl:value-of select="title"/>
      <xsl:value-of select="$newline"/>
  </xsl:for-each>
  <xsl:value-of select="$newline"/>
</xsl:template>

<xsl:template match="book" mode="number-2">
  <xsl:text>Test #2: level="any",
       count="chapter|sect1|sect2|sect3",
       format="1. "</xsl:text>
  <xsl:value-of select="$newline"/>
  <xsl:value-of select="$newline"/>
  <xsl:for-each select="chapter|.//sect1|.//sect2|.//sect3">
    <xsl:number level="any" count="chapter|sect1|sect2|sect3"
      format="1. "/>
      <xsl:value-of select="title"/>
      <xsl:value-of select="$newline"/>
  </xsl:for-each>
  <xsl:value-of select="$newline"/>
</xsl:template>

<xsl:template match="book" mode="number-3">
  <xsl:text>Test #3: level="single",
       count="chapter|sect1|sect2|sect3",
       format="1.1.1.1. "</xsl:text>
  <xsl:value-of select="$newline"/>
  <xsl:value-of select="$newline"/>
  <xsl:for-each select="chapter|.//sect1|.//sect2|.//sect3">
    <xsl:number level="single" count="chapter|sect1|sect2|sect3"
      format="1.1.1.1. "/>
      <xsl:value-of select="title"/>
      <xsl:value-of select="$newline"/>
  </xsl:for-each>
  <xsl:value-of select="$newline"/>
</xsl:template>
```

```
<xsl:template match="book" mode="number-4">
  <xsl:text>Test #4: level="multiple",
       select=".//sect2",
       count="chapter|sect1|sect2",
       format="I-A-i: "</xsl:text>
  <xsl:value-of select="$newline"/>
  <xsl:value-of select="$newline"/>
  <xsl:for-each select=".//sect2">
    <xsl:number level="multiple" count="chapter|sect1|sect2"
      format="I-A-i: "/>
      <xsl:value-of select="title"/>
      <xsl:value-of select="$newline"/>
  </xsl:for-each>
  <xsl:value-of select="$newline"/>
</xsl:template>

<xsl:template match="book" mode="number-5">
  <xsl:text>Test #5: level="any",
       count="[various elements]"
       from="[various elements]"
       format="1.1.1.1. "</xsl:text>
  <xsl:value-of select="$newline"/>
  <xsl:value-of select="$newline"/>
  <xsl:for-each select=".//sect3">
    <xsl:number level="any" from="book" count="chapter" format="1."/>
    <xsl:number level="any" from="chapter" count="sect1" format="1."/>
    <xsl:number level="any" from="sect1" count="sect2" format="1."/>
    <xsl:number level="any" from="sect2" count="sect3" format="1. "/>
    <xsl:value-of select="title"/>
    <xsl:value-of select="$newline"/>
  </xsl:for-each>
  <xsl:value-of select="$newline"/>
</xsl:template>

<xsl:template match="book" mode="number-6">
  <xsl:text>Test #6: level="any",
       count="chapter|sect1|sect2|sect3",
       grouping-separator=",",
       using a variable to start counting at 1000.</xsl:text>
  <xsl:value-of select="$newline"/>
  <xsl:value-of select="$newline"/>
  <xsl:for-each select="chapter|.//sect1|.//sect2|.//sect3">
    <xsl:variable name="value1">
      <xsl:number level="any" count="chapter|sect1|sect2|sect3"/>
    </xsl:variable>
    <xsl:number value="$value1 + 999"
      grouping-separator="." grouping-size="3"/>
    <xsl:text>. </xsl:text>
    <xsl:value-of select="title"/>
    <xsl:value-of select="$newline"/>
```

```
    </xsl:for-each>
    <xsl:value-of select="$newline"/>
  </xsl:template>

  <xsl:template match="book" mode="number-7">
    <xsl:text>Test #7: level="multiple",
        count="chapter|sect1|sect2|sect3",
        format="1.1.1.1. ",
        selecting up to the first two <sect1> elements from chapter 2.</xsl:text>
    <xsl:value-of select="$newline"/>
    <xsl:value-of select="$newline"/>
    <xsl:for-each select="chapter[2]/sect1[position() < 3]">
      <xsl:for-each select="chapter|.//sect1|.//sect2|.//sect3">
        <xsl:number level="multiple" count="chapter|sect1|sect2|sect3"
          format="1.1.1.1. "/>
        <xsl:value-of select="title"/>
        <xsl:value-of select="$newline"/>
      </xsl:for-each>
    </xsl:for-each>
  </xsl:template>

</xsl:stylesheet>
```

Here are our results:

```
Test #1: level="multiple",
         count="chapter|sect1|sect2|sect3",
         format="1.1.1.1. "

1. Alfa Romeo
1.1. Bentley
1.2. Chevrolet
1.2.1. Dodge
1.2.1.1. Eagle
2. Ford
2.1. GMC
2.1.1. Honda
2.1.1.1. Isuzu
2.1.1.2. Javelin
2.1.1.3. K-Car
2.1.1.4. Lincoln
2.1.2. Mercedes
2.1.3. Nash
2.1.3.1. Opel
2.1.3.2. Pontiac
2.1.4. Quantum
2.1.4.1. Rambler
2.1.4.2. Studebaker
2.2. Toyota
```

```
2.2.1. Um, is there a car that starts with "U"?
2.3. Volkswagen

Test #2: level="any",
         count="chapter|sect1|sect2|sect3",
         format="1. "

1. Alfa Romeo
2. Bentley
3. Chevrolet
4. Dodge
5. Eagle
6. Ford
7. GMC
8. Honda
9. Isuzu
10. Javelin
11. K-Car
12. Lincoln
13. Mercedes
14. Nash
15. Opel
16. Pontiac
17. Quantum
18. Rambler
19. Studebaker
20. Toyota
21. Um, is there a car that starts with "U"?
22. Volkswagen

Test #3: level="single",
         count="chapter|sect1|sect2|sect3",
         format="1.1.1.1. "

1. Alfa Romeo
1. Bentley
2. Chevrolet
1. Dodge
1. Eagle
2. Ford
1. GMC
1. Honda
1. Isuzu
2. Javelin
3. K-Car
4. Lincoln
2. Mercedes
3. Nash
1. Opel
2. Pontiac
```

```
4. Quantum
1. Rambler
2. Studebaker
2. Toyota
1. Um, is there a car that starts with "U"?
3. Volkswagen

Test #4: level="multiple",
         select=".//sect2",
         count="chapter|sect1|sect2",
         format="I-A-i: "

I-B-i: Dodge
II-A-i: Honda
II-A-ii: Mercedes
II-A-iii: Nash
II-A-iv: Quantum
II-B-i: Um, is there a car that starts with "U"?

Test #5: level="any",
         count="[various elements]"
         from="[various elements]"
         format="1.1.1.1. "

1.2.1.1. Eagle
2.1.1.1. Isuzu
2.1.1.2. Javelin
2.1.1.3. K-Car
2.1.1.4. Lincoln
2.1.3.1. Opel
2.1.3.2. Pontiac
2.1.4.1. Rambler
2.1.4.2. Studebaker

Test #6: level="any",
         count="chapter|sect1|sect2|sect3",
         grouping-separator=",",
         using a variable to start counting at 1000.

1,000. Alfa Romeo
1,001. Bentley
1,002. Chevrolet
1,003. Dodge
1,004. Eagle
1,005. Ford
1,006. GMC
1,007. Honda
1,008. Isuzu
1,009. Javelin
1,010. K-Car
```

```
1,011. Lincoln
1,012. Mercedes
1,013. Nash
1,014. Opel
1,015. Pontiac
1,016. Quantum
1,017. Rambler
1,018. Studebaker
1,019. Toyota
1,020. Um, is there a car that starts with "U"?
1,021. Volkswagen

Test #7: level="multiple",
         count="chapter|sect1|sect2|sect3",
         format="1.1.1.1. ",
         selecting up to the first two <sect1> elements from chapter 2.

2.1. GMC
2.1.1. Honda
2.1.1.1. Isuzu
2.1.1.2. Javelin
2.1.1.3. K-Car
2.1.1.4. Lincoln
2.1.2. Mercedes
2.1.3. Nash
2.1.3.1. Opel
2.1.3.2. Pontiac
2.1.4. Quantum
2.1.4.1. Rambler
2.1.4.2. Studebaker
2.2. Toyota
2.2.1. Um, is there a car that starts with "U"?
```

In Test 1, we used `level="multiple"` to count the <chapter>, <sect1>, <sect2>, and <sect3> elements. Numbering these at multiple levels gives us a dotted-decimal number for each element. We can look at the number next to `Studebaker` and know that it is the second <sect3> element inside the fourth <sect2> element inside the first <sect1> element inside the second <chapter> element.

Test 2 uses `level="any"` to count all of the <chapter>, <sect1>, <sect2>, and <sect3> elements in order.

Test 3 uses `level="single"` to count the elements at each level. This means that the fourth <sect3> element inside a given <sect2> element will be numbered with a `4` (or `iv` or `D` or whatever the appropriate value would be). Notice that the number used for each element is the same as the last number beside each element in Test 1.

Test 4 does a couple of things differently: first, it uses the uppercase-alpha and lowercase-roman numbering styles. Second, it counts elements at multiple levels (for the <chapter>,

<sect1>, and <sect2> elements), but we only process the <sect2> elements. Even though we only output the title text for the <sect2> elements, we can still generate the appropriate multilevel numbers.

Test 5 generates numbers similarly to Test 4, except that it uses the from attribute. We generate numbers for <sect3> elements in four stages; first, we count the <chapter> ancestors, starting at the first <book> ancestor; then we count the <sect1> ancestors, starting at the first <chapter> ancestor, etc.

Test 6 starts counting at 1000 instead of 1. To do this, we have to store the value generated by <xsl:number> in a variable, then output the value of the variable plus 1000. Notice that we can use an expression in the value attribute of the <xsl:number> element. We also used the grouping-separator attribute to use a comma to separate groups of three digits.

Last but not least, Test 7 only numbers items from the first and second <sect1> elements (<sect1> elements whose position() is less than 3) in the second <chapter> element. Even though we're only processing these sections, we can still use <xsl:number> to generate the correct numbers for the elements.

<xsl:otherwise> — Defines the else or default case in an <xsl:choose> element. This element always appears inside an <xsl:choose> element, and it must always appear last.

Category

Subinstruction (<xsl:otherwise> always appears as part of an <xsl:choose> element).

Required Attributes

None.

Optional Attributes

None.

Content

A template.

Appears in

The <xsl:choose> element.

Defined in

XSLT section 9.2, Conditional Processing with xsl:choose.

Example

As an example, we'll use an <xsl:choose> element that cycles through a set of values for the background color of a cell in an HTML table. We'll use this XML document as our input:

```
<?xml version="1.0"?>
<list xml:lang="en">
  <title>Albums I've bought recently:</title>
  <listitem>The Sacred Art of Dub</listitem>
  <listitem>Only the Poor Man Feel It</listitem>
```

```
    <listitem>Excitable Boy</listitem>
    <listitem xml:lang="sw">Aki Special</listitem>
    <listitem xml:lang="en-gb">Combat Rock</listitem>
    <listitem xml:lang="zu">Talking Timbuktu</listitem>
    <listitem xml:lang="jz">The Birth of the Cool</listitem>
  </list>
```

Here is our stylesheet, which uses `<xsl:choose>` inside an `<xsl:attribute>` element to determine the correct value for the `bgcolor` attribute. We have an `<xsl:otherwise>` element that generates the value `whitesmoke` for every fourth `<listitem>` in our source document:

```
<?xml version="1.0"?>
<xsl:stylesheet version="1.0" xmlns:xsl="http://www.w3.org/1999/XSL/Transform">

  <xsl:output method="html"/>

  <xsl:template match="/">
    <html>
      <head>
        <title>
          <xsl:value-of select="list/title"/>
        </title>
      </head>
      <body>
        <h1><xsl:value-of select="list/title"/></h1>
        <table border="1">
          <xsl:for-each select="list/listitem">
            <tr>
              <td>
                <xsl:attribute name="bgcolor">
                  <xsl:choose>
                    <xsl:when test="@bgcolor">
                      <xsl:value-of select="@bgcolor"/>
                    </xsl:when>
                    <xsl:when test="position() mod 4 = 0">
                      <xsl:text>papayawhip</xsl:text>
                    </xsl:when>
                    <xsl:when test="position() mod 4 = 1">
                      <xsl:text>mintcream</xsl:text>
                    </xsl:when>
                    <xsl:when test="position() mod 4 = 2">
                      <xsl:text>lavender</xsl:text>
                    </xsl:when>
                    <xsl:otherwise>
                      <xsl:text>whitesmoke</xsl:text>
                    </xsl:otherwise>
                  </xsl:choose>
                </xsl:attribute>
                <xsl:value-of select="."/>
              </td>
```

```
            </tr>
          </xsl:for-each>
        </table>
      </body>
    </html>
  </xsl:template>

</xsl:stylesheet>
```

Here is our generated HTML document. Notice that every fourth row has a background color of whitesmoke; that value was generated by the <xsl:otherwise> element:

```
<html>
<head>
<META http-equiv="Content-Type" content="text/html; charset=UTF-8">
<title>Albums I've bought recently:</title>
</head>
<body>
<h1>Albums I've bought recently:</h1>
<table border="1">
<tr>
<td bgcolor="mintcream">The Sacred Art of Dub</td>
</tr>
<tr>
<td bgcolor="lavender">Only the Poor Man Feel It</td>
</tr>
<tr>
<td bgcolor="whitesmoke">Excitable Boy</td>
</tr>
<tr>
<td bgcolor="papayawhip">Aki Special</td>
</tr>
<tr>
<td bgcolor="mintcream">Combat Rock</td>
</tr>
<tr>
<td bgcolor="lavender">Talking Timbuktu</td>
</tr>
<tr>
<td bgcolor="whitesmoke">The Birth of the Cool</td>
</tr>
</table>
</body>
</html>
```

When rendered, our HTML document looks like Figure A-7.

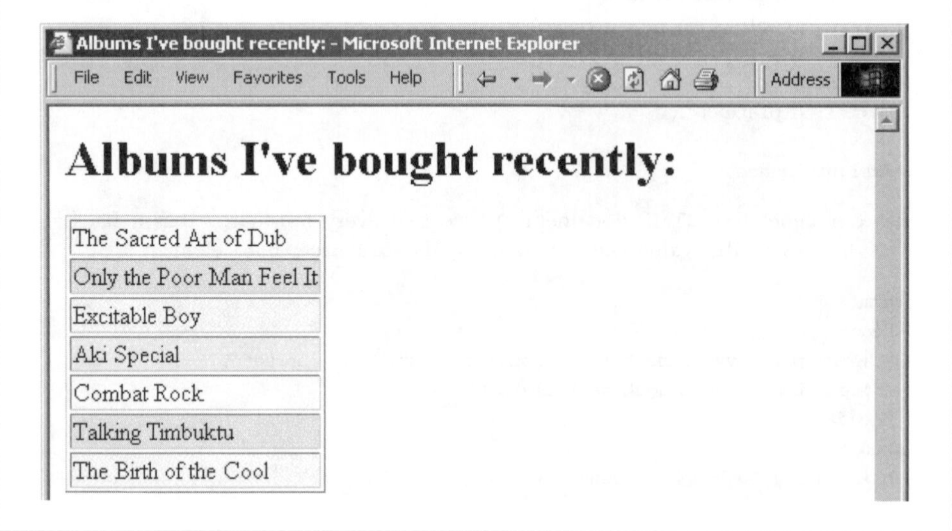

Figure A-7. Document cycling among different background colors

<xsl:output> — Defines the characteristics of the output document.

Category

Top-level element

Required Attributes

None.

Optional Attributes

method

Typically has one of three values: `xml`, `html`, or `text`. This value indicates the type of document that is generated. An XSLT processor can add other values to this list; how those values affect the generated document is determined by the XSLT processor.

version

Defines the value of the `version` attribute of the XML or HTML declaration in the output document. This attribute is used only when `method="html"` or `method="xml"`.

encoding

Defines the value of the `encoding` attribute of the XML declaration in the output document.

omit-xml-declaration

Defines whether the XML declaration is omitted in the output document. Allowable values are `yes` and `no`. This attribute is used only when `method="xml"`.

standalone
Defines the value of the `standalone` attribute of the XML declaration in the output document. Valid values are `yes` and `no`. This attribute is used only when `method="xml"`.

doctype-public
Defines the value of the `PUBLIC` attribute of the `DOCTYPE` declaration in the output document. This attribute defines the public identifier of the output document's DTD. It is used only when `method="html"` or `method="xml"`.

doctype-system
Defines the value of the `SYSTEM` attribute of the `DOCTYPE` declaration in the output document. It defines the system identifier of the output document's DTD. This attribute is used only when `method="html"` or `method="xml"`.

cdata-section-elements
Lists the elements that should be written as `CDATA` sections in the output document. All restrictions and escaping conventions of `CDATA` sections are handled by the XSLT processor. If you need to list more than one element, separate the element names with one or more whitespace characters. This attribute is used only when `method="xml"`.

indent
Specifies whether the tags in the output document should be indented. Allowable values are `yes` and `no`. This attribute is used only when `method="xml"` or `method="html"`, and the XSLT processor is not required to honor it.

media-type
Defines the MIME type of the output document.

Content

None. `<xsl:output>` is an empty element.

Appears in

`<xsl:output>` is a top-level element and can only appear as a child of `<xsl:stylesheet>`.

Defined in

XSLT section 16, Output.

Example

To illustrate the three output methods defined in the XSLT specification, we'll create three stylesheets, each of which uses one of the three methods. We'll use the following XML document in all three examples:

```
<?xml version="1.0"?>
<list>
  <title>A few of my favorite albums</title>
  <listitem>A Love Supreme</listitem>
  <listitem>Beat Crazy</listitem>
  <listitem>Here Come the Warm Jets</listitem>
  <listitem>Kind of Blue</listitem>
  <listitem>London Calling</listitem>
  <listitem>Remain in Light</listitem>
```

```
    <listitem>The Joshua Tree</listitem>
    <listitem>The Indestructible Beat of Soweto</listitem>
</list>
```

We'll now look at our three stylesheets and the results produced by each. First, let's look at the `method="xml"` stylesheet:

```
<?xml version="1.0"?>
<xsl:stylesheet version="1.0" xmlns:xsl="http://www.w3.org/1999/XSL/Transform">

  <xsl:output
    method="xml"
    doctype-public="-//W3C/DTD XHTML 1.0//EN"
    doctype-system="file:///d:/xhtml.dtd"
    encoding="ISO-8859-1"
    indent="no"/>

  <xsl:template match="/">
    <html>
      <head>
        <title><xsl:value-of select="/list/title"/></title>
      </head>
      <body>
        <h1><xsl:value-of select="/list/title"/></h1>
        <p>
          <xsl:for-each select="/list/listitem">
            <xsl:number format="1. "/>
            <xsl:value-of select="."/>
            <br/>
          </xsl:for-each>
        </p>
      </body>
    </html>
  </xsl:template>

</xsl:stylesheet>
```

This stylesheet generates the following results:

```
<?xml version="1.0" encoding="ISO-8859-1"?>
<!DOCTYPE html PUBLIC "-//W3C/DTD XHTML 1.0//EN" "file:///d:/xhtml.dtd">
<html><head><title>A few of my favorite albums</title>
</head><body><h1>A few of my favorite albums</h1>
<p>1. A Love Supreme<br/>2. Beat Crazy<br/>3. Here Come the
Warm Jets<br/>4. Kind of Blue<br/>5. London Calling<br/>6.
Remain in Light<br/>7. The Joshua Tree<br/>8. The Indestructible
Beat of Soweto<br/></p></body></html>
```

(We actually added line breaks to this listing; the original output put everything from `<html>` through `</html>` on a single line.)

The output document has the encoding we specified in our stylesheet, and the DOCTYPE declaration includes the PUBLIC and SYSTEM identifiers we requested as well. Even with the line breaks we added, it's still obvious that this document has not been formatted with any extra whitespace whatsoever. We also have empty <br/> elements in our output document; those elements will be handled differently when we specify method="html". Speaking of which, here is our method="html" stylesheet:

```
<?xml version="1.0"?>
<xsl:stylesheet version="1.0" xmlns:xsl="http://www.w3.org/1999/XSL/Transform">

  <xsl:output
    method="html"
    encoding="ISO-8859-1"
    doctype-public="-//W3C/DTD HTML 1.0 Transitional//EN"/>

  <xsl:template match="/">
    <html>
      <head>
        <title><xsl:value-of select="/list/title"/></title>
      </head>
      <body>
        <h1><xsl:value-of select="/list/title"/></h1>
        <p>
          <xsl:for-each select="/list/listitem">
            <xsl:number format="1. "/>
            <xsl:value-of select="."/>
            <br/>
          </xsl:for-each>
        </p>
      </body>
    </html>
  </xsl:template>

</xsl:stylesheet>
```

Here is the HTML document generated by this stylesheet:

```
<!DOCTYPE HTML PUBLIC "-//W3C/DTD HTML 1.0 Transitional//EN">
<html>
<head>
<META http-equiv="Content-Type" content="text/html; charset=ISO-8859-1">
<title>A few of my favorite albums</title>
</head>
<body>
<h1>A few of my favorite albums</h1>
<p>1. A Love Supreme<br>2. Beat Crazy<br>3. Here Come
the Warm Jets<br>4. Kind of Blue<br>5. London Calling<br>6.
Remain in Light<br>7. The Joshua Tree<br>8. The Indestructible
Beat of Soweto<br>
```

```
</p>
</body>
</html>
```

(As before, we added line breaks to make the listing legible.) Notice that the XSLT processor has automatically inserted a <META> element in the <head> of our HTML document. The <br> elements that were empty in our previous stylesheet are now old-fashioned <br> tags. Even though this style of XSLT output results in a document that is not valid XML (or XHTML), the document will work with existing HTML browsers.

Our final stylesheet will use `method="text"`:

```
<?xml version="1.0"?>
<xsl:stylesheet version="1.0" xmlns:xsl="http://www.w3.org/1999/XSL/Transform">

  <xsl:output method="text"/>

  <xsl:template match="/">
    <html>
      <head>
        <title><xsl:value-of select="/list/title"/></title>
      </head>
      <body>
        <h1><xsl:value-of select="/list/title"/></h1>
        <p>
          <xsl:for-each select="/list/listitem">
            <xsl:number format="1. "/>
            <xsl:value-of select="."/>
            <br/>
          </xsl:for-each>
        </p>
      </body>
    </html>
  </xsl:template>

</xsl:stylesheet>
```

Here are the results, such as they are, from this stylesheet:

```
A few of my favorite albumsA few of my favorite albums1. A Love Supreme2. Beat
Crazy3. Here Come the Warm Jets4. Kind of Blue5. London Calling6. Remain in
Light7. The Joshua Tree8. The Indestructible Beat of Soweto
```

(As before, we inserted line breaks so the document would fit on the page.) These results are basically worthless. Why weren't our carefully coded HTML elements output to the text document? The reason is that the `text` output method only outputs text nodes to the result tree. Even though we requested that various HTML elements be generated along the way, they're ignored because we specified `method="text"`.

<xsl:param>

— Defines the name and value of a parameter to be used by a template. This element can appear as a top-level element or inside the `<xsl:template>` element. If the `<xsl:param>` appears as a top-level element, it is a global parameter, visible to all areas of the stylesheet. The value of the parameter can be defined in one of two ways: specified in the `select` attribute, or defined in an XSLT template inside the `<xsl:param>` element itself.

Category

Instruction

Required Attributes

name

Defines the name of this parameter.

Optional Attributes

select

Contains an XPath expression that defines the value of this parameter.

Content

If the `select` attribute is used, `<xsl:param>` should be empty. Otherwise, it contains an XSLT template.

Appears in

`<xsl:stylesheet>` and `<xsl:template>`. If an `<xsl:param>` appears as a child of `<xsl:stylesheet>`, then it is a global parameter visible throughout the stylesheet. XSLT doesn't define the way global parameters are passed to the XSLT processor, so check the documentation for your processor to see how this is done. (See the section "Global Parameters" in Chapter 4 for an overview of how to pass parameters to the most popular XSLT processors.)

Defined in

XSLT section 11, Variables and Parameters.

Example

Here is a stylesheet that defines several `<xsl:param>` elements, both global and local. Notice that one of the parameters is a node-set; parameters can be of any XPath or XSLT datatype:

```
<?xml version="1.0"?>
<xsl:stylesheet version="1.0" xmlns:xsl="http://www.w3.org/1999/XSL/Transform">

  <xsl:output method="text"/>

  <xsl:variable name="newline">
<xsl:text>
</xsl:text>
  </xsl:variable>
```

```
  <xsl:param name="favoriteNumber" select="23"/>
  <xsl:param name="favoriteColor"/>

  <xsl:template match="/">
    <xsl:value-of select="$newline"/>
    <xsl:value-of select="list/title"/>
    <xsl:value-of select="$newline"/>
    <xsl:variable name="listitems" select="list/listitem"/>
    <xsl:call-template name="processListitems">
      <xsl:with-param name="items" select="$listitems"/>
      <xsl:with-param name="color" select="'yellow'"/>
      <xsl:with-param name="number" select="$favoriteNumber"/>
    </xsl:call-template>
  </xsl:template>

  <xsl:template name="processListitems">
    <xsl:param name="items"/>
    <xsl:param name="color" select="'blue'"/>

    <xsl:for-each select="$items">
      <xsl:value-of select="position()"/>
      <xsl:text>.  </xsl:text>
      <xsl:value-of select="."/>
      <xsl:value-of select="$newline"/>
    </xsl:for-each>

    <xsl:value-of select="$newline"/>

    <xsl:text>Your favorite color is </xsl:text>
    <xsl:value-of select="$favoriteColor"/>
    <xsl:text>.</xsl:text>
    <xsl:value-of select="$newline"/>
    <xsl:text>The color passed to this template is </xsl:text>
    <xsl:value-of select="$color"/>
    <xsl:text>.</xsl:text>
    <xsl:value-of select="$newline"/>
  </xsl:template>

</xsl:stylesheet>
```

We'll use this stylesheet to transform the following document:

```
<?xml version="1.0"?>
<list>
  <title>A few of my favorite albums</title>
  <listitem>A Love Supreme</listitem>
  <listitem>Beat Crazy</listitem>
  <listitem>Here Come the Warm Jets</listitem>
  <listitem>Kind of Blue</listitem>
  <listitem>London Calling</listitem>
```

```
    <listitem>Remain in Light</listitem>
    <listitem>The Joshua Tree</listitem>
    <listitem>The Indestructible Beat of Soweto</listitem>
  </list>
```

Here are the results:

```
A few of my favorite albums
1.  A Love Supreme
2.  Beat Crazy
3.  Here Come the Warm Jets
4.  Kind of Blue
5.  London Calling
6.  Remain in Light
7.  The Joshua Tree
8.  The Indestructible Beat of Soweto

Your favorite color is purple.
The color passed to this template is yellow.
```

To generate these results, we passed the value `purple` to the XSLT processor. With Xalan, the value is passed like this:

```
java org.apache.xalan.xslt.Process -in test4.xml -xsl param.xsl
  -param favoriteColor purple
```

(The command should be entered on a single line.) See the section "Global Parameters" in Chapter 4 for a more complete discussion of global parameters and how they can be set for various XSLT processors.

<xsl:preserve-space> — Defines the source document elements for which whitespace should be preserved.

Category

Top-level element

Required Attributes

elements

This attribute defines the elements for which whitespace should be preserved. If you need to define more than one element, separate the element names with one or more whitespace characters.

Optional Attributes

None.

Content

None. `<xsl:preserve-space>` is an empty element.

Appears in

<preserve-space> is a top-level element and can only appear as a child of <xsl:stylesheet>.

Defined in

XSLT section 3.4, Whitespace Stripping.

Example

We'll illustrate how <preserve-space> works with the following stylesheet:

```
<?xml version="1.0"?>
<xsl:stylesheet version="1.0" xmlns:xsl="http://www.w3.org/1999/XSL/Transform">

  <xsl:output method="text"/>
  <xsl:preserve-space elements="listing"/>

  <xsl:variable name="newline">
<xsl:text>
</xsl:text>
  </xsl:variable>

  <xsl:template match="/">
    <xsl:value-of select="$newline"/>
    <xsl:value-of select="/code-sample/title"/>
    <xsl:value-of select="$newline"/>
    <xsl:for-each select="/code-sample/listing">
      <xsl:value-of select="."/>
    </xsl:for-each>
  </xsl:template>

</xsl:stylesheet>
```

We'll use this stylesheet to process the following document:

```
<?xml version="1.0"?>
<code-sample>
  <title>Conditional variable initialization</title>
  <listing>
  <type>int</type> <variable>y</variable> = <constant>23</constant>;
  <type>int</type> <variable>x</variable>;
    <keyword>if</keyword> (<variable>y</variable> > <constant>10</constant>)
    <variable>x</variable> = <constant>5</constant>;
  <keyword>else</keyword>
    <keyword>if</keyword> (<variable>y</variable> > <constant>5</constant>)
      <variable>x</variable> = <constant>3</constant>;
  <keyword>else</keyword>
    <variable>x</variable> = <constant>1</constant>;
  </listing>
</code-sample>
```

When we process this document with our stylesheet, we get these results:

```
Conditional variable initialization

  int y = 23;
  int x;
    if (y > 10)
    x = 5;
  else
    if (y > 5)
      x = 3;
  else
    x = 1;
```

Compare this example to the one for the `<strip-space>` element.

<xsl:processing-instruction> — Creates a processing instruction in the output document.

Category

Instruction

Required Attributes

name
Defines the name of this processing instruction.

Optional Attributes

None.

Content

An XSLT template. The contents of the template become the data of the processing instruction.

Appears in

`<xsl:processing-instruction>` appears inside a template.

Defined in

XSLT section 7.3, Creating Processing Instructions.

Example

We'll demonstrate a stylesheet that adds a processing instruction to an XML document. The processing instruction will associate the stylesheet *template.xsl* with this XML document. Here is our stylesheet:

```
<?xml version="1.0"?>
<xsl:stylesheet xmlns:xsl="http://www.w3.org/1999/XSL/Transform" version="1.0">
  <xsl:output method="xml"/>
```

```
  <xsl:template match="/">
    <xsl:processing-instruction name="xml-stylesheet">href="docbook/html/docbook.xsl"
       type="text/xsl"</xsl:processing-instruction>
    <xsl:copy-of select="."/>
  </xsl:template>

</xsl:stylesheet>
```

This stylesheet simply uses the <xsl:copy-of> element to copy the input document to the result tree, adding a processing instruction along the way. We'll use our stylesheet with this XML document:

```
<?xml version="1.0"?>
<list>
  <title>A few of my favorite albums</title>
  <listitem>A Love Supreme</listitem>
  <listitem>Beat Crazy</listitem>
  <listitem>Here Come the Warm Jets</listitem>
  <listitem>Kind of Blue</listitem>
  <listitem>London Calling</listitem>
  <listitem>Remain in Light</listitem>
  <listitem>The Joshua Tree</listitem>
  <listitem>The Indestructible Beat of Soweto</listitem>
</list>
```

When we run this transformation, here are the results:

```
<?xml version="1.0" encoding="UTF-8"?>
<?xml-stylesheet href="docbook/html/docbook.xsl" type="text/xsl"?>
<list>
  <title>A few of my favorite albums</title>
  <listitem>A Love Supreme</listitem>
  <listitem>Beat Crazy</listitem>
  <listitem>Here Come the Warm Jets</listitem>
  <listitem>Kind of Blue</listitem>
  <listitem>London Calling</listitem>
  <listitem>Remain in Light</listitem>
  <listitem>The Joshua Tree</listitem>
  <listitem>The Indestructible Beat of Soweto</listitem>
</list>
```

Note that the contents of a processing instruction are text. Even though the processing instruction we just generated looks like it contains two attributes, you can't create the processing instruction like this:

```
<?xml version="1.0"?>
<xsl:stylesheet xmlns:xsl="http://www.w3.org/1999/XSL/Transform" version="1.0">
  <xsl:output method="xml"/>

  <xsl:template match="/">
    <xsl:processing-instruction name="xml-stylesheet">
```

```
    <!-- This doesn't work!  You can't put <xsl:attribute>
         elements inside a <xsl:processing-instruction> element. -->

    <xsl:attribute name="href">
      <xsl:text>docbook/html/docbook.xsl</xsl:text>
    </xsl:attribute>
    <xsl:attribute name="type">
      <xsl:text>text/xsl</xsl:text>
    </xsl:attribute>
  </xsl:processing-instruction>
  <xsl:copy-of select="."/>
</xsl:template>

</xsl:stylesheet>
```

If you try this, you'll get an exception from the XSLT processor.

<xsl:sort> — Defines a sort key for the current context. This element appears as a child of the `<xsl:apply-templates>` or `<xsl:for-each>` elements. Within those elements, the first `<xsl:sort>` defines the primary sort key, the second `<xsl:sort>` defines the secondary sort key, etc.

Category

Subinstruction (`<xsl:sort>` always appears as a child of the `<xsl:apply-templates>` or `<xsl:for-each>` elements)

Required Attributes

None.

Optional Attributes

select
: An XPath expression that defines the nodes to be sorted.

lang
: A string that defines the language used by the sort. The language codes are defined in RFC1766, available at *http://www.ietf.org/rfc/rfc1766.txt*.

data-type
: An attribute that defines the type of the items to be sorted. Allowable values are `number` and `text`; the default is `text`. An XSLT processor has the option of supporting other values as well. Sorting the values `32 10 120` with `data-type="text"` returns `10 120 32`, while `data-type="number"` returns `10 32 120`.

order
: An attribute that defines the order of the sort. Allowable values are `ascending` and `descending`.

case-order
: An attribute that defines the order in which upper- and lowercase letters are sorted. Allowable values are `upper-first` and `lower-first`.

Content

None.

Appears in

<xsl:apply-templates> and <xsl:for-each>.

Defined in

XSLT section 10, Sorting.

Example

We'll illustrate <xsl:sort> with this stylesheet:

```
<?xml version="1.0"?>
<xsl:stylesheet version="1.0" xmlns:xsl="http://www.w3.org/1999/XSL/Transform">

  <xsl:output method="text"/>

  <xsl:variable name="newline">
<xsl:text>
</xsl:text>
  </xsl:variable>

  <xsl:template match="/">
    <xsl:value-of select="$newline"/>
    <xsl:call-template name="ascending-alpha-sort">
      <xsl:with-param name="items" select="/sample/textlist/listitem"/>
    </xsl:call-template>
    <xsl:call-template name="ascending-alpha-sort">
      <xsl:with-param name="items" select="/sample/numericlist/listitem"/>
    </xsl:call-template>
    <xsl:call-template name="ascending-numeric-sort">
      <xsl:with-param name="items" select="/sample/numericlist/listitem"/>
    </xsl:call-template>
    <xsl:call-template name="descending-alpha-sort">
      <xsl:with-param name="items" select="/sample/textlist/listitem"/>
    </xsl:call-template>
  </xsl:template>

  <xsl:template name="ascending-alpha-sort">
    <xsl:param name="items"/>
    <xsl:text>Ascending text sort:</xsl:text>
    <xsl:value-of select="$newline"/>
    <xsl:for-each select="$items">
      <xsl:sort select="."/>
      <xsl:value-of select="."/>
      <xsl:value-of select="$newline"/>
    </xsl:for-each>
    <xsl:value-of select="$newline"/>
  </xsl:template>
```

```
  <xsl:template name="descending-alpha-sort">
    <xsl:param name="items"/>
    <xsl:text>Descending text sort:</xsl:text>
    <xsl:value-of select="$newline"/>
    <xsl:for-each select="$items">
      <xsl:sort select="." order="descending"/>
      <xsl:value-of select="."/>
      <xsl:value-of select="$newline"/>
    </xsl:for-each>
    <xsl:value-of select="$newline"/>
  </xsl:template>

  <xsl:template name="ascending-numeric-sort">
    <xsl:param name="items"/>
    <xsl:text>Ascending numeric sort:</xsl:text>
    <xsl:value-of select="$newline"/>
    <xsl:for-each select="$items">
      <xsl:sort select="." data-type="number"/>
      <xsl:value-of select="."/>
      <xsl:value-of select="$newline"/>
    </xsl:for-each>
    <xsl:value-of select="$newline"/>
  </xsl:template>

</xsl:stylesheet>
```

Our stylesheet defines three named templates, each of which sorts <listitem>s in a different order or with a different data-type. We'll use this stylesheet against this document:

```
<?xml version="1.0"?>
<sample>
  <numericlist>
    <listitem>1</listitem>
    <listitem>3</listitem>
    <listitem>23</listitem>
    <listitem>120</listitem>
    <listitem>2</listitem>
  </numericlist>
  <textlist>
    <listitem>3</listitem>
    <listitem>apple</listitem>
    <listitem>orange</listitem>
    <listitem>dragonfruit</listitem>
    <listitem>carambola</listitem>
  </textlist>
</sample>
```

Here are the results:

```
Ascending text sort:
3
apple
carambola
dragonfruit
orange

Ascending text sort:
1
120
2
23
3

Ascending numeric sort:
1
2
3
23
120

Descending text sort:
orange
dragonfruit
carambola
apple
3
```

Notice that the `data-type="numeric"` attribute causes data to be sorted in numeric order.

<xsl:strip-space> — Defines the source-document elements for which whitespace should be removed.

Category

Top-level element

Required Attributes

elements

Contains a space-separated list of source document elements for which nonsignificant whitespace should be removed. Nonsignificant whitespace typically means text nodes that contain nothing but whitespace; whitespace that appears in and around text is preserved.

Optional Attributes

None.

Content

None. <xsl:strip-space> is an empty element.

Appears in

<xsl:strip-space> is a top-level element, and can only appear as a child of <xsl:stylesheet>.

Defined in

XSLT section 3.4, Whitespace Stripping.

Example

We'll illustrate the <xsl:strip-space> element with the following stylesheet:

```
<?xml version="1.0"?>
<xsl:stylesheet version="1.0" xmlns:xsl="http://www.w3.org/1999/XSL/Transform">

  <xsl:output method="text"/>
  <xsl:strip-space elements="listing"/>

  <xsl:variable name="newline">
<xsl:text>
</xsl:text>
  </xsl:variable>

  <xsl:template match="/">
    <xsl:value-of select="$newline"/>
    <xsl:value-of select="/code-sample/title"/>
    <xsl:value-of select="$newline"/>
    <xsl:for-each select="/code-sample/listing">
      <xsl:value-of select="."/>
    </xsl:for-each>
  </xsl:template>

</xsl:stylesheet>
```

We'll use this stylesheet to process the following document:

```
<?xml version="1.0"?>
<code-sample>
  <title>Conditional variable initialization</title>
  <listing>
  <type>int</type> <variable>y</variable> = <constant>23</constant>;
  <type>int</type> <variable>x</variable>;
```

```
    <keyword>if</keyword> (<variable>y</variable> > <constant>10</constant>)
    <variable>x</variable> = <constant>5</constant>;
  <keyword>else</keyword>
    <keyword>if</keyword> (<variable>y</variable> > <constant>5</constant>)
      <variable>x</variable> = <constant>3</constant>;
  <keyword>else</keyword>
    <variable>x</variable> = <constant>1</constant>;
  </listing>
</code-sample>
```

Here are the results:

```
Conditional variable initialization
inty = 23;
  intx;
    if (y > 10)
    x = 5;
  elseif (y > 5)
      x = 3;
  elsex = 1;
```

Notice that all the extra whitespace from the `<listing>` element has been removed. This includes the space between the various elements contained inside `<listing>`, such as `<keyword>`, `<constant>`, and `<variable>`. Compare this example to the one for the `<preserve-space>` element.

<xsl:stylesheet> — The root element of an XSLT stylesheet. It is identical to the `<xsl:transform>` element, which was included in the XSLT specification for historical purposes.

Category

Contains the entire stylesheet

Required Attributes

version

Indicates the version of XSLT that the stylesheet requires. For XSLT version 1.0, its value should always be `"1.0"`. As later versions of the XSLT specification are defined, the required values for the `version` attribute will be defined along with them.

xmlns:xsl

Defines the URI for the XSL namespace. For XSLT Version 1.0, this attribute's value should be `http://www.w3.org/1999/XSL/Transform`. Note that most XSLT processors will give you a warning message if your `xmlns:xsl` declaration does not have the proper value.

Optional Attributes

id

Defines an ID for this stylesheet.

extension-element-prefixes

Defines any namespace prefixes used to invoke extension elements. Multiple namespace prefixes are separated by whitespace.

exclude-result-prefixes

Defines namespace prefixes that should not be sent to the output document. Multiple namespace prefixes are separated by whitespace.

Content

This element contains the entire stylesheet. The following items can be children of `<xsl:stylesheet>`:

- `<xsl:import>`
- `<xsl:include>`
- `<xsl:strip-space>`
- `<xsl:preserve-space>`
- `<xsl:output>`
- `<xsl:key>`
- `<xsl:decimal-format>`
- `<xsl:namespace-alias>`
- `<xsl:attribute-set>`
- `<xsl:variable>`
- `<xsl:param>`
- `<xsl:template>`

Appears in

None. `<xsl:stylesheet>` is the root element of the stylesheet.

Defined in

XSLT section 2.2, Stylesheet Element.

Example

For the sake of completeness, we'll include an example here. We'll use the Hello World document from the XML 1.0 specification for our example:

```
<?xml version="1.0"?>
<greeting>
  Hello, World!
</greeting>
```

We'll transform our document with this stylesheet:

```
<xsl:stylesheet xmlns:xsl="http://www.w3.org/1999/XSL/Transform" version="1.0">
  <xsl:output method="html"/>

  <xsl:template match="/">
    <xsl:apply-templates select="greeting"/>
  </xsl:template>

  <xsl:template match="greeting">
    <html>
      <body>
        <h1>
          <xsl:value-of select="."/>
        </h1>
      </body>
    </html>
  </xsl:template>
</xsl:stylesheet>
```

When we transform our document with this stylesheet, here are the results:

```
<html>
<body>
<h1>
  Hello, World!
</h1>
</body>
</html>
```

<xsl:template> — Defines an output template. For templates that begin `<xsl:template match="x"`, the template defines a transformation for a given element. Templates that begin `<xsl:template name="x"` define a set of output elements that are processed whenever the template is invoked. All `<xsl:template>` elements must have either the `match` or the `name` attribute defined. Although not common, it is also possible to create `<xsl:template>` elements that have both a `match` and a `name`.

Category

Top-level element

Required Attributes

None.

Optional Attributes

match
: A pattern that defines the elements for which this template should be invoked. For example, `<xsl:template match="xyz">` defines a template for processing `<xyz>` elements.

name
: An attribute that names this template. Named templates are invoked with the `<xsl:call-template>` element.

mode
: An attribute that defines a mode for this template. A mode is a convenient syntax that allows you to write specific templates for specific purposes. For example, I could write an `<xsl:template>` with `mode="toc"` to process a node for the table of contents of a document and other `<xsl:template>`s with `mode="print"`, `mode="online"`, `mode="index"`, etc. to process the same information for different purposes.

priority
: An attribute that assigns a numeric priority to this template. The value can be any numeric value except `Infinity`. If the XSLT processor cannot determine which template to use (in other words, more than one template has the same default priority), the `priority` attribute allows you to define a tiebreaker.

Content

An XSLT template.

Appears in

`<xsl:stylesheet>`. `<xsl:template>` is a top-level element and can only appear as a child of `<xsl:stylesheet>`.

Defined in

XSLT section 5.3, Defining Template Rules.

Example

We'll use a template that copies all nodes from the input document to the output document, with one important difference: all attributes in the original document are converted to elements in the output document. The name of each generated element is the name of the original attribute, and the text of each element is the attribute's value. Here's our stylesheet:

```
<?xml version="1.0"?>
<xsl:stylesheet xmlns:xsl="http://www.w3.org/1999/XSL/Transform" version="1.0">
  <xsl:output method="xml"/>
  <xsl:template match="*">
    <xsl:element name="{name()}">
      <xsl:for-each select="@*">
        <xsl:element name="{name()}">
          <xsl:value-of select="."/>
        </xsl:element>
      </xsl:for-each>
      <xsl:apply-templates select="*|text()"/>
```

```
    </xsl:element>
  </xsl:template>
</xsl:stylesheet>
```

Our stylesheet contains a single `<xsl:template>` that transforms every node in the original document. We'll use our stylesheet to transform the following XML document:

```
<?xml version="1.0"?>
<report>
  <title>Miles Flown in 2001</title>
  <month sequence="01">
    <miles-flown>12379</miles-flown>
    <miles-earned>35215</miles-earned>
  </month>
  <month sequence="02">
    <miles-flown>32857</miles-flown>
    <miles-earned>92731</miles-earned>
  </month>
  <month sequence="03">
    <miles-flown>19920</miles-flown>
    <miles-earned>76725</miles-earned>
  </month>
  <month sequence="04">
    <miles-flown>18903</miles-flown>
    <miles-earned>31781</miles-earned>
  </month>
</report>
```

Here are the results of our transformation:

```
<?xml version="1.0" encoding="UTF-8"?>
<report>
  <title>Miles Flown in 2001</title>
  <month><sequence>01</sequence>
    <miles-flown>12379</miles-flown>
    <miles-earned>35215</miles-earned>
  </month>
  <month><sequence>02</sequence>
    <miles-flown>32857</miles-flown>
    <miles-earned>92731</miles-earned>
  </month>
  <month><sequence>03</sequence>
    <miles-flown>19920</miles-flown>
    <miles-earned>76725</miles-earned>
  </month>
  <month><sequence>04</sequence>
    <miles-flown>18903</miles-flown>
    <miles-earned>31781</miles-earned>
  </month>
</report>
```

<xsl:text> — Allows you to write literal text to the output document.

Category

Instruction

Required Attributes

None.

Optional Attributes

disable-output-escaping
: Defines whether special characters are escaped when they are written to the output document. For example, if the literal text contains the character >, it is normally written to the output document as `>`. If you code `disable-output-escaping="yes"`, the character > is written instead. The XSLT processor uses this attribute only if you're using the `html` or `xml` output methods. If you're using `<xsl:output method="text">`, the attribute is ignored because output escaping is not done for the `text` output method.

Content

`#PCDATA`, literal text, and entity references.

Appears in

`<xsl:text>` appears inside a template.

Defined in

XSLT section 7.2, Creating Text.

Example

This sample stylesheet generates text with `<xsl:text>`. We intermingle `<xsl:text>` elements and `<xsl:value-of>` elements to create a coherent sentence. In this case, we simply generate a text document, but this technique works equally well to create the text of an HTML or XML element. Here is the stylesheet:

```
<?xml version="1.0"?>
<xsl:stylesheet version="1.0" xmlns:xsl="http://www.w3.org/1999/XSL/Transform">

  <xsl:output method="text"/>

  <xsl:variable name="newline">
<xsl:text>
</xsl:text>
  </xsl:variable>

  <xsl:template match="/">
    <xsl:text>Your document contains </xsl:text>
    <xsl:value-of select="count(//*)"/>
    <xsl:text> elements and </xsl:text>
    <xsl:value-of select="count(//@*)"/>
    <xsl:text> attributes. </xsl:text>
    <xsl:value-of select="$newline"/>
```

```
    <xsl:text disable-output-escaping="yes"><Have a great day!></xsl:text>
  </xsl:template>
</xsl:stylesheet>
```

Also notice our use of <xsl:variable> to generate line breaks. The <xsl:text> element inside the <xsl:variable> element contains a line break, so writing the value of that variable to the result tree gives us the line break we want. Given this XML document:

```
<?xml version="1.0"?>
<list xml:lang="en">
  <title>Albums I've bought recently:</title>
  <listitem>The Sacred Art of Dub</listitem>
  <listitem>Only the Poor Man Feel It</listitem>
  <listitem>Excitable Boy</listitem>
  <listitem xml:lang="sw">Aki Special</listitem>
  <listitem xml:lang="en-gb">Combat Rock</listitem>
  <listitem xml:lang="zu">Talking Timbuktu</listitem>
  <listitem xml:lang="jz">The Birth of the Cool</listitem>
</list>
```

Our stylesheet produces these results:

```
Your document contains 9 elements and 5 attributes.
<Have a great day!>
```

Since we use the `text` output method, the `disable-output-escaping` attribute has no effect. If you change the stylesheet to use `<xsl:output method="html"/>` or `<xsl:output method="xml"/>`, then `disable-output-escaping` is used. Here are the results for `disable-output-escaping="yes"`:

```
Your document contains 10 elements and 2 attributes.
<Have a great day!>
```

And here are the results for `disable-output-escaping="no"`, the default:

```
Your document contains 10 elements and 2 attributes.
&lt;Have a great day!&gt;
```

<xsl:transform> — This is a synonym for <xsl:stylesheet>. It was included in the XSLT 1.0 spec for historical purposes. Its attributes, content, and all other properties are the same as those for <xsl:stylesheet>. See <xsl:stylesheet> for more information.

<xsl:value-of> — Calculates the value of an XPath expression, converts that value to a string, and then writes the value to the result tree.

Category

Instruction

Required Attributes

select
The XPath expression that is evaluated and written to the output document.

Optional Attributes

disable-output-escaping
An attribute that defines whether special characters are escaped when written to the output document. For example, if the literal text contains the character >, it is normally written to the output document as `>`. If you code `disable-output-escaping="yes"`, the character > is written instead. The XSLT processor uses this attribute only if you use the `html` or `xml` output methods. If you use `<xsl:output method="test">`, the attribute is ignored becasue output escaping is not done for the `text` output method. See `<xsl:text>` for a more thorough discussion of the `disable-output-escaping` attribute.

Content

None. `<xsl:value-of>` is an empty element.

Appears in

`<xsl:value-of>` appears inside a template.

Defined in

XSLT section 7.6.1, Generating Text with `xsl:value-of`.

Example

We'll use the `<xsl:value-of>` element to generate some text. Here is our stylesheet:

```
<?xsl version="1.0"?>
<xsl:stylesheet version="1.0" xmlns:xsl="http://www.w3.org/1999/XSL/Transform">

  <xsl:output method="text"/>

  <xsl:variable name="newline">
<xsl:text>
</xsl:text>
  </xsl:variable>

  <xsl:template match="/">
    <xsl:text>Your document contains</xsl:text>
    <xsl:value-of select="count(//*)"/>
    <xsl:text> elements and </xsl:text>
    <xsl:value-of select="count(//@*)"/>
    <xsl:text> attributes.  </xsl:text>
    <xsl:value-of select="$newline"/>
```

```
    <xsl:text>Have a great day!</xsl:text>
  </xsl:template>
</xsl:stylesheet>
```

We'll use this XML document as input:

```
<?xml version="1.0"?>
<report>
  <title>Miles Flown in 2001</title>
  <month sequence="01">
    <miles-flown>12379</miles-flown>
    <miles-earned>35215</miles-earned>
  </month>
  <month sequence="02">
    <miles-flown>32857</miles-flown>
    <miles-earned>92731</miles-earned>
  </month>
  <month sequence="03">
    <miles-flown>19920</miles-flown>
    <miles-earned>76725</miles-earned>
  </month>
  <month sequence="04">
    <miles-flown>18903</miles-flown>
    <miles-earned>31781</miles-earned>
  </month>
</report>
```

Here are the results:

```
Your document contains 14 elements and 4 attributes.
Have a great day!
```

<xsl:variable> — Defines a variable. If `<xsl:variable>` occurs as a top-level element, it is a global variable that is accessible throughout the stylesheet. Otherwise, the variable is local and exists only in the element that contains the `<xsl:variable>`. The value of the variable can be defined in one of two ways: specified in the `select` attribute or defined in an XSLT template inside the `<xsl:variable>` element itself. If neither method is used, the value of the variable is an empty string.

Category

Either a top-level element or an instruction

Required Attributes

name
: An attribute that names this variable.

Optional Attributes

select

An XPath expression that defines the value of this variable.

Content

The <xsl:variable> element can be empty, or it can contain an XSLT template. If it contains an XSLT template, the value of the `select` attribute (if any exists) is ignored.

Appears in

<xsl:stylesheet> as a top-level element or in a template.

Defined in

XSLT section 11, Variables and Parameters.

Example

Here is a stylesheet that defines a number of variables:

```
<?xml version="1.0"?>
<xsl:stylesheet version="1.0" xmlns:xsl="http://www.w3.org/1999/XSL/Transform">

  <xsl:output method="text"/>

  <xsl:variable name="newline">
<xsl:text>
</xsl:text>
  </xsl:variable>

  <xsl:variable name="favoriteNumber" select="23"/>
  <xsl:variable name="favoriteColor" select="'blue'"/>
  <xsl:variable name="complicatedVariable">
    <xsl:choose>
      <xsl:when test="count(//listitem) > 10">
        <xsl:text>really long list</xsl:text>
      </xsl:when>
      <xsl:when test="count(//listitem) > 5">
        <xsl:text>moderately long list</xsl:text>
      </xsl:when>
      <xsl:otherwise>
        <xsl:text>fairly short list</xsl:text>
      </xsl:otherwise>
    </xsl:choose>
  </xsl:variable>

  <xsl:template match="/">
    <xsl:text>Hello!  Your favorite number is </xsl:text>
    <xsl:value-of select="$favoriteNumber"/>
    <xsl:text>.</xsl:text>
    <xsl:value-of select="$newline"/>
    <xsl:text>Your favorite color is </xsl:text>
```

```
    <xsl:value-of select="$favoriteColor"/>
    <xsl:text>.</xsl:text>
    <xsl:value-of select="$newline"/>
    <xsl:value-of select="$newline"/>
    <xsl:text>Here is a </xsl:text>
    <xsl:value-of select="$complicatedVariable"/>
    <xsl:text>:</xsl:text>
    <xsl:value-of select="$newline"/>
    <xsl:variable name="listitems" select="list/listitem"/>
    <xsl:call-template name="processListitems">
      <xsl:with-param name="items" select="$listitems"/>
    </xsl:call-template>
  </xsl:template>

  <xsl:template name="processListitems">
    <xsl:param name="items"/>
    <xsl:variable name="favoriteColor">
      <xsl:text>chartreuse</xsl:text>
    </xsl:variable>

    <xsl:text>    (Your favorite color is now </xsl:text>
    <xsl:value-of select="$favoriteColor"/>
    <xsl:text>.)</xsl:text>
    <xsl:value-of select="$newline"/>
    <xsl:for-each select="$items">
      <xsl:value-of select="position()"/>
      <xsl:text>.  </xsl:text>
      <xsl:value-of select="."/>
      <xsl:value-of select="$newline"/>
    </xsl:for-each>
  </xsl:template>

</xsl:stylesheet>
```

We'll use our stylesheet to transform the following document:

```
<?xml version="1.0"?>
<list xml:lang="en">
  <title>Albums I've bought recently:</title>
  <listitem>The Sacred Art of Dub</listitem>
  <listitem>Only the Poor Man Feel It</listitem>
  <listitem>Excitable Boy</listitem>
  <listitem xml:lang="sw">Aki Special</listitem>
  <listitem xml:lang="en-gb">Combat Rock</listitem>
  <listitem xml:lang="zu">Talking Timbuktu</listitem>
  <listitem xml:lang="jz">The Birth of the Cool</listitem>
</list>
```

Here are the results of our transformation:

```
Hello!  Your favorite number is 23.
Your favorite color is blue.

Here is a moderately long list:
    (Your favorite color is now chartreuse.)
1.  The Sacred Art of Dub
2.  Only the Poor Man Feel It
3.  Excitable Boy
4.  Aki Special
5.  Combat Rock
6.  Talking Timbuktu
7.  The Birth of the Cool
```

Several things are worth mentioning in our stylesheet. First, notice that when we defined values for the first two variables (`favoriteNumber` and `favoriteColor`), we had to quote the string "blue", but didn't have to quote `23`. If we don't quote `blue`, the XSLT processor assumes we mean all the `<blue>` elements in the current context. We don't have to quote `23` because XML element names can't start with a number. It's a good idea to always quote literals, even those that can't be element names; chances are good that you'll forget this process at some point.

Also notice that we have two variables named `favoriteColor`. One is a global variable because its parent is the `<xsl:stylesheet>` element; the other is a local variable because it is defined in a `<xsl:template>`. When we access `favoriteColor` in the `match="/"` template, it has one value; when we access it inside the `name="processListitems"` template, it has another. Having two variables at the same level with the same name is an error. It's also an error to define an `<xsl:variable>` and an `<xsl:param>` with the same name at the same level.

Using an `<xsl:choose>` element to initialize an `<xsl:variable>` is a common technique. This technique is the equivalent of this procedural programming construct:

```
String complicatedVariable;
if (count(listitems) > 10)
  complicatedVariable = "really long list";
else if (count(listitems)) > 5)
  complicatedVariable = "moderately long list";
else
  complicatedVariable = "fairly short list";
```

The last point we'll make is that a variable can be any of the XPath or XSLT variable types, including a node-set. When we call the `processListitems` template, the parameter we pass to it is a variable containing the node-set of all the `<listitem>` elements in our document. Inside the `processListitems` template, our variable (which is now technically a parameter) can be used inside an `<xsl:for-each>` element.

<xsl:when> — Defines one branch of an <xsl:choose> element. It is equivalent to the Java case statement.

Category

Subinstruction (<xsl:when> always appears as a child of an <xsl:choose> element)

Required Attributes

test

Contains a boolean expression that is evaluated. If the expression evaluates to true, the contents of the <xsl:when> element are processed; otherwise, the contents of the <xsl:when> are ignored.

Optional Attributes

None.

Content

An XSLT template.

Appears in

The <xsl:choose> element only.

Defined in

XSLT section 9.2, Conditional Processing with xsl:choose.

Example

This example uses an <xsl:choose> element and three <xsl:when> elements to cycle through a set of values. Now we will generate rows of an HTML table for each <listitem>:

```
<?xml version="1.0"?>
<list xml:lang="en">
  <title>Albums I've bought recently:</title>
  <listitem>The Sacred Art of Dub</listitem>
  <listitem>Only the Poor Man Feel It</listitem>
  <listitem>Excitable Boy</listitem>
  <listitem xml:lang="sw">Aki Special</listitem>
  <listitem xml:lang="en-gb">Combat Rock</listitem>
  <listitem xml:lang="zu">Talking Timbuktu</listitem>
  <listitem xml:lang="jz">The Birth of the Cool</listitem>
</list>
```

In our stylesheet, we'll generate table rows with the background colors of mintcream, lavender, whitesmoke, and papayawhip. For each <listitem> in our source document, one of the <xsl:when> elements (or the <xsl:otherwise> element) generates the appropriate color.

```
<?xml version="1.0"?>
<xsl:stylesheet version="1.0" xmlns:xsl="http://www.w3.org/1999/XSL/Transform">
```

```
  <xsl:output method="html"/>

  <xsl:template match="/">
    <html>
      <head>
        <title>
          <xsl:value-of select="list/title"/>
        </title>
      </head>
      <body>
        <h1><xsl:value-of select="list/title"/></h1>
        <table border="1">
          <xsl:for-each select="list/listitem">
            <tr>
              <td>
                <xsl:attribute name="bgcolor">
                  <xsl:choose>
                    <xsl:when test="@bgcolor">
                      <xsl:value-of select="@bgcolor"/>
                    </xsl:when>
                    <xsl:when test="position() mod 4 = 0">
                      <xsl:text>papayawhip</xsl:text>
                    </xsl:when>
                    <xsl:when test="position() mod 4 = 1">
                      <xsl:text>mintcream</xsl:text>
                    </xsl:when>
                    <xsl:when test="position() mod 4 = 2">
                      <xsl:text>lavender</xsl:text>
                    </xsl:when>
                    <xsl:otherwise>
                      <xsl:text>whitesmoke</xsl:text>
                    </xsl:otherwise>
                  </xsl:choose>
                </xsl:attribute>
                <xsl:value-of select="."/>
              </td>
            </tr>
          </xsl:for-each>
        </table>
      </body>
    </html>
  </xsl:template>

</xsl:stylesheet>
```

When we process our XML source document with this stylesheet, here are the results:

```
<html>
<head>
<META http-equiv="Content-Type" content="text/html; charset=UTF-8">
<title>Albums I've bought recently:</title>
</head>
<body>
<h1>Albums I've bought recently:</h1>
<table border="1">
<tr>
<td bgcolor="mintcream">The Sacred Art of Dub</td>
</tr>
<tr>
<td bgcolor="lavender">Only the Poor Man Feel It</td>
</tr>
<tr>
<td bgcolor="whitesmoke">Excitable Boy</td>
</tr>
<tr>
<td bgcolor="papayawhip">Aki Special</td>
</tr>
<tr>
<td bgcolor="mintcream">Combat Rock</td>
</tr>
<tr>
<td bgcolor="lavender">Talking Timbuktu</td>
</tr>
<tr>
<td bgcolor="whitesmoke">The Birth of the Cool</td>
</tr>
</table>
</body>
</html>
```

All `<td>` elements with a background color of `papayawhip`, `mintcream`, or `lavender` were generated by one of the `<xsl:when>` elements.

<xsl:with-param> — Defines a parameter to be passed to a template. When the template is invoked, values can be passed in for the parameter.

Category

Subinstruction (`<xsl:with-param>` always appears inside an `<xsl:apply-templates>` or `<xsl:call-template>` element)

Description

<xsl:with-param> defines a parameter to be passed to a template. When the template is invoked, values can be passed in for the parameter. The value of the parameter can be defined in one of three ways:

- If the <xsl:with-param> element is empty and does not contain a select attribute, then no value is passed to the template.
- If the <xsl:with-param> element is empty and has a select attribute, the value of the parameter is the value of the select attribute.
- If the <xsl:with-param> element contains an XSLT template, the value of the parameter is the result of processing the template.

If no value is passed to the template (<xsl:with-param name="x"/>), then the default value of the parameter, if any, is used instead. The default value of the parameter is defined on the <xsl:param> element inside the <xsl:template> itself; see the description of the <xsl:param> element for more details.

Required Attributes

name
Names this parameter.

Optional Attributes

select
An XPath expression that defines the value of this parameter.

Content

The <xsl:with-param> element can be empty, or it can contain an XSLT template. If it contains an XSLT template, the value of the select attribute (if any exists) is ignored.

Appears in

<xsl:apply-templates> and <xsl:call-template>.

Defined in

XSLT section 11.6, Passing Parameters to Templates.

Example

Here is a stylesheet with a number of parameters. Notice that some parameters are global and defined outside the stylesheet:

```
<?xml version="1.0"?>
<xsl:stylesheet version="1.0" xmlns:xsl="http://www.w3.org/1999/XSL/Transform">

  <xsl:output method="text"/>

  <xsl:variable name="newline">
<xsl:text>
</xsl:text>
  </xsl:variable>
```

```
  <xsl:param name="favoriteNumber" select="23"/>
  <xsl:param name="favoriteColor"/>

  <xsl:template match="/">
    <xsl:value-of select="$newline"/>
    <xsl:value-of select="list/title"/>
    <xsl:value-of select="$newline"/>
    <xsl:variable name="listitems" select="list/listitem"/>
    <xsl:call-template name="processListitems">
      <xsl:with-param name="items" select="$listitems"/>
      <xsl:with-param name="color" select="'yellow'"/>
      <xsl:with-param name="number" select="$favoriteNumber"/>
    </xsl:call-template>
  </xsl:template>

  <xsl:template name="processListitems">
    <xsl:param name="items"/>
    <xsl:param name="color" select="'blue'"/>

    <xsl:for-each select="$items">
      <xsl:value-of select="position()"/>
      <xsl:text>.  </xsl:text>
      <xsl:value-of select="."/>
      <xsl:value-of select="$newline"/>
    </xsl:for-each>

    <xsl:value-of select="$newline"/>

    <xsl:text>Your favorite color is </xsl:text>
    <xsl:value-of select="$favoriteColor"/>
    <xsl:text>.</xsl:text>
    <xsl:value-of select="$newline"/>
    <xsl:text>The color passed to this template is </xsl:text>
    <xsl:value-of select="$color"/>
    <xsl:text>.</xsl:text>
    <xsl:value-of select="$newline"/>
  </xsl:template>

</xsl:stylesheet>
```

We'll use this stylesheet to transform this document:

```
<?xml version="1.0"?>
<list xml:lang="en">
  <title>Albums I've bought recently:</title>
  <listitem>The Sacred Art of Dub</listitem>
  <listitem>Only the Poor Man Feel It</listitem>
  <listitem>Excitable Boy</listitem>
  <listitem xml:lang="sw">Aki Special</listitem>
  <listitem xml:lang="en-gb">Combat Rock</listitem>
```

```
  <listitem xml:lang="zu">Talking Timbuktu</listitem>
  <listitem xml:lang="jz">The Birth of the Cool</listitem>
</list>
```

Our stylesheet contains two global parameters, `favoriteNumber` and `favoriteColor`, and defines a default value for `favoriteNumber`. The stylesheet also passes a parameter from the `match="/"` template to the `name="processListitems"` template; that parameter contains a node-set. Here are the results of the transformation:

```
Albums I've bought recently:
1.  The Sacred Art of Dub
2.  Only the Poor Man Feel It
3.  Excitable Boy
4.  Aki Special
5.  Combat Rock
6.  Talking Timbuktu
7.  The Birth of the Cool

Your favorite color is orange.
The color passed to this template is yellow.
```

To generate these results with Xalan, we use this command:

```
java org.apache.xalan.xslt.Process -in test4.xml -xsl with-param.xsl
  -param favoriteColor orange
```

The command should appear on a single line. See the section "Global Parameters" in Chapter 4 for a complete discussion of global parameters and how you define them for various XSLT processors.

B

XPath Reference

This appendix contains reference information from the XPath specification. The XPath node types, axes, and operators are defined here. The datatypes used in XSLT stylesheets, including the `result tree fragment` type (technically defined in the XSLT specification, not in XPath), are defined here as well. This appendix concludes with a definition of the XPath context.

XPath Node Types

There are seven types of nodes in XPath. We'll stick to the reference material here; for more information on the different node types, see our earlier discussion of the XPath data model.

The Root Node

The root node is the root of the tree. Unlike all other nodes, it does not have a parent. Its children are the element node for the document, along with any comments or processing instructions that appear outside the document element. The root node does not have an expanded name.

Element Nodes

Each element in the original XML document is represented by an element node. The expanded name of the element is its local name, combined with any namespace that is in effect for the element. You can access the different parts of the element name with the `name()`, `local-name()`, and `namespace-uri()` functions. Here is an element from an XML document:

```
<xyz:report xmlns:xyz="http://www.xyz.com/">
```

The values of the three functions for this element node are:

`name()`
: `xyz:report`

`local-name()`
: `report`

`namespace-uri()`
: `http://www.xyz.com/`

Attribute Nodes

Attributes of elements in the XML document become XPath attribute nodes. An attribute has an expanded name, just as an element node has. The attribute nodes of a given element node are the attributes explicitly coded on the XML element and any attributes defined with default values in the DTD.

Taking a different approach from the Document Object Model, an element node is the parent of its attributes, although the attributes are not the children of the element. In other words, selecting all the children of an element node does not select any attribute nodes that the element node might have.

Text Nodes

Text nodes simply contain text from an element. If the original text in the XML document contained character or entity references, they are resolved before the XPath text node is created. Similarly, any existing CDATA sections appear as text nodes. You have no way of knowing if a given portion of a text node was originally a character or entity reference or a CDATA section.

Comment Nodes

A comment node is also very simple; it contains some text. Every comment in the source document (except for any comments in the DTD) becomes a comment node. The text of the comment node (returned with the `text()` node test) contains everything inside the comment except the opening `<!--` and the closing `-->`.

Processing-Instruction Nodes

A processing-instruction node has two parts: a name (returned by the `name()` function) and a string value. The string value is everything after the name, including the whitespace, but not including the `?>` that closes the processing instruction.

Namespace Nodes

Namespace nodes are almost never used in XSLT stylesheets; they exist primarily for the XSLT processor's benefit. One thing to keep in mind is that the declaration of a namespace (such as `xmlns:auth="http://www.authors.net"`), even though it is technically an attribute in the XML source, becomes a namespace node and not an attribute node. Namespace nodes exist for both the namespace prefixes that are defined and any default namespaces.

XPath Node Tests

XPath defines several node tests that can be used to select nodes from the source tree. Strictly speaking, any XPath expression can be considered a node test; the expression `para`, for example, selects all `<para>` elements from the context node. Several special node tests allow you to select nodes that can't be selected any other way. (Although they look and work like functions, they are technically node tests.) These special node tests are described here:

`text()`
: Selects all the text-node children of the context node.

`comment()`
: Selects all the comment-node children of the context node.

`processing-instruction()`
: Selects all the processing-instruction children of the context node. Unlike the other node tests defined here, `processing-instruction()` can have an optional argument; `processing-instruction('xml-stylesheet')` selects all processing instructions with a name of `xml-stylesheet`.

`node()`
: Is true for all nodes, regardless of type. Using this node test selects all element nodes, attribute nodes, processing-instruction nodes, etc.

XPath Axes

The XPath specification defines thirteen different axes; each axis contains various nodes. The nodes that are in a given axis depend on the context node. All 13 axes, excerpted from our more involved discussion in the section "The XPath Data Model" in Chapter 3, are listed here.

`child` *axis*
: Contains the children of the context node. As we've already mentioned, the XPath expressions `child::lines/child::line` and `lines/line` are equivalent. If an XPath expression (such as `/sonnet`) doesn't have an axis specifier, the `child` axis is used by default.

`parent` *axis*
: Contains the parent of the context node, if there is one. (If the context node is the root node, the parent axis returns an empty node-set.) This axis can be abbreviated with a double period (`..`). The expressions `parent::sonnet` and `../sonnet` are equivalent. If the context node does not have a `<sonnet>` element as its parent, these XPath expressions return an empty node-set.

`self` *axis*
: Contains the context node itself. The `self` axis can be abbreviated with a single period (`.`).

`attribute` *axis*
: Contains the attributes of the context node. If the context node is not an element node, this axis is empty. The `attribute` axis can be abbreviated with the at sign (`@`). The expressions `attribute::type` and `@type` are equivalent.

`ancestor` *axis*
: Contains the parent of the context node, the parent's parent, and so on. The `ancestor` axis always contains the root node, unless the context node is the root node.

`ancestor-or-self` *axis*
: Contains the context node, its parent, its parent's parent, and so on. This axis always includes the root node.

`descendant` *axis*
: Contains all children of the context node, all children of all the children of the context node, and so on. Be aware that the `descendant` axis does not include any attribute or namespace nodes. (As we discussed earlier, an attribute node has an element node as its parent, even though the attribute node is not considered a child of its parent.)

`descendant-or-self` *axis*
: Contains the context node and all children of the context node, all children of all the children of the context node, and so on.

`preceding-sibling` *axis*
: Contains all of the preceding siblings of the context node—in other words, all nodes that have the same parent as the context node and appear before the context node in the XML document. If the context node is an attribute node or a namespace node, the `preceding-sibling` axis is empty.

`following-sibling` *axis*
: Contains all of the following siblings of the context node—in other words, all nodes that have the same parent as the context node and appear after the context node in the XML document. If the context node is an attribute node or a namespace node, the `following-sibling` axis is empty.

`preceding` *axis*
: Contains all nodes that appear before the context node in the document, except any ancestors, attribute nodes, and namespace nodes.

`following` *axis*
: Contains all nodes that appear after the context node in the document, except any descendants, attribute nodes, and namespace nodes.

`namespace` *axis*
: Contains the namespace nodes of the context node. If the context node is not an element node, this axis is empty.

The five axes `ancestor`, `descendant`, `following`, `preceding`, and `self` partition everything in the XML document (with the exception of any attribute or namespace nodes). Any node in the XPath tree appears in one of these five axes, and the five axes do not overlap.

XPath Operators

All operators defined by XPath are listed here.

Mathematical Operators

`+` *(plus)*
: Adds one number to another

`-` *(minus)*
: Subtracts one number from another

* *(multiplication)*
: Multiplies one number by another

div
: Performs a floating-point division between two numbers

mod
: Returns the floating-point remainder of dividing one number by another

Boolean Operators

=
: Tests whether two expressions are equal.

<
: Tests whether the first expression is less than the second. Within an attribute, this operator must be coded <.

<=
: Tests whether the first expression is less than or equal to the second. Within an attribute, this operator must be coded <=.

>
: Tests whether the first expression is greater than the second. Within an attribute, this operator can be coded >.

>=
: Tests whether the first expression is greater than or equal to the second. Within an attribute, this operator can be coded >=.

!=
: Tests whether the two expressions are not equal.

and
: Tests whether both the first and second expressions are true. If the first expression is false, the second is not evaluated.

or
: Tests whether either the first or second expressions are true. If the first expression is true, the second is not evaluated.

Comparing values of various datatypes

For the first six boolean operators, comparing values of various datatypes is complicated. We explain the various possibilities here:

If both objects are boolean values
: Then they are equal if they have the same value. For less-than and greater-than comparisons, false is considered less than true (the function call number(false()) returns 0, while number(true()) returns 1).

If both objects are numbers
: Then the operators work just the way you'd think they would.

If both objects are strings
: Then they are equal if their Unicode characters are identical. For less-than and greater-than comparisons, the character codes are compared.

If neither object is a node-set and the operator is `=` *or* `!=`
: Then the two objects are converted to the same object type, and the comparison works as described previously. If one of the objects is a boolean, then the objects are converted to boolean values as if by a call to the `boolean()` function. If none of the objects are boolean, the next attempted conversion is to a number. If one of the objects is a number, then the objects are converted to numeric values as if by a call to the `number()` function. Otherwise, all objects are converted to strings as if by a call to the `string()` function.

If neither object is a node-set and the operator is <, >, *or* >=
: Then the objects are converted to numbers and compared.

If one or both of the objects is a node-set
: Then things really get complicated. If both objects are node-sets, a comparison is true when the string value of at least one node in the first node-set is equal to the string value of at least one node in the second node-set. If one object is a node-set and the other is a number, string, or boolean, the comparison is true when there is at least one node in the node set whose number, string, or boolean value is equal to that number, string, or boolean value.

Expression Operators

`/`
: The stepping operator, which is used to separate steps in a location path. If an XPath expression begins with `/`, it represents the root of the document.

`//`
: The abbreviated syntax for the `descendant-or-self` axis.

`.`
: The abbreviated syntax for the `self` axis.

`..`
: The abbreviated syntax for the `parent` axis.

`@`
: The abbreviated syntax for the `attribute` axis.

|
: The union operator. For example, the `match` attribute in the element `<xsl:template match="a|b">` matches all <a> and <b> elements.

`*`
: A wildcard that represents any node of the principal node type. `child::*` selects all element children of the context node, `attribute::*` selects all attributes of the context node, etc. Using the abbreviated syntax, `*` selects all element children of the context node, and `@*` selects all attributes of the context node. Contrast the wildcard operator with the `node()` node test, which matches any node, regardless of type.

`[]`
: The predicate operator, used to contain a predicate expression that filters a group of nodes.

`$`
: The variable operator, used to indicate that a given symbol is a variable name.

Datatypes

XPath and XSLT define five datatypes, listed here. The `result tree fragment` type is defined by XSLT and is specific to transformations; the other four are defined by XPath and are generic to any technology that uses XPath. The four XPath datatypes are tersely defined in Section 1 of the XPath specification; section 11.1 of the XSLT specification defines result tree fragments.

`node-set`
: A set of nodes. The set can be empty, or it can contain any number of nodes.

`boolean`
: The value `true` or `false`. Be aware that the strings `true` and `false` have no special meaning or value in XPath. If you need to use the boolean values themselves, use the functions `true()` and `false()`.

`number`
: A floating-point number. All numbers in XPath and XSLT are implemented as floating-point numbers; the `integer` or `int` datatype does not exist in XPath and XSLT. To be specific, all numbers are implemented as IEEE 754 floating-point numbers, the same standard used by the Java `float` and `double` primitive types. In addition to ordinary numbers, there are five special values for numbers: positive and negative infinity, positive and negative zero, and `NaN`, the special symbol for anything that is not a number.

`string`

Zero or more characters, as defined in the XML specification.

`result tree fragment`

A temporary tree. You can create one with an `<xsl:variable>` element that uses content (instead of the `select` attribute) to initialize its value. A result tree fragment can be copied to the result tree with the `<xsl:copy-of>` element. It may also be converted to a string with the `<xsl:value-of>` element.

The XPath Context

The context in an XPath expression consists of several things:

Context node

The node currently being evaluated.

Context position

A nonzero positive integer that indicates the position of the context node within the set of context nodes.

Context size

A nonzero positive integer that indicates the number of nodes in the current context.

Variable bindings

A set of variables that are in scope for the current context. Each one is represented by a variable name and an object that represents its value. The object might be one of the four XPath datatypes, some additional type defined by an extension, or some other entity.

Functions

A set of functions visible to the current context. Each function is represented by a mapping between a function name and the actual code to be invoked. Each function takes zero or more arguments and returns a single result. XPath defines a number of core functions that are always available; XSLT defines additional functions that go beyond those defined in the XPath specification.

Namespace declarations

The set of namespace declarations visible to the current context. Each one consists of a namespace prefix and the URI with which it is associated.

XSLT and XPath Function Reference

This section lists all functions defined by XSLT and XPath.

boolean() Function — Converts its argument to a boolean value.

Synopsis

```
boolean boolean(object)
```

Inputs

An object. The object is converted to a boolean value. This conversion is described in the following subsection.

Output

The boolean value corresponding to the input object. Objects are converted to boolean values as follows:

- A number is `true` if and only if it is not zero, negative zero, or `NaN` (not a number).
- A node-set is `true` if and only if it is not empty.
- A string is `true` if and only if its length is greater than zero.
- All other datatypes are converted in a way specific to those datatypes.

Defined in

XPath section 4.3, Boolean Functions.

Example

The following example demonstrates the results of invoking the `boolean()` function against a variety of argument types. Here's our XML document:

```
<?xml version="1.0"?>
<test>
<p>This is a test XML document used by several
of our sample stylesheets.</p>
<question>
<text>When completed, the Eiffel Tower was the
tallest building in the world.</text>
<true>Yes!  The Eiffel Tower was the world's
tallest building until 1932, when
New York's Empire State Building opened. </true>
<false>No, the Eiffel Tower was the world's tallest
building for over 30 years.</false>
</question>
</test>
```

We'll process this document with the following stylesheet:

```
<?xml version="1.0"?>
<xsl:stylesheet version="1.0" xmlns:xsl="http://www.w3.org/1999/XSL/Transform">

  <xsl:output method="text"/>

  <xsl:variable name="newline">
<xsl:text>
</xsl:text>
  </xsl:variable>

  <xsl:template match="/">
    <xsl:value-of select="$newline"/>
    <xsl:text>Tests of the boolean() function:</xsl:text>

    <xsl:value-of select="$newline"/>
    <xsl:value-of select="$newline"/>
    <xsl:choose>
      <xsl:when test="boolean(true())">
        <xsl:text>   "boolean(true())"   returned true!</xsl:text>
      </xsl:when>
      <xsl:otherwise>
        <xsl:text>   "boolean(true())"   returned false!</xsl:text>
      </xsl:otherwise>
    </xsl:choose>

    <xsl:value-of select="$newline"/>
    <xsl:choose>
      <xsl:when test="boolean(true)">
```

```
      <xsl:text>   "boolean(true)"     returned true!</xsl:text>
    </xsl:when>
    <xsl:otherwise>
      <xsl:text>   "boolean(true)"     returned false!</xsl:text>
    </xsl:otherwise>
  </xsl:choose>

  <xsl:value-of select="$newline"/>
  <xsl:choose>
    <xsl:when test="boolean('false')">
      <xsl:text>   "boolean('false')"  returned true!</xsl:text>
    </xsl:when>
    <xsl:otherwise>
      <xsl:text>   "boolean('false')"  returned false!</xsl:text>
    </xsl:otherwise>
  </xsl:choose>

  <xsl:value-of select="$newline"/>
  <xsl:choose>
    <xsl:when test="boolean('7')">
      <xsl:text>   "boolean('7')"      returned true!</xsl:text>
    </xsl:when>
    <xsl:otherwise>
      <xsl:text>   "boolean('7')"      returned false!</xsl:text>
    </xsl:otherwise>
  </xsl:choose>

  <xsl:value-of select="$newline"/>
  <xsl:choose>
    <xsl:when test="boolean(/true)">
      <xsl:text>   "boolean(/true)"    returned true!</xsl:text>
    </xsl:when>
    <xsl:otherwise>
      <xsl:text>   "boolean(/true)"    returned false!</xsl:text>
    </xsl:otherwise>
  </xsl:choose>

  <xsl:value-of select="$newline"/>
  <xsl:choose>
    <xsl:when test="boolean(//true)">
      <xsl:text>   "boolean(//true)"   returned true!</xsl:text>
    </xsl:when>
    <xsl:otherwise>
      <xsl:text>   "boolean(//true)"   returned false!</xsl:text>
    </xsl:otherwise>
  </xsl:choose>
</xsl:template>

</xsl:stylesheet>
```

Here are the results:

```
Tests of the boolean() function:

   "boolean(true())"   returned true!
   "boolean(true)"     returned false!
   "boolean('false')"  returned true!
   "boolean('7')"      returned true!
   "boolean(/true)"    returned false!
   "boolean(//true)"   returned true!
```

See the section "Boolean examples" in Chapter 4 for more examples and information.

ceiling() Function — Returns the smallest integer that is not less than the argument.

Synopsis

`number` **`ceiling(`**`number`**`)`**

Inputs

A number. If the argument is not a number, it is transformed into a number as if it had been processed by the `number()` function. If the argument cannot be transformed into a number, the `ceiling()` function returns the value `NaN` (not a number).

Output

The smallest integer that is not less than the argument, or `NaN` if the argument cannot be converted to a number.

Defined in

XPath section 4.4, Number Functions.

Example

The following stylesheet shows the results of invoking the `ceiling()` function against a variety of values. We'll use this XML document as input:

```
<?xml version="1.0"?>
<report>
  <title>Miles Flown in 2001</title>
  <month sequence="01">
    <miles-flown>12379</miles-flown>
    <miles-earned>35215</miles-earned>
  </month>
  <month sequence="02">
    <miles-flown>32857</miles-flown>
    <miles-earned>92731</miles-earned>
  </month>
  <month sequence="03">
    <miles-flown>19920</miles-flown>
    <miles-earned>76725</miles-earned>
```

```
  </month>
  <month sequence="04">
    <miles-flown>18903</miles-flown>
    <miles-earned>31781</miles-earned>
  </month>
</report>
```

Here's the stylesheet that uses the `ceiling()` function:

```
<?xml version="1.0"?>
<xsl:stylesheet version="1.0"
  xmlns:xsl="http://www.w3.org/1999/XSL/Transform"
  xmlns:months="Lookup table for month names">

  <months:name sequence="01">January</months:name>
  <months:name sequence="02">February</months:name>
  <months:name sequence="03">March</months:name>
  <months:name sequence="04">April</months:name>
  <months:name sequence="05">May</months:name>
  <months:name sequence="06">June</months:name>
  <months:name sequence="07">July</months:name>
  <months:name sequence="08">August</months:name>
  <months:name sequence="09">September</months:name>
  <months:name sequence="10">October</months:name>
  <months:name sequence="11">November</months:name>
  <months:name sequence="12">December</months:name>

  <xsl:output method="text"/>

  <xsl:variable name="newline">
<xsl:text>
</xsl:text>
  </xsl:variable>

  <xsl:template match="/">
    <xsl:value-of select="$newline"/>
    <xsl:text>Tests of the ceiling() function:</xsl:text>

    <xsl:value-of select="$newline"/>
    <xsl:value-of select="$newline"/>
    <xsl:text>   "ceiling('7.983')" = </xsl:text>
    <xsl:value-of select="ceiling('7.983')"/>

    <xsl:value-of select="$newline"/>
    <xsl:text>   "ceiling('-7.893')" = </xsl:text>
    <xsl:value-of select="ceiling('-7.893')"/>

    <xsl:value-of select="$newline"/>
    <xsl:text>   "ceiling(/report/month[@sequence='01']/miles-flown)" = </xsl:text>
    <xsl:value-of select="ceiling(/report/month[@sequence='01']/miles-flown)"/>
```

```
      <xsl:value-of select="$newline"/>
      <xsl:text>   "ceiling(document('')/*/</xsl:text>
      <xsl:text>months:name[@sequence='02'])" = </xsl:text>
      <xsl:value-of select="ceiling(document('')/*/months:name[@sequence='02'])"/>

      <xsl:value-of select="$newline"/>
      <xsl:value-of select="$newline"/>
      <xsl:for-each select="/report/month">
        <xsl:text>   </xsl:text>
        <xsl:value-of
          select="document('')/*/months:name[@sequence=current()/@sequence]"/>
        <xsl:text> - </xsl:text>
        <xsl:value-of select="format-number(miles-flown, '##,###')"/>
        <xsl:text> miles flown, </xsl:text>
        <xsl:value-of select="format-number(miles-earned, '##,###')"/>
        <xsl:text> miles earned.</xsl:text>
        <xsl:value-of select="$newline"/>
        <xsl:text>      (Averaged </xsl:text>
        <xsl:value-of select="ceiling(miles-earned div miles-flown)"/>
        <xsl:text> miles earned for each mile flown.)</xsl:text>
        <xsl:value-of select="$newline"/>
        <xsl:value-of select="$newline"/>
      </xsl:for-each>
    </xsl:template>

  </xsl:stylesheet>
```

When we transform the XML document with our stylesheet, here are the results:

```
Tests of the ceiling() function:

   "ceiling('7.983')" = 8
   "ceiling('-7.893')" = -7
   "ceiling(/report/month[@sequence='01']/miles-flown)" = 12379
   "ceiling(document('')/*/months:name[@sequence='02'])" = NaN

   January - 12,379 miles flown, 35,215 miles earned.
      (Averaged 3 miles earned for each mile flown.)

   February - 32,857 miles flown, 92,731 miles earned.
      (Averaged 3 miles earned for each mile flown.)

   March - 19,920 miles flown, 76,725 miles earned.
      (Averaged 4 miles earned for each mile flown.)

   April - 18,903 miles flown, 31,781 miles earned.
      (Averaged 2 miles earned for each mile flown.)
```

Notice that when we invoked the `ceiling()` function against the string "February" (what `document('')/*/months:name[@sequence='02']` resolves to), the function returned `NaN`. You can compare these results to those from the `floor()` function and the `round()` function.

concat() Function — Takes all of its arguments and concatenates them. Any arguments that are not strings are converted to strings as if processed by the `string()` function.

Synopsis

string **concat(***string*, *string*, *string****)**

Inputs

Two or more strings.

Output

The concatenation of all of the input strings.

Defined in

XPath section 4.2, String Functions.

Example

We'll use this XML file to demonstrate how `concat()` works:

```
<?xml version="1.0"?>
<list>
  <title>A few of my favorite albums</title>
  <listitem>A Love Supreme</listitem>
  <listitem>Beat Crazy</listitem>
  <listitem>Here Come the Warm Jets</listitem>
  <listitem>Kind of Blue</listitem>
  <listitem>London Calling</listitem>
  <listitem>Remain in Light</listitem>
  <listitem>The Joshua Tree</listitem>
  <listitem>The Indestructible Beat of Soweto</listitem>
</list>
```

In our stylesheet, we'll use the `concat()` function to create filenames for various JPEG files. The filenames are composed from several pieces of information, concatenated by the `concat()` function:

```
<?xml version="1.0"?>
<xsl:stylesheet version="1.0" xmlns:xsl="http://www.w3.org/1999/XSL/Transform">

  <xsl:output method="text"/>

  <xsl:variable name="newline">
<xsl:text>
</xsl:text>
  </xsl:variable>

  <xsl:template match="/">
    <xsl:value-of select="$newline"/>
    <xsl:for-each select="list/listitem">
      <xsl:text>See the file </xsl:text>
```

```
      <xsl:value-of select="concat('album', position(), '.jpg')"/>
      <xsl:text> to see the title of album #</xsl:text>
      <xsl:value-of select="position()"/>
      <xsl:value-of select="$newline"/>
    </xsl:for-each>
  </xsl:template>

</xsl:stylesheet>
```

Our stylesheet generates these results:

```
See the file album1.jpg to see the title of album #1
See the file album2.jpg to see the title of album #2
See the file album3.jpg to see the title of album #3
See the file album4.jpg to see the title of album #4
See the file album5.jpg to see the title of album #5
See the file album6.jpg to see the title of album #6
See the file album7.jpg to see the title of album #7
See the file album8.jpg to see the title of album #8
```

contains() Function — Determines if the first argument string contains the second.

Synopsis

boolean **contains(***string*, *string***)**

Inputs

Two strings. If the first string contains the second string, the function returns the boolean value `true`.

Output

The boolean value `true` if the first argument contains the second; `false` otherwise.

Defined in

XPath section 4.2, String Functions.

Example

This stylesheet uses the `replace-substring` named template. It passes three arguments to the `replace-substring` template: the original string, the substring to be searched for in the original string, and the substring to replace the target substring in the original string. The `replace-substring` template uses the `contains()`, `substring-after()`, and `substring-before()` functions extensively.

Here is our sample stylesheet. It replaces all occurrences of `World` with the string "Mundo":

```
<?xml version="1.0"?>
<xsl:stylesheet xmlns:xsl="http://www.w3.org/1999/XSL/Transform" version="1.0">

  <xsl:output method="text"/>
```

```
<xsl:template match="/">
  <xsl:variable name="test">
    <xsl:call-template name="replace-substring">
      <xsl:with-param name="original">Hello World!</xsl:with-param>
      <xsl:with-param name="substring">World</xsl:with-param>
      <xsl:with-param name="replacement">Mundo</xsl:with-param>
    </xsl:call-template>
  </xsl:variable>
  <xsl:value-of select="$test"/>
</xsl:template>

<xsl:template name="replace-substring">
  <xsl:param name="original"/>
  <xsl:param name="substring"/>
  <xsl:param name="replacement" select="''"/>
  <xsl:variable name="first">
    <xsl:choose>
      <xsl:when test="contains($original, $substring)">
        <xsl:value-of select="substring-before($original, $substring)"/>
      </xsl:when>
      <xsl:otherwise>
        <xsl:value-of select="$original"/>
      </xsl:otherwise>
    </xsl:choose>
  </xsl:variable>
  <xsl:variable name="middle">
    <xsl:choose>
      <xsl:when test="contains($original, $substring)">
        <xsl:value-of select="$replacement"/>
      </xsl:when>
      <xsl:otherwise>
        <xsl:text></xsl:text>
      </xsl:otherwise>
    </xsl:choose>
  </xsl:variable>
  <xsl:variable name="last">
    <xsl:choose>
      <xsl:when test="contains($original, $substring)">
        <xsl:choose>
          <xsl:when test="contains(substring-after($original,
                                   $substring), $substring)">
            <xsl:call-template name="replace-substring">
              <xsl:with-param name="original">
                <xsl:value-of
                  select="substring-after($original, $substring)"/>
              </xsl:with-param>
              <xsl:with-param name="substring">
                <xsl:value-of select="$substring"/>
              </xsl:with-param>
              <xsl:with-param name="replacement">
```

```
                  <xsl:value-of select="$replacement"/>
                </xsl:with-param>
              </xsl:call-template>
            </xsl:when>
            <xsl:otherwise>
              <xsl:value-of
                select="substring-after($original, $substring)"/>
            </xsl:otherwise>
          </xsl:choose>
        </xsl:when>
        <xsl:otherwise>
          <xsl:text></xsl:text>
        </xsl:otherwise>
      </xsl:choose>
    </xsl:variable>
    <xsl:value-of select="concat($first, $middle, $last)"/>
  </xsl:template>

</xsl:stylesheet>
```

The stylesheet produces these results, regardless of the XML document used as input:

```
Hello Mundo!
```

count() Function — Counts the number of nodes in a given node-set.

Synopsis

number **count(***node-set***)**

Inputs

A node-set.

Output

The number of nodes in the node-set.

Defined in

XPath section 4.1, Node Set Functions.

Examples

Here's the XML document we'll use to illustrate the `count()` function:

```
<?xml version="1.0"?>
<test>
  <p>This is a test XML document used by
  several of our sample stylesheets.</p>
  <question>
    <text>When completed, the Eiffel Tower was the
    tallest building in the world.</text>
    <true>You're correct!  The Eiffel Tower was the
```

```
      world's tallest building until 1930.</true>
      <false>No, the Eiffel Tower was the world's
      tallest building for over 30 years.</false>
    </question>
    <question>
      <text>New York's Empire State Building knocked
      the Eiffel Tower from its pedestal.</text>
      <true>No, that's not correct.</true>
      <false>Correct!  New York's Chrysler Building,
      completed in 1930, became the world's tallest.</false>
    </question>
  </test>
```

Here's a stylesheet that illustrates the count() function:

```
<?xml version="1.0"?>
<xsl:stylesheet version="1.0" xmlns:xsl="http://www.w3.org/1999/XSL/Transform">

  <xsl:output method="text"/>

  <xsl:variable name="newline">
<xsl:text>
</xsl:text>
  </xsl:variable>

  <xsl:template match="/">
    <xsl:value-of select="$newline"/>
    <xsl:text>Tests of the count() function:</xsl:text>

    <xsl:value-of select="$newline"/>
    <xsl:value-of select="$newline"/>
    <xsl:text>   count(/test)=</xsl:text>
    <xsl:value-of select="count(/test)"/>
    <xsl:value-of select="$newline"/>
    <xsl:text>   count(/true)=</xsl:text>
    <xsl:value-of select="count(/true)"/>
    <xsl:value-of select="$newline"/>
    <xsl:text>   count(//true)=</xsl:text>
    <xsl:value-of select="count(//true)"/>
    <xsl:value-of select="$newline"/>
    <xsl:text>   count(//test|//true|//text)=</xsl:text>
    <xsl:value-of select="count(//test|//true|//text)"/>
    <xsl:value-of select="$newline"/>
    <xsl:variable name="numberOfQuestions" select="count(/test/question)"/>
    <xsl:for-each select="/test/question">
      <xsl:text>   This is question number </xsl:text>
      <xsl:value-of select="position()"/>
      <xsl:text> of </xsl:text>
      <xsl:value-of select="$numberOfQuestions"/>
```

```
      <xsl:value-of select="$newline"/>
    </xsl:for-each>
  </xsl:template>

</xsl:stylesheet>
```

Here are the results of our stylesheet:

```
Tests of the count() function:

   count(/test)=1
   count(/true)=0
   count(//true)=2
   count(//test|//true|//text)=5
   This is question number 1 of 2
   This is question number 2 of 2
```

The first four invocations of the `count()` function merely use XPath expressions to count something in the XML document. The last use of `count()` counts the number of `<question>` elements in our document and stores that value in a variable. Generating text like item x of y is a common technique; our use of the `count()` and `position()` is how this generation is commonly done.

---

current() Function — Returns a node-set that has the current node as its only member.

Synopsis

node-set **current()**

Inputs

None.

Output

A node-set that has the current node as its only member. Most of the time, the current node is no different than the context node. These two XSLT elements have the same meaning:

```
<xsl:value-of select="current()"/>
<xsl:value-of select="."/>
```

Within a predicate expression, however, the current node and the context node are usually different. The example section that follows illustrates when you need to use the `current()` function.

Defined in

XSLT section 12.4, Miscellaneous Additional Functions.

Example

We'll use the `current()` function along with a lookup table. Here's the document we'll transform:

```
<?xml version="1.0"?>
<report>
  <title>Miles Flown in 2001</title>
  <month sequence="01">
    <miles-flown>12379</miles-flown>
    <miles-earned>35215</miles-earned>
  </month>
  <month sequence="02">
    <miles-flown>32857</miles-flown>
    <miles-earned>92731</miles-earned>
  </month>
  <month sequence="03">
    <miles-flown>19920</miles-flown>
    <miles-earned>76725</miles-earned>
  </month>
  <month sequence="04">
    <miles-flown>18903</miles-flown>
    <miles-earned>31781</miles-earned>
  </month>
</report>
```

Here's our stylesheet. We'll do the same transform twice, one time with the `current()` function and one time without it:

```
<?xml version="1.0"?>
<xsl:stylesheet version="1.0"
  xmlns:xsl="http://www.w3.org/1999/XSL/Transform"
  xmlns:months="Lookup table for month names">

  <months:name sequence="12">December</months:name>
  <months:name sequence="01">January</months:name>
  <months:name sequence="02">February</months:name>
  <months:name sequence="03">March</months:name>
  <months:name sequence="04">April</months:name>
  <months:name sequence="05">May</months:name>
  <months:name sequence="06">June</months:name>
  <months:name sequence="07">July</months:name>
  <months:name sequence="08">August</months:name>
  <months:name sequence="09">September</months:name>
  <months:name sequence="10">October</months:name>
  <months:name sequence="11">November</months:name>

  <xsl:output method="text"/>
```

```
  <xsl:variable name="newline">
<xsl:text>
</xsl:text>
  </xsl:variable>

  <xsl:template match="/">
    <xsl:value-of select="$newline"/>
    <xsl:text>A test of the current() function:</xsl:text>

    <xsl:value-of select="$newline"/>
    <xsl:value-of select="$newline"/>
    <xsl:for-each select="/report/month">
      <xsl:text>   </xsl:text>
      <xsl:value-of
        select="document('')/*/months:name[@sequence=current()/@sequence]"/>
      <xsl:text> - </xsl:text>
      <xsl:value-of select="format-number(miles-flown, '##,###')"/>
      <xsl:text> miles flown, </xsl:text>
      <xsl:value-of select="format-number(miles-earned, '##,###')"/>
      <xsl:text> miles earned.</xsl:text>
      <xsl:value-of select="$newline"/>
      <xsl:text>      (Averaged </xsl:text>
      <xsl:value-of
        select="format-number(miles-earned div miles-flown, '##.#')"/>
      <xsl:text> miles earned for each mile flown.)</xsl:text>
      <xsl:value-of select="$newline"/>
      <xsl:value-of select="$newline"/>
    </xsl:for-each>
    <xsl:value-of select="$newline"/>

    <xsl:text>Let's try it again, without using current() this time:</xsl:text>
    <xsl:value-of select="$newline"/>
    <xsl:value-of select="$newline"/>

    <xsl:for-each select="/report/month">
      <xsl:text>   </xsl:text>
      <xsl:value-of
        select="document('')/*/months:name[@sequence=./@sequence]"/>
      <xsl:text> - </xsl:text>
      <xsl:value-of select="format-number(miles-flown, '##,###')"/>
      <xsl:text> miles flown, </xsl:text>
      <xsl:value-of select="format-number(miles-earned, '##,###')"/>
      <xsl:text> miles earned.</xsl:text>
      <xsl:value-of select="$newline"/>
      <xsl:text>      (Averaged </xsl:text>
      <xsl:value-of
        select="format-number(miles-earned div miles-flown, '##.#')"/>
      <xsl:text> miles earned for each mile flown.)</xsl:text>
```

```
        <xsl:value-of select="$newline"/>
        <xsl:value-of select="$newline"/>
      </xsl:for-each>
    </xsl:template>

  </xsl:stylesheet>
```

Here are the results:

```
  A test of the current() function:

     January - 12,379 miles flown, 35,215 miles earned.
        (Averaged 2.8 miles earned for each mile flown.)

     February - 32,857 miles flown, 92,731 miles earned.
        (Averaged 2.8 miles earned for each mile flown.)

     March - 19,920 miles flown, 76,725 miles earned.
        (Averaged 3.9 miles earned for each mile flown.)

     April - 18,903 miles flown, 31,781 miles earned.
        (Averaged 1.7 miles earned for each mile flown.)


  Let's try it again, without using current() this time:

     December - 12,379 miles flown, 35,215 miles earned.
        (Averaged 2.8 miles earned for each mile flown.)

     December - 32,857 miles flown, 92,731 miles earned.
        (Averaged 2.8 miles earned for each mile flown.)

     December - 19,920 miles flown, 76,725 miles earned.
        (Averaged 3.9 miles earned for each mile flown.)

     December - 18,903 miles flown, 31,781 miles earned.
        (Averaged 1.7 miles earned for each mile flown.)
```

The second time around, our stylesheet matched each `<month>` element to the month `December`. The difference is that the dot syntax (`.`) represents the current node at that point in the XPath expression, while the `current()` function represents the current node before the XSLT processor began evaluating the XPath expression.

In other words, the XSLT processor starts with the first `<months:name>` element, attempting to find the element whose `sequence` attribute matches another `sequence` attribute we're examining. If we specify the other `sequence` attribute with `./@sequence`, it indicates the `sequence` attribute of the current node at this point in the expression, which is the first `<months:name>` element. That always returns the value of the first `<months:name>` element. Using the `current()` function, on the other hand, returns the node that was current when we started to evaluate this expression; `current()` gives us the behavior we want.

document() Function — Allows you to process multiple source documents in a single stylesheet. This extremely powerful and flexible function is the subject of Chapter 7, so we'll only include a brief overview of the function here.

Synopsis

node-set **document(***object*, *node-set?***)**

Inputs

The `document()` function most commonly takes a string as its argument; that string is treated as a URI, and the XSLT processor attempts to open that URI and parse it. If the string is empty (the function call is `document('')`), the `document()` function parses the stylesheet itself. See the section "Invoking the document() Function" in Chapter 7 for all the details on the parameters to the `document()` function.

Output

A node-set containing the nodes identified by the input argument. Again, Chapter 7 has all the details, so we won't rehash them here.

Defined in

XSLT section 12.1, Multiple Source Documents.

Example

The following example uses the `document()` function with an empty string to implement a lookup table. Here is our XML document:

```
<?xml version="1.0"?>
<report>
  <title>Miles Flown in 2001</title>
  <month sequence="01">
    <miles-flown>12379</miles-flown>
    <miles-earned>35215</miles-earned>
  </month>
  <month sequence="02">
    <miles-flown>32857</miles-flown>
    <miles-earned>92731</miles-earned>
  </month>
  <month sequence="03">
    <miles-flown>19920</miles-flown>
    <miles-earned>76725</miles-earned>
  </month>
  <month sequence="04">
    <miles-flown>18903</miles-flown>
    <miles-earned>31781</miles-earned>
  </month>
</report>
```

We can use the `document()` function to convert the `sequence` attribute of the `<month>` element into the name of the corresponding month. Here is our stylesheet:

```
<?xml version="1.0"?>
<xsl:stylesheet version="1.0"
  xmlns:xsl="http://www.w3.org/1999/XSL/Transform"
  xmlns:months="Lookup table for month names">

  <months:name sequence="01">January</months:name>
  <months:name sequence="02">February</months:name>
  <months:name sequence="03">March</months:name>
  <months:name sequence="04">April</months:name>
  <months:name sequence="05">May</months:name>
  <months:name sequence="06">June</months:name>
  <months:name sequence="07">July</months:name>
  <months:name sequence="08">August</months:name>
  <months:name sequence="09">September</months:name>
  <months:name sequence="10">October</months:name>
  <months:name sequence="11">November</months:name>
  <months:name sequence="12">December</months:name>

  <xsl:output method="text"/>

  <xsl:variable name="newline">
<xsl:text>
</xsl:text>
  </xsl:variable>

  <xsl:template match="/">
    <xsl:value-of select="$newline"/>
    <xsl:text>A test of the document() function:</xsl:text>

    <xsl:value-of select="$newline"/>
    <xsl:value-of select="$newline"/>
    <xsl:for-each select="/report/month">
      <xsl:text>   </xsl:text>
      <xsl:value-of
        select="document('')/*/months:name[@sequence=current()/@sequence]"/>
      <xsl:text> - </xsl:text>
      <xsl:value-of select="format-number(miles-flown, '##,###')"/>
      <xsl:text> miles flown, </xsl:text>
      <xsl:value-of select="format-number(miles-earned, '##,###')"/>
      <xsl:text> miles earned.</xsl:text>
      <xsl:value-of select="$newline"/>
      <xsl:text>      (Averaged </xsl:text>
      <xsl:value-of
        select="format-number(miles-earned div miles-flown, '##.#')"/>
      <xsl:text> miles earned for each mile flown.)</xsl:text>
```

```
      <xsl:value-of select="$newline"/>
      <xsl:value-of select="$newline"/>
    </xsl:for-each>
  </xsl:template>

</xsl:stylesheet>
```

Here are the results, with the correct month names included in the output:

```
A test of the document() function:

   January - 12,379 miles flown, 35,215 miles earned.
      (Averaged 2.8 miles earned for each mile flown.)

   February - 32,857 miles flown, 92,731 miles earned.
      (Averaged 2.8 miles earned for each mile flown.)

   March - 19,920 miles flown, 76,725 miles earned.
      (Averaged 3.9 miles earned for each mile flown.)

   April - 18,903 miles flown, 31,781 miles earned.
      (Averaged 1.7 miles earned for each mile flown.)
```

element-available() Function — Determines if a given element is available to the XSLT processor. This function allows you to design stylesheets that react gracefully if a particular element is not available to process an XML document.

Synopsis

boolean **element-available(***string***)**

Inputs

The element's name. The name should be qualified with a namespace; if the namespace URI is the same as the XSLT namespace URI, then the element name refers to an element defined by XSLT. Otherwise, the name refers to an extension element. If the element name has a null namespace URI, then the `element-available` function returns `false`.

Output

The boolean value `true` if the element is available; `false` otherwise.

Defined in

XSLT section 15, Fallback.

Example

We'll use the following example to test the `element-available()` function:

```
<?xml version="1.0"?>
<book>
  <title>XSLT</title>
  <chapter>
    <title>Getting Started</title>
    <para>If this chapter had any text, it would appear here.</para>
  </chapter>
  <chapter>
    <title>The Hello World Example</title>
    <para>If this chapter had any text, it would appear here.</para>
  </chapter>
  <chapter>
    <title>XPath</title>
    <para>If this chapter had any text, it would appear here.</para>
  </chapter>
  <chapter>
    <title>Stylesheet Basics</title>
    <para>If this chapter had any text, it would appear here.</para>
  </chapter>
  <chapter>
    <title>Branching and Control Elements</title>
    <para>If this chapter had any text, it would appear here.</para>
  </chapter>
  <chapter>
    <title>Functions</title>
    <para>If this chapter had any text, it would appear here.</para>
  </chapter>
  <chapter>
    <title>Creating Links and Cross-References</title>
    <para>If this chapter had any text, it would appear here.</para>
  </chapter>
  <chapter>
    <title>Sorting and Grouping Elements</title>
    <para>If this chapter had any text, it would appear here.</para>
  </chapter>
  <chapter>
    <title>Combining XML Documents</title>
    <para>If this chapter had any text, it would appear here.</para>
  </chapter>
</book>
```

Here is our stylesheet:

```
<?xml version="1.0"?>
<xsl:stylesheet version="1.0" xmlns:xsl="http://www.w3.org/1999/XSL/Transform"
  xmlns:redirect="org.apache.xalan.xslt.extensions.Redirect"
```

```
xmlns:saxon="http://icl.com/saxon"
extension-element-prefixes="redirect saxon">

<xsl:output method="html"/>

<xsl:template match="/">
  <xsl:choose>
    <xsl:when test="element-available('redirect:write')">
      <xsl:for-each select="/book/chapter">
        <redirect:write select="concat('chapter', position(), '.html')">
          <html>
            <head>
              <title><xsl:value-of select="title"/></title>
            </head>
            <body>
              <h1><xsl:value-of select="title"/></h1>
              <xsl:apply-templates select="para"/>
              <xsl:if test="not(position()=1)">
                <p>
                  <a href="chapter{position()-1}.html">Previous</a>
                </p>
              </xsl:if>
              <xsl:if test="not(position()=last())">
                <p>
                  <a href="chapter{position()+1}.html">Next</a>
                </p>
              </xsl:if>
            </body>
          </html>
        </redirect:write>
      </xsl:for-each>
    </xsl:when>
    <xsl:when test="element-available('saxon:output')">
      <xsl:for-each select="/book/chapter">
        <saxon:output file="chapter{position()}.html">
          <html>
            <head>
              <title><xsl:value-of select="title"/></title>
            </head>
            <body>
              <h1><xsl:value-of select="title"/></h1>
              <xsl:apply-templates select="para"/>
              <xsl:if test="not(position()=1)">
                <p>
                  <a href="chapter{position()-1}.html">Previous</a>
                </p>
              </xsl:if>
              <xsl:if test="not(position()=last())">
```

```
                <p>
                  <a href="chapter{position()+1}.html">Next</a>
                </p>
              </xsl:if>
            </body>
          </html>
        </saxon:output>
      </xsl:for-each>
    </xsl:when>
    <xsl:otherwise>
      <html>
        <head>
          <title><xsl:value-of select="/book/title"/></title>
        </head>
        <xsl:for-each select="/book/chapter">
          <h1><xsl:value-of select="title"/></h1>
          <xsl:apply-templates select="para"/>
        </xsl:for-each>
      </html>
    </xsl:otherwise>
  </xsl:choose>
  <xsl:if test="not(element-available('write'))">
    <xsl:message terminate="no">
      The <write> element is not available!
    </xsl:message>
  </xsl:if>
</xsl:template>

<xsl:template match="para">
  <p><xsl:apply-templates select="*|text()"/></p>
</xsl:template>

</xsl:stylesheet>
```

This stylesheet attempts to take the content in the XML file and write portions of it out to different HTML files. The first `<chapter>` element is written to the file *chapter1.html*, the second `<chapter>` element is written to the file *chapter2.html*, and so on. Our stylesheet attempts to use Xalan's `<redirect:write>` element first; if that element is not available, it checks for Saxon's `<saxon:output>` element. If neither of those elements is available, it writes the contents of all `<chapter>` elements to the same output stream. The stylesheet also calls the `element-available()` function with the nonqualified element name `write`; this call always returns `false` because the element name is not namespace qualified.

When we use Xalan to process the XML file with our stylesheet, here are the results on the console:

```
file:///D:/O'Reilly/XSLT/bookSamples/AppendixC/elementavailable.xsl; Line 66;
Column 35; The <write> element is not available!
```

The stylesheet generates the files *chapter1.html* through *chapter9.html*, with each file containing data from one of the <chapter> elements in the original file. Our stylesheet also generates hyperlinks between the chapter files; here's what *chapter3.html* looks like:

```
<html>
   <head>
      <meta http-equiv="Content-Type" content="text/html; charset=utf-8">

      <title>XPath</title>
   </head>
   <body>
      <h1>XPath</h1>
      <p>If this chapter had any text, it would appear here.</p>
      <p><a href="chapter2.html">Previous</a></p>
      <p><a href="chapter4.html">Next</a></p>
   </body>
</html>
```

When rendered in a browser, the file looks like Figure C-1.

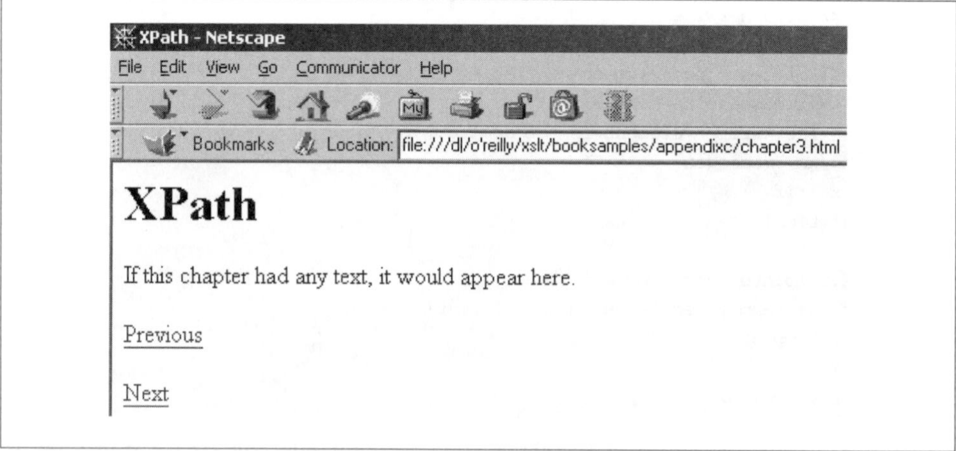

Figure C-1. Sample HTML output file

Clicking on the Previous link takes you to the file *chapter2.html*, while clicking on the Next link takes you to *chapter4.html*.

Using our stylesheet with Saxon (using the command `java com.icl.saxon.StyleSheet chapterlist.xml elementavailable.xsl`) produces similar results on the console:

```
The <write> element is not available!
```

Although the format of the message is slightly different, the output in the multiple HTML files is the same.

Finally, if we use the Oracle XML parser, none of the elements we query will be available, so all the output is written to a single file. We'll invoke the processor with this command. (The command should be on one line.)

```
java oracle.xml.parser.v2.oraxsl chapterlist.xml
  elementavailable.xsl chapters.html
```

Here's the console output:

```
Message: The <write> element is not available!
```

The output file, *chapters.html*, looks like this:

```
<html xmlns:redirect="org.apache.xalan.xslt.extensions.Redirect"
  xmlns:saxon="http://icl.com/saxon">
   <head>
      <META http-equiv="Content-Type" content="text/html">
      <title>XSLT</title>
   </head>
   <h1>Getting Started</h1>
   <p>If this chapter had any text, it would appear here.</p>
   <h1>The Hello World Example</h1>
   <p>If this chapter had any text, it would appear here.</p>
   <h1>XPath</h1>
   <p>If this chapter had any text, it would appear here.</p>
   <h1>Stylesheet Basics</h1>
   <p>If this chapter had any text, it would appear here.</p>
   <h1>Branching and Control Elements</h1>
   <p>If this chapter had any text, it would appear here.</p>
   <h1>Functions</h1>
   <p>If this chapter had any text, it would appear here.</p>
   <h1>Creating Links and Cross-References</h1>
   <p>If this chapter had any text, it would appear here.</p>
   <h1>Sorting and Grouping Elements</h1>
   <p>If this chapter had any text, it would appear here.</p>
   <h1>Combining XML Documents</h1>
   <p>If this chapter had any text, it would appear here.</p>
</html>
```

When rendered, our output looks like Figure C-2.

In this example, the `element-available()` function allows us to determine what processing capabilities are available and respond gracefully to whatever we find.

false() Function

— Always returns the boolean value `false`. Remember that the strings "true" and "false" don't have any special significance in XSLT. This function (and the `true()` function) allow you to generate boolean values directly when you need them.

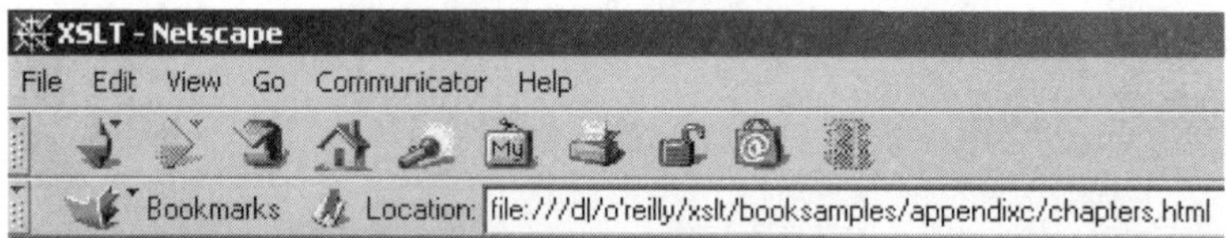

Figure C-2. HTML document listing all chapters

Synopsis

boolean **false()**

Inputs

None.

Output

The boolean value `false`.

Defined in

XPath section 4.3, Boolean Functions.

Example

Here's a brief example that uses the `false()` function:

```
<?xml version="1.0"?>
<xsl:stylesheet version="1.0" xmlns:xsl="http://www.w3.org/1999/XSL/Transform">

  <xsl:output method="text"/>
```

```
  <xsl:variable name="newline">
<xsl:text>
</xsl:text>
  </xsl:variable>

  <xsl:template match="/">
    <xsl:value-of select="$newline"/>
    <xsl:text>A test of the false() function:</xsl:text>

    <xsl:value-of select="$newline"/>
    <xsl:value-of select="$newline"/>
    <xsl:choose>
      <xsl:when test="false()">
        <xsl:text>   "false()"   returned true!</xsl:text>
      </xsl:when>
      <xsl:otherwise>
        <xsl:text>   "false()"   returned false!</xsl:text>
      </xsl:otherwise>
    </xsl:choose>
  </xsl:template>
</xsl:stylesheet>
```

When using this stylesheet against any XML document, it generates this less-than-exciting result:

```
A test of the false() function:

   "false()"   returned false!
```

floor() Function — Returns the largest integer that is not greater than the argument.

Synopsis

`number` **`floor(`**`*number*`**`)`**

Inputs

A number. If the argument is not a number, it is transformed into a number as if it had been processed by the `number()` function. If the argument cannot be transformed into a number, the `floor()` function returns `NaN` (not a number).

Output

The largest integer that is not greater than the argument, or `NaN` if the argument cannot be converted into a number.

Defined in

XPath section 4.4, Number Functions.

Example

The following stylesheet shows the results of invoking the `floor()` function against a variety of values. We'll use this XML document as input:

```
<?xml version="1.0"?>
<report>
  <title>Miles Flown in 2001</title>
  <month sequence="01">
    <miles-flown>12379</miles-flown>
    <miles-earned>35215</miles-earned>
  </month>
  <month sequence="02">
    <miles-flown>32857</miles-flown>
    <miles-earned>92731</miles-earned>
  </month>
  <month sequence="03">
    <miles-flown>19920</miles-flown>
    <miles-earned>76725</miles-earned>
  </month>
  <month sequence="04">
    <miles-flown>18903</miles-flown>
    <miles-earned>31781</miles-earned>
  </month>
</report>
```

Here's the stylesheet that uses the `floor()` function:

```
<?xml version="1.0"?>
<xsl:stylesheet version="1.0"
  xmlns:xsl="http://www.w3.org/1999/XSL/Transform"
  xmlns:months="Lookup table for month names">

  <months:name sequence="01">January</months:name>
  <months:name sequence="02">February</months:name>
  <months:name sequence="03">March</months:name>
  <months:name sequence="04">April</months:name>
  <months:name sequence="05">May</months:name>
  <months:name sequence="06">June</months:name>
  <months:name sequence="07">July</months:name>
  <months:name sequence="08">August</months:name>
  <months:name sequence="09">September</months:name>
  <months:name sequence="10">October</months:name>
  <months:name sequence="11">November</months:name>
  <months:name sequence="12">December</months:name>

  <xsl:output method="text"/>
```

```
  <xsl:variable name="newline">
<xsl:text>
</xsl:text>
  </xsl:variable>

  <xsl:template match="/">
    <xsl:value-of select="$newline"/>
    <xsl:text>Tests of the floor() function:</xsl:text>

    <xsl:value-of select="$newline"/>
    <xsl:value-of select="$newline"/>
    <xsl:text>   "floor('7.983')" = </xsl:text>
    <xsl:value-of select="floor('7.983')"/>

    <xsl:value-of select="$newline"/>
    <xsl:text>   "floor('-7.893')" = </xsl:text>
    <xsl:value-of select="floor('-7.893')"/>

    <xsl:value-of select="$newline"/>
    <xsl:text>   "floor(/report/month[@sequence='01']</xsl:text>
    <xsl:text>/miles-flown)" = </xsl:text>
    <xsl:value-of select="floor(/report/month[@sequence='01']/miles-flown)"/>

    <xsl:value-of select="$newline"/>
    <xsl:text>   "floor(document('')/*/months:name</xsl:text>
    <xsl:text>[@sequence='02'])" = </xsl:text>
    <xsl:value-of select="floor(document('')/*/months:name[@sequence='02'])"/>

    <xsl:value-of select="$newline"/>
    <xsl:value-of select="$newline"/>
    <xsl:for-each select="/report/month">
      <xsl:text>   </xsl:text>
      <xsl:value-of
        select="document('')/*/months:name[@sequence=current()/@sequence]"/>
      <xsl:text> - </xsl:text>
      <xsl:value-of select="format-number(miles-flown, '##,###')"/>
      <xsl:text> miles flown, </xsl:text>
      <xsl:value-of select="format-number(miles-earned, '##,###')"/>
      <xsl:text> miles earned.</xsl:text>
      <xsl:value-of select="$newline"/>
      <xsl:text>      (Averaged </xsl:text>
      <xsl:value-of select="floor(miles-earned div miles-flown)"/>
      <xsl:text> miles earned for each mile flown.)</xsl:text>
      <xsl:value-of select="$newline"/>
      <xsl:value-of select="$newline"/>
    </xsl:for-each>
  </xsl:template>

</xsl:stylesheet>
```

Here is the output of our stylesheet:

```
Tests of the floor() function:

   "floor('7.983')" = 7
   "floor('-7.893')" = -8
   "floor(/report/month[@sequence='01']/miles-flown)" = 12379
   "floor(document('')/*/months:name[@sequence='02'])" = NaN

   January - 12,379 miles flown, 35,215 miles earned.
     (Averaged 2 miles earned for each mile flown.)

   February - 32,857 miles flown, 92,731 miles earned.
     (Averaged 2 miles earned for each mile flown.)

   March - 19,920 miles flown, 76,725 miles earned.
     (Averaged 3 miles earned for each mile flown.)

   April - 18,903 miles flown, 31,781 miles earned.
     (Averaged 1 miles earned for each mile flown.)
```

Notice that when we invoked the `ceiling()` function against the string "February" (that's what `document('')/*/months:name[@sequence='02']` resolves to), the function returned `NaN`. You can compare these results to those from the `ceiling()` function and the `round()` function.

format-number() Function — Takes a number and formats it as a string.

Synopsis

`string` **`format-number(`**`*number*, *string*, *string?*`**`)`**

Inputs

The number to be formatted and the format pattern string are required. The third argument is the optional name of a decimal format; if the third argument is not supplied, the default decimal format is used.

Output

The number, formatted according to the rules supplied by the other arguments. The special characters used in the second argument are:

`#`

Represents a digit. Trailing or leading zeroes are not displayed. Formatting the number `4.0` with the string "#.##" returns the string "4".

`0`

Represents a digit. Unlike the `#` character, the `0` always displays a zero. Formatting the number `4.1` with the string "#.00" returns the string "4.10".

`.`
: Represents the decimal point.

`-`
: Represents the minus sign.

`,`
: Is the grouping separator.

`;`
: Separates the positive-number pattern from the negative-number pattern.

`%`
: Indicates that a number should be displayed as a percentage. The value will be multiplied by 100, then displayed as a percentage. Formatting the number `.76` with the string "##%" returns the string "76%".

`\u2030`
: Is the Unicode character for the per-thousand (per-mille) sign. The value will be multiplied by 1000, then displayed as a per mille. Formatting the number `.768` with the string "###\u2030" returns the string "768‰".

The third argument, if given, must be the name of an `<xsl:decimal-format>` element. The `<xsl:decimal-format>` element lets you define the character that should be used for the decimal point and the grouping separator, the string used to represent infinity, and other formatting options. See `<xsl:decimal-format>` for more information.

Defined in

XSLT section 12.3, Number Formatting.

Example

The following stylesheet uses the `format-number()` function in various ways:

```
<?xml version="1.0" encoding="ISO-8859-1" ?>
<xsl:stylesheet version="1.0"
  xmlns:xsl="http://www.w3.org/1999/XSL/Transform"
  xmlns:months="Lookup table for month names">

  <xsl:output method="text"/>

  <months:name sequence="01">January</months:name>
  <months:name sequence="02">February</months:name>
  <months:name sequence="03">March</months:name>
  <months:name sequence="04">April</months:name>

  <xsl:variable name="newline">
<xsl:text>
</xsl:text>
  </xsl:variable>
```

```
<xsl:decimal-format name="f1"
  decimal-separator=":"
  grouping-separator="/"/>

<xsl:decimal-format name="f2"
  infinity="Really, really big"
  NaN="[not a number]"/>

<xsl:template match="/">
  <xsl:value-of select="$newline"/>
  <xsl:text>Tests of the format-number() function:</xsl:text>

  <xsl:value-of select="$newline"/>
  <xsl:value-of select="$newline"/>
  <xsl:text>   format-number(528.3, '#.#;-#.#')=</xsl:text>
  <xsl:value-of select="format-number(528.3, '#.#;-#.#')"/>
  <xsl:value-of select="$newline"/>
  <xsl:text>   format-number(528.3, '0,000.00;-0,000.00')=</xsl:text>
  <xsl:value-of select="format-number(528.3, '0,000.00;-0,000.00')"/>
  <xsl:value-of select="$newline"/>
  <xsl:text>   format-number(-23528.3, '$#,###.00;($#,###.00)')=</xsl:text>
  <xsl:value-of select="format-number(-23528.3, '$#,###.00;($#,###.00)')"/>
  <xsl:value-of select="$newline"/>
  <xsl:text>   format-number(1528.3, '#/###:00', 'f1')=</xsl:text>
  <xsl:value-of select="format-number(1528.3, '#/###:00;-#/###:00', 'f1')"/>
  <xsl:value-of select="$newline"/>
  <xsl:text>   format-number(1 div 0, '###,###.00', 'f2')=</xsl:text>
  <xsl:value-of select="format-number(1 div 0, '###,###.00', 'f2')"/>
  <xsl:value-of select="$newline"/>
  <xsl:text>   format-number(blue div orange, '#.##', 'f2')=</xsl:text>
  <xsl:value-of select="format-number(blue div orange, '#.##', 'f2')"/>
  <xsl:value-of select="$newline"/>
  <xsl:value-of select="$newline"/>
  <xsl:for-each select="report/month">
    <xsl:text>   </xsl:text>
    <xsl:value-of
      select="document('')/*/months:name[@sequence=current()/@sequence]"/>
    <xsl:text> - </xsl:text>
    <xsl:value-of select="format-number(miles-flown, '##,###')"/>
    <xsl:text> miles flown, </xsl:text>
    <xsl:value-of select="format-number(miles-earned, '##,###')"/>
    <xsl:text> miles earned.</xsl:text>
    <xsl:value-of select="$newline"/>
    <xsl:text>     (</xsl:text>
    <xsl:value-of
      select="format-number(miles-flown div sum(//miles-flown), '##%')"/>
    <xsl:text> of all miles flown, </xsl:text>
    <xsl:value-of
      select="format-number(miles-earned div sum(//miles-earned), '##%')"/>
    <xsl:text> of all miles earned.)</xsl:text>
```

```
      <xsl:value-of select="$newline"/>
      <xsl:value-of select="$newline"/>
    </xsl:for-each>
    <xsl:text>   Total miles flown: </xsl:text>
    <xsl:value-of select="format-number(sum(//miles-flown), '##,###')"/>
    <xsl:text>, total miles earned: </xsl:text>
    <xsl:value-of select="format-number(sum(//miles-earned), '##,###')"/>
  </xsl:template>

</xsl:stylesheet>
```

We'll use this XML document with our stylesheet:

```
<?xml version="1.0"?>
<report>
  <title>Miles Flown in 2001</title>
  <month sequence="01">
    <miles-flown>12379</miles-flown>
    <miles-earned>35215</miles-earned>
  </month>
  <month sequence="02">
    <miles-flown>32857</miles-flown>
    <miles-earned>92731</miles-earned>
  </month>
  <month sequence="03">
    <miles-flown>19920</miles-flown>
    <miles-earned>76725</miles-earned>
  </month>
  <month sequence="04">
    <miles-flown>18903</miles-flown>
    <miles-earned>31781</miles-earned>
  </month>
</report>
```

When we run this stylesheet, here are the results:

```
Tests of the format-number() function:

   format-number(528.3, '#.#;-#.#')=528.3
   format-number(528.3, '0,000.00;-0,000.00')=0,528.30
   format-number(-23528.3, '$#,###.00;($#,###.00)')=($23,528.30)
   format-number(1528.3, '#/###:00', 'f1')=1/528:30
   format-number(1 div 0, '###,###.00', 'f2')=Really, really big
   format-number(blue div orange, '#.##', 'f2')=[not a number]

   January - 12,379 miles flown, 35,215 miles earned.
     (15% of all miles flown, 15% of all miles earned.)

   February - 32,857 miles flown, 92,731 miles earned.
     (39% of all miles flown, 39% of all miles earned.)
```

```
March - 19,920 miles flown, 76,725 miles earned.
  (24% of all miles flown, 32% of all miles earned.)

April - 18,903 miles flown, 31,781 miles earned.
  (22% of all miles flown, 13% of all miles earned.)

Total miles flown: 84,059, total miles earned: 236,452
```

The first few examples illustrate some of the more complicated formatting options available, along with references to the `<xsl:decimal-format>` elements in the stylesheet. The last section is a more typical use of the `format-number` function: formatting values selected or calculated from an XML document.

function-available() Function — Determines if a given function is available to the XSLT processor. This function allows you to design stylesheets that react gracefully if a particular function is not available to process an XML document.

Synopsis

boolean **function-available(***string***)**

Inputs

The name function's name. The name is usually qualified with a namespace; if the namespace of the function name is non-null, the function is an extension function. Otherwise, the function is one of the functions defined in the XSLT or XPath specifications.

Output

The boolean value `true` if the function is available, `false` otherwise.

Defined in

XSLT section 15, Fallback.

Example

We'll use the following XML document to test the `function-available()` function:

```
<?xml version="1.0"?>
<list>
  <title>A few of my favorite albums</title>
  <listitem>A Love Supreme</listitem>
  <listitem>Beat Crazy</listitem>
  <listitem>Here Come the Warm Jets</listitem>
  <listitem>Kind of Blue</listitem>
  <listitem>London Calling</listitem>
  <listitem>Remain in Light</listitem>
```

```
    <listitem>The Joshua Tree</listitem>
    <listitem>The Indestructible Beat of Soweto</listitem>
  </list>
```

Here's our stylesheet:

```
<?xml version="1.0"?>
<xsl:stylesheet version="1.0" xmlns:xsl="http://www.w3.org/1999/XSL/Transform"
  xmlns:jpeg="class:JPEGWriter"
  extension-element-prefixes="jpeg">

  <xsl:output method="text"/>

  <xsl:variable name="newline">
<xsl:text>
</xsl:text>
  </xsl:variable>

  <xsl:template match="/">
    <xsl:value-of select="$newline"/>
    <xsl:for-each select="list/listitem">
      <xsl:choose>
        <xsl:when test="function-available('jpeg:createJPEG')">
          <xsl:value-of
            select="jpeg:createJPEG(., 'bg.jpg',
            concat('album', position(), '.jpg'),
            'Swiss 721 Bold Condensed', 'BOLD', 22, 52, 35)"/>
          <xsl:text>See the file </xsl:text>
          <xsl:value-of select="concat('album', position(), '.jpg')"/>
          <xsl:text> to see the title of album #</xsl:text>
          <xsl:value-of select="position()"/>
          <xsl:value-of select="$newline"/>
        </xsl:when>
        <xsl:otherwise>
          <xsl:value-of select="position()"/>
          <xsl:text>. </xsl:text>
          <xsl:value-of select="."/>
          <xsl:value-of select="$newline"/>
        </xsl:otherwise>
      </xsl:choose>
    </xsl:for-each>
  </xsl:template>

</xsl:stylesheet>
```

In our stylesheet, if the `createJPEG()` function is available, we'll invoke it to create JPEG files for the titles of all our favorite albums. If the function is not available, we'll simply write those titles to the output stream. Here are the results we get when the `createJPEG()` function is available:

```
See the file album1.jpg to see the title of album #1
See the file album2.jpg to see the title of album #2
See the file album3.jpg to see the title of album #3
See the file album4.jpg to see the title of album #4
See the file album5.jpg to see the title of album #5
See the file album6.jpg to see the title of album #6
See the file album7.jpg to see the title of album #7
See the file album8.jpg to see the title of album #8
```

All album titles (the text of the `<listitem>` elements) are converted to JPEG graphics. In this example, the file *album8.jpg* looks like Figure C-3.

:-) The Indestructible Beat of Soweto

Figure C-3. Generated graphic for the eighth <listitem> element

If we delete the file *JPEGWriter.class* (if the *.class* file is missing, the function isn't available), we get these results instead:

```
1. A Love Supreme
2. Beat Crazy
3. Here Come the Warm Jets
4. Kind of Blue
5. London Calling
6. Remain in Light
7. The Joshua Tree
8. The Indestructible Beat of Soweto
```

generate-id() Function — Generates a unique ID (an XML name) for a given node. If no node-set is given, `generate-id()` generates an ID for the context node.

Synopsis

string **generate-id(***node-set?***)**

Inputs

An optional node-set. If no node-set is given, this function generates an ID for the context node. If the node-set is empty, `generate-id()` returns an empty string.

Output

A unique ID, or an empty string if an empty node-set is given. Several things about the `generate-id()` function are important to know:

- For a given transformation, every time you invoke `generate-id()` against a given node, the XSLT processor must return the same ID. The ID can't change while you're doing a transformation. If you ask the XSLT processor to transform your document with this stylesheet tomorrow, there's no guarantee that `generate-id()` will generate the same ID the second time around. All of tomorrow's calls to `generate-id()` will generate the same ID, but that ID might not be the one generated today.
- The `generate-id()` function is not required to check if its generated ID duplicates an ID that's already in the document. In other words, if an element in your document has an attribute of type `ID` with the value `sdk3829a`, there's a remote possibility that an ID returned by `generate-id()` would have the value `sdk3829a`. It's not likely, but it could happen.
- If you invoke `generate-id()` against two different nodes, the two generated IDs must be different.
- Given a node-set, `generate-id()` returns an ID for the node in the node-set that occurs first in document order.
- If the node-set you pass to the function is empty (you invoke `generate-id(fleeber)`, but there are no `<fleeber>` elements in the current context), `generate-id()` returns an empty string.

Defined in

XSLT section 12.4, Miscellaneous Additional Functions.

Example

Here's a simple stylesheet that uses the `document('')` function to access all of its own `<xsl:text>` nodes. It then uses `generate-id()` to generate a unique ID for each of those nodes, then calls `generate-id()` again to illustrate that the function generates the same ID for a given node. Here's the stylesheet:

```
<?xml version="1.0"?>
<xsl:stylesheet version="1.0"
  xmlns:xsl="http://www.w3.org/1999/XSL/Transform">

  <xsl:output method="text"/>

  <xsl:variable name="newline">
<xsl:text>
</xsl:text>
  </xsl:variable>

  <xsl:template match="/">
    <xsl:value-of select="$newline"/>
    <xsl:text>A test of the generate-id() function:</xsl:text>
```

```
      <xsl:value-of select="$newline"/>
      <xsl:value-of select="$newline"/>
      <xsl:for-each select="document('')//xsl:text">
        <xsl:text>Node name: </xsl:text>
        <xsl:value-of select="name()"/>
        <xsl:text> - generated id: </xsl:text>
        <xsl:value-of select="generate-id()"/>
        <xsl:value-of select="$newline"/>
      </xsl:for-each>
      <xsl:value-of select="$newline"/>
      <xsl:value-of select="$newline"/>
      <xsl:text>Now we'll try it again...</xsl:text>
      <xsl:value-of select="$newline"/>
      <xsl:value-of select="$newline"/>
      <xsl:for-each select="document('')//xsl:text">
        <xsl:text>Node name: </xsl:text>
        <xsl:value-of select="name()"/>
        <xsl:text> - generated id: </xsl:text>
        <xsl:value-of select="generate-id()"/>
        <xsl:value-of select="$newline"/>
      </xsl:for-each>
    </xsl:template>

  </xsl:stylesheet>
```

Our stylesheet generates these results:

```
A test of the generate-id() function:

Node name: xsl:text - generated id: NC
Node name: xsl:text - generated id: N16
Node name: xsl:text - generated id: N22
Node name: xsl:text - generated id: N28
Node name: xsl:text - generated id: N38
Node name: xsl:text - generated id: N44
Node name: xsl:text - generated id: N4A


Now we'll try it again...

Node name: xsl:text - generated id: NC
Node name: xsl:text - generated id: N16
Node name: xsl:text - generated id: N22
Node name: xsl:text - generated id: N28
Node name: xsl:text - generated id: N38
Node name: xsl:text - generated id: N44
Node name: xsl:text - generated id: N4A
```

The IDs generated each time are the same.

id() Function — Returns the node in the source tree whose ID attribute matches the value passed in as input.

Synopsis

node-set **id(***object***)**

Inputs

An object. If the input object is a node-set, the result is a node-set that contains the result of applying the `id()` function to the string value of each node in the argument node-set. Usually, the argument is some other node type, which is (or is converted to) a string. That string is then used as the search value while all attributes of type ID are searched.

Remember that a limitation of the XML `ID` datatype is that a single set of names across all attributes is declared to be of type `ID`. The XSLT `key()` function and the associated `<xsl:key>` element address this and other limitations; see the `key()` function and `<xsl:key>` for more information.

Output

A node-set containing all nodes whose attributes of type `ID` match the string values of the input node-set. In practice, this node-set is a single node, the node whose attribute of type `ID` matches a string value.

Defined in

XPath section 4.1, Node Set Functions.

Example

For our example, we'll take this shortened version of the glossary we discussed earlier:

```
<?xml version="1.0" ?>
<!DOCTYPE glossary SYSTEM "glossary.dtd">
<glossary>
  <glentry>
    <term id="applet">applet</term>
    <defn>
      An application program,
      written in the Java programming language, that can be
      retrieved from a web server and executed by a web browser.
      A reference to an applet appears in the markup for a web
      page, in the same way that a reference to a graphics
      file appears; a browser retrieves an applet in the same
      way that it retrieves a graphics file.
      For security reasons, an applet's access rights are limited
      in two ways: the applet cannot access the filesystem of the
      client upon which it is executing, and the applet's
      communication across the network is limited to the server
      from which it was downloaded.
      Contrast with <xref refid="servlet"/>.
    </defn>
  </glentry>
```

```
    <glentry>
      <term id="servlet">servlet</term>
      <defn>
        An application program, written in the Java programming language,
        that is executed on a web server. A reference to a servlet
        appears in the markup for a web page, in the same way that a
        reference to a graphics file appears. The web server executes
        the servlet and sends the results of the execution (if there are
        any) to the web browser. Contrast with <xref refid="applet" />.
      </defn>
    </glentry>
  </glossary>
```

Here's the stylesheet we'll use to resolve the references:

```
<?xml version="1.0"?>
<xsl:stylesheet version="1.0" xmlns:xsl="http://www.w3.org/1999/XSL/Transform">
<xsl:output method="html" indent="yes"/>
<xsl:strip-space elements="*"/>

  <xsl:template match="/">
    <xsl:apply-templates select="glossary"/>
  </xsl:template>

  <xsl:template match="glossary">
    <html>
      <head>
        <title>
          <xsl:text>Glossary Listing </xsl:text>
        </title>
      </head>
      <body>
        <h1>
          <xsl:text>Glossary Listing </xsl:text>
        </h1>
        <xsl:apply-templates select="glentry"/>
      </body>
    </html>
  </xsl:template>

  <xsl:template match="glentry">
    <p>
      <b>
        <a>
          <xsl:attribute name="name">
            <xsl:value-of select="term/@id" />
          </xsl:attribute>
        </a>
```

```
        <xsl:value-of select="term"/>
        <xsl:text>: </xsl:text>
      </b>
      <xsl:apply-templates select="defn"/>
    </p>
  </xsl:template>

  <xsl:template match="defn">
    <xsl:apply-templates
     select="*|comment()|processing-instruction()|text()"/>
  </xsl:template>

  <xsl:template match="xref">
    <a>
      <xsl:attribute name="href">
        <xsl:text>#</xsl:text><xsl:value-of select="@refid"/>
      </xsl:attribute>
      <xsl:choose>
        <xsl:when test="id(@refid)/@xreftext">
          <xsl:value-of select="id(@refid)/@xreftext"/>
        </xsl:when>
        <xsl:otherwise>
          <xsl:value-of select="id(@refid)"/>
        </xsl:otherwise>
      </xsl:choose>
    </a>
  </xsl:template>

</xsl:stylesheet>
```

Our stylesheet generates these results:

```
<html>
<head>
<META http-equiv="Content-Type" content="text/html; charset=UTF-8">
<title>Glossary Listing </title>
</head>
<body>
<h1>Glossary Listing </h1>
<p>
<b><a name="applet"></a>applet: </b>
      An application program,
      written in the Java programming language, that can be
      retrieved from a web server and executed by a web browser.
      A reference to an applet appears in the markup for a web
      page, in the same way that a reference to a graphics
      file appears; a browser retrieves an applet in the same
      way that it retrieves a graphics file.
```

```
      For security reasons, an applet's access rights are limited
      in two ways: the applet cannot access the filesystem of the
      client upon which it is executing, and the applet's
      communication across the network is limited to the server
      from which it was downloaded.
      Contrast with <a href="#servlet">servlet</a>.
    </p>
  <p>
  <b><a name="servlet"></a>servlet: </b>
      An application program, written in the Java programming language,
      that is executed on a web server. A reference to a servlet
      appears in the markup for a web page, in the same way that a
      reference to a graphics file appears. The web server executes
      the servlet and sends the results of the execution (if there are
      any) to the web browser. Contrast with <a href="#applet">applet</a>.
    </p>
  </body>
  </html>
```

When rendered in a browser, our hyperlinked document looks like Figure C-4.

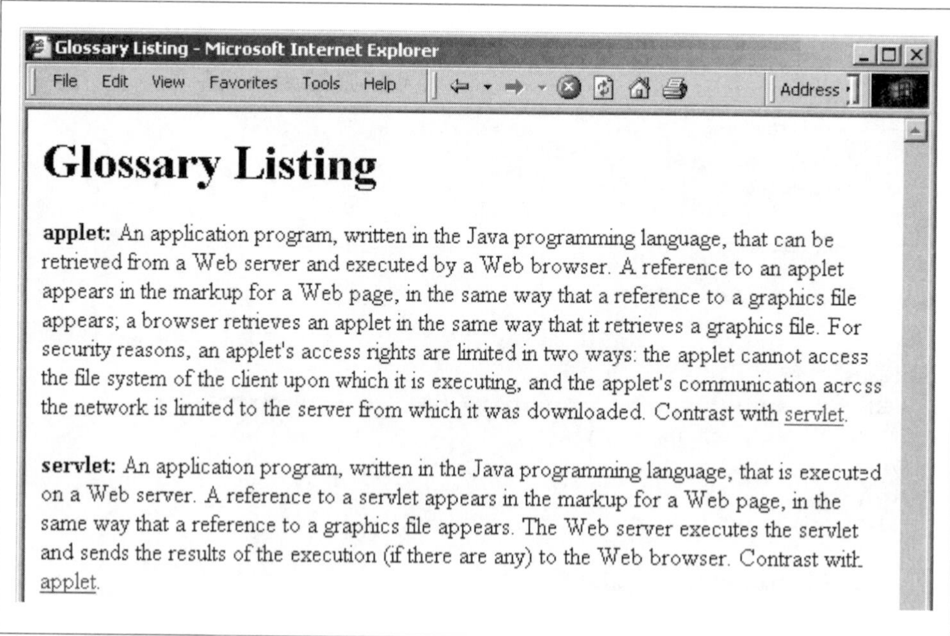

Figure C-4. Generated HTML glossary

key() Function — References a relation defined with an <xsl:key> element. Conceptually, the `key()` function works similarly to the `id()` function, although keys are more flexible than IDs.

Synopsis

node-set **key(***string*, *object***)**

Inputs

The name of the key (defined by an <xsl:key> element) and an object. If the object is a node-set, then the `key()` function applies itself to the string value of each node in the node-set and returns the node-set of the result of all those `key()` function invocations. If the object is any other type, it is converted to a string as if by a call to the `string()` function.

Output

A node-set containing the nodes in the same document as the context node whose values for the requested key match the search argument(s). In other words, if our stylesheet has an <xsl:key> element that defines a key named `postalcodes` based on the <postalcode> child of all <address> elements in the current document, the function call `key(postalcodes, '34829')` returns a node-set containing all the <address> elements with a <postalcode> element whose value is `34829`.

Defined in

XSLT section 12.2, Keys.

Example

To illustrate the power of the `key()` function, we'll use this document—a truncated version of the glossary we discussed in Chapter 5:

```
<?xml version="1.0" ?>
<glossary>
  <glentry>
    <term id="applet">applet</term>
    <defn topic="Java" language="en">
      An application program,
      written in the Java programming language, that can be
      retrieved from a web server and executed by a web browser.
      A reference to an applet appears in the markup for a web
      page, in the same way that a reference to a graphics
      file appears; a browser retrieves an applet in the same
      way that it retrieves a graphics file.
      For security reasons, an applet's access rights are limited
      in two ways: the applet cannot access the filesystem of the
      client upon which it is executing, and the applet's
      communication across the network is limited to the server
      from which it was downloaded.
      Contrast with <xref refid="servlet"/>.
    </defn>
```

```
    <defn topic="Java" language="it">
      [Pretend this is an Italian definition of applet.]
    </defn>
    <defn topic="Java" language="es">
      [Pretend this is a Spanish definition of applet.]
    </defn>
  </glentry>

  <glentry>
    <term id="DMZlong" xreftext="demilitarized zone">demilitarized
      zone (DMZ)</term>
    <defn topic="security" language="en">
      In network security, a network that is isolated from, and
      serves as a neutral zone between, a trusted network (for example,
      a private intranet) and an untrusted network (for example, the
      Internet). One or more secure gateways usually control access
      to the DMZ from the trusted or the untrusted network.
    </defn>
    <defn topic="security" language="it">
      [Pretend this is an Italian definition of DMZ.]
    </defn>
    <defn topic="security" language="es">
      [Pretend this is a Spanish definition of DMZ.]
    </defn>
    <defn topic="security" language="jp">
      [Pretend this is a Japanese definition of DMZ.]
    </defn>
    <defn topic="security" language="de">
      [Pretend this is a German definition of DMZ.]
    </defn>
  </glentry>

  <glentry>
    <term id="servlet">servlet</term>
    <defn topic="Java" language="en">
      An application program, written in the Java programming language,
      that is executed on a web server. A reference to a servlet
      appears in the markup for a web page, in the same way that a
      reference to a graphics file appears. The web server executes
      the servlet and sends the results of the execution (if there are
      any) to the web browser. Contrast with <xref refid="applet" />.
    </defn>
    <defn topic="Java" language="es">
      [Pretend this is a Spanish definition of servlet.]
    </defn>
    <defn topic="Java" language="it">
      [Pretend this is an Italian definition of servlet.]
    </defn>
```

```
    <defn topic="Java" language="de">
      [Pretend this is a German definition of servlet.]
    </defn>
    <defn topic="Java" language="jp">
      [Pretend this is a Japanese definition of servlet.]
    </defn>
  </glentry>
</glossary>
```

Here's the stylesheet we'll use to process this document. Notice that we define two `<xsl:key>` elements to index the XML document in two different ways:

```
<?xml version="1.0"?>
<xsl:stylesheet version="1.0" xmlns:xsl="http://www.w3.org/1999/XSL/Transform">
<xsl:output method="html" indent="yes"/>
<xsl:strip-space elements="*"/>

  <xsl:key name="language-index" match="defn" use="@language"/>
  <xsl:key name="term-ids"       match="term" use="@id"/>

  <xsl:param name="targetLanguage"/>

  <xsl:template match="/">
    <xsl:apply-templates select="glossary"/>
  </xsl:template>

  <xsl:template match="glossary">
    <html>
      <head>
        <title>
          <xsl:text>Glossary Listing: </xsl:text>
        </title>
      </head>
      <body>
        <h1>
          <xsl:text>Glossary Listing: </xsl:text>
        </h1>
        <xsl:for-each select="key('language-index', $targetLanguage)">
          <xsl:apply-templates select="ancestor::glentry"/>
        </xsl:for-each>
      </body>
    </html>
  </xsl:template>

  <xsl:template match="glentry">
    <p>
      <b>
        <a>
          <xsl:attribute name="name">
            <xsl:value-of select="term/@id" />
```

```
          </xsl:attribute>
        </a>
        <xsl:value-of select="term"/>
        <xsl:text>: </xsl:text>
      </b>
      <xsl:apply-templates select="defn[@language=$targetLanguage]"/>
    </p>
  </xsl:template>

  <xsl:template match="defn">
    <xsl:apply-templates
     select="*|comment()|processing-instruction()|text()"/>
  </xsl:template>

  <xsl:template match="xref">
    <a>
      <xsl:attribute name="href">
        <xsl:text>#</xsl:text><xsl:value-of select="@refid"/>
      </xsl:attribute>
      <xsl:choose>
        <xsl:when test="key('term-ids', @refid)[1]/@xreftext">
          <xsl:value-of select="key('term-ids', @refid)[1]/@xreftext"/>
        </xsl:when>
        <xsl:otherwise>
          <xsl:value-of select="key('term-ids', @refid)[1]"/>
        </xsl:otherwise>
      </xsl:choose>
    </a>
  </xsl:template>

</xsl:stylesheet>
```

Transforming the glossary with a `targetLanguage` of `en` gives these results:

```
<html>
<head>
<META http-equiv="Content-Type" content="text/html; charset=UTF-8">
<title>Glossary Listing: </title>
</head>
<body>
<h1>Glossary Listing: </h1>
<p>
<b><a name="applet"></a>applet: </b>
      An application program,
      written in the Java programming language, that can be
      retrieved from a web server and executed by a web browser.
      A reference to an applet appears in the markup for a web
      page, in the same way that a reference to a graphics
      file appears; a browser retrieves an applet in the same
      way that it retrieves a graphics file.
```

```
        For security reasons, an applet's access rights are limited
        in two ways: the applet cannot access the filesystem of the
        client upon which it is executing, and the applet's
        communication across the network is limited to the server
        from which it was downloaded.
        Contrast with <a href="#servlet">servlet</a>.
      </p>
<p>
<b><a name="DMZlong"></a>demilitarized
        zone (DMZ): </b>
        In network security, a network that is isolated from, and
        serves as a neutral zone between, a trusted network (for example,
        a private intranet) and an untrusted network (for example, the
        Internet). One or more secure gateways usually control access
        to the DMZ from the trusted or the untrusted network.
      </p>
<p>
<b><a name="servlet"></a>servlet: </b>
        An application program, written in the Java programming language,
        that is executed on a web server. A reference to a servlet
        appears in the markup for a web page, in the same way that a
        reference to a graphics file appears. The web server executes
        the servlet and sends the results of the execution (if there are
        any) to the web browser. Contrast with <a href="#applet">applet</a>.
      </p>
</body>
</html>
```

Figure C-5 shows how this document looks when it's rendered in a browser. Using a targetLanguage of jp gives us these results instead:

```
<html>
<head>
<META http-equiv="Content-Type" content="text/html; charset=UTF-8">
<title>Glossary Listing: </title>
</head>
<body>
<h1>Glossary Listing: </h1>
<p>
<b><a name="DMZlong"></a>demilitarized
        zone (DMZ): </b>
        [Pretend this is a Japanese definition of DMZ.]
      </p>
<p>
<b><a name="servlet"></a>servlet: </b>
        [Pretend this is a Japanese definition of servlet.]
      </p>
</body>
</html>
        </programlisting>
```

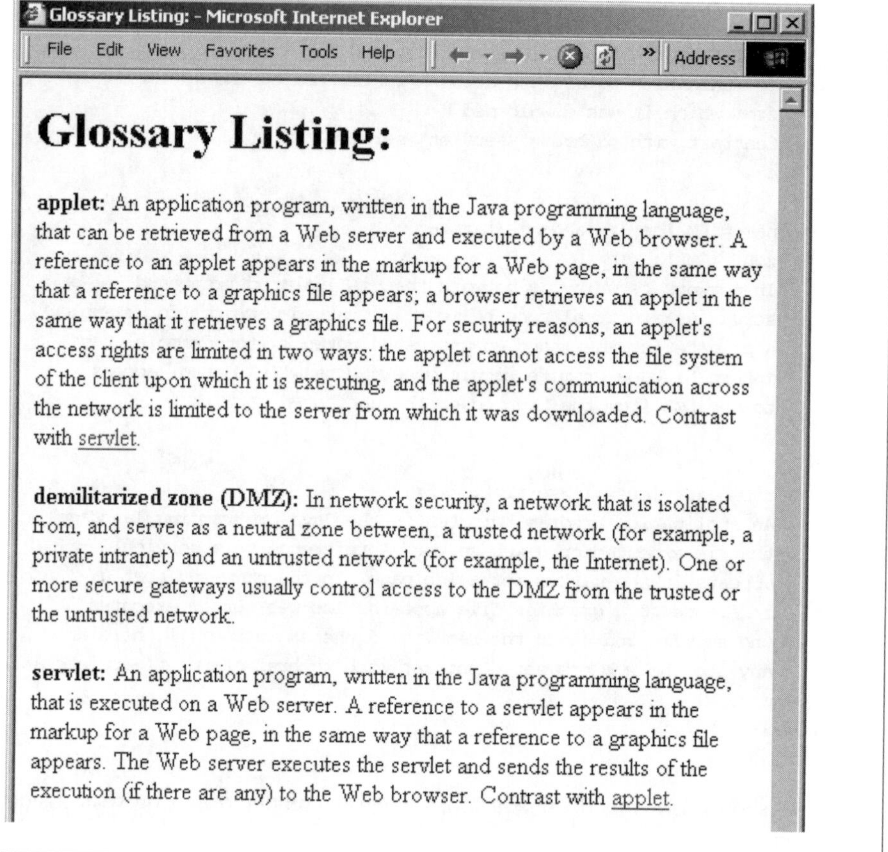

Figure C-5. Generated HTML glossary

When rendered, the document looks like Figure C-6. Notice that we get entirely different results when we change the `targetLanguage`.

lang() Function — Determines whether a given language string is the same as, or is a sublanguage of, the language of the context node, as defined by an `xml:lang` attribute.

Synopsis

```
boolean lang(string)
```

Inputs

A string representing a language code. If the context node has a language of `xml:lang="en-us"`, invoking the `lang()` function with any of the values `en`, `EN`, and `en-us` returns the boolean value `true`, while invoking `lang()` with the value `en-gb` returns the boolean value `false`.

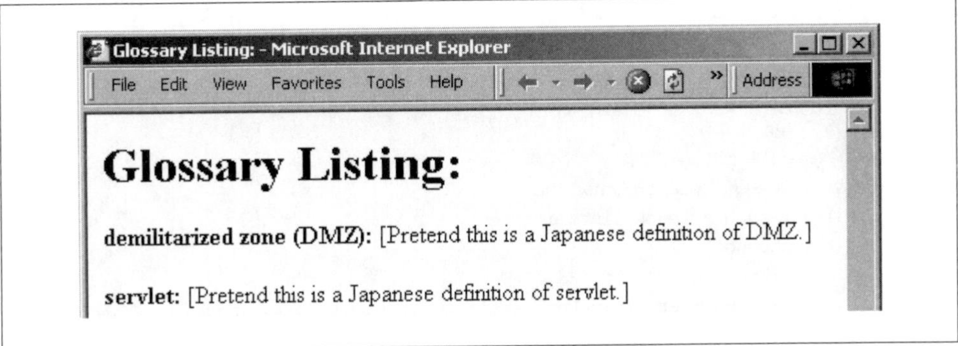

Figure C-6. Generated HTML glossary

Output

If the argument string is the same as, or is a sublanguage of, the context node's language, `lang()` returns the boolean value `true`. If the context node does not have an `xml:lang` attribute, then the value of the `xml:lang` attribute of its nearest ancestor is used instead. If there is no such attribute, then the `lang()` function returns the boolean value `false`. When comparing the language code of the context node with the argument string, the `lang()` function ignores case.

Defined in

XPath section 4.3, Boolean Functions.

Example

Here is an XML document that uses language codes:

```
<?xml version="1.0"?>
<list xml:lang="en">
  <title>Albums I've bought recently:</title>
  <listitem>The Sacred Art of Dub</listitem>
  <listitem>Only the Poor Man Feel It</listitem>
  <listitem>Excitable Boy</listitem>
  <listitem xml:lang="sw">Aki Special</listitem>
  <listitem xml:lang="en-gb">Combat Rock</listitem>
  <listitem xml:lang="zu">Talking Timbuktu</listitem>
  <listitem xml:lang="jz">The Birth of the Cool</listitem>
</list>
```

Here's a stylesheet that uses the `lang()` function:

```
<?xml version="1.0"?>
<xsl:stylesheet version="1.0" xmlns:xsl="http://www.w3.org/1999/XSL/Transform">

  <xsl:output method="text"/>
```

```
  <xsl:variable name="newline">
<xsl:text>
</xsl:text>
  </xsl:variable>

  <xsl:template match="/">
    <xsl:value-of select="$newline"/>
    <xsl:for-each select="list/listitem">
      <xsl:choose>
        <xsl:when test="lang('EN')">
          <xsl:text>Here's an English-language album: </xsl:text>
        </xsl:when>
        <xsl:otherwise>
          <xsl:text>-------> Here's some World music: </xsl:text>
        </xsl:otherwise>
      </xsl:choose>
      <xsl:value-of select="."/>
      <xsl:value-of select="$newline"/>
    </xsl:for-each>
  </xsl:template>

</xsl:stylesheet>
```

Finally, here are the results:

```
Here's an English-language album: The Sacred Art of Dub
Here's an English-language album: Only the Poor Man Feel It
Here's an English-language album: Excitable Boy
-------> Here's some World music: Aki Special
Here's an English-language album: Combat Rock
-------> Here's some World music: Talking Timbuktu
-------> Here's some World music: The Birth of the Cool
```

last() Function — Returns the position of the last node in the current context. This function is useful for defining templates for the last occurrence of a given element or for testing if a given node is the last in the node-set to which it belongs.

Synopsis

`number` **`last()`**

Inputs

None.

Output

A number equal to the number of nodes in the current context. For example, if the current context contains 12 `<li>` nodes, `last()` returns 12.

Defined in

XPath section 4.1, Node Set Functions.

Example

We'll use the `last()` function to handle the last item in a list in a special way. Here's the XML document we'll use:

```
<?xml version="1.0"?>
<list>
  <title>A few of my favorite albums</title>
  <listitem>A Love Supreme</listitem>
  <listitem>Beat Crazy</listitem>
  <listitem>Here Come the Warm Jets</listitem>
  <listitem>Kind of Blue</listitem>
  <listitem>London Calling</listitem>
  <listitem>Remain in Light</listitem>
  <listitem>The Joshua Tree</listitem>
  <listitem>The Indestructible Beat of Soweto</listitem>
</list>
```

Here is the stylesheet that handles the last `<listitem>` in the list differently:

```
<?xml version="1.0"?>
<xsl:stylesheet version="1.0" xmlns:xsl="http://www.w3.org/1999/XSL/Transform">

  <xsl:output method="html"/>

  <xsl:template match="/">
    <html>
      <head>
        <title>
          <xsl:value-of select="/list/title"/>
        </title>
      </head>
      <body>
        <h1>
          <xsl:value-of select="/list/title"/>
        </h1>
        <ul>
          <xsl:for-each select="/list/listitem">
            <xsl:choose>
              <xsl:when test="position()=last()">
                <li><b>Last, but not least: </b><xsl:value-of select="."/></li>
              </xsl:when>
              <xsl:otherwise>
                <li><xsl:value-of select="."/></li>
              </xsl:otherwise>
            </xsl:choose>
          </xsl:for-each>
        </ul>
```

```
      </body>
    </html>
  </xsl:template>

</xsl:stylesheet>
```

When we transform the XML document with this stylesheet, here are the results:

```
<html>
<head>
<META http-equiv="Content-Type" content="text/html; charset=UTF-8">
<title>A few of my favorite albums</title>
</head>
<body>
<h1>A few of my favorite albums</h1>
<ul>
<li>A Love Supreme</li>
<li>Beat Crazy</li>
<li>Here Come the Warm Jets</li>
<li>Kind of Blue</li>
<li>London Calling</li>
<li>Remain in Light</li>
<li>The Joshua Tree</li>
<li>
<b>Last, but not least: </b>The Indestructible Beat of Soweto</li>
</ul>
</body>
</html>
```

When rendered, the HTML file looks like Figure C-7.

local-name() Function — Returns the local part of the first node in the argument node-set.

Synopsis

string **local-name(***node-set?***)**

Inputs

A node-set. If the node-set is empty, the function returns an empty string. If the node-set is omitted, the function uses a node-set with the context node as its only member.

Output

A string corresponding to the local name of the first element in the argument node-set. If the node-set is empty, the `local-name()` function returns an empty string.

Defined in

XPath section 4.1, Node Set Functions.

Figure C-7. Generated HTML document

Example

Here is a stylesheet that uses the `document()` function to process all its own nodes. It then calls the `local-name()` function against each node.

```
<?xml version="1.0"?>
<xsl:stylesheet version="1.0"
  xmlns:xsl="http://www.w3.org/1999/XSL/Transform"
  xmlns:months="Lookup table for month names">

  <months:name sequence="12">December</months:name>
  <months:name sequence="01">January</months:name>
  <months:name sequence="02">February</months:name>
  <months:name sequence="03">March</months:name>
  <months:name sequence="04">April</months:name>
  <months:name sequence="05">May</months:name>
  <months:name sequence="06">June</months:name>
  <months:name sequence="07">July</months:name>
  <months:name sequence="08">August</months:name>
  <months:name sequence="09">September</months:name>
  <months:name sequence="10">October</months:name>
  <months:name sequence="11">November</months:name>

  <xsl:output method="text"/>

  <xsl:variable name="newline">
<xsl:text>
</xsl:text>
  </xsl:variable>
```

```
  <xsl:template match="/">
    <xsl:value-of select="$newline"/>
    <xsl:text>A test of the local-name() function:</xsl:text>

    <xsl:value-of select="$newline"/>
    <xsl:value-of select="$newline"/>
    <xsl:for-each select="document('')//*">
      <xsl:text>local-name: </xsl:text>
      <xsl:value-of select="local-name()"/>
      <xsl:value-of select="$newline"/>
    </xsl:for-each>
  </xsl:template>

</xsl:stylesheet>
```

The stylesheet generates these results:

```
A test of the local-name() function:

local-name: stylesheet
local-name: name
local-name: name
local-name: name
local-name: name
local-name: name
local-name: name
local-name: name
local-name: name
local-name: name
local-name: name
local-name: name
local-name: name
local-name: output
local-name: variable
local-name: text
local-name: template
local-name: value-of
local-name: text
local-name: value-of
local-name: value-of
local-name: for-each
local-name: text
local-name: value-of
local-name: value-of
```

name() Function — Returns the qualified name of a node. The qualified name includes the appropriate namespace prefix. For information on the namespace URI (not the prefix), XPath provides the `namespace-uri()` function.

Synopsis

`string` **`name(`***`node-set?`***`)`**

Inputs

An optional node-set. If no node-set is given, the `name()` function creates a node-set with the context node as its only member.

Output

The expanded name of the node. If the argument node-set is empty, or if the first node in the node-set does not have an expanded name, an empty string is returned.

Defined in

XPath section 4.1, Node Set Functions.

Example

Here is the XML document we'll use to demonstrate the `name()` function:

```
<?xml version="1.0"?>
<report>
  <title>Miles Flown in 2001</title>
  <month sequence="01">
    <miles-flown>12379</miles-flown>
    <miles-earned>35215</miles-earned>
  </month>
  <month sequence="02">
    <miles-flown>32857</miles-flown>
    <miles-earned>92731</miles-earned>
  </month>
  <month sequence="03">
    <miles-flown>19920</miles-flown>
    <miles-earned>76725</miles-earned>
  </month>
  <month sequence="04">
    <miles-flown>18903</miles-flown>
    <miles-earned>31781</miles-earned>
  </month>
</report>
```

We'll use this stylesheet to output the value of the `name()` function for each node in the XML document:

```
<?xml version="1.0"?>
<xsl:stylesheet version="1.0"
  xmlns:xsl="http://www.w3.org/1999/XSL/Transform"
  xmlns:months="Lookup table for month names">
```

```
  <months:name sequence="12">December</months:name>
  <months:name sequence="01">January</months:name>
  <months:name sequence="02">February</months:name>
  <months:name sequence="03">March</months:name>
  <months:name sequence="04">April</months:name>
  <months:name sequence="05">May</months:name>
  <months:name sequence="06">June</months:name>
  <months:name sequence="07">July</months:name>
  <months:name sequence="08">August</months:name>
  <months:name sequence="09">September</months:name>
  <months:name sequence="10">October</months:name>
  <months:name sequence="11">November</months:name>

  <xsl:output method="text"/>

  <xsl:variable name="newline">
<xsl:text>
</xsl:text>
  </xsl:variable>

  <xsl:template match="/">
    <xsl:value-of select="$newline"/>
    <xsl:text>A test of the name() function:</xsl:text>

    <xsl:value-of select="$newline"/>
    <xsl:value-of select="$newline"/>
    <xsl:for-each select="document('')//*">
      <xsl:text>name: </xsl:text>
      <xsl:value-of select="name()"/>
      <xsl:value-of select="$newline"/>
    </xsl:for-each>
  </xsl:template>

</xsl:stylesheet>
```

When we transform the XML document with this stylesheet, here are the results:

```
A test of the name() function:

name: xsl:stylesheet
name: months:name
name: months:name
name: months:name
name: months:name
name: months:name
name: months:name
name: months:name
name: months:name
name: months:name
name: months:name
```

```
name: months:name
name: months:name
name: xsl:output
name: xsl:variable
name: xsl:text
name: xsl:template
name: xsl:value-of
name: xsl:text
name: xsl:value-of
name: xsl:value-of
name: xsl:for-each
name: xsl:text
name: xsl:value-of
name: xsl:value-of
```

namespace-uri() Function — Returns the namespace URI of the first node in the argument node-set.

Synopsis

string **namespace-uri(***node-set?***)**

Inputs

A node-set. If the node-set is omitted, the `namespace-uri()` function creates a node-set that has the context node as its only member.

Output

The namespace URI of the first node in the argument node-set. If the argument node-set is empty, the first node has no namespace URI, or the first node has a namespace URI that is null, an empty string is returned. Be aware that the `namespace-uri()` function returns an empty string for all nodes other than element and attribute nodes.

Defined in

XPath section 4.1, Node Set Functions.

Example

Here is a stylesheet that uses the `document()` function to examine its own nodes and then invoke the `namespace-uri()` against each of them:

```
<?xml version="1.0"?>
<xsl:stylesheet version="1.0"
  xmlns:xsl="http://www.w3.org/1999/XSL/Transform"
  xmlns:months="Lookup table for month names">

  <months:name sequence="01">January</months:name>
  <months:name sequence="02">February</months:name>
  <months:name sequence="03">March</months:name>
  <months:name sequence="04">April</months:name>
  <months:name sequence="05">May</months:name>
```

```
  <months:name sequence="06">June</months:name>
  <months:name sequence="07">July</months:name>
  <months:name sequence="08">August</months:name>
  <months:name sequence="09">September</months:name>
  <months:name sequence="10">October</months:name>
  <months:name sequence="11">November</months:name>
  <months:name sequence="12">December</months:name>

  <xsl:output method="text"/>

  <xsl:variable name="newline">
<xsl:text>
</xsl:text>
  </xsl:variable>

  <xsl:template match="/">
    <xsl:value-of select="$newline"/>
    <xsl:text>A test of the namespace-uri() function:</xsl:text>

    <xsl:value-of select="$newline"/>
    <xsl:value-of select="$newline"/>
    <xsl:for-each select="document('')//*">
      <xsl:text>namespace URI: </xsl:text>
      <xsl:value-of select="namespace-uri()"/>
      <xsl:value-of select="$newline"/>
    </xsl:for-each>
  </xsl:template>

</xsl:stylesheet>
```

Here are the results of our stylesheet:

```
A test of the namespace-uri() function:

namespace URI: http://www.w3.org/1999/XSL/Transform
namespace URI: Lookup table for month names
namespace URI: Lookup table for month names
namespace URI: Lookup table for month names
namespace URI: Lookup table for month names
namespace URI: Lookup table for month names
namespace URI: Lookup table for month names
namespace URI: Lookup table for month names
namespace URI: Lookup table for month names
namespace URI: Lookup table for month names
namespace URI: Lookup table for month names
namespace URI: Lookup table for month names
namespace URI: Lookup table for month names
namespace URI: http://www.w3.org/1999/XSL/Transform
namespace URI: http://www.w3.org/1999/XSL/Transform
namespace URI: http://www.w3.org/1999/XSL/Transform
```

```
namespace URI: http://www.w3.org/1999/XSL/Transform
namespace URI: http://www.w3.org/1999/XSL/Transform
namespace URI: http://www.w3.org/1999/XSL/Transform
namespace URI: http://www.w3.org/1999/XSL/Transform
namespace URI: http://www.w3.org/1999/XSL/Transform
namespace URI: http://www.w3.org/1999/XSL/Transform
namespace URI: http://www.w3.org/1999/XSL/Transform
namespace URI: http://www.w3.org/1999/XSL/Transform
namespace URI: http://www.w3.org/1999/XSL/Transform
```

normalize-space() Function — Removes extra whitespace from its argument string.

Synopsis

string **normalize-space(***string?***)**

Inputs

An optional string. If the argument is omitted, the `normalize-space()` function uses the string value of the context node.

Output

The argument string, with whitespace removed as follows:

- All leading whitespace is removed.
- All trailing whitespace is removed.
- Within the string, any sequence of whitespace characters is replaced with a single space.

Defined in

XPath section 4.2, String Functions.

Example

Here is a short example that demonstrates how `normalize-space()` works:

```
<?xml version="1.0"?>
<xsl:stylesheet version="1.0" xmlns:xsl="http://www.w3.org/1999/XSL/Transform">

  <xsl:output method="text"/>

  <xsl:variable name="newline">
<xsl:text>
</xsl:text>
  </xsl:variable>
```

```
  <xsl:variable name="testString">
    <xsl:text>                    This
is


a string
with lots of


whitespace.

</xsl:text>
    </xsl:variable>

  <xsl:template match="/">
    <xsl:value-of select="$newline"/>
    <xsl:text>Tests of the normalize-space() function:</xsl:text>

    <xsl:value-of select="$newline"/>
    <xsl:value-of select="$newline"/>
    <xsl:text>   normalize-space('       Hello,            World!')="</xsl:text>
    <xsl:value-of select="normalize-space('       Hello,            World!')"/>
    <xsl:text>"</xsl:text>
    <xsl:value-of select="$newline"/>
    <xsl:text>   normalize-space($newline)="</xsl:text>
    <xsl:value-of select="normalize-space($newline)"/>
    <xsl:text>"</xsl:text>
    <xsl:value-of select="$newline"/>
    <xsl:text>   normalize-space($testString)="</xsl:text>
    <xsl:value-of select="normalize-space($testString)"/>
    <xsl:text>"</xsl:text>
    <xsl:value-of select="$newline"/>
  </xsl:template>

</xsl:stylesheet>
```

The stylesheet generates this output:

```
Tests of the normalize-space() function:

   normalize-space('       Hello,            World!')="Hello, World!"
   normalize-space($newline)=""
   normalize-space($testString)="This is a string with lots of whitespace."
```

not() Function — Returns the negation of its argument. If the argument is not a boolean value already, it is converted to a boolean value using the rules described in the `boolean()` function entry.

Synopsis

`boolean` **`not(`**`*boolean*`**`)`**

Inputs

A boolean value, or more commonly, an XPath expression that evaluates to a boolean value.

Output

`false` if the input parameter is `true`; `true` if the input parameter is `false`.

Defined in

XPath section 4.3, Boolean Functions.

Example

To demonstrate the `not()` function, we'll use the same stylesheet and XML document we used for the `boolean()` function. Here's our XML document:

```
<?xml version="1.0"?>
<test>
<p>This is a test XML document used by several
of our sample stylesheets.</p>
<question>
<text>When completed, the Eiffel Tower was the
tallest building in the world.</text>
<true>Yes!  The Eiffel Tower was the world's
tallest building until 1932, when
New York's Empire State Building opened. </true>
<false>No, the Eiffel Tower was the world's
tallest building for over 30 years.</false>
</question>
</test>
```

We'll process this document with the following stylesheet, which uses the `not()` to negate all `boolean()` function calls:

```
<?xml version="1.0"?>
<xsl:stylesheet version="1.0" xmlns:xsl="http://www.w3.org/1999/XSL/Transform">

  <xsl:output method="text"/>

  <xsl:variable name="newline">
<xsl:text>
</xsl:text>
  </xsl:variable>

  <xsl:template match="/">
```

```
<xsl:value-of select="$newline"/>
<xsl:text>Tests of the not() function:</xsl:text>

<xsl:value-of select="$newline"/>
<xsl:value-of select="$newline"/>
<xsl:choose>
  <xsl:when test="not(boolean(true()))">
    <xsl:text>   "not(boolean(true()))"   returned true!</xsl:text>
  </xsl:when>
  <xsl:otherwise>
    <xsl:text>   "not(boolean(true()))"   returned false!</xsl:text>
  </xsl:otherwise>
</xsl:choose>

<xsl:value-of select="$newline"/>
<xsl:choose>
  <xsl:when test="not(boolean(true))">
    <xsl:text>   "not(boolean(true))"     returned true!</xsl:text>
  </xsl:when>
  <xsl:otherwise>
    <xsl:text>   "not(boolean(true))"     returned false!</xsl:text>
  </xsl:otherwise>
</xsl:choose>

<xsl:value-of select="$newline"/>
<xsl:choose>
  <xsl:when test="not(boolean('false'))">
    <xsl:text>   "not(boolean('false'))"  returned true!</xsl:text>
  </xsl:when>
  <xsl:otherwise>
    <xsl:text>   "not(boolean('false'))"  returned false!</xsl:text>
  </xsl:otherwise>
</xsl:choose>

<xsl:value-of select="$newline"/>
<xsl:choose>
  <xsl:when test="not(boolean('7'))">
    <xsl:text>   "not(boolean('7'))"      returned true!</xsl:text>
  </xsl:when>
  <xsl:otherwise>
    <xsl:text>   "not(boolean('7'))"      returned false!</xsl:text>
  </xsl:otherwise>
</xsl:choose>

<xsl:value-of select="$newline"/>
<xsl:choose>
  <xsl:when test="not(boolean(/true))">
    <xsl:text>   "not(boolean(/true))"    returned true!</xsl:text>
  </xsl:when>
  <xsl:otherwise>
```

```
        <xsl:text>   "not(boolean(/true))"   returned false!</xsl:text>
      </xsl:otherwise>
    </xsl:choose>

    <xsl:value-of select="$newline"/>
    <xsl:choose>
      <xsl:when test="not(boolean(//true))">
        <xsl:text>   "not(boolean(//true))"  returned true!</xsl:text>
      </xsl:when>
      <xsl:otherwise>
        <xsl:text>   "not(boolean(//true))"  returned false!</xsl:text>
      </xsl:otherwise>
    </xsl:choose>
  </xsl:template>

</xsl:stylesheet>
```

Here are the results:

```
Tests of the not() function:

   "not(boolean(true()))"   returned false!
   "not(boolean(true))"     returned true!
   "not(boolean('false'))"  returned false!
   "not(boolean('7'))"      returned false!
   "not(boolean(/true))"    returned true!
   "not(boolean(//true))"   returned false!
```

As you'd expect, these results are the exact opposite of the results we got when we tested the `boolean()` function.

number() Function — Converts its argument to a number.

Synopsis

`number` **`number(`**`*object?*`**`)`**

Inputs

An object. The object is converted to a number as described in the following subsection.

Output

A number. The object is converted to a number as follows:

- If the argument is a boolean value, the value `true` is converted to the number `1`; the value `false` is converted to the number `0`.
- If the argument is a node-set, the node-set is converted to a string as if it were passed to the `string()` function, then that string is converted to a number like any other string. (Remember that the `string()` function returns the string value of the first node in the node-set.)

- If the argument is a string, it is converted as follows:
  - If the string consists of optional whitespace, followed by an optional minus sign (-), followed by a number, followed by whitespace, it is converted to the floating-point value nearest to the mathematical value represented by the string. (The IEEE 754 standard defines a `round-to-nearest` rule; see the standard for more information.)
  - Any other string is converted to the value `NaN` (not a number).
- If the argument is any other type, it is converted to a number in a way that depends on that type. See the documentation for your XSLT processor to find out what other types are supported and how they are converted to numbers.

Defined in

XPath section 4.4, Number Functions.

Example

Here is the XML document we'll use to test the `number()` function:

```
<?xml version="1.0"?>
<report>
  <title>Miles Flown in 2001</title>
  <month sequence="01">
    <miles-flown>12379</miles-flown>
    <miles-earned>35215</miles-earned>
  </month>
  <month sequence="02">
    <miles-flown>32857</miles-flown>
    <miles-earned>92731</miles-earned>
  </month>
  <month sequence="03">
    <miles-flown>19920</miles-flown>
    <miles-earned>76725</miles-earned>
  </month>
  <month sequence="04">
    <miles-flown>18903</miles-flown>
    <miles-earned>31781</miles-earned>
  </month>
</report>
```

We'll test the `number()` function with a variety of arguments:

```
<?xml version="1.0"?>
<xsl:stylesheet version="1.0"
  xmlns:xsl="http://www.w3.org/1999/XSL/Transform">

  <xsl:output method="text"/>
```

```
  <xsl:variable name="newline">
<xsl:text>
</xsl:text>
  </xsl:variable>

  <xsl:template match="/">
    <xsl:value-of select="$newline"/>
    <xsl:text>Tests of the number() function:</xsl:text>

    <xsl:value-of select="$newline"/>
    <xsl:value-of select="$newline"/>
    <xsl:text>   number(true())=</xsl:text>
    <xsl:value-of select="number(true())"/>
    <xsl:value-of select="$newline"/>
    <xsl:text>   number(false())=</xsl:text>
    <xsl:value-of select="number(false())"/>
    <xsl:value-of select="$newline"/>
    <xsl:text>   number(/report/month[2]/miles-flown)=</xsl:text>
    <xsl:value-of select="number(/report/month[2]/miles-flown)"/>
    <xsl:value-of select="$newline"/>
    <xsl:text>   number(//miles-flown)=</xsl:text>
    <xsl:value-of select="number(//miles-flown)"/>
    <xsl:value-of select="$newline"/>
    <xsl:text>   number(/report/title)=</xsl:text>
    <xsl:value-of select="number(/report/title)"/>
  </xsl:template>

</xsl:stylesheet>
```

The output of our stylesheet looks like this:

```
Tests of the number() function:

   number(true())=1
   number(false())=0
   number(/report/month[2]/miles-flown)=32857
   number(//miles-flown)=12379
   number(/report/title)=NaN
```

---

position() Function — Returns a number equal to the context position from the current context.

Synopsis

number **position()**

Inputs

None.

Output

A number equal to the position of the current node in the evaluation context.

Defined in

XPath section 4.1, Node Set Functions.

Examples

This example uses the `position()` function to determine the background color of the rows of a table. The background colors cycle through the options `white`, `darkgray`, and `light-green`. Here's the XML document we'll use:

```
<?xml version="1.0"?>
<list>
  <title>A few of my favorite albums</title>
  <listitem>A Love Supreme</listitem>
  <listitem>Beat Crazy</listitem>
  <listitem>Here Come the Warm Jets</listitem>
  <listitem>Kind of Blue</listitem>
  <listitem>London Calling</listitem>
  <listitem>Remain in Light</listitem>
  <listitem>The Joshua Tree</listitem>
  <listitem>The Indestructible Beat of Soweto</listitem>
</list>
```

We'll use this stylesheet to generate our HTML document:

```
<?xml version="1.0"?>
<xsl:stylesheet version="1.0" xmlns:xsl="http://www.w3.org/1999/XSL/Transform">

  <xsl:output method="html"/>

  <xsl:template match="/">
    <html>
      <head>
        <title>
          <xsl:value-of select="/list/title"/>
        </title>
      </head>
      <body>
        <h1>
          <xsl:value-of select="/list/title"/>
        </h1>
        <table border="1">
          <xsl:for-each select="/list/listitem">
            <xsl:variable name="background-color">
              <xsl:choose>
                <xsl:when test="position() mod 3 = 1">white</xsl:when>
```

```
                <xsl:when test="position() mod 3 = 2">darkgray</xsl:when>
                <xsl:otherwise>lightgreen</xsl:otherwise>
              </xsl:choose>
            </xsl:variable>
            <tr bgcolor="{$background-color}">
              <td>
                <b><xsl:value-of select="."/></b>
              </td>
            </tr>
          </xsl:for-each>
        </table>
      </body>
    </html>
  </xsl:template>

</xsl:stylesheet>
```

Our stylesheet generates the following results:

```
<html>
<head>
<META http-equiv="Content-Type" content="text/html; charset=UTF-8">
<title>A few of my favorite albums</title>
</head>
<body>
<h1>A few of my favorite albums</h1>
<table border="1">
<tr bgcolor="white">
<td><b>A Love Supreme</b></td>
</tr>
<tr bgcolor="darkgray">
<td><b>Beat Crazy</b></td>
</tr>
<tr bgcolor="lightgreen">
<td><b>Here Come the Warm Jets</b></td>
</tr>
<tr bgcolor="white">
<td><b>Kind of Blue</b></td>
</tr>
<tr bgcolor="darkgray">
<td><b>London Calling</b></td>
</tr>
<tr bgcolor="lightgreen">
<td><b>Remain in Light</b></td>
</tr>
<tr bgcolor="white">
<td><b>The Joshua Tree</b></td>
</tr>
<tr bgcolor="darkgray">
<td><b>The Indestructible Beat of Soweto</b></td>
```

```
</tr>
</table>
</body>
</html>
```

When rendered, the HTML file looks like Figure C-8.

Figure C-8. HTML file displaying items with different background colors

round() Function — Returns the integer closest to the argument.

Synopsis

`number **round(**number**)**`

Description

If two numbers are equally close to the argument (`1` and `2` are equally close to `1.5`), the number closest to positive infinity is returned. Various argument values are handled as follows:

- If the argument is `NaN` (not a number), the `round()` function returns `NaN`.
- If the argument is positive infinity, then positive infinity is returned.
- If the argument is negative infinity, then negative infinity is returned.
- If the argument is positive zero, then positive zero is returned.

- If the argument is negative zero, then negative zero is returned.
- If the argument is between zero and -0.5, then negative zero is returned.

Inputs

A number. If the argument is not a number, it is converted to a number as if it were passed to the `number()` function.

Output

The integer that is closest to the argument. Special cases are handled as described in this section.

Defined in

XPath section 4.4, Number Functions.

Example

The following stylesheet shows the results of invoking the `round()` function against a variety of values. We'll use this XML document as input:

```
<?xml version="1.0"?>
<report>
  <title>Miles Flown in 2001</title>
  <month sequence="01">
    <miles-flown>12379</miles-flown>
    <miles-earned>35215</miles-earned>
  </month>
  <month sequence="02">
    <miles-flown>32857</miles-flown>
    <miles-earned>92731</miles-earned>
  </month>
  <month sequence="03">
    <miles-flown>19920</miles-flown>
    <miles-earned>76725</miles-earned>
  </month>
  <month sequence="04">
    <miles-flown>18903</miles-flown>
    <miles-earned>31781</miles-earned>
  </month>
</report>
```

Here's the stylesheet that uses the `round()` function:

```
<?xml version="1.0"?>
<xsl:stylesheet version="1.0"
  xmlns:xsl="http://www.w3.org/1999/XSL/Transform"
  xmlns:months="Lookup table for month names">

  <months:name sequence="01">January</months:name>
  <months:name sequence="02">February</months:name>
  <months:name sequence="03">March</months:name>
```

```
  <months:name sequence="04">April</months:name>
  <months:name sequence="05">May</months:name>
  <months:name sequence="06">June</months:name>
  <months:name sequence="07">July</months:name>
  <months:name sequence="08">August</months:name>
  <months:name sequence="09">September</months:name>
  <months:name sequence="10">October</months:name>
  <months:name sequence="11">November</months:name>
  <months:name sequence="12">December</months:name>

  <xsl:output method="text"/>

  <xsl:variable name="newline">
<xsl:text>
</xsl:text>
  </xsl:variable>

  <xsl:template match="/">
    <xsl:value-of select="$newline"/>
    <xsl:text>Tests of the round() function:</xsl:text>

    <xsl:value-of select="$newline"/>
    <xsl:value-of select="$newline"/>
    <xsl:text>   "round('7.983')" = </xsl:text>
    <xsl:value-of select="round('7.983')"/>

    <xsl:value-of select="$newline"/>
    <xsl:text>   "round('7.5')" = </xsl:text>
    <xsl:value-of select="round('7.5')"/>

    <xsl:value-of select="$newline"/>
    <xsl:text>   "round('-7.893')" = </xsl:text>
    <xsl:value-of select="round('-7.893')"/>

    <xsl:value-of select="$newline"/>
    <xsl:text>   "round('-7.5')" = </xsl:text>
    <xsl:value-of select="round('-7.5')"/>

    <xsl:value-of select="$newline"/>
    <xsl:text>   "round(/report/month[@sequence='01']/miles-flown)" = </xsl:text>
    <xsl:value-of select="round(/report/month[@sequence='01']/miles-flown)"/>

    <xsl:value-of select="$newline"/>
    <xsl:text>   "round(document('')/*/months:name[@sequence='02'])" = </xsl:text>
    <xsl:value-of select="round(document('')/*/months:name[@sequence='02'])"/>

    <xsl:value-of select="$newline"/>
    <xsl:value-of select="$newline"/>
```

```
    <xsl:for-each select="/report/month">
      <xsl:text>    </xsl:text>
      <xsl:value-of
        select="document('')/*/months:name[@sequence=current()/@sequence]"/>
      <xsl:text> - </xsl:text>
      <xsl:value-of select="format-number(miles-flown, '##,###')"/>
      <xsl:text> miles flown, </xsl:text>
      <xsl:value-of select="format-number(miles-earned, '##,###')"/>
      <xsl:text> miles earned.</xsl:text>
      <xsl:value-of select="$newline"/>
      <xsl:text>        (Averaged </xsl:text>
      <xsl:value-of select="round(miles-earned div miles-flown)"/>
      <xsl:text> miles earned for each mile flown.)</xsl:text>
      <xsl:value-of select="$newline"/>
    </xsl:for-each>
  </xsl:template>

</xsl:stylesheet>
```

When we process our XML document with this stylesheet, the results are:

```
Tests of the round() function:

   "round('7.983')" = 8
   "round('7.5')" = 8
   "round('-7.893')" = -8
   "round('-7.5')" = -7
   "round(/report/month[@sequence='01']/miles-flown)" = 12379
   "round(document('')/*/months:name[@sequence='02'])" = NaN

   January - 12,379 miles flown, 35,215 miles earned.
       (Averaged 3 miles earned for each mile flown.)

   February - 32,857 miles flown, 92,731 miles earned.
       (Averaged 3 miles earned for each mile flown.)

   March - 19,920 miles flown, 76,725 miles earned.
       (Averaged 4 miles earned for each mile flown.)

   April - 18,903 miles flown, 31,781 miles earned.
       (Averaged 2 miles earned for each mile flown.)
```

You can compare these results to those from the `ceiling()` and `floor()` functions.

starts-with() Function — Determines if the first argument string begins with the second argument.

Synopsis

boolean **starts-with(***string*, *string***)**

Inputs

Two strings.

Output

If the first string begins with the second, `starts-with()` returns the boolean value `true`; otherwise it returns `false`.

Defined in

XPath section 4.2, String Functions.

Example

We'll use this sample XML document:

```
<?xml version="1.0"?>
<list>
  <title>A few of my favorite albums</title>
  <listitem>A Love Supreme</listitem>
  <listitem>Beat Crazy</listitem>
  <listitem>Here Come the Warm Jets</listitem>
  <listitem>Kind of Blue</listitem>
  <listitem>London Calling</listitem>
  <listitem>Remain in Light</listitem>
  <listitem>The Joshua Tree</listitem>
  <listitem>The Indestructible Beat of Soweto</listitem>
</list>
```

This stylesheet outputs contents of all `<listitem>` elements that begin with the string "The":

```
<?xml version="1.0"?>
<xsl:stylesheet version="1.0" xmlns:xsl="http://www.w3.org/1999/XSL/Transform">

  <xsl:output method="text"/>

  <xsl:variable name="newline">
<xsl:text>
</xsl:text>
  </xsl:variable>

  <xsl:template match="/">
    <xsl:value-of select="$newline"/>
    <xsl:for-each select="list/listitem">
      <xsl:if test="starts-with(., 'The')">
        <xsl:value-of select="position()"/>
        <xsl:text>. </xsl:text>
```

```
        <xsl:value-of select="."/>
        <xsl:value-of select="$newline"/>
      </xsl:if>
    </xsl:for-each>
  </xsl:template>

</xsl:stylesheet>
```

Our stylesheet generates this result:

```
7. The Joshua Tree
8. The Indestructible Beat of Soweto
```

string() Function — Returns the string value of the argument.

Synopsis

`string` **`string(`**`object`**`)`**

Inputs

An object. The object is converted to a string, as described in the following subsection.

Output

A string. The input argument is converted to a string as follows:

- If the argument is a node-set, the first node in the node-set is converted to a string. (The first node in the node-set is the one that occurs first in document order.)
- If the argument is a number, it is converted to a string as follows:
  - The value `NaN` is converted to the string "NaN".
  - Positive zero is converted to the string "0".
  - Negative zero is converted to the string "0".
  - Positive infinity is converted to the string "Infinity".
  - Negative infinity is converted to the string "-Infinity".
  - An integer is converted to a string representing that integer, using no decimal point and no leading zeros. If the integer is negative, it will be preceded by a minus sign (-).
  - Any other number is converted to a string with a decimal point, at least one number before the decimal point, and at least one number after the decimal point. If the number is negative, it will be preceded by a minus sign (-). There will not be any leading zeros before the decimal point (with the possible exception of the one required digit before the decimal point). After the decimal point, there will be only as many digits as needed to distinguish this number from all other numeric values defined by the IEEE 754 standard, the same standard used by the Java `float` and `double` types.

- If the argument is a boolean value, the value `true` is represented by the string "true" and the value `false` is represented by the string "false".
- If the argument is any other type, it is converted to a string in a way that depends on that type. See the documentation for your XSLT processor to find out what other types are supported and how they are converted to strings.

Defined in

XPath section 4.2, String Functions.

Example

Here is the XML document we'll use to test the `string()` function:

```
<?xml version="1.0"?>
<test>
  <p>This is a test XML document used by several
  of our sample stylesheets.</p>
  <question>
    <text>When completed, the Eiffel Tower was the
    tallest building in the world.</text>
    <true>You're correct!  The Eiffel Tower was the
    world's tallest building until 1930.</true>
    <false>No, the Eiffel Tower was the world's
    tallest building for over 30 years.</false>
  </question>
  <question>
    <text>New York's Empire State Building knocked
    the Eiffel Tower from its pedestal.</text>
    <true>No, that's not correct.</true>
    <false>Correct!  New York's Chrysler Building,
    completed in 1930, became the world's tallest.</false>
  </question>
</test>
```

We'll test the `string()` function with a variety of arguments:

```
<?xml version="1.0"?>
<xsl:stylesheet version="1.0" xmlns:xsl="http://www.w3.org/1999/XSL/Transform">

  <xsl:output method="text"/>

  <xsl:variable name="newline">
<xsl:text>
</xsl:text>
  </xsl:variable>

  <xsl:template match="/">
    <xsl:value-of select="$newline"/>
    <xsl:text>Tests of the string() function:</xsl:text>
```

```
    <xsl:value-of select="$newline"/>
    <xsl:value-of select="$newline"/>
    <xsl:text>   string(count(/test))=</xsl:text>
    <xsl:value-of select="string(count(/test))"/>
    <xsl:value-of select="$newline"/>
    <xsl:text>   string(count(/test/question))=</xsl:text>
    <xsl:value-of select="string(count(/test/question))"/>
    <xsl:value-of select="$newline"/>
    <xsl:text>   string('4')=</xsl:text>
    <xsl:value-of select="string('4')"/>
    <xsl:value-of select="$newline"/>
    <xsl:text>   string(true())=</xsl:text>
    <xsl:value-of select="string(true())"/>
    <xsl:value-of select="$newline"/>
    <xsl:text>   string(false())=</xsl:text>
    <xsl:value-of select="string(false())"/>
    <xsl:value-of select="$newline"/>
    <xsl:text>   string(count(/test/question) > 5)=</xsl:text>
    <xsl:value-of select="string(count(/test/question) > 5)"/>
    <xsl:value-of select="$newline"/>
    <xsl:value-of select="$newline"/>
    <xsl:text>Here are the string values of some <text> elements:</xsl:text>
    <xsl:value-of select="$newline"/>
    <xsl:for-each select="/test/question/text">
      <xsl:text>   </xsl:text>
      <xsl:value-of select="string(.)"/>
      <xsl:value-of select="$newline"/>
    </xsl:for-each>
  </xsl:template>

</xsl:stylesheet>
```

Here are the results of our stylesheet:

```
Tests of the string() function:

   string(count(/test))=1
   string(count(/test/question))=2
   string('4')=4
   string(true())=true
   string(false())=false
   string(count(/test/question) > 5)=false

Here are the string values of some <text> elements:
   When completed, the Eiffel Tower was the tallest building in the world.
   New York's Empire State Building knocked the Eiffel Tower from its pedestal.
```

string-length() Function — Returns the number of characters in the string passed in as the argument to this function. If no argument is specified, the context node is converted to a string and the length of that string is returned.

Synopsis

number **string-length(***string?***)**

Inputs

An optional string.

Output

The number of characters defined in the string.

Defined in

XPath section 4.2, String Functions.

Example

The following example demonstrates the results of invoking the `string-length()` function against various argument types. Here's the XML document we'll use for our example:

```
<?xml version="1.0"?>
<test>
  <p>This is a test XML document used by several
  of our sample stylesheets.</p>
  <question>
    <text>When completed, the Eiffel Tower was the
    tallest building in the world.</text>
    <true>You're correct!  The Eiffel Tower was the
    world's tallest building until 1930.</true>
    <false>No, the Eiffel Tower was the world's
    tallest building for over 30 years.</false>
  </question>
  <question>
    <text>New York's Empire State Building knocked
    the Eiffel Tower from its pedestal.</text>
    <true>No, that's not correct.</true>
    <false>Correct!  New York's Chrysler Building,
    completed in 1930, became the world's tallest.</false>
  </question>
</test>
```

We'll process this document with the following stylesheet:

```
<?xml version="1.0"?>
<xsl:stylesheet version="1.0" xmlns:xsl="http://www.w3.org/1999/XSL/Transform">
```

```
  <xsl:output method="text"/>

  <xsl:variable name="newline">
<xsl:text>
</xsl:text>
  </xsl:variable>

  <xsl:template match="/">
    <xsl:value-of select="$newline"/>
    <xsl:text>Tests of the string-length() function:</xsl:text>

    <xsl:value-of select="$newline"/>
    <xsl:value-of select="$newline"/>
    <xsl:text>   string-length(/test)=</xsl:text>
    <xsl:value-of select="string-length(/test)"/>
    <xsl:value-of select="$newline"/>
    <xsl:text>   string-length(/true)=</xsl:text>
    <xsl:value-of select="string-length(/true)"/>
    <xsl:value-of select="$newline"/>
    <xsl:text>   string-length(//true)=</xsl:text>
    <xsl:value-of select="string-length(//true)"/>
    <xsl:value-of select="$newline"/>
    <xsl:text>   string-length(//test|//true|//text)=</xsl:text>
    <xsl:value-of select="string-length(//test|//true|//text)"/>
    <xsl:value-of select="$newline"/>
    <xsl:value-of select="$newline"/>
    <xsl:for-each select="/test/question">
      <xsl:text>   Question #</xsl:text>
      <xsl:value-of select="position()"/>
      <xsl:text> contains </xsl:text>
      <xsl:value-of select="string-length()"/>
      <xsl:text> characters.</xsl:text>
      <xsl:value-of select="$newline"/>
    </xsl:for-each>
  </xsl:template>

</xsl:stylesheet>
```

Here are the results of our stylesheet:

```
Tests of the string-length() function:

   string-length(/test)=522
   string-length(/true)=0
   string-length(//true)=78
   string-length(//test|//true|//text)=522

   Question #1 contains 239 characters.
   Question #2 contains 203 characters.
```

When we invoked the `string-length()` function without any arguments, the context node was converted to a string, then the length of that string was returned. The two `<question>` elements were handled this way inside the `<xsl:for-each>` element.

substring() Function — Returns a portion of a given string. The second and third arguments determine what portion of the string is returned. The second argument specifies the position of the first character of the substring, and the optional third argument specifies how many characters should be returned.

Synopsis

string **substring(***string*, *number*, *number?***)**

Inputs

The `substring()` function takes a string and one or two numbers as arguments. The string is the string from which the substring will be extracted. The second argument is used as the starting position of the returned substring, and the optional third argument specifies how many characters are returned.

Output

With two arguments (a string and a starting position), the `substring()` function returns all characters in the string, starting with the starting position. Be aware that the first character in an XPath string is at position 1, not 0.

With three arguments (a string, a starting position, and a length), the `substring()` function returns all characters in the string whose position is greater than or equal to the starting position and whose position is less than or equal to the starting position plus the length.

Normally, the arguments to the `substring()` function are integers, although they may be more complicated expressions. See the "Example" section that follows for some unusual cases.

Defined in

XPath section 4.2, String Functions.

Example

We'll use this XML document to demonstrate how the `substring()` function works:

```
<?xml version="1.0"?>
<test>
  <p>This is a test XML document used by several
    of our sample stylesheets.</p>
  <question>
    <text>When completed, the Eiffel Tower was the
    tallest building in the world.</text>
    <true>You're correct!  The Eiffel Tower was the
    world's tallest building until 1930.</true>
```

```
    <false>No, the Eiffel Tower was the world's
    tallest building for over 30 years.</false>
  </question>
  <question>
    <text>New York's Empire State Building knocked the
    Eiffel Tower from its pedestal.</text>
    <true>No, that's not correct.</true>
    <false>Correct!  New York's Chrysler Building,
    completed in 1930, became the world's tallest.</false>
  </question>
</test>
```

Here's the stylesheet we'll use:

```
<?xml version="1.0"?>
<xsl:stylesheet version="1.0" xmlns:xsl="http://www.w3.org/1999/XSL/Transform">

  <xsl:output method="text"/>

  <xsl:variable name="newline">
<xsl:text>
</xsl:text>
  </xsl:variable>

  <xsl:template match="/">
    <xsl:value-of select="$newline"/>
    <xsl:text>Tests of the substring() function:</xsl:text>

    <xsl:value-of select="$newline"/>
    <xsl:value-of select="$newline"/>
    <xsl:text>   substring('Now is the time', 4)="</xsl:text>
    <xsl:value-of select="substring('Now is the time', 4)"/>
    <xsl:text>"</xsl:text>
    <xsl:value-of select="$newline"/>
    <xsl:text>   substring('Now is the time', 4, 6)="</xsl:text>
    <xsl:value-of select="substring('Now is the time', 4, 6)"/>
    <xsl:text>"</xsl:text>
    <xsl:value-of select="$newline"/>
    <xsl:text>   substring('Now is the time', 4, -6)="</xsl:text>
    <xsl:value-of select="substring('Now is the time', 4, -6)"/>
    <xsl:text>"</xsl:text>
    <xsl:value-of select="$newline"/>
    <xsl:text>   substring('Now is the time', -3, 6)="</xsl:text>
    <xsl:value-of select="substring('Now is the time', -3, 6)"/>
    <xsl:text>"</xsl:text>
    <xsl:value-of select="$newline"/>
    <xsl:text>   substring('Now is the time', 54, 6)="</xsl:text>
    <xsl:value-of select="substring('Now is the time', 54, 6)"/>
    <xsl:text>"</xsl:text>
```

```
    <xsl:value-of select="$newline"/>
    <xsl:value-of select="$newline"/>
    <xsl:text>   count(//*)=</xsl:text>
    <xsl:value-of select="count(//*)"/>
    <xsl:value-of select="$newline"/>
    <xsl:text>   substring('Here is a really long string', </xsl:text>
    <:xsl:text>count(//*))="</xsl:text>
    <xsl:value-of
      select="substring('Here is a really long string', count(//*))"/>
    <xsl:text>"</xsl:text>
    <xsl:value-of select="$newline"/>
    <xsl:text>   substring('Here is a less long string', </xsl:text>
    <xsl:text>count(//*) mod 7, 7)="</xsl:text>
    <xsl:value-of
      select="substring('Here is a less long string', count(//*) mod 7, 7)"/>
    <xsl:text>"</xsl:text>
    <xsl:value-of select="$newline"/>
    <xsl:text>   substring(/test/question[1]/text, 3, 7)="</xsl:text>
    <xsl:value-of select="substring(//*, 3, 7)"/>
    <xsl:text>"</xsl:text>
    <xsl:value-of select="$newline"/>
  </xsl:template>

</xsl:stylesheet>
```

When using the Saxon processor, here are the results:

```
Tests of the substring() function:

   substring('Now is the time', 4)=" is the time"
   substring('Now is the time', 4, 6)=" is th"
   substring('Now is the time', 4, -6)=""
   substring('Now is the time', -3, 6)="No"
   substring('Now is the time', 54, 6)=""

   count(//*)=10
   substring('Here is a really long string', count(//*))=" really long string"
   substring('Here is a less long string', count(//*) mod 7, 7)="re is a"
   substring(/test/question[1]/text, 3, 7)=" This i"
```

When running the same transformation with Xalan, we get a runtime error:

```
file:///D:/O'Reilly/XSLT/bookSamples/AppendixC/substringfunction.xsl; Line 26;
  Column 65;
Tests of the substring() function:
```

```
    substring('Now is the time', 4)=" is the time"
    substring('Now is the time', 4, 6)=" is th"
    substring('Now is the time', 4, -6)="
XSLT Error (javax.xml.transform.TransformerException): String index out of range
: -3
```

As of this writing, XT, Saxon, and Oracle's processors all gave the correct results; both Xalan and Microsoft's XSLT tools generated runtime exceptions. The lesson here is to use reasonable arguments to the `substring()` function so you won't be at the mercy of different implementations.

substring-after() Function — Returns the substring of the first argument after the first occurrence of the second argument in the first argument. If the second argument does not occur in the first argument, the `substring-after()` function returns an empty string.

Synopsis

string **substring-after(***string*, *string***)**

Inputs

Two strings. The first string is the string to be searched, and the second string is the string to be searched for in the first string.

Output

The portion of the first argument that occurs after the first occurrence of the second argument. If the second argument does not appear in the first argument, the function returns an empty string.

Defined in

XPath section 4.2, String Functions.

Example

This stylesheet uses the `replace-substring` named template. It passes three arguments to the `replace-substring` template: the original string, the substring to be searched for in the original string, and the substring to replace the target substring in the original string. The `replace-substring` template uses the `contains()`, `substring-after()`, and `substring-before()` functions extensively.

Here is our sample stylesheet. It replaces all occurrences of `World` with the string "Mundo":

```
<?xml version="1.0"?>
<xsl:stylesheet xmlns:xsl="http://www.w3.org/1999/XSL/Transform" version="1.0">

  <xsl:output method="text"/>

  <xsl:template match="/">
    <xsl:variable name="test">
      <xsl:call-template name="replace-substring">
        <xsl:with-param name="original">Hello World!</xsl:with-param>
        <xsl:with-param name="substring">World</xsl:with-param>
        <xsl:with-param name="replacement">Mundo</xsl:with-param>
      </xsl:call-template>
    </xsl:variable>
    <xsl:value-of select="$test"/>
  </xsl:template>

  <xsl:template name="replace-substring">
    <xsl:param name="original"/>
    <xsl:param name="substring"/>
    <xsl:param name="replacement" select="''"/>
    <xsl:variable name="first">
      <xsl:choose>
        <xsl:when test="contains($original, $substring)">
          <xsl:value-of select="substring-before($original, $substring)"/>
        </xsl:when>
        <xsl:otherwise>
          <xsl:value-of select="$original"/>
        </xsl:otherwise>
      </xsl:choose>
    </xsl:variable>


    <xsl:variable name="middle">
      <xsl:choose>
        <xsl:when test="contains($original, $substring)">
          <xsl:value-of select="$replacement"/>
        </xsl:when>
        <xsl:otherwise>
          <xsl:text></xsl:text>
        </xsl:otherwise>
      </xsl:choose>
    </xsl:variable>
    <xsl:variable name="last">
      <xsl:choose>
        <xsl:when test="contains($original, $substring)">
          <xsl:choose>
            <xsl:when test="contains(substring-after($original, $substring),
                             $substring)">
```

```
              <xsl:call-template name="replace-substring">
                <xsl:with-param name="original">
                  <xsl:value-of
                    select="substring-after($original, $substring)"/>
                </xsl:with-param>
                <xsl:with-param name="substring">
                  <xsl:value-of select="$substring"/>
                </xsl:with-param>
                <xsl:with-param name="replacement">
                  <xsl:value-of select="$replacement"/>
                </xsl:with-param>
              </xsl:call-template>
            </xsl:when>
            <xsl:otherwise>
              <xsl:value-of select="substring-after($original, $substring)"/>
            </xsl:otherwise>
          </xsl:choose>
        </xsl:when>
        <xsl:otherwise>
          <xsl:text></xsl:text>
        </xsl:otherwise>
      </xsl:choose>
    </xsl:variable>
    <xsl:value-of select="concat($first, $middle, $last)"/>
  </xsl:template>

</xsl:stylesheet>
```

The stylesheet produces these results, regardless of the XML document used as input:

```
Hello Mundo!
```

substring-before() Function — Returns the substring of the first argument before the first occurrence of the second argument in the first argument. If the second argument does not occur in the first argument, the `substring-before()` function returns an empty string.

Synopsis

string **`substring-before(`***`string`*, *`string`***`)`**

Inputs

Two strings. The first string is the string to be searched, and the second string is the string to be searched for in the first string.

Output

The portion of the first argument that occurs before the first occurrence of the second argument. If the second argument does not appear in the first argument, the function returns an empty string.

Defined in

XPath section 4.2, String Functions.

Example

This stylesheet uses the `replace-substring` named template. It passes three arguments to the `replace-substring` template: the original string, the substring to be searched for in the original string, and the substring to replace the target substring in the original string. The `replace-substring` template uses the `contains()`, `substring-after()`, and `substring-before()` functions extensively.

Here is our sample stylesheet. It replaces all occurrences of `World` with the string "Mundo":

```
<?xml version="1.0"?>
<xsl:stylesheet xmlns:xsl="http://www.w3.org/1999/XSL/Transform" version="1.0">

  <xsl:output method="text"/>

  <xsl:template match="/">
    <xsl:variable name="test">
      <xsl:call-template name="replace-substring">
        <xsl:with-param name="original">Hello World!</xsl:with-param>
        <xsl:with-param name="substring">World</xsl:with-param>
        <xsl:with-param name="replacement">Mundo</xsl:with-param>
      </xsl:call-template>
    </xsl:variable>
    <xsl:value-of select="$test"/>
  </xsl:template>

  <xsl:template name="replace-substring">
    <xsl:param name="original"/>
    <xsl:param name="substring"/>
    <xsl:param name="replacement" select="''"/>
    <xsl:variable name="first">
      <xsl:choose>
        <xsl:when test="contains($original, $substring)">
          <xsl:value-of select="substring-before($original, $substring)"/>
        </xsl:when>
        <xsl:otherwise>
          <xsl:value-of select="$original"/>
        </xsl:otherwise>
      </xsl:choose>
    </xsl:variable>
    <xsl:variable name="middle">
      <xsl:choose>
        <xsl:when test="contains($original, $substring)">
```

```
          <xsl:value-of select="$replacement"/>
        </xsl:when>
        <xsl:otherwise>
          <xsl:text></xsl:text>
        </xsl:otherwise>
      </xsl:choose>
    </xsl:variable>
    <xsl:variable name="last">
      <xsl:choose>
        <xsl:when test="contains($original, $substring)">
          <xsl:choose>
            <xsl:when test="contains(substring-after($original, $substring),
                                     $substring)">
              <xsl:call-template name="replace-substring">
                <xsl:with-param name="original">
                  <xsl:value-of
                    select="substring-after($original, $substring)"/>
                </xsl:with-param>
                <xsl:with-param name="substring">
                  <xsl:value-of select="$substring"/>
                </xsl:with-param>
                <xsl:with-param name="replacement">
                  <xsl:value-of select="$replacement"/>
                </xsl:with-param>
              </xsl:call-template>
            </xsl:when>
            <xsl:otherwise>
              <xsl:value-of select="substring-after($original, $substring)"/>
            </xsl:otherwise>
          </xsl:choose>
        </xsl:when>
        <xsl:otherwise>
          <xsl:text></xsl:text>
        </xsl:otherwise>
      </xsl:choose>
    </xsl:variable>
    <xsl:value-of select="concat($first, $middle, $last)"/>
  </xsl:template>

</xsl:stylesheet>
```

The stylesheet produces these results, regardless of the XML document used as input:

```
Hello Mundo!
```

sum() Function — Converts all nodes in the argument node-set to numbers, and then returns the sum of all of those numbers. If any node in the node-set can't be converted to numbers (passing them to the `number()` function returns `NaN`), the `sum()` function returns `NaN`.

Synopsis

`number` **`sum(`***`node-set`***`)`**

Inputs

A node-set. Any node in the node-set that is not a number is converted to a number as if it were passed to the `number()` function, then the numeric values of all of the nodes are summed.

Output

The sum of the numeric values of all of the nodes in the argument node-set. If any node in the argument node-set cannot be converted to a number, the `sum()` function returns `NaN`.

Defined in

XPath section 4.4, Number Functions.

Example

We'll demonstrate the `sum()` function against the following XML document:

```
<?xml version="1.0"?>
<report>
  <title>Miles Flown in 2001</title>
  <month sequence="01">
    <miles-flown>12379</miles-flown>
    <miles-earned>35215</miles-earned>
  </month>
  <month sequence="02">
    <miles-flown>32857</miles-flown>
    <miles-earned>92731</miles-earned>
  </month>
  <month sequence="03">
    <miles-flown>19920</miles-flown>
    <miles-earned>76725</miles-earned>
  </month>
  <month sequence="04">
    <miles-flown>18903</miles-flown>
    <miles-earned>31781</miles-earned>
  </month>
</report>
```

Here is a stylesheet that uses the `sum()` function:

```
<?xml version="1.0"?>
<xsl:stylesheet version="1.0"
  xmlns:xsl="http://www.w3.org/1999/XSL/Transform">

  <xsl:output method="text"/>

  <xsl:variable name="newline">
<xsl:text>
</xsl:text>
  </xsl:variable>

  <xsl:template match="/">
    <xsl:value-of select="$newline"/>
    <xsl:text>A test of the sum() function:</xsl:text>

    <xsl:value-of select="$newline"/>
    <xsl:value-of select="$newline"/>
    <xsl:text>Total miles flown this year:  </xsl:text>
    <xsl:value-of
      select="format-number(sum(/report/month/miles-flown), '###,###')"/>
    <xsl:value-of select="$newline"/>
    <xsl:value-of select="$newline"/>
    <xsl:text>Total miles earned this year: </xsl:text>
    <xsl:value-of
      select="format-number(sum(/report/month/miles-earned), '###,###')"/>
    <xsl:value-of select="$newline"/>
    <xsl:value-of select="$newline"/>
  </xsl:template>

</xsl:stylesheet>
```

Processing the XML document with this stylesheet generates these results:

```
A test of the sum() function:

Total miles flown this year:  84,059

Total miles earned this year: 236,452
```

system-property() Function — Returns the value of the system property named by the argument to the function.

Synopsis

object **system-property(***string***)**

Description

By definition, all XSLT processors must support three system properties:

`xsl:version`
: A floating-point number representing the version of XSLT implemented by this XSLT processor. As of this writing, the only official version of XSLT supported by any XSLT processors is `1.0`.

`xsl:vendor`
: A string that identifies the vendor of this XSLT processor.

`xsl:vendor-url`
: A string containing the URL identifying the vendor of the XSLT processor. This string is typically the home page of the vendor's web site.

Inputs

The XSLT 1.0 specification defines three properties: `xsl:version`, `xsl:vendor`, and `xsl:vendor-url`. These properties must be supported by all XSLT processors. Other properties may be supported by individual processors; check your processor's documentation for more information.

Output

The value of the queried property.

Defined in

XSLT section 12.4, Miscellaneous Additional Functions.

Example

Here is a stylesheet that queries different properties of the XSLT processor:

```
<?xml version="1.0"?>
<xsl:stylesheet version="1.0" xmlns:xsl="http://www.w3.org/1999/XSL/Transform">

  <xsl:output method="text"/>

  <xsl:variable name="newline">
<xsl:text>
</xsl:text>
  </xsl:variable>

  <xsl:template match="/">
    <xsl:text>xsl:version = "</xsl:text>
    <xsl:value-of select="system-property('xsl:version')"/>
    <xsl:text>"</xsl:text><xsl:value-of select="$newline"/>
    <xsl:text>xsl:vendor = "</xsl:text>
    <xsl:value-of select="system-property('xsl:vendor')"/>
    <xsl:text>"</xsl:text><xsl:value-of select="$newline"/>
    <xsl:text>xsl:vendor-url = "</xsl:text>
```

```
    <xsl:value-of select="system-property('xsl:vendor-url')"/>
    <xsl:text>"</xsl:text><xsl:value-of select="$newline"/>
  </xsl:template>

</xsl:stylesheet>
```

When the stylesheet is applied toward any XML document with the Xalan XSLT processor (invoked by the following command):

```
java org.apache.xalan.xslt.Process -in test1.xml -xsl systemproperties.xsl
```

The results are:

```
xsl:version = "1"
xsl:vendor = "Apache Software Foundation"
xsl:vendor-url = "http://xml.apache.org/xalan"
```

The following command invokes the results for Michael Kay's Saxon processor:

```
java com.icl.saxon.StyleSheet test1.xml systemproperties.xsl
```

Here are the results:

```
xsl:version = "1"
xsl:vendor = "SAXON 6.4.3 from Michael Kay"
xsl:vendor-url = "http://saxon.sourceforge.net"
```

We invoked Oracle's XML parser with:

```
java oracle.xml.parser.v2.oraxsl test1.xml systemproperties.xsl
```

Here are the results:

```
xsl:version = "1"
xsl:vendor = "Oracle Corporation."
xsl:vendor-url = "http://www.oracle.com"
```

We invoked James Clark's XT processor with:

```
java com.jclark.xsl.sax.Driver test1.xml systemproperties.xsl
```

Here are the results:

```
xsl:version = "1"
xsl:vendor = "James Clark"
xsl:vendor-url = "http://www.jclark.com/"
```

Finally, we invoked Microsoft's XSLT processor with:

```
msxsl test1.xml systemproperties.xsl
```

Here are the results:

```
xsl:version = "1"
xsl:vendor = "Microsoft"
xsl:vendor-url = "http://www.microsoft.com"
```

translate() Function — Allows you to convert individual characters in a string from one value to another. In many languages, this function is powerful enough to convert characters from one case to another.

Synopsis

string **translate(***string, string, string***)**

Inputs

Three strings. The first is the original, untranslated string, and the second and third strings define the characters to be converted.

Output

The original string, translated as follows:

- If a character in the original string appears in the second argument string, it is replaced with the corresponding character in the third argument string. In other words, if the character `J` appears in the original string and `J` appears as the fourth character in the second argument string, the `J` is replaced with the fourth character from the third argument string. (Don't worry, we'll have some examples to clear this up in just a minute.)
- If a character in the original string appears in the second argument string and there is no corresponding character in the third argument string (the second argument string is longer than the third), then that character is deleted. In other words, if the character `J` appears in the original string, and `J` appears as the fourth character in the second argument string, and the third argument string is three characters long, the `J` is deleted.
- If a character in the second argument string appears more than once, the first occurrence determines the replacement character.
- If the third argument string is longer than the second argument string, the extra characters are ignored.

Defined in

XPath section 4.2, String Functions.

Example

Here's a stylesheet with several examples of the `translate()` function:

```
<?xml version="1.0"?>
<xsl:stylesheet version="1.0" xmlns:xsl="http://www.w3.org/1999/XSL/Transform">

  <xsl:output method="text"/>
```

```
  <xsl:variable name="newline">
<xsl:text>
</xsl:text>
  </xsl:variable>

  <xsl:template match="/">
    <xsl:value-of select="$newline"/>
    <xsl:text>Tests of the translate() function:</xsl:text>

    <xsl:value-of select="$newline"/>
    <xsl:value-of select="$newline"/>
    <xsl:text>Convert a string to uppercase:</xsl:text>
    <xsl:value-of select="$newline"/>
    <xsl:text>   translate('Doug', 'abcdefghijklmnopqrstuvwxyz', </xsl:text>
    <xsl:value-of select="$newline"/>
    <xsl:text>                'ABCDEFGHIJKLMNOPQRSTUVWXYZ')=</xsl:text>
    <xsl:value-of select="translate('Doug',
      'abcdefghijklmnopqrstuvwxyz', 'ABCDEFGHIJKLMNOPQRSTUVWXYZ')"/>
    <xsl:value-of select="$newline"/>
    <xsl:value-of select="$newline"/>
    <xsl:text>Convert a string to lowercase:</xsl:text>
    <xsl:value-of select="$newline"/>
    <xsl:text>   translate('Doug', 'ABCDEFGHIJKLMNOPQRSTUVWXYZ', </xsl:text>
    <xsl:value-of select="$newline"/>
    <xsl:text>                'abcdefghijklmnopqrstuvwxyz')=</xsl:text>
    <xsl:value-of
      select="translate('Doug', 'ABCDEFGHIJKLMNOPQRSTUVWXYZ',
                       'abcdefghijklmnopqrstuvwxyz')"/>
    <xsl:value-of select="$newline"/>
    <xsl:value-of select="$newline"/>
    <xsl:text>Remove parentheses, spaces, and dashes</xsl:text>
    <xsl:text> from a U.S. phone number:</xsl:text>
    <xsl:value-of select="$newline"/>
    <xsl:text>   translate('(555) 555-1212', '() -', '')=</xsl:text>
    <xsl:value-of select="translate('(555) 555-1212', '() -', '')"/>
    <xsl:value-of select="$newline"/>
    <xsl:value-of select="$newline"/>
    <xsl:text>Replace all but the last four digits of a </xsl:text>
    <xsl:text>credit card number with Xs:</xsl:text>
    <xsl:value-of select="$newline"/>
    <xsl:variable name="credit" select="'4918 3829 9920 1810'"/>
    <xsl:text>   $credit='</xsl:text>
    <xsl:value-of select="$credit"/>
    <xsl:text>'</xsl:text>
    <xsl:value-of select="$newline"/>
    <xsl:text>   translate(substring($credit, 1, 15), </xsl:text>
    <xsl:text>'1234567890 ', 'XXXXXXXXXX-')</xsl:text>
    <xsl:value-of select="$newline"/>
    <xsl:text>   substring($credit, 16)</xsl:text>
    <xsl:value-of select="$newline"/>
```

```
      <xsl:value-of select="$newline"/>
      <xsl:text>   The first part is </xsl:text>
      <xsl:value-of
        select="translate(substring($credit, 1, 15), '123457890 ',
          'XXXXXXXXXX-')"/>
      <xsl:value-of select="$newline"/>
      <xsl:text>   The second part is </xsl:text>
      <xsl:value-of select="substring($credit, 16)"/>
      <xsl:value-of select="$newline"/>
      <xsl:value-of select="$newline"/>
      <xsl:text>   Here's how they look together: </xsl:text>
      <xsl:value-of
        select="translate(substring($credit, 1, 15), '123457890 ',
          'XXXXXXXXXX-')"/>
      <xsl:value-of select="substring($credit, 16)"/>
    </xsl:template>

  </xsl:stylesheet>
```

When we use this stylesheet with any XML document, here are the results:

```
Tests of the translate() function:

Convert a string to uppercase:
   translate('Doug', 'abcdefghijklmnopqrstuvwxyz',
             'ABCDEFGHIJKLMNOPQRSTUVWXYZ')=DOUG

Convert a string to lowercase:
   translate('Doug', 'ABCDEFGHIJKLMNOPQRSTUVWXYZ',
             'abcdefghijklmnopqrstuvwxyz')=doug

Remove parentheses, spaces, and dashes from a U.S. phone number:
   translate('(555) 555-1212', '() -', '')=5555551212

Replace all but the last four digits of a credit card number with Xs:
   $credit='4918 3829 9920 1810'
   translate(substring($credit, 1, 15), '1234567890 ', 'XXXXXXXXXXX-')
   substring($credit, 16)

   The first part is XXXX-XXXX-XXXX-
   The second part is 1810

   Here's how they look together: XXXX-XXXX-XXXX-1810
```

true() Function — Always returns the boolean value `true`.

Synopsis

boolean **true()**

Inputs

None.

Output

The boolean value `true`.

Defined in

XPath section 4.3, Boolean Functions.

Example

Here's a brief example that uses the `true()` function:

```
<?xml version="1.0"?>
<xsl:stylesheet version="1.0" xmlns:xsl="http://www.w3.org/1999/XSL/Transform">

  <xsl:output method="text"/>

  <xsl:variable name="newline">
<xsl:text>
</xsl:text>
  </xsl:variable>

  <xsl:template match="/">
    <xsl:value-of select="$newline"/>
    <xsl:text>A test of the true() function:</xsl:text>

    <xsl:value-of select="$newline"/>
    <xsl:value-of select="$newline"/>
    <xsl:choose>
      <xsl:when test="true()">
        <xsl:text>   "true()"   returned true!</xsl:text>
      </xsl:when>
      <xsl:otherwise>
        <xsl:text>   "true()"   returned false!</xsl:text>
      </xsl:otherwise>
    </xsl:choose>
  </xsl:template>
</xsl:stylesheet>
```

When using this stylesheet against any XML document, it generates this less-than-exciting result:

```
A test of the true() function:

   "true()"   returned true!
```

unparsed-entity-uri() Function — Returns the URI of the unparsed entity with the specified name. If there is no such entity, `unparsed-entity-uri` returns an empty string.

Synopsis

string **unparsed-entity-uri(***string***)**

Inputs

The name of the unparsed entity.

Output

The URI of the unparsed entity with the specified name.

Defined in

XSLT section 12.4, Miscellaneous Additional Functions.

Example

Unparsed entities are rarely used; they refer to non-XML data, as in the entity `author-picture` in this XML document:

```
<?xml version="1.0"?>
<!DOCTYPE book [
  <!ENTITY author-picture SYSTEM "dougtidwell.jpg" NDATA JPEG>
]>
<book>
  <prolog cover-image="author-picture"/>
  <body>
    <p>Pretend that lots of useful content appears here.</p>
  </body>
</book>
```

We'll use this stylesheet to process our unparsed entity:

```
<?xml version="1.0"?>
<xsl:stylesheet version="1.0"
  xmlns:xsl="http://www.w3.org/1999/XSL/Transform">

  <xsl:output method="text"/>
```

```
  <xsl:variable name="newline">
<xsl:text>
</xsl:text>
  </xsl:variable>

  <xsl:template match="/">
    <xsl:value-of select="$newline"/>
    <xsl:text>A test of the unparsed-entity-uri() function:</xsl:text>

    <xsl:value-of select="$newline"/>
    <xsl:value-of select="$newline"/>
    <xsl:text>   The cover image is located at </xsl:text>
    <xsl:value-of select="unparsed-entity-uri(/book/prolog/@cover-image)"/>
    <xsl:text>.</xsl:text>
    <xsl:value-of select="$newline"/>
  </xsl:template>

</xsl:stylesheet>
```

When we transform the XML document with our stylesheet, the results look like this:

```
A test of the unparsed-entity-uri() function:

   The cover image is located at file:///D:/O'Reilly/dougtidwell.jpg.
```

The URI of the unparsed entity is based on the base URI of the XML document itself.

D

XSLT Guide

This appendix is a short, task-oriented guide to common stylesheet tasks. It is organized by task; find what you want to do, and this guide will show you how to do it.

How Do I Put Quotes Inside an Attribute Value?

First, remember that attribute values can be quoted with either single quotes or double quotes. If you need to define an attribute with the value `"Doug's car,"` you can do what we just did: use double quotes to contain a value with single quotes inside it. If, however, you need to quote an attribute value that contains both single and double quotes, use the predefined entities `"` for double quotes and `'` for single quotes. Here's a sample document that contains some examples:

```
<?xml version="1.0"?>
<sampledoc>
  <head>
    <title>Attributes with Quotes</title>
  </head>
  <body>
    <p>This is an XML document that contains elements with attributes.
    The values of some of those attributes, interestingly enough, contain
    quotes. Look at the source of the document to see how we did this.</p>
    <tag1 author="Doug 'Gone' Tidwell"
      editor="Breanna & Meghan's Mom">
      Here's some text
    </tag1>
    <tag2 author='Doug "Geek of the Week" Tidwell'
      test="$x<7">
```

```
    Here's some more text
  </tag2>
  <tag3 author='Doug "The Slug" Tidwell' test="$x>9">
    A final example
  </tag3>
 </body>
</sampledoc>
```

How Do I Convert All Attributes to Elements?

Here's a short stylesheet that does the job:

```
<?xml version="1.0"?>
<xsl:stylesheet xmlns:xsl="http://www.w3.org/1999/XSL/Transform" version="1.0">
  <xsl:output method="xml"/>

  <xsl:template match="*">
    <xsl:element name="{name()}">
      <xsl:for-each select="@*">
        <xsl:element name="{name()}">
          <xsl:value-of select="."/>
        </xsl:element>
      </xsl:for-each>
      <xsl:apply-templates select="*|text()"/>
    </xsl:element>
  </xsl:template>

</xsl:stylesheet>
```

This example is about as short a stylesheet as you'll ever see. The XSLT processor uses the single `<xsl:template>` to process every element in the document. For each element, we output:

- A new element, whose name is the name of the current element
- For each attribute of the current element (selected with `@*`), a new element whose name is the name of the current attribute. The text of our newly created element is the text of the current attribute.

Once we've processed all the attributes, we process all of the child elements and text nodes beneath the current element. Processing them in this way means that the text and generated elements in the output document will be in the same sequence in the original document and the generated one.

As an example, we'll use our stylesheet to transform this XML document:

```
<?xml version="1.0"?>
<report>
  <title>Database Access Sample</title>
  <section>
```

```
      <title>Employees by Last Name</title>
      <dbaccess driver="COM.ibm.db2.jdbc.app.DB2Driver"
        database="jdbc:db2:sample" tablename="wstkadmin.employee" where="*"
        fieldnames='lastname as "Last Name",
        firstnme as "First Name", workdept as "Department"'
        order-by="lastname" group-by="lastname, firstnme, workdept"/>
    </section>
  </report>
```

When we transform our document, here are the results:

```
<?xml version="1.0" encoding="UTF-8"?>
<report>
  <title>Database Access Sample</title>
  <section>
    <title>Employees by Last Name</title>
    <dbaccess>
      <driver>COM.ibm.db2.jdbc.app.DB2Driver</driver>
      <database>jdbc:db2:sample</database>
      <tablename>wstkadmin.employee</tablename>
      <where>*</where>
      <fieldnames>lastname as "Last Name", firstnme as "First Name",
        workdept as "Department"</fieldnames>
      <order-by>lastname</order-by>
      <group-by>lastname, firstnme, workdept</group-by>
    </dbaccess>
  </section>
</report>
```

In the output, all attributes of the original document are now elements. (We've added line breaks and indenting to make the output more readable.) With that exception, everything else in the document is unchanged.

How Do I List All the Elements in an XML Document?

As in our last example, this job is for generic XPath expressions. We'll use the grouping techniques described in the section "Grouping Nodes" in Chapter 6, along with the `name()` function, to accomplish this. Our stylesheet sorts all element names alphabetically, and then groups them to list each unique element once, along with a count of how many times that element appears:

```
<?xml version="1.0"?>
<xsl:stylesheet xmlns:xsl="http://www.w3.org/1999/XSL/Transform" version="1.0">
  <xsl:output method="text"/>

  <xsl:variable name="newline">
<xsl:text>
</xsl:text>
  </xsl:variable>
```

```
  <xsl:key name="elements" match="*" use="name()"/>

  <xsl:template match="/">
    <xsl:value-of select="$newline"/>
    <xsl:text>Summary of Elements</xsl:text>
    <xsl:value-of select="$newline"/>
    <xsl:value-of select="$newline"/>
    <xsl:for-each
      select="//*[generate-id(.)=generate-id(key('elements',name())[1])]">
      <xsl:sort select="name()"/>
      <xsl:for-each select="key('elements', name())">
        <xsl:if test="position()=1">
          <xsl:text>Element </xsl:text>
          <xsl:value-of select="name()"/>
          <xsl:text> occurs </xsl:text>
          <xsl:value-of select="count(//*[name()=name(current())])"/>
          <xsl:text> times.</xsl:text>
          <xsl:value-of select="$newline"/>
        </xsl:if>
      </xsl:for-each>
    </xsl:for-each>
    <xsl:value-of select="$newline"/>
    <xsl:text>There are </xsl:text>
    <xsl:value-of select="count(//*)"/>
    <xsl:text> elements in all.</xsl:text>
  </xsl:template>

</xsl:stylesheet>
```

When we run this stylesheet against the XML source file for Appendix C, here are the results:

```
Summary of Elements

Element appendix occurs 1 times.
Element emphasis occurs 9 times.
Element filename occurs 11 times.
Element funcdef occurs 36 times.
Element funcprototype occurs 36 times.
Element funcsynopsis occurs 36 times.
Element function occurs 181 times.
Element graphic occurs 8 times.
Element itemizedlist occurs 9 times.
Element link occurs 1 times.
Element listitem occurs 52 times.
Element literal occurs 14 times.
Element para occurs 338 times.
Element paramdef occurs 45 times.
Element programlisting occurs 110 times.
Element quote occurs 4 times.
Element refentry occurs 36 times.
Element refname occurs 36 times.
Element refnamediv occurs 36 times.
Element refpurpose occurs 36 times.
```

```
Element refsect1 occurs 144 times.
Element refsynopsisdiv occurs 36 times.
Element literal occurs 184 times.
Element term occurs 13 times.
Element title occurs 146 times.
Element variablelist occurs 2 times.
Element varlistentry occurs 13 times.
Element xref occurs 14 times.

There are 1587 elements in all.
```

This stylesheet works against any valid XML document, regardless of the elements that document uses. For more information on the technique we used to group the element names (popularly known as the Muench method), see the section "Grouping Nodes" in Chapter 6.

How Do I Implement an if Statement?

Use the cleverly named `<xsl:if>` element. See the "`<xsl:if>`" entry in Appendix A for information and examples.

How Do I Implement an if-else Statement?

For whatever reason, XSLT doesn't provide an `<xsl:else>` element. To create an `if-else` statement, you need an `<xsl:choose>` element with a single `<xsl:when>` element and a single `<xsl:otherwise>` element. If the `test` attribute of the `<xsl:when>` element is true, then the contents of the `<xsl:when>` are evaluated; if not, the contents of the `<xsl:otherwise>` element are.

See the "`<xsl:choose>`" entry in Appendix A for a complete discussion of this element and some examples.

How Do I Implement a for Loop?

The simple answer: you don't. What XSLT calls variables are variables in the mathematical sense of the term. An `<xsl:variable>` can be assigned an initial value, but it can't be changed. The upshot of this situation is that you can't implement a `for` loop as you typically do in most procedural programming languages. However, earlier in the book we did implement a stylesheet that emulates a `for` loop. See the section "A Stylesheet That Emulates a for Loop" in Chapter 4 for a complete discussion of this example.

It's much more likely that you need to iterate across a group of nodes in an XML document. If that's the case, see the section "The <xsl:for-each> Element" in Chapter 4 for more information.

How Do I Implement a case Statement?

The XSLT `<xsl:choose>` element works very similarly to the `case` or `switch` statement you might know from procedural programming languages. See the section "The <xsl:choose> Element" in Chapter 4 for more information.

How Do I Group Elements in an XML Document?

Unlike sorting, grouping is not directly supported in XSLT. Most axes and functions you'd like to use for grouping work only with the document order of the XML document, not with the sorted order you'd need for grouping. That being said, you can use some tricks to group elements in your output document. This subject is discussed in great detail in the section "Grouping Nodes" in Chapter 6.

How Do I Group Elements Pulled from Multiple XML Documents?

Unfortunately, grouping these elements is more difficult than grouping elements in the same document. It's not pretty or efficient, but you can do it. This subject is discussed in the section "Grouping Across Multiple Documents" in Chapter 7.

How Do I Combine XML Documents into a Single Master Document?

This is actually pretty straightforward. See Chapter 7 for a discussion of the XSLT `document()` function in all its glory.

How Do I Resolve Cross-References?

The most common ways of resolving cross-references require use of the `id()` and `key()` functions, assuming there is some structure to your document to begin with. See Chapter 5 for a discussion of the various techniques for generating cross-references.

How Do I Generate Some Text?

You can generate text in your output in several different ways. The simplest way is to use the <xsl:text> element. This element generates text to the output stream automatically. The <xsl:text> element is often necessary because many elements in the XSLT vocabulary can't contain text.

A second way is to use the <xsl:value-of> element with various string functions. Say we're going to generate a string that is the concatenation of several items in the current context. Combining <xsl:value-of> with the concat() function allows us to do this. Here's an example:

```
<xsl:value-of select="concat('abc ', 'easy as ',123)">
```

This element is replaced with the text "abc easy as 123."

How Do I Control Angle Brackets and Quote Marks in My Output?

The XML 1.0 Specification defines five entities you can use to generate special characters: the apostrophe, or single quote mark (defined as '); the ampersand (defined as &); the less-than sign, or left angle bracket (defined as <); the double-quote mark (defined as "); and the greater-than sign, or right angle bracket (defined as >). You can use these entities to output one of these special symbols without an eager XML parser attempting to process them as metacharacters along the way.

If using the predefined entities doesn't do the trick, use the disable-output-escaping attribute of the <xsl:text> element. If you set this attribute to yes, the XSLT processor will not convert entities such as < and > to their associated characters.

Here's an <xsl:text> element with the normal setting and the results it generates:

```
<xsl:text>Hey, y&apos;all!</xsl:text>
```

Output:

```
Hey, y'all!
```

Here's the same listing with output escaping disabled:

```
<xsl:text disable-output-escaping="yes">Hey, y&apos;all!</xsl:text>
```

Output:

```
Hey, y&apos;all!
```

Be aware that the `disable-output-escaping` attribute may not be supported by all XSLT processors, and it may result in XML that is not well formed. For these reasons, the XSLT specification advises that `disable-output-escaping` "should be used only when there is no alternative."

Glossary

absolute location path
: A location path that begins with `/`, followed by one or more location steps separated by `/`. All location paths that begin with `/` are evaluated from the root node, so they always return the same result, regardless of the context node. Compare with *location path* and *relative location path.*

ancestor
: A node that appears above a given node. Ancestors include a node's parent, its parent's parent, its parent's parent's parent, etc. XPath also defines the `ancestor` axis, which includes a node's parent, its parent's parent, its parent's parent's parent, etc., but not the node itself. Contrast with *parent.*

attribute node
: The XPath node type that represents an attribute from an XML document. Attributes are different from other nodes because an attribute node is not considered a child of the element node that contains it. Despite this fact, the element node is considered the parent of the attribute node.

attribute set
: A named group of attributes. You can create an attribute set (with the `<xsl:attribute-set>` element), then reference that attribute set elsewhere. For more information, see the description of the `<xsl:attribute-set>` element in Appendix A.

attribute value template
: An expression that contains an XPath expression in curly braces (`{}`). The XPath expression is evaluated at runtime, and its value replaces the expression. For an example of an attribute value template, see the discussion of the `<xsl:attribute>` element in Appendix A; Chapter 3 contains a complete discussion of attribute value templates.

axis
: A relationship between the context node and other nodes in the document. XPath defines 13 different axes; see the section "Axes" in Chapter 3 for a complete discussion of them.

base URI

The URI associated with every node in the XPath source tree. In certain circumstances, the base URI is used to resolve references to other resources. If a given node is an element or processing-instruction node and that node occurs in an external entity, then the base URI for that node is the base URI of the external entity. If an element or processing-instruction node does not occur in an external entity, then its base URI is the base URI of the document in which it appears. The base URI of a document node is the base URI of the document itself, and the base URI of an attribute, comment, namespace, or text node is the base URI of that node's parent.

CDATA section

A section of an XML document in which all markup is ignored. A CDATA section begins with the characters `<![CDATA[`, and ends with the characters `]]>`. If two right brackets appear in the content of a CDATA section, they must be escaped. Within a stylesheet, determining if a given text node was originally a CDATA section is not possible. It is possible to generate certain elements as CDATA sections with the `cdata-section-elements` attribute of the `<xsl:output>` element.

child

An immediate descendant of a given node. Contrast with *descendant*. `child` is also the name of one of the XPath axes. The children of a node include all comment, element, processing-instruction, and text nodes. Attribute nodes and namespace nodes are not considered children.

comment node

A node that represents a comment from the original XML document. This is one of the seven kinds of nodes defined by XPath.

context

A data structure that determines how XPath expressions are evaluated. The context consists of five items: the context node, a pair of nonzero positive integers (the context position and context size), a set of variable bindings, a function library, and the set of namespace declarations that are in scope.

context node

The node from which all XPath expressions are evaluated. The context node is analogous to the current directory at a command prompt; all commands you type at a command prompt are evaluated in terms of the current directory. Compare with *current node*.

context position

A nonzero positive integer that indicates the position of the current node. The context position is always less than or equal to the context size.

context size

The number of nodes in the current node list.

current node

The node currently being processed. The node is defined by the `select` attribute of the `<xsl:apply-templates>` or `<xsl:for-each>` elements. Except within a predicate expression, the current node and the context node are the same.

current node list

The list of nodes selected by the `select` attribute of the `<xsl:apply-templates>` or `<xsl:for-each>` element currently being processed. By default, the current node list is in document order, but it may be reordered with one or more `<xsl:sort>` elements.

descendant

A given node's children, its children's children, its children's children's children, etc. `descendant` is also the name of one of the axes defined by XPath. Contrast with *child*.

document element

The element in the XML source document that contains the entire XML document. The node that represents the document element is a child of the root node; the root node and the element node for the document element are not the same.

element node

An XPath node that represents an element from the XML source document.

encoding

A set of characters, referenced in the XML declaration to describe the characters used in a particular document. The range of values for encodings is defined in *http://www.ietf.org/rfc/rfc2278.txt*. The range of values supported by a given XML parser or XSLT processor varies.

expanded name

The complete name of an element or attribute, including the local name and a possibly null namespace URI.

extension element

An element in an XSLT stylesheet whose namespace prefix references an extension. The XSLT specification defines how extension elements are identified in the stylesheet, but does not specify how they are implemented. Extension elements are implemented with a piece of code that is referenced in the stylesheet; each XSLT processor defines how that code is invoked to handle the transformation of the extension element. See Chapter 8 for an extensive discussion of extension elements and extension functions.

extension function

A function whose namespace prefix references an extension. The XSLT specification defines how extension functions are identified in the stylesheet, but does not specify how they are implemented. Extension functions are implemented with a piece of code that is referenced in the stylesheet; each XSLT processor defines how that code is invoked to handle the invocation of the extension function. See Chapter 8 for an extensive discussion of extension elements and extension functions.

fallback processing

Processing designed to handle the absence of an extension element or an extension function gracefully. This processing is typically accomplished with the `element-available()` or the `function-available()` function. When either function returns false, a stylesheet can respond gracefully to the absence of the requested function. XSLT also defines the `<xsl:fallback>` element, which can be used when an extension element is not available.

ID

One of the basic datatypes defined by the XML specification. In an XML document, one attribute of an element can be declared to be of type `ID`; this means that the value of that attribute must be unique across all attributes of type `ID` for all elements in the document. No more than one attribute on a given element can be of type `ID`. Attributes of type `ID` are useful for generating cross-references with the `id()` function. See Chapter 5 for an extensive discussion of the `ID`, `IDREF`, and `IDREFS` datatypes.

IDREF

One of the basic datatypes defined by the XML specification. In an XML document, an attribute declared to be of type `IDREF` must have a value that matches an `ID` attribute elsewhere in the document. Attributes of type IDREF are useful for generating cross-references with the id() function. See Chapter 5 for an extensive discussion of the ID, IDREF, and IDREFS datatypes.

IDREFS

One of the basic datatypes defined by the XML specification. In an XML document, an IDREFS attribute must contain one or more whitespace-separated values, each of which matches an ID attribute elsewhere in the document. Attributes of type IDREFS are useful for generating cross-references with the id() function. See Chapter 5 for an extensive discussion of the ID, IDREF, and IDREFS datatypes.

key

A key is similar to a database index. It has three components: a *name*, used to identify the key (specified with the name attribute of the <xsl:key> element); the *nodes*, which will be returned by the key (specified with the use attribute of the <xsl:key> element); and the *values*, used to search for things in the key (specified with the match attribute of the <xsl:key> element)

The key <key name="language-index" match="defn" use="@language"/>, for example, defines a new key named language-index. Given a value for the language attribute, the key returns all <defn> elements whose language attributes match the given value. See the section "Generating Links with the key() Function" in Chapter 5 for a complete discussion of keys and how they are used.

literal result element (LRE)

An element in an XSLT stylesheet that does not belong to the XSLT namespace and is not an extension element. Literal elements are simply copied to the result tree.

local name

The nonqualified portion of an element or attribute name. For example, in the element <xsl:template>, template is the local name.

location path

An XPath expression that selects a set of nodes relative to the context node. Compare with *absolute location path* and *relative location path.*

location step

Consists of three parts: an axis name, a node test, and zero or more predicate expressions. There are three location steps in the XPath expression preceding-sibling::region/product[@name="Sandpiper"]/text().

The first location step is preceding-sibling::region; it has an axis name of preceding-sibling and a node test of region. It selects all <region> elements that are preceding siblings of the context node. It does not have a predicate expression.

The second location step, product[@name="Sandpiper"], has an axis name of child, the default axis. Its node test is product and it has the predicate [@name="Sandpiper"]. It selects all <product> children of the previous location step that have an attribute named name with a value of Sandpiper.

The third location step, text(), has an axis name of child and a node test of text(). It selects all text node children of the previous location step. It does not have a predicate expression.

mode

An XSLT feature that allows an element to be processed multiple times, using a different template and producing a different result each time. See the discussion of the <xsl:apply-templates> element in Appendix A for a detailed example of modes.

namespace
A collection of element and attribute names that are associated with a URI.

namespace node
The XPath node type that corresponds to a namespace declaration in an XML document.

namespace prefix
Part of a qualified name used to associate an element or attribute with a namespace URI.

namespace URI
The string associated with a collection of element and attribute names. Although commonly referred to as a URI, a namespace URI can actually be any string.

NCName
An XML name, used for local names and namespace prefixes. An NCName must start with a letter or an underscore (_).

node test
An XPath expression that selects certain nodes. The expressions `child::*`, `para`, and `@id` select all child nodes, all `<para>` child nodes, and any attribute named `id`, respectively. Four node tests—(`text()`, `comment()`, `node()`, and `processing-instruction()`)—look like functions, even though they technically aren't. They allow you to select parts of an XML document not accessible through the various axes defined by XPath. See the section "XPath Node Tests" in Appendix B for a complete discussion of these node tests.

output escaping
The process of changing reserved characters (such as <, >, and &) into their entity references (such as `<`, `>`, and `&`).

parameter
An XSLT mechanism used to bind a name to a value, defined with the `<xsl:param>` element. The difference between a parameter and a variable is that the value specified in the definition of a parameter is a default value. When the template or stylesheet that contains the parameter is invoked, the default value can be overridden. Like variables, though, once the value of a parameter is set, it cannot be changed.

parent
A node that appears immediately above a given node. A parent is a node's first ancestor. XPath also defines the `parent` axis, which contains a node's parent. With the exception of the root node, all nodes have a parent. Contrast with *ancestor*.

predicate expression
An XPath expression that appears in square brackets (`[]`). Predicate expressions filter a node-set, selecting only nodes that match the expression in square brackets. See the section "Predicates" in Chapter 3 for more information.

prefix
An abbreviation for *namespace prefix*.

processing instruction
Part of an XML document containing instructions for applications. Here is a sample processing instruction:

```
<?xml-stylesheet href="docbook/html/docbook.xsl"
  type="text/xsl"?>
```

This processing instruction associates an XSLT stylesheet with an XML document. See the section "Associating stylesheets with XML documents" in Chapter 1 for a complete discussion of processing instructions.

processing-instruction node
The XPath node type that represents a processing instruction from an XML document.

qualified name
An element or attribute name that has been qualified with a namespace prefix. The format of a qualified name is `prefix:local-name`, where `prefix` and `local-name` are both NCNames. For example, `<xsl:template>` is a qualified name, while `<template>` is not. The names in an XSLT stylesheet (variable names, template names, mode names, etc.) must be qualified names.

QNAME
An abbreviation for *qualified name*.

relative location path
A location path that consists of one or more location steps separated by `/`. Compare with *location path* and *absolute location path*.

result-tree fragment
A fragment of the is result tree that can be associated with a variable. See the section "Datatypes" in Appendix B for a more complete discussion of result-tree fragments.

root node
The XPath node that represents the root of an XML document. Note that the root node is not the same as the element node for the document element. The root node is specified with the XPath expression `/`. The children of the root node are the element node for the document element, as well as any comments or processing instructions that occur outside the document element.

sibling
Two nodes that have the same parent. XPath defines the `preceding-sibling` and `following-sibling` axes.

stylesheet
An XML document, written with the XSLT vocabulary, that specifies how an XML document should be transformed.

template
A rule in an XSLT stylesheet that defines how part of an XML document should be transformed. Templates are defined with the `<xsl:template>` element.

text node
A group of characters from an XML document. Text nodes are one of the seven types of nodes defined by XPath. The XPath specification states that as much text as possible must be combined into a single text node. In other words, a text node will never have a preceding or following sibling that is also a text node.

top-level element
An element whose parent is the `<xsl:stylesheet>` element.

unparsed entity
A resource in an XML document whose contents may or may not be text, and if text, may not be XML. Every unparsed entity has an associated XML notation. See the discussion of the `unparsed-entity-uri()` function in Appendix C for more details on unparsed entities.

valid document
An XML document that follows the basic rules of XML documents and additionally follows all rules of its associated document type definition or schema. See the section "XML Document Rules" in Chapter 1 for a complete discussion of the XML document rules; the section "Document Type Definitions (DTDs) and XML Schemas," also in Chapter 1, discusses document type definitions and schemas.

variable

An XSLT mechanism used to bind a name to a value, defined with the `<xsl:variable>` element. Variables are different from parameters because parameters can have default values. One significant difference between XSLT variables and variables in most other programming languages is that once an XSLT variable is initialized, its value cannot be changed. See the section "Variables" in Chapter 4 for a complete discussion of the `<xsl:variable>` element and how it is used.

well-formed document

An XML document that follows the basic rules of XML documents. See the section "XML Document Rules" in Chapter 1 for a complete discussion of those rules.

whitespace

One of four characters: space (` `), tab (`	`), return (`
`), or linefeed (`
`).

XML declaration

Part of an XML document that defines the version of XML being used. Although the XML declaration looks like a processing instruction, it is not. For that reason, you cannot access the XML declaration from an XSLT stylesheet or an XPath expression.

Index

Symbols

A

We'd like to hear your suggestions for improving our indexes. Send email to *index@oreilly.com.*

T

Z

About the Author

Doug Tidwell is a senior programmer at IBM. He has more than a sixth of a century of programming experience, and has been working with markup languages for more than a decade. He was a speaker at the first XML conference in 1997, and has taught XML classes around the world. His job as a Cyber Evangelist is to look busy and to help people use new technologies to solve problems. Using a pair of zircon-encrusted tweezers, he holds a master's degree in computer science from Vanderbilt University and a bachelor's degree in English from the University of Georgia. He lives in Raleigh, North Carolina, with his wife, cooking teacher Sheri Castle (see her web site at *http://www.sheri-inc.com*) and their daughter Lily.

Colophon

Our look is the result of reader comments, our own experimentation, and feedback from distribution channels. Distinctive covers complement our distinctive approach to technical topics, breathing personality and life into potentially dry subjects.

The animal on the cover of *XSLT* is a jabiru. Standing up to five feet tall and with a wingspan of eight feet, this wading stork is the largest flying bird in the western hemisphere. The bird's habitat ranges from southern Mexico to northern Argentina, and much of its migrating population is found in Belize from November through July. Its habitat generally includes coastal areas, savannas, and marshes. The jabiru population has steadily decreased over the past decades due to hunting and deforestation, but some areas of Central America have seen a slow recovery in the bird's population.

Ann Schirmer was the production editor and copyeditor for *XSLT*. Linley Dolby and Jeffrey Holcomb were the proofreaders. Claire Cloutier, Emily Quill, and Rachel Wheeler provided quality control. Brenda Miller wrote the index. Interior composition was done by Ann Schirmer. Emma Colby designed the cover of this book, based on a series design by Edie Freedman. The cover image is an original antique engraving from the 19th century. Emma Colby produced the cover layout with QuarkXPress 4.1 using Adobe's ITC Garamond font.

David Futato designed the interior layout, based on a series design by Nancy Priest. This book was written entirely in XML. The book's print version was created by translating the XML source into a set of gtroff macros using a Perl filter developed by Norman Walsh. Erik Ray wrote extensions to the filter. Steve Talbott designed and wrote the underlying macro set on the basis of the GNU gtroff -ms macros; Lenny Muellner adapted them to XML and implemented the book design. The GNU groff text formatter Version 1.11 was used to generate PostScript output. The text and heading fonts are ITC Garamond Light and Garamond Book; the code font is Constant Willison. The illustrations that appear in the book were produced by Robert Romano and Jessamyn Read using Macromedia FreeHand 9 and Adobe Photoshop 6. This colophon was written by Ann Schirmer.

Whenever possible, our books use a durable and flexible lay-flat binding. If the page count exceeds this binding's limit, perfect binding is used.

Other Titles Available from O'Reilly

XML

XML in a Nutshell, 2nd Edition

By Elliotte Rusty Harold & W. Scott Means
1st Edition December 2000
400 pages, ISBN 0-596-00058-8

This powerful new edition provides developers with a comprehensive guide to the rapidly evolving XML space. Serious users of XML will find topics on just about everything they need, from fundamental syntax rules, to details of DTD and XML Schema creation, to XSLT transformations, to APIs used for processing XML documents. Simply put, this is the only reference of its kind among XML books.

XSLT Cookbook

By Sal Mangano
1st Edition December 2002
670 pages, ISBN 0-596-00372-2

This book offers the definitive collection of solutions and examples that developers at any level can use immediately to solve a wide variety of XML processing issues. As with our other Cookbook titles, *XSLT Cookbook* contains code recipes for specific programming problems. But more than just a book of cut-and-paste code, *XSLT Cookbook* enables developers to build their programming skills and their understanding of XSLT through the detailed explanations provided with each recipe.

Learning XML

By Erik T. Ray with Christopher R. Maden
1st Edition January 2001
368 pages, ISBN 0-596-00046-4

XML (Extensible Markup Language) is a flexible way to create "self-describing data"—and to share both the format and the data on the World Wide Web, intranets, and elsewhere. In *Learning XML*, the authors explain XML and its capabilities succinctly and professionally, with references to real-life projects and other cogent examples. *Learning XML* shows the purpose of XML markup itself, the CSS and XSL styling languages, and the XLink and XPointer specifications for creating rich link structures.

XML Schema

By Eric van der Vlist
1st Edition June 2002
400 pages, 0-596-00252-1

The W3C's XML Schema offers a powerful set of tools for defining acceptable XML document structures and content. While schemas are powerful, that power comes with substantial complexity. This book explains XML Schema foundations, a variety of different styles for writing schemas, simple and complex types, datatypes and facets, keys, extensibility, documentation, design choices, best practices, and limitations. Complete with references, a glossary, and examples throughout.

Java & XML, 2nd Edition

By Brett McLaughlin
2nd Edition September 2001
528 pages, ISBN 0-596-00197-5

New chapters on Advanced SAX, Advanced DOM, SOAP, and data binding, as well as new examples throughout, bring the second edition of *Java & XML* thoroughly up to date. Except for a concise introduction to XML basics, the book focuses entirely on using XML from Java applications. It's a worthy companion for Java developers working with XML or involved in messaging, web services, or the new peer-to-peer movement.

How to stay in touch with O'Reilly

1. Visit our award-winning web site

http://www.oreilly.com/

★ "Top 100 Sites on the Web"—PC Magazine
★ CIO Magazine's Web Business 50 Awards

Our web site contains a library of comprehensive product information (including book excerpts and tables of contents), downloadable software, background articles, interviews with technology leaders, links to relevant sites, book cover art, and more. File us in your bookmarks or favorites!

2. Join our email mailing lists

Sign up to get email announcements of new books and conferences, special offers, and O'Reilly Network technology newsletters at:

http://elists.oreilly.com

It's easy to customize your free elists subscription so you'll get exactly the O'Reilly news you want.

3. Get examples from our books

To find example files for a book, go to:

http://www.oreilly.com/catalog

select the book, and follow the "Examples" link.

4. Work with us

Check out our web site for current employment opportunities:

http://jobs.oreilly.com/

5. Register your book

Register your book at:

http://register.oreilly.com

6. Contact us

O'Reilly & Associates, Inc.
1005 Gravenstein Hwy North
Sebastopol, CA 95472 USA
TEL: 707-827-7000 or 800-998-9938
(6am to 5pm PST)
FAX: 707-829-0104

order@oreilly.com
For answers to problems regarding your order or our products. To place a book order online visit:

http://www.oreilly.com/order_new/

catalog@oreilly.com
To request a copy of our latest catalog.

booktech@oreilly.com
For book content technical questions or corrections.

corporate@oreilly.com
For educational, library, government, and corporate sales.

proposals@oreilly.com
To submit new book proposals to our editors and product managers.

international@oreilly.com
For information about our international distributor or translation queries. For a list of our distributors outside of North America check out:

http://international.oreilly.com/distributors.html

adoption@oreilly.com
For information about academic use of O'Reilly books, visit:

http://academic.oreilly.com